DOGS BULLETS & CARNAGE

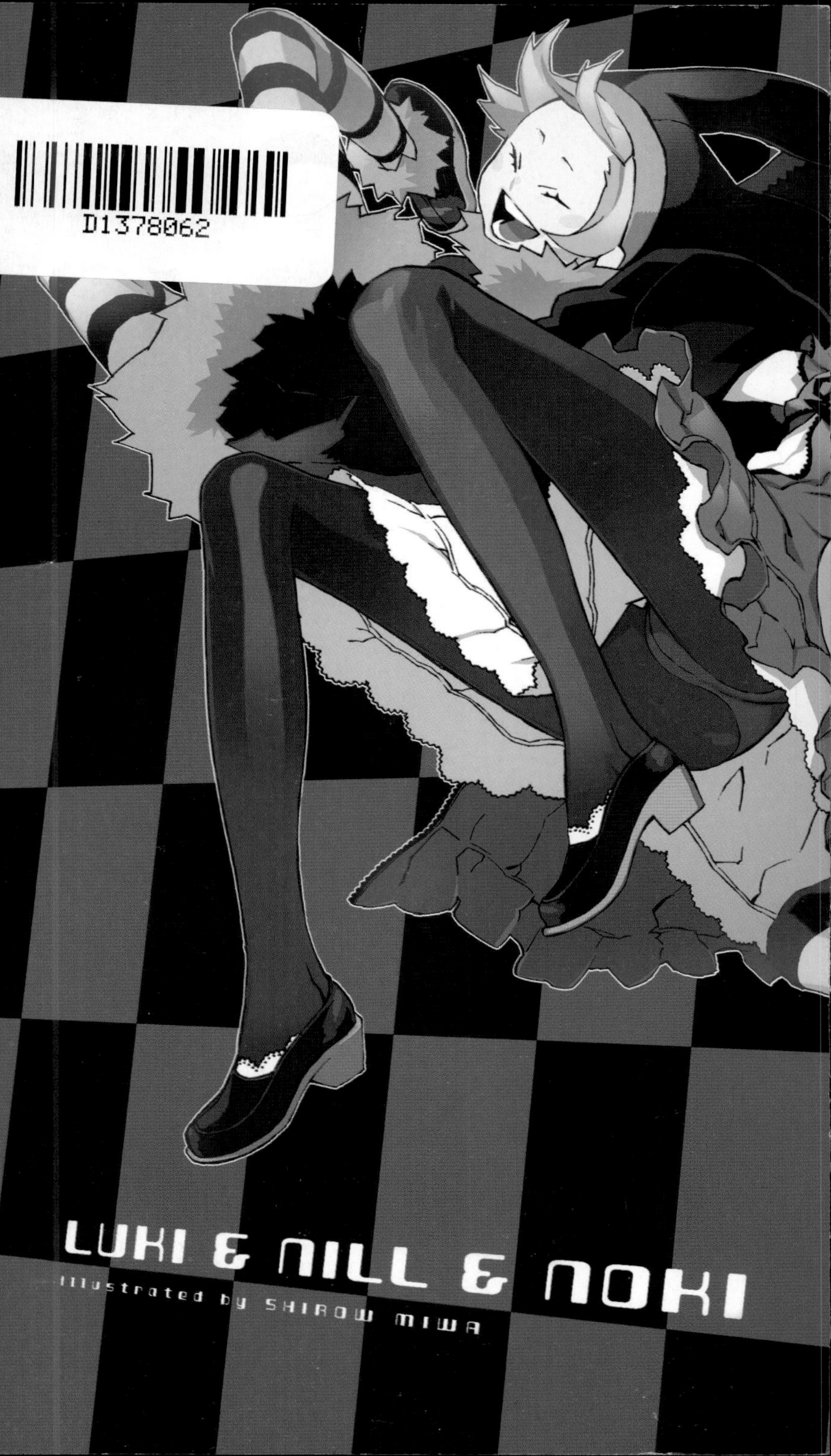

LUKI & NILL & NOKI

illustrated by SHIROW MIWA

DOGS
BULLETS & CARNAGE

2

CONTENTS

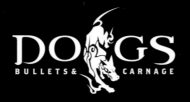

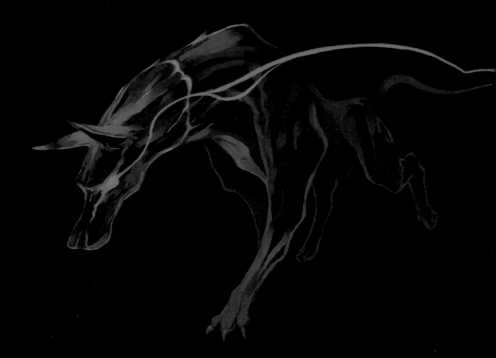

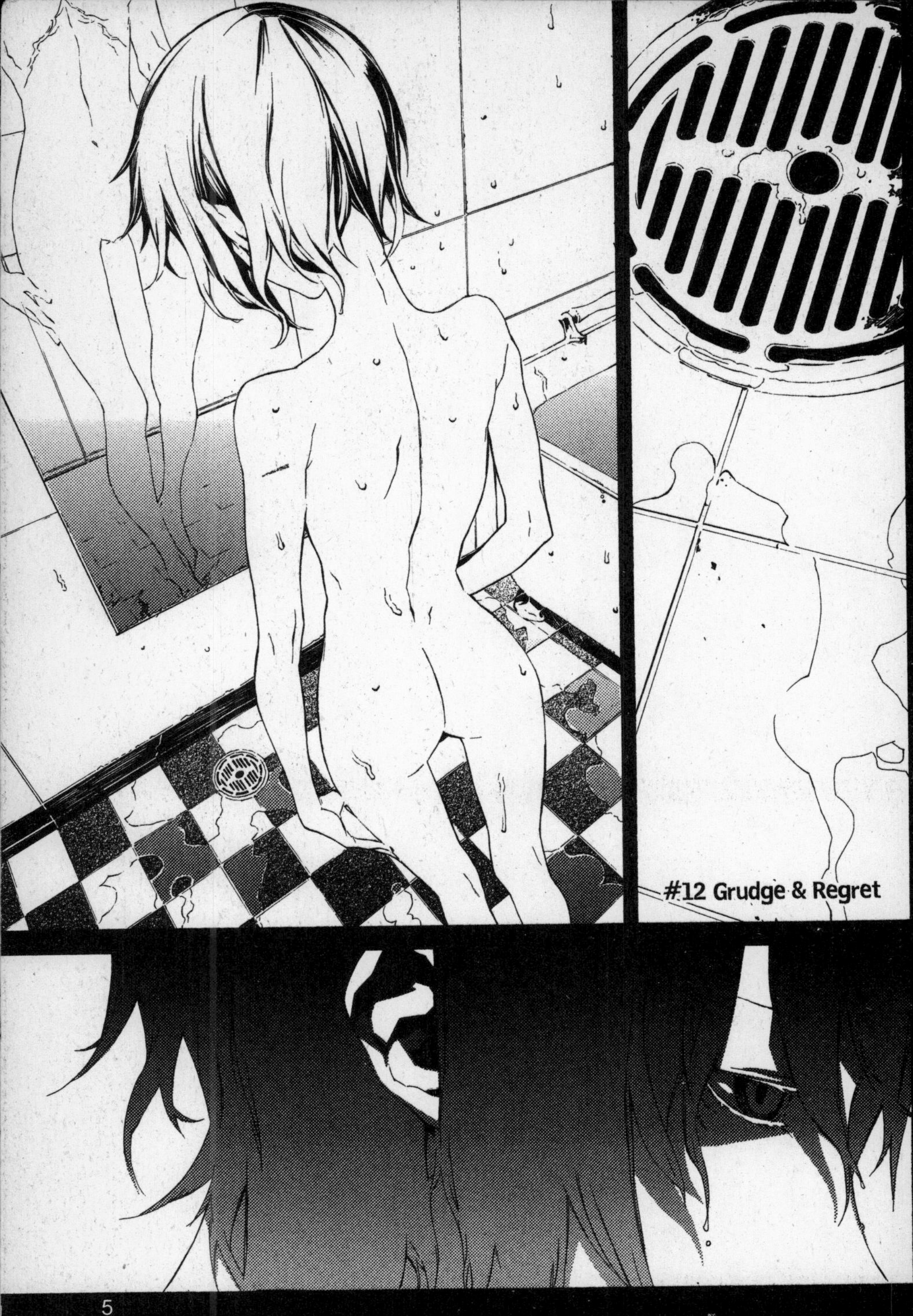
#12 Grudge & Regret

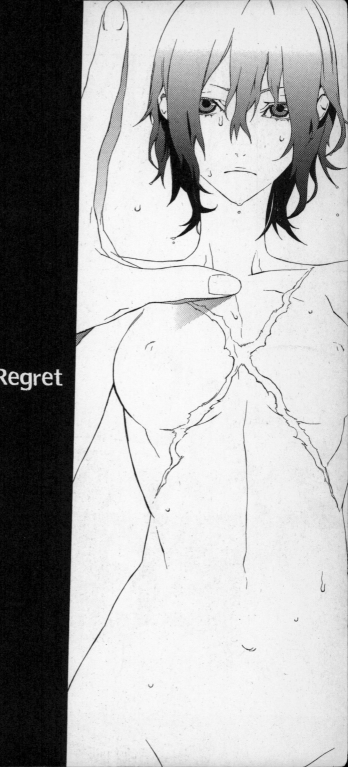

#12 Grudge & Regret

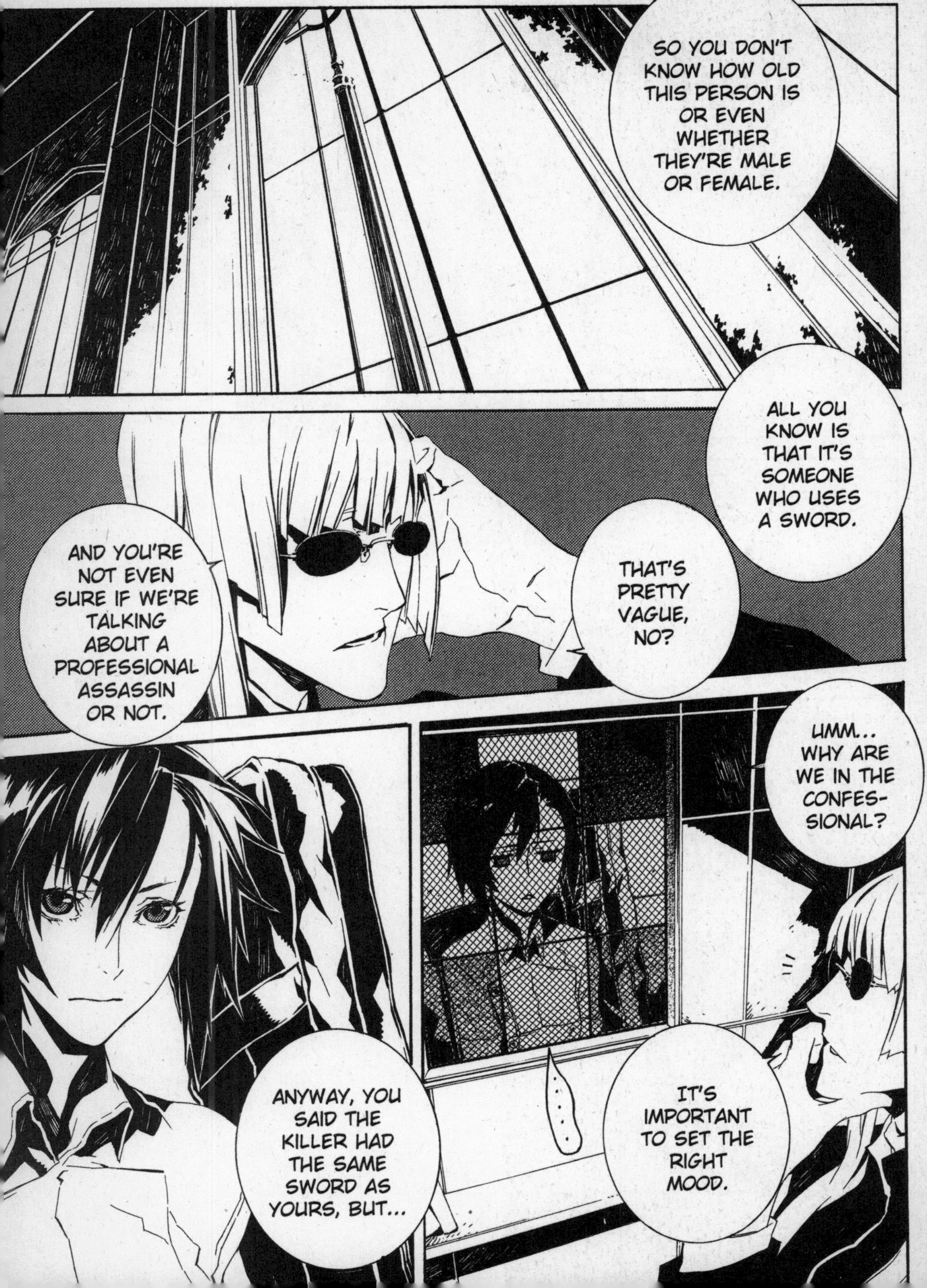
SO YOU DON'T KNOW HOW OLD THIS PERSON IS OR EVEN WHETHER THEY'RE MALE OR FEMALE.
ALL YOU KNOW IS THAT IT'S SOMEONE WHO USES A SWORD.
THAT'S PRETTY VAGUE, NO?
AND YOU'RE NOT EVEN SURE IF WE'RE TALKING ABOUT A PROFESSIONAL ASSASSIN OR NOT.
UMM... WHY ARE WE IN THE CONFES-SIONAL?
IT'S IMPORTANT TO SET THE RIGHT MOOD.
ANYWAY, YOU SAID THE KILLER HAD THE SAME SWORD AS YOURS, BUT...

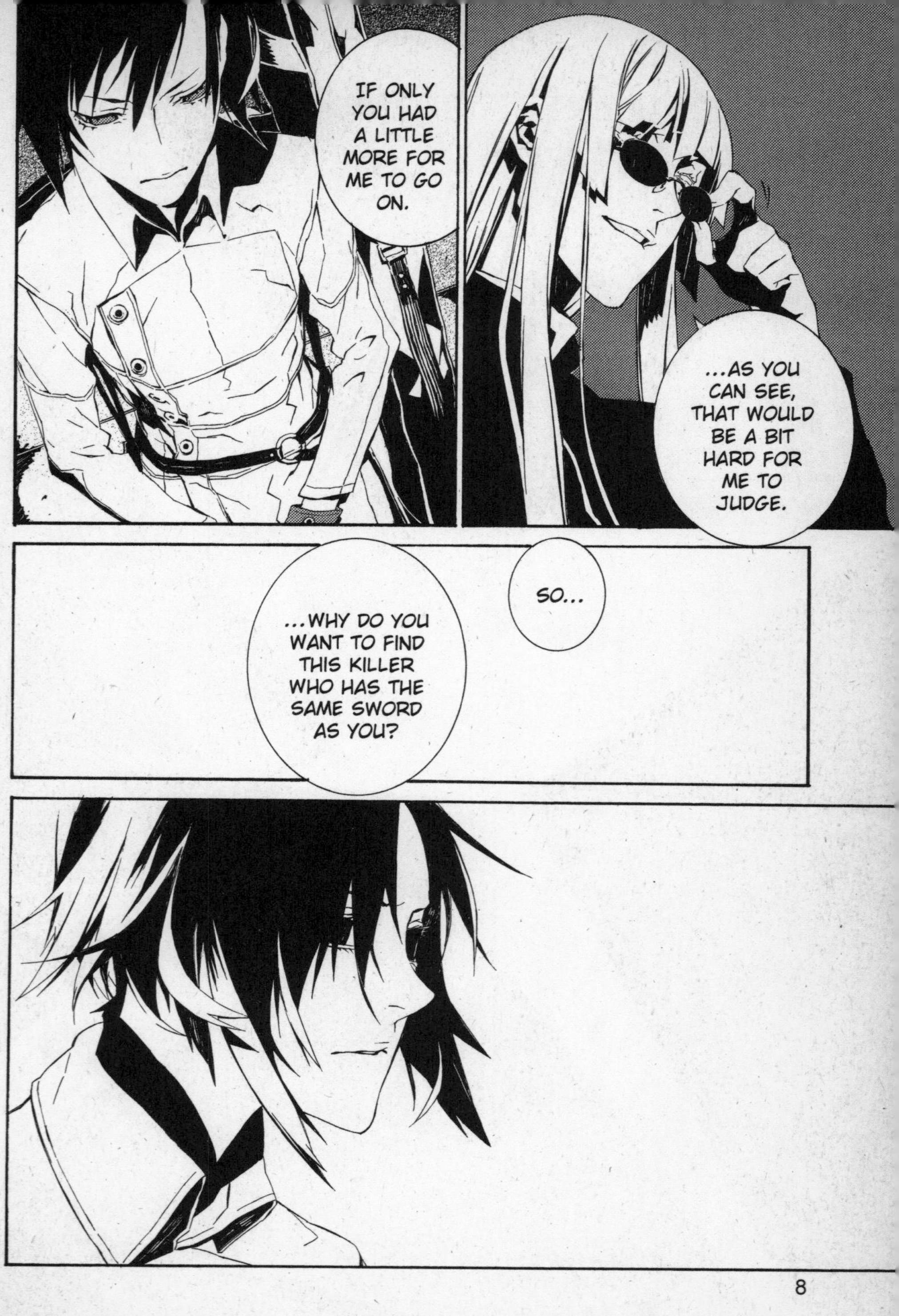
...AS YOU CAN SEE, THAT WOULD BE A BIT HARD FOR ME TO JUDGE.
IF ONLY YOU HAD A LITTLE MORE FOR ME TO GO ON.
SO...
...WHY DO YOU WANT TO FIND THIS KILLER WHO HAS THE SAME SWORD AS YOU?

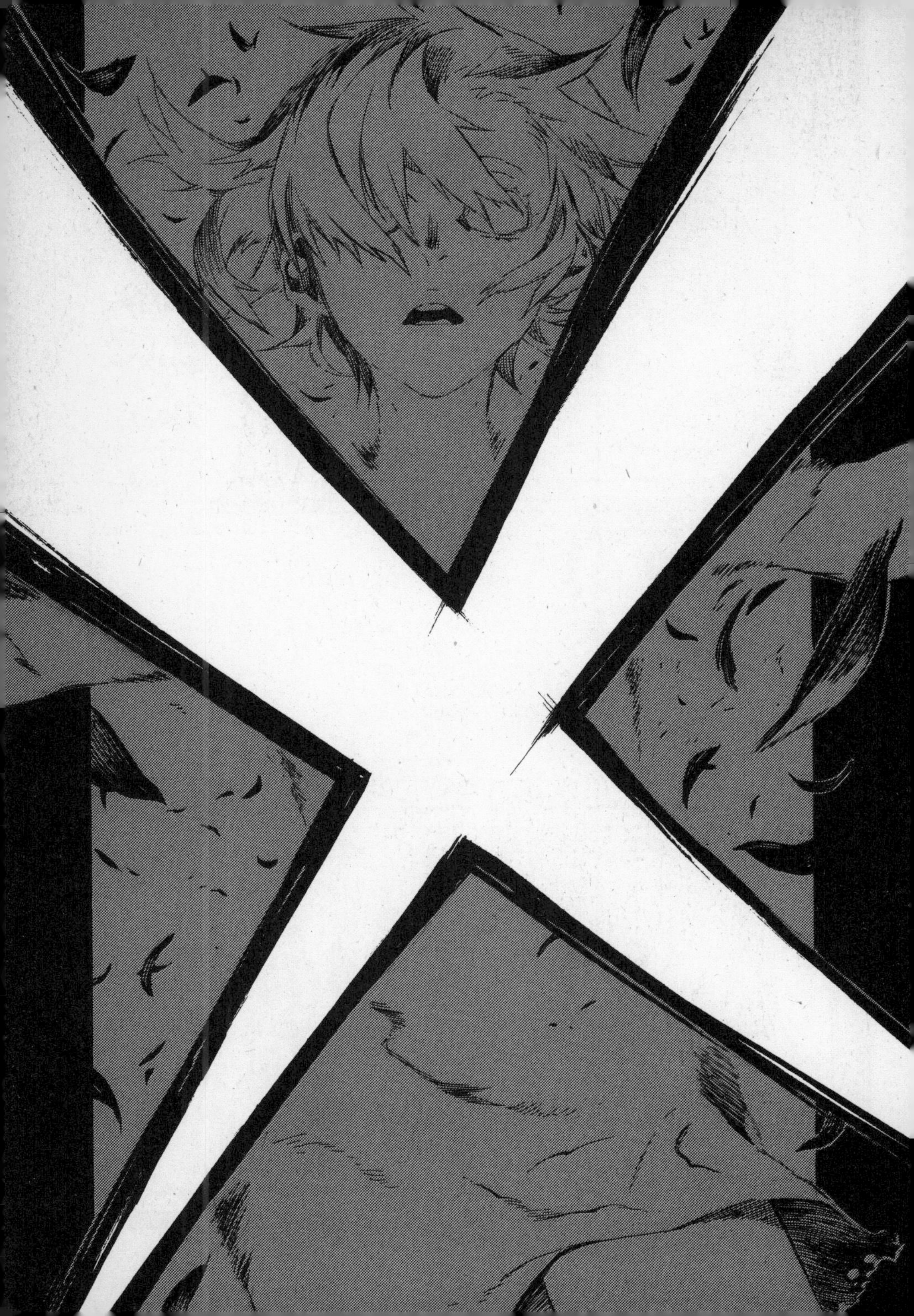

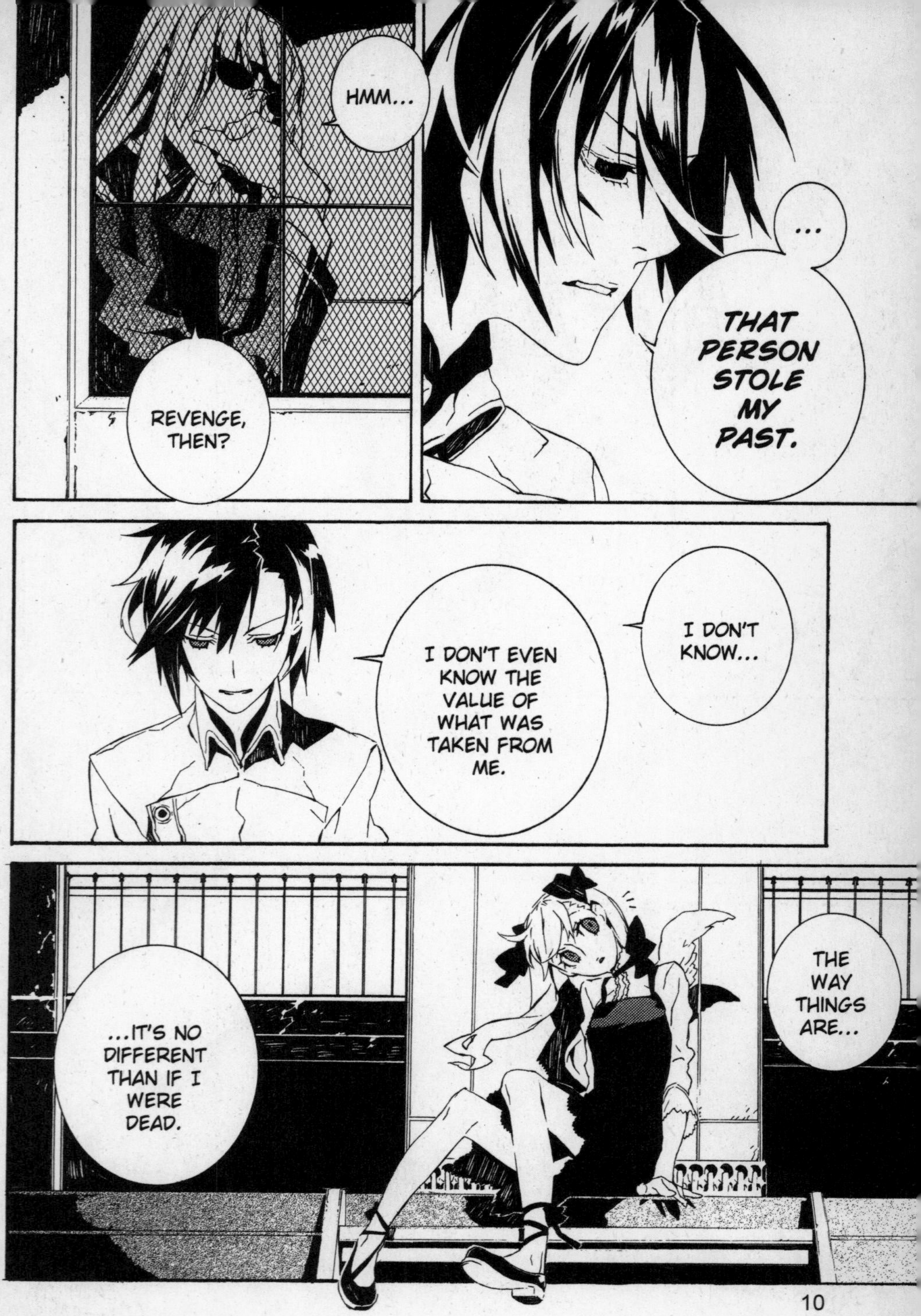
...
THAT PERSON STOLE MY PAST.
HMM...
REVENGE, THEN?
I DON'T KNOW...
I DON'T EVEN KNOW THE VALUE OF WHAT WAS TAKEN FROM ME.
THE WAY THINGS ARE...
...IT'S NO DIFFERENT THAN IF I WERE DEAD.

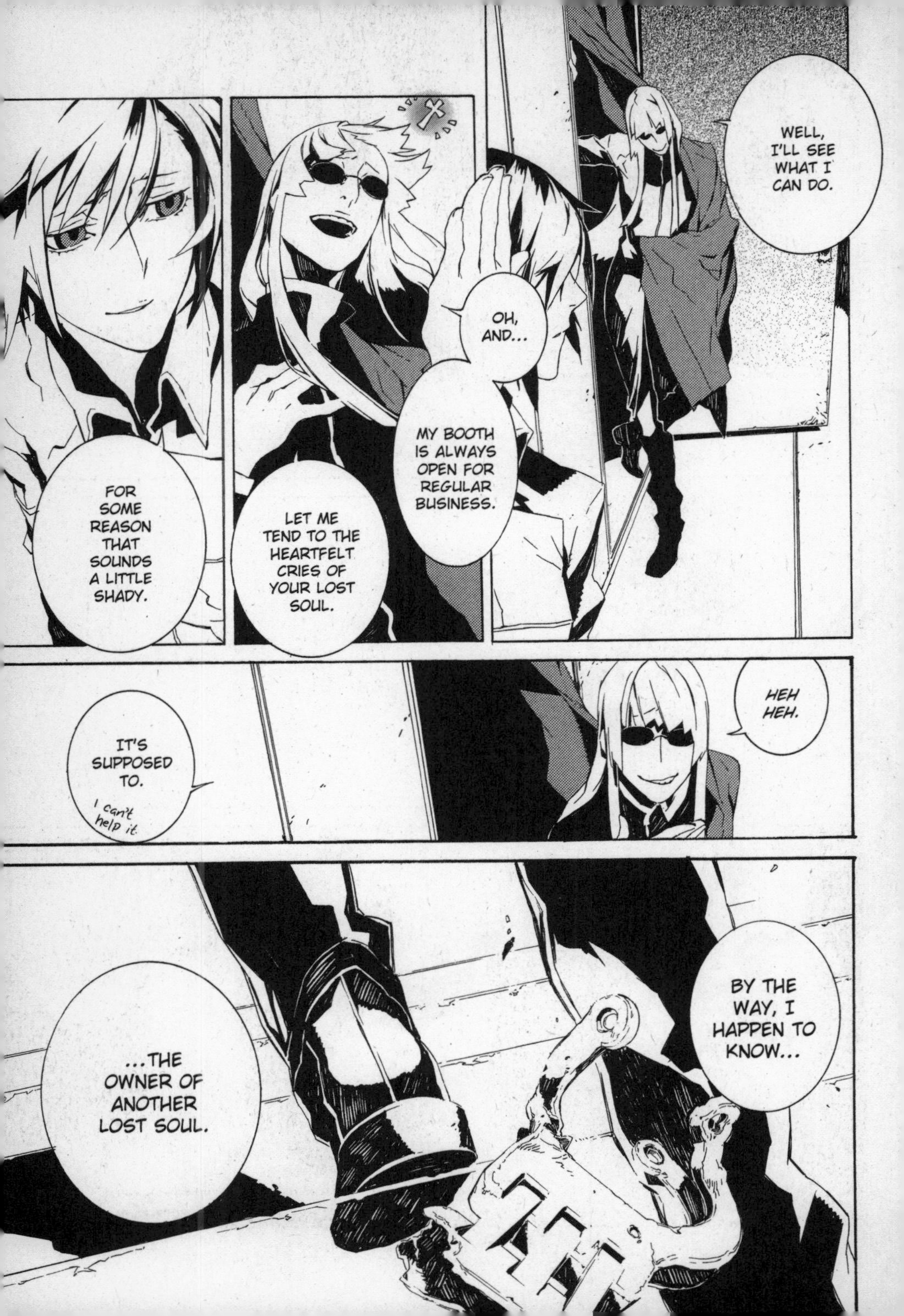
WELL, I'LL SEE WHAT I CAN DO.
OH, AND...
MY BOOTH IS ALWAYS OPEN FOR REGULAR BUSINESS.
LET ME TEND TO THE HEARTFELT CRIES OF YOUR LOST SOUL.
FOR SOME REASON THAT SOUNDS A LITTLE SHADY.
HEH HEH.
IT'S SUPPOSED TO.
I can't help it.
BY THE WAY, I HAPPEN TO KNOW...
...THE OWNER OF ANOTHER LOST SOUL.

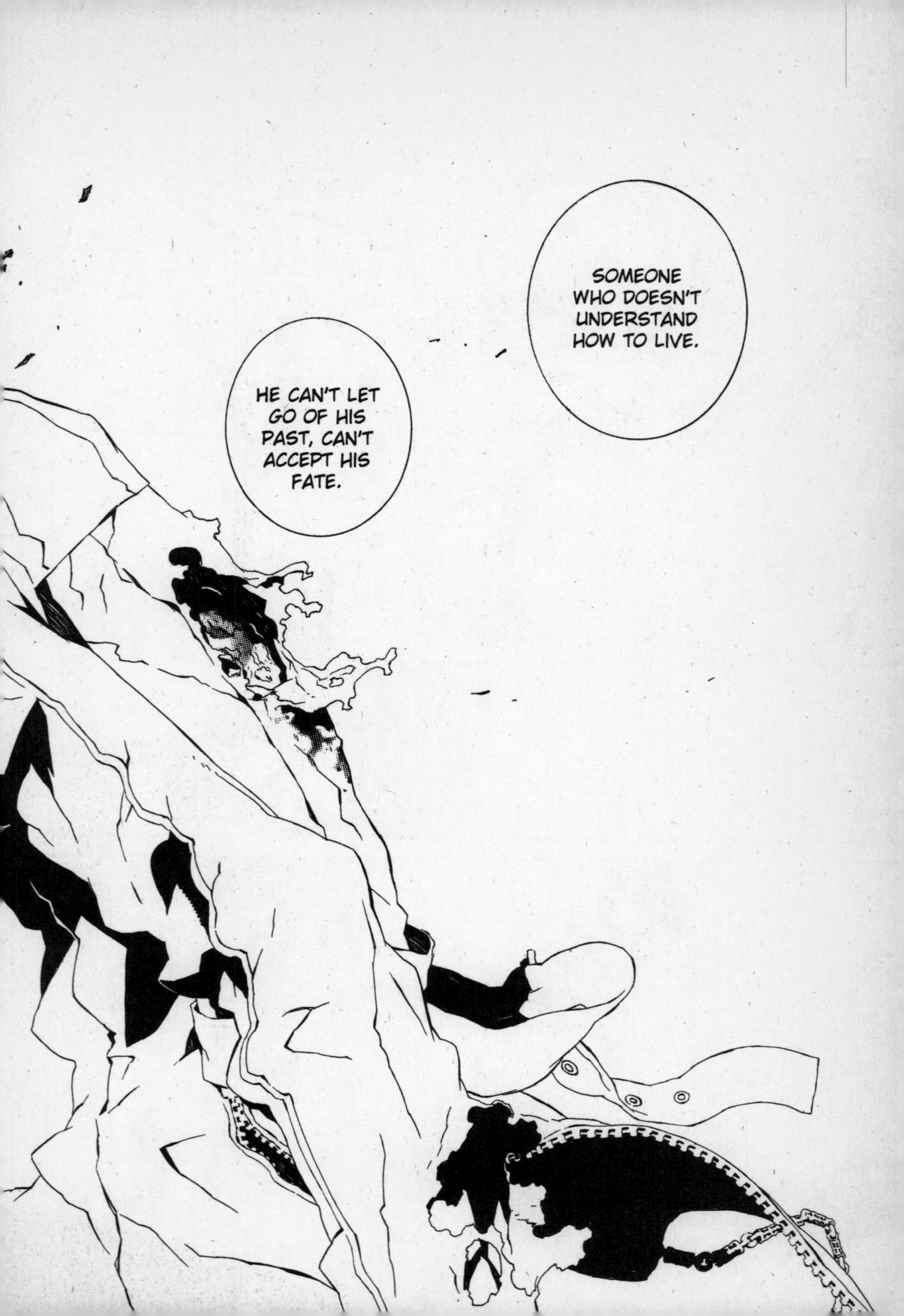
SOMEONE WHO DOESN'T UNDERSTAND HOW TO LIVE.
HE CAN'T LET GO OF HIS PAST, CAN'T ACCEPT HIS FATE.

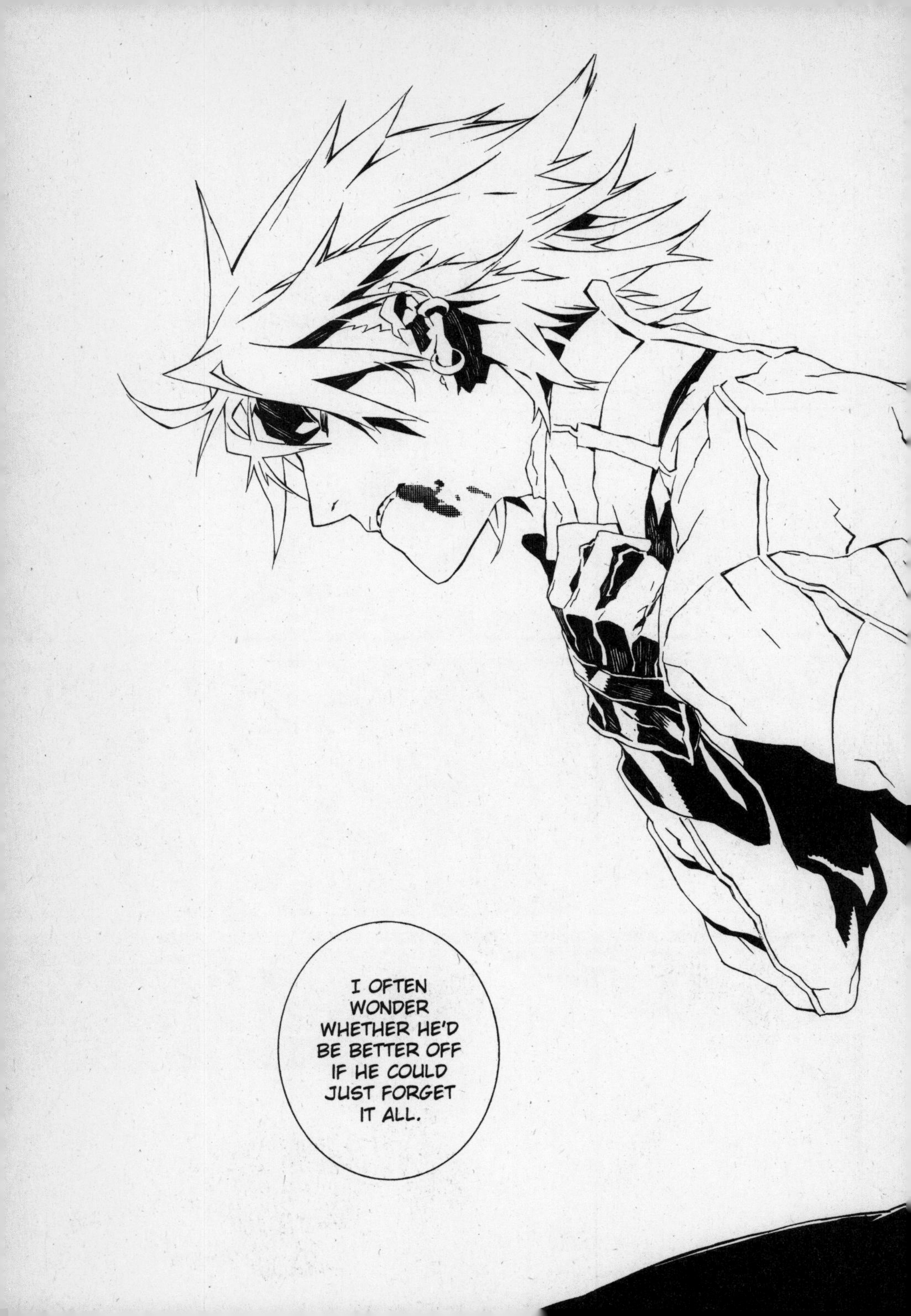
I OFTEN WONDER WHETHER HE'D BE BETTER OFF IF HE COULD JUST FORGET IT ALL.

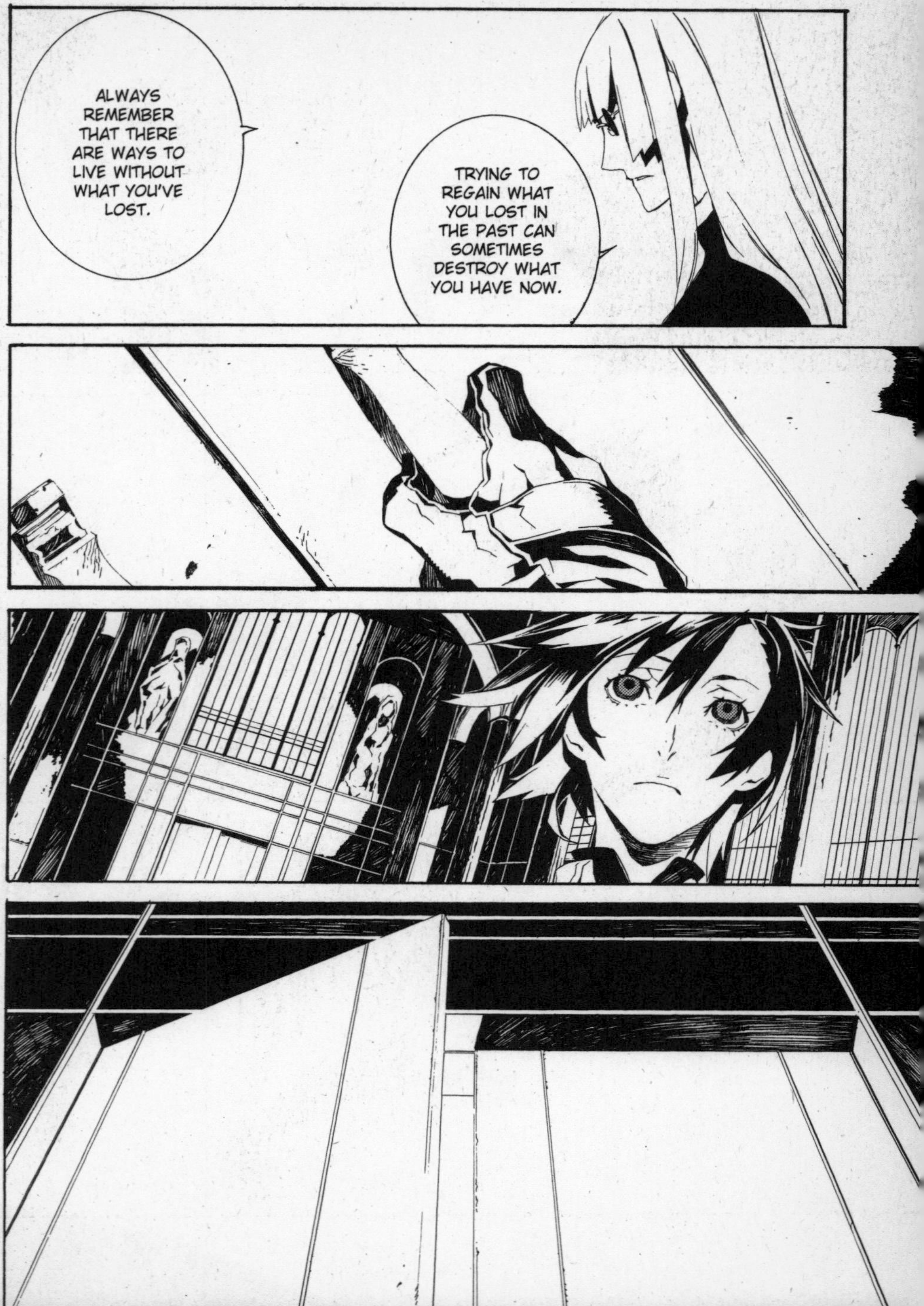
TRYING TO REGAIN WHAT YOU LOST IN THE PAST CAN SOMETIMES DESTROY WHAT YOU HAVE NOW.
ALWAYS REMEMBER THAT THERE ARE WAYS TO LIVE WITHOUT WHAT YOU'VE LOST.

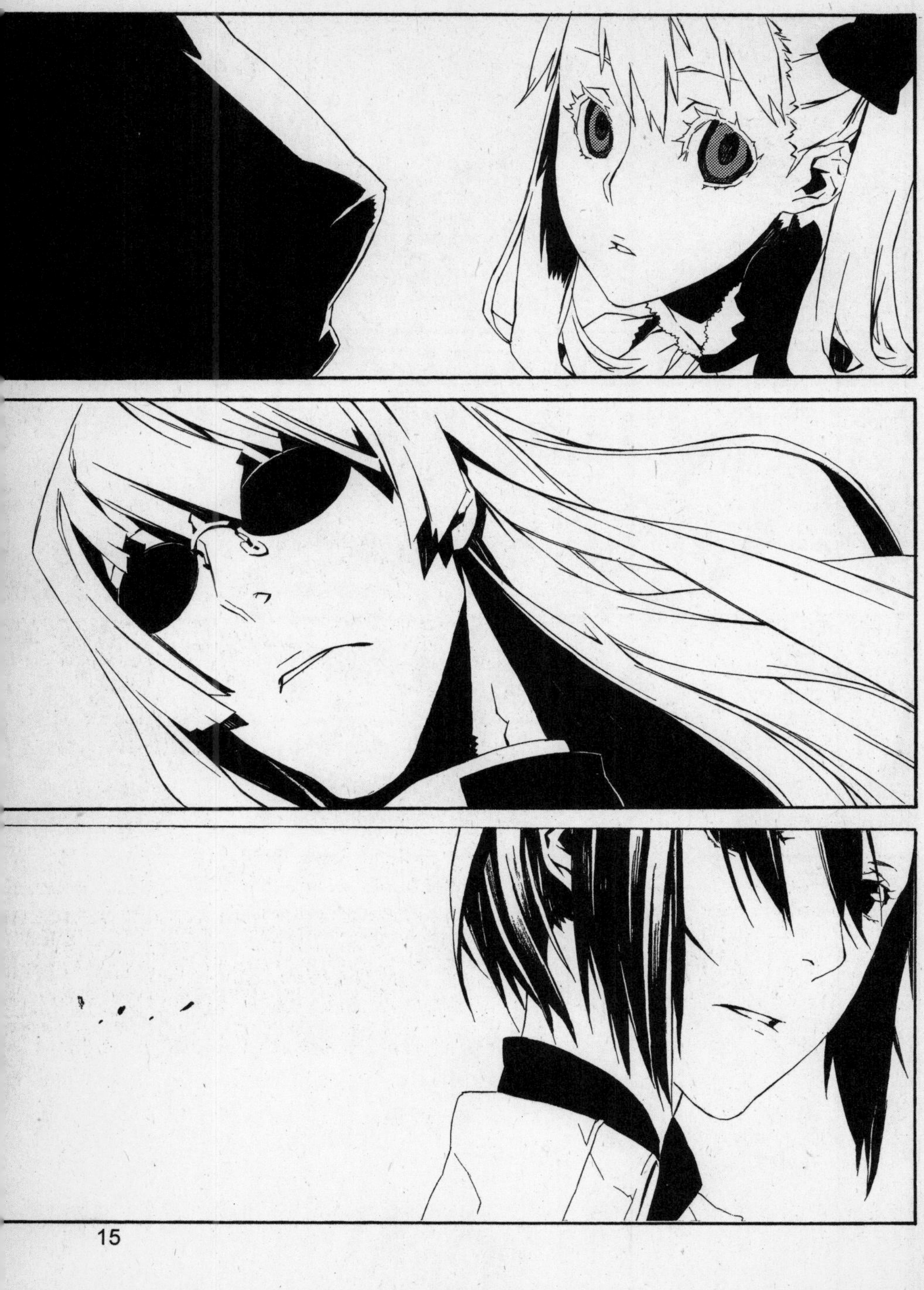
...

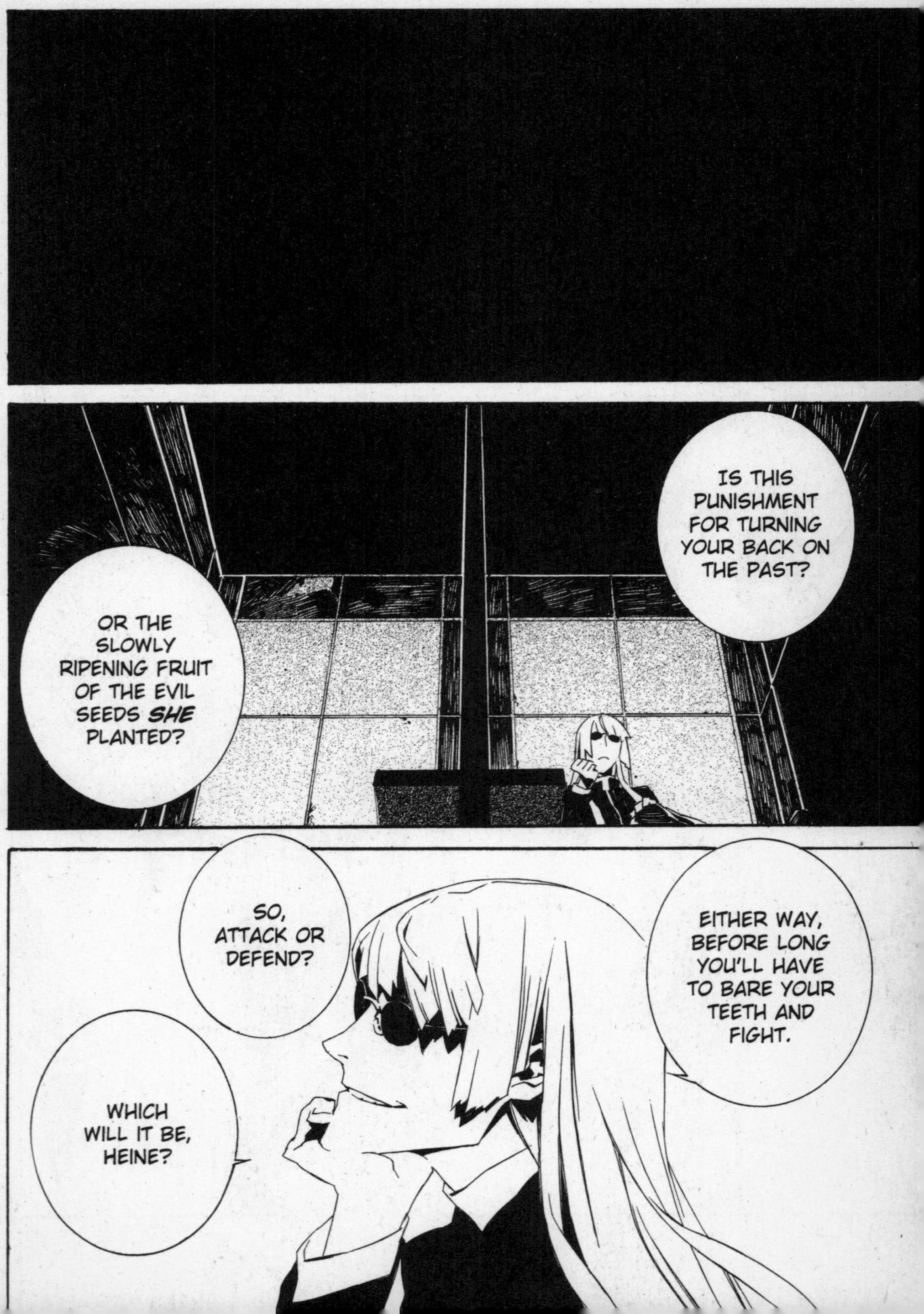
IS THIS PUNISHMENT FOR TURNING YOUR BACK ON THE PAST?
OR THE SLOWLY RIPENING FRUIT OF THE EVIL SEEDS *SHE* PLANTED?
EITHER WAY, BEFORE LONG YOU'LL HAVE TO BARE YOUR TEETH AND FIGHT.
SO, ATTACK OR DEFEND?
WHICH WILL IT BE, HEINE?

#13 Silver & Steel Ⅰ

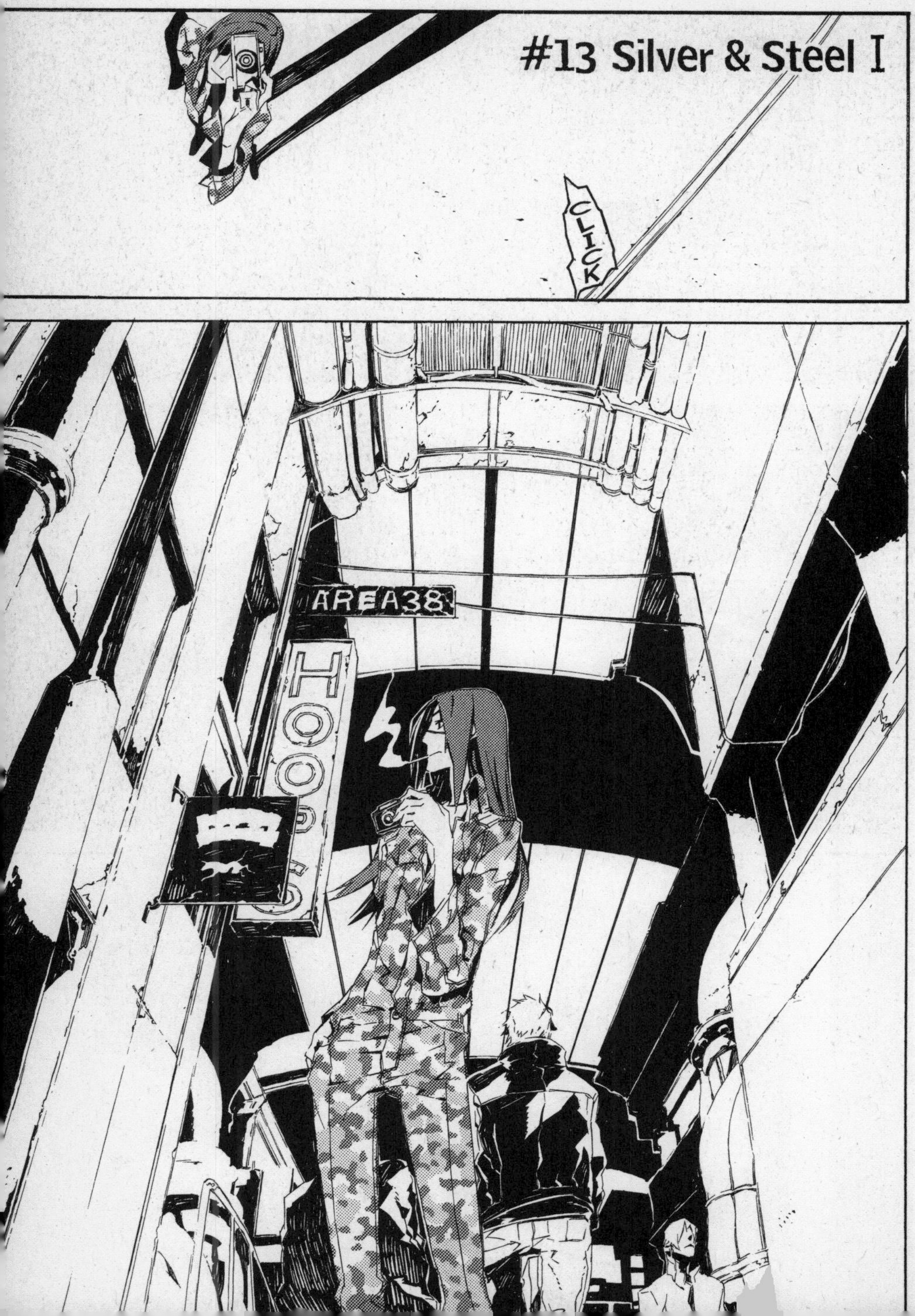
CLICK
AREA38

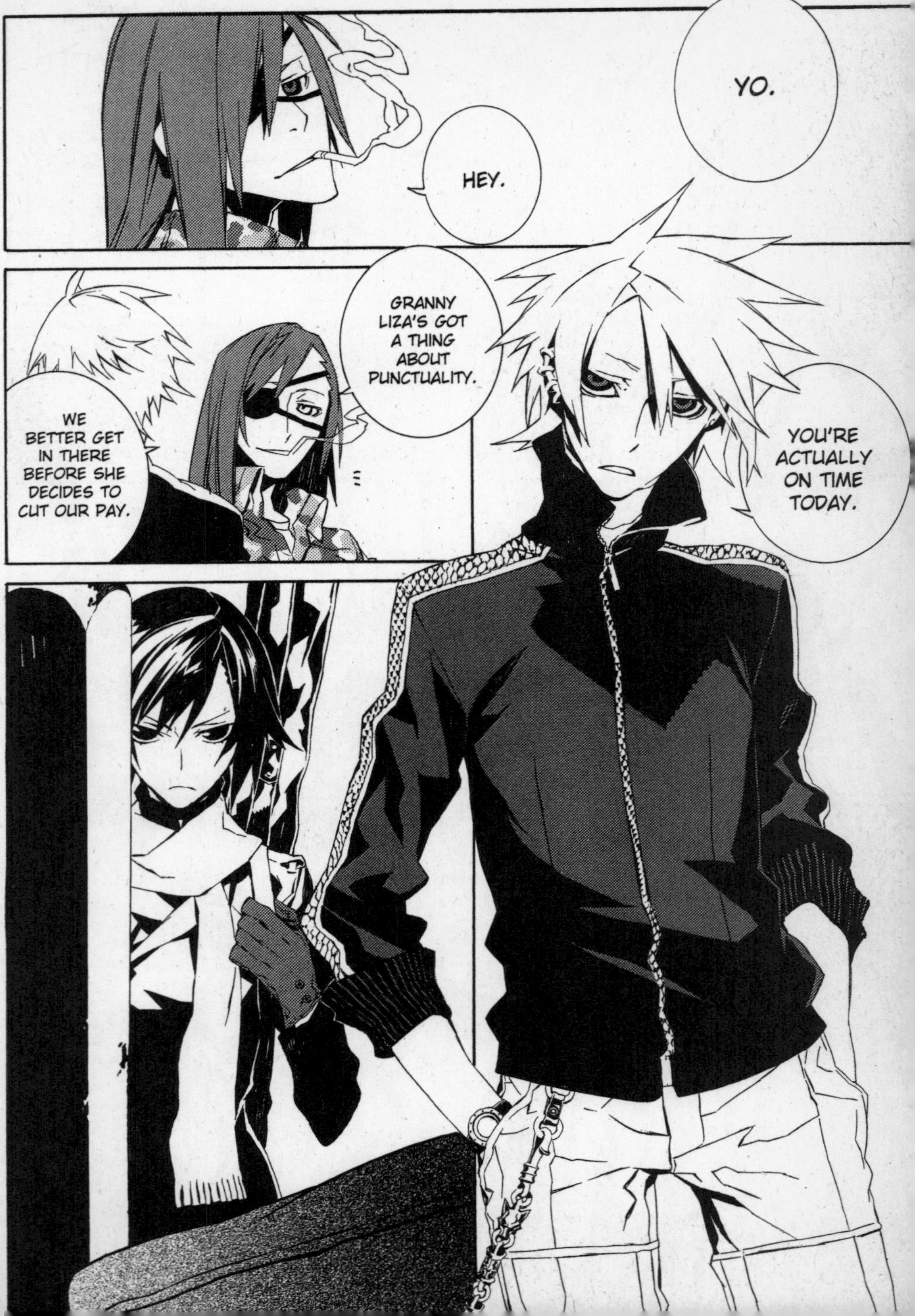
YO.
HEY.
YOU'RE ACTUALLY ON TIME TODAY.
GRANNY LIZA'S GOT A THING ABOUT PUNCTUALITY.
WE BETTER GET IN THERE BEFORE SHE DECIDES TO CUT OUR PAY.

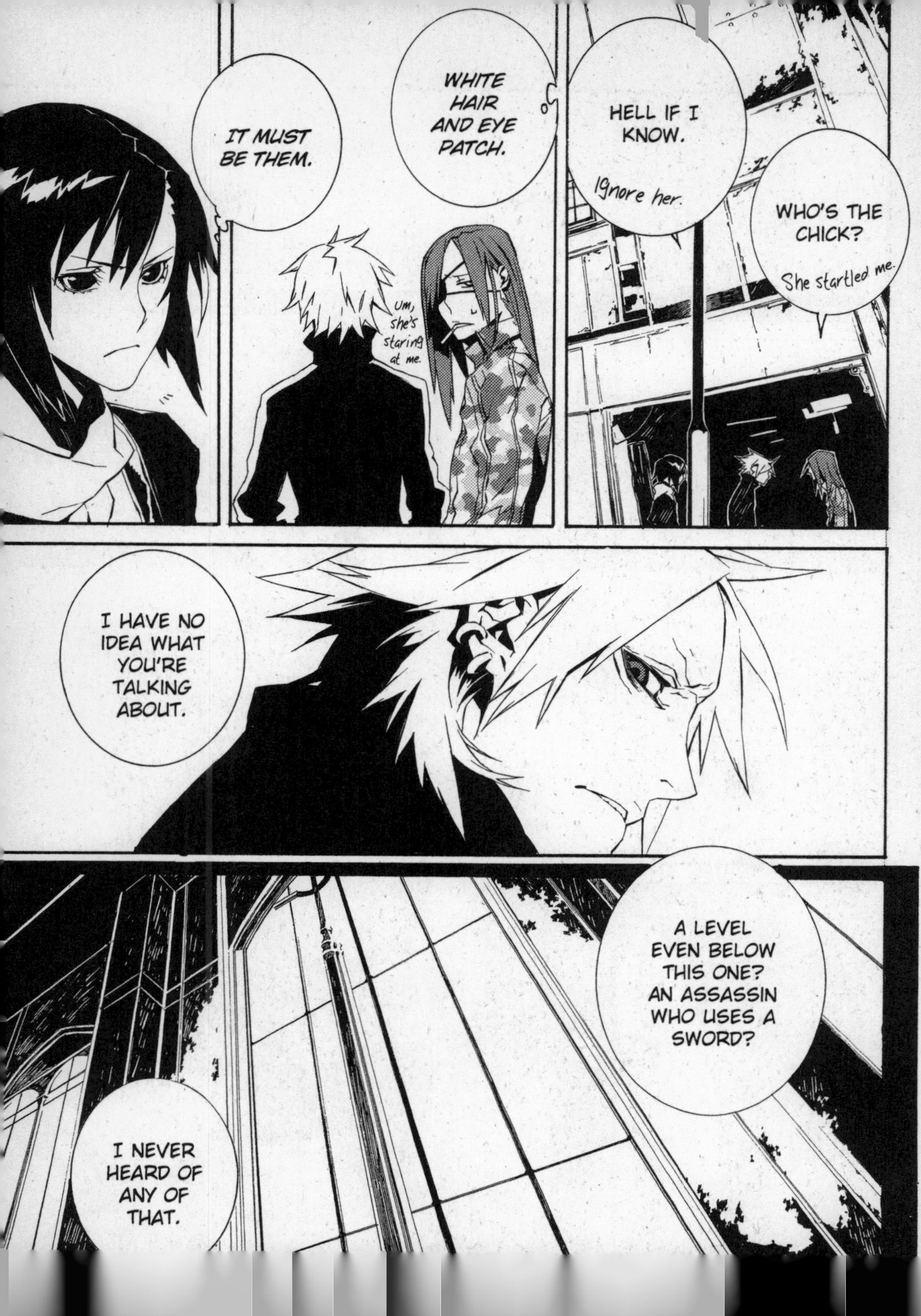
WHO'S THE CHICK?
She startled me.
HELL IF I KNOW.
Ignore her.
WHITE HAIR AND EYE PATCH.
Um, she's staring at me.
IT MUST BE THEM.
I HAVE NO IDEA WHAT YOU'RE TALKING ABOUT.
A LEVEL EVEN BELOW THIS ONE? AN ASSASSIN WHO USES A SWORD?
I NEVER HEARD OF ANY OF THAT.

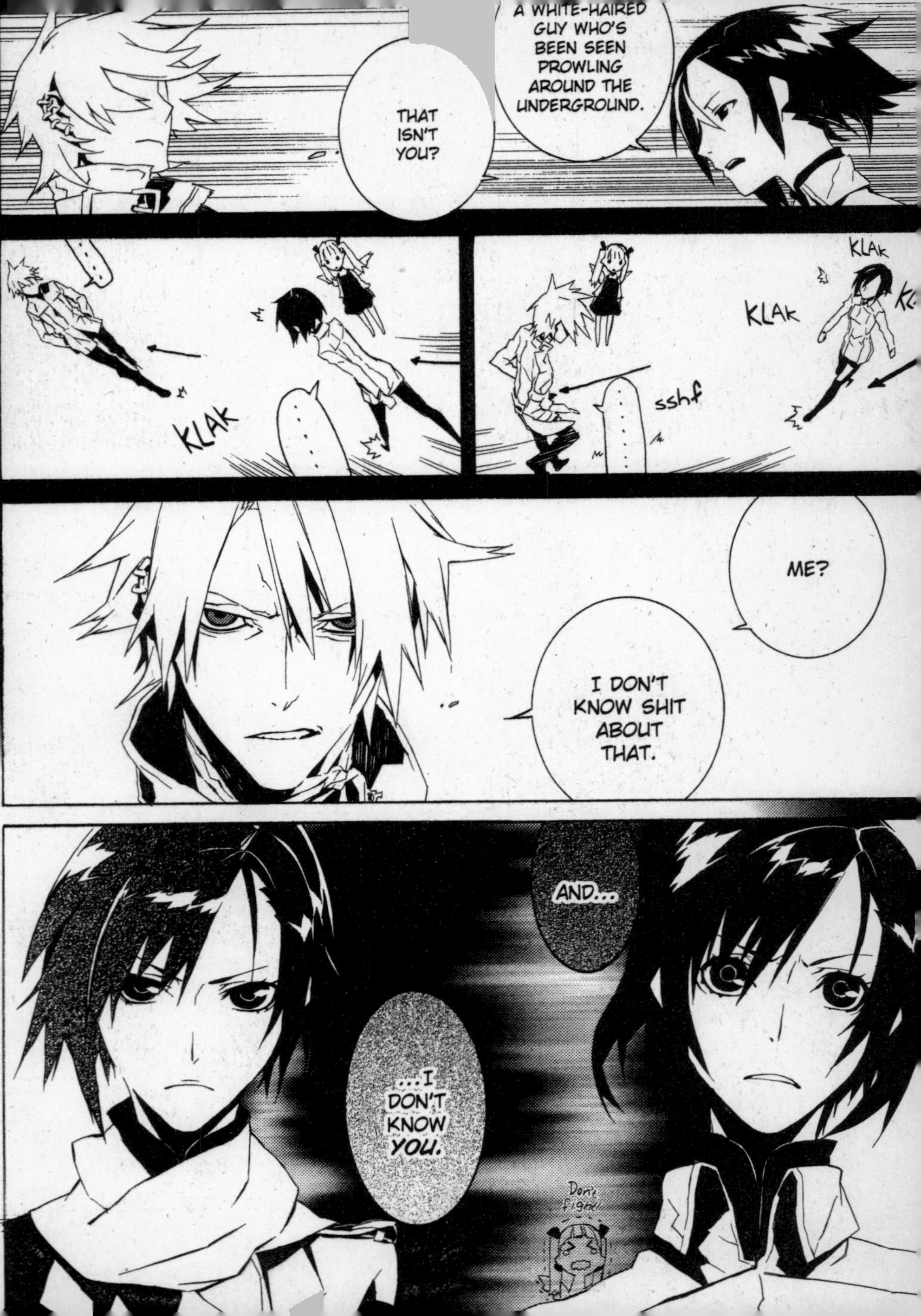
A WHITE-HAIRED GUY WHO'S BEEN SEEN PROWLING AROUND THE UNDERGROUND.
THAT ISN'T YOU?
KLAK
KLAK
sshf
...
...
KLAK
...
ME?
I DON'T KNOW SHIT ABOUT THAT.
AND...
...I DON'T KNOW YOU.
Don't fight!

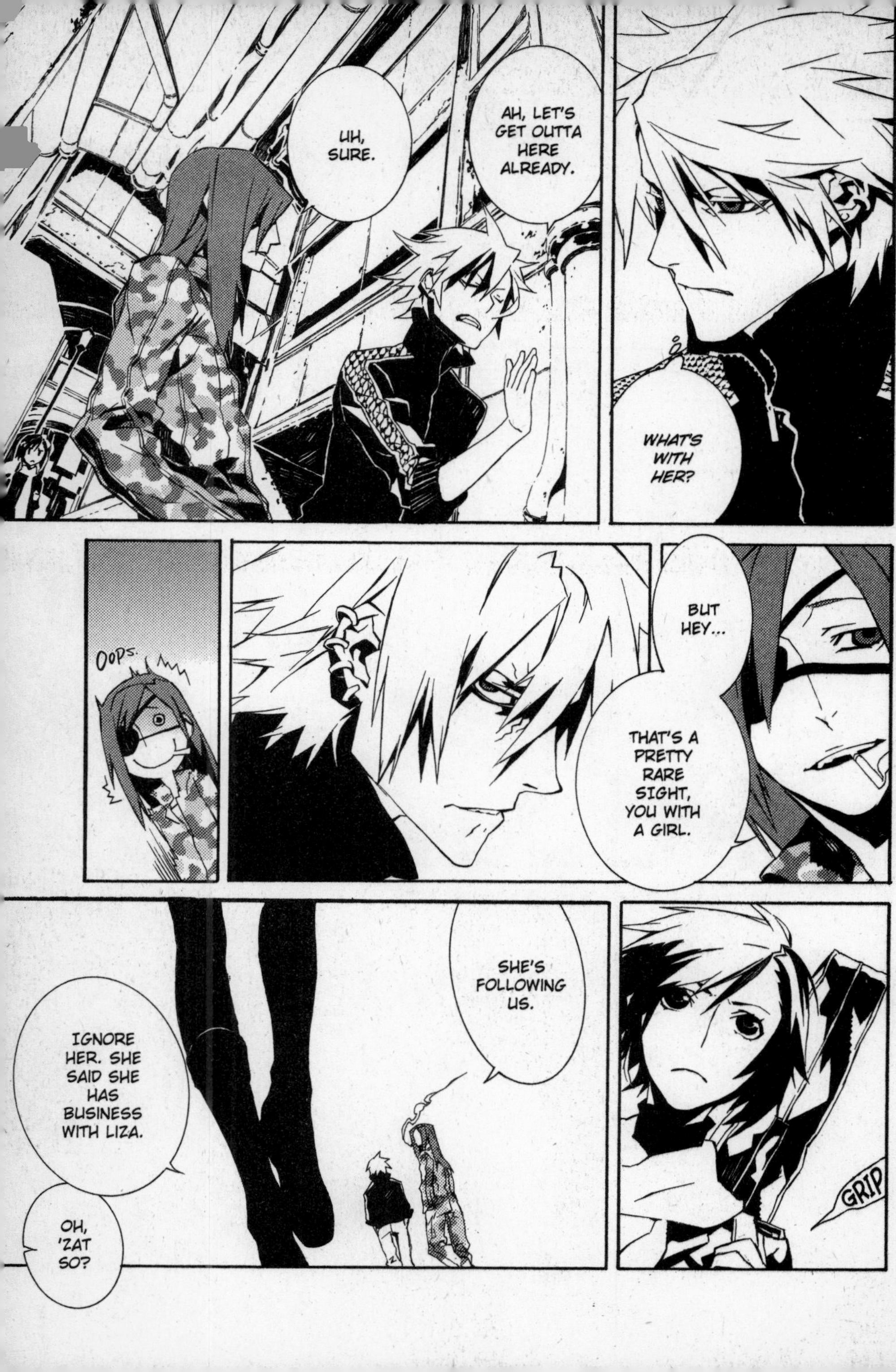
WHAT'S WITH HER?
AH, LET'S GET OUTTA HERE ALREADY.
UH, SURE.
BUT HEY...
THAT'S A PRETTY RARE SIGHT, YOU WITH A GIRL.
OOPS.
GRIP
SHE'S FOLLOWING US.
IGNORE HER. SHE SAID SHE HAS BUSINESS WITH LIZA.
OH, 'ZAT SO?

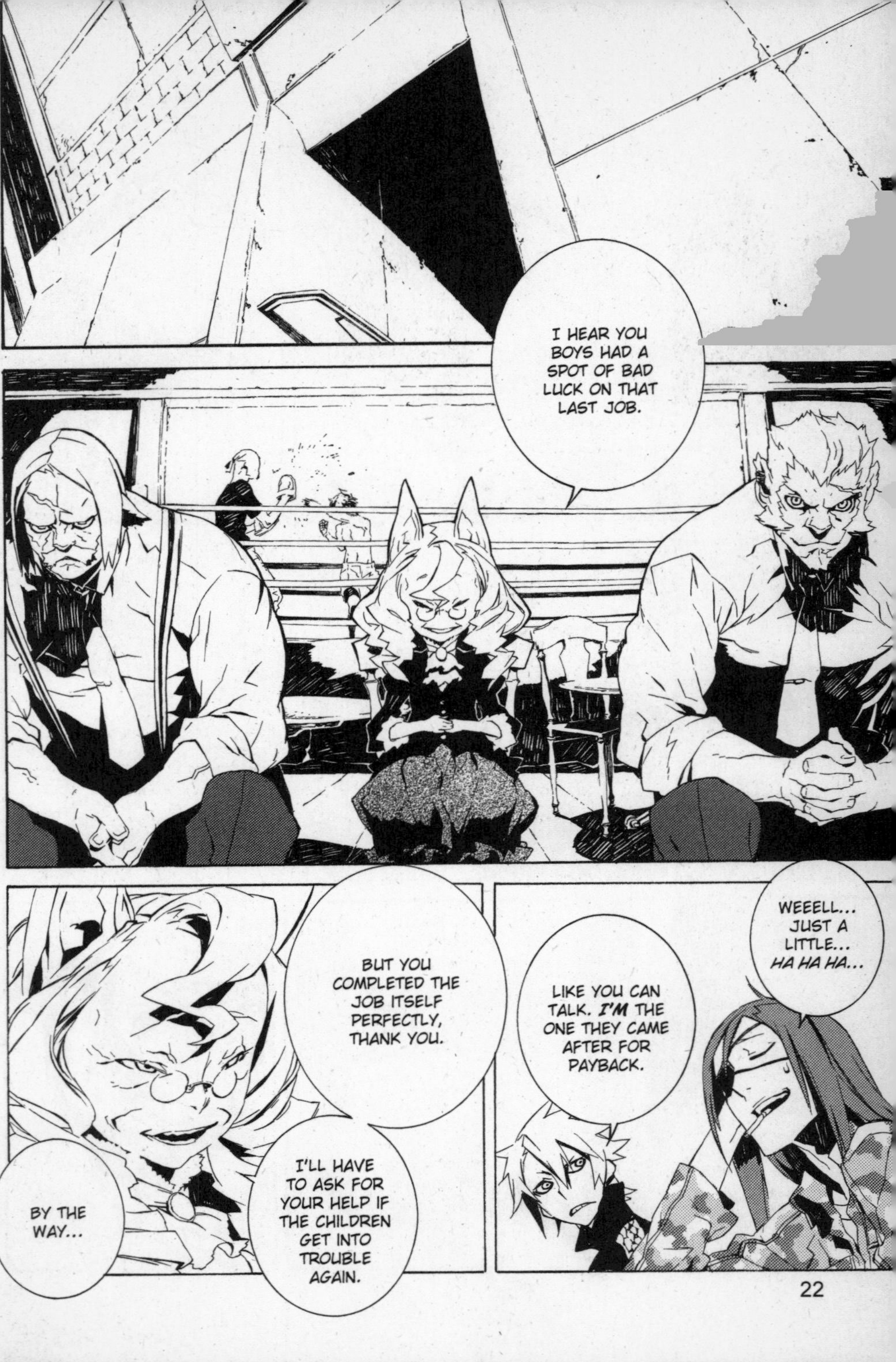
I HEAR YOU BOYS HAD A SPOT OF BAD LUCK ON THAT LAST JOB.
WEEELL... JUST A LITTLE... *HA HA HA...*
LIKE YOU CAN TALK. ***I'M*** THE ONE THEY CAME AFTER FOR PAYBACK.
BUT YOU COMPLETED THE JOB ITSELF PERFECTLY, THANK YOU.
I'LL HAVE TO ASK FOR YOUR HELP IF THE CHILDREN GET INTO TROUBLE AGAIN.
BY THE WAY...

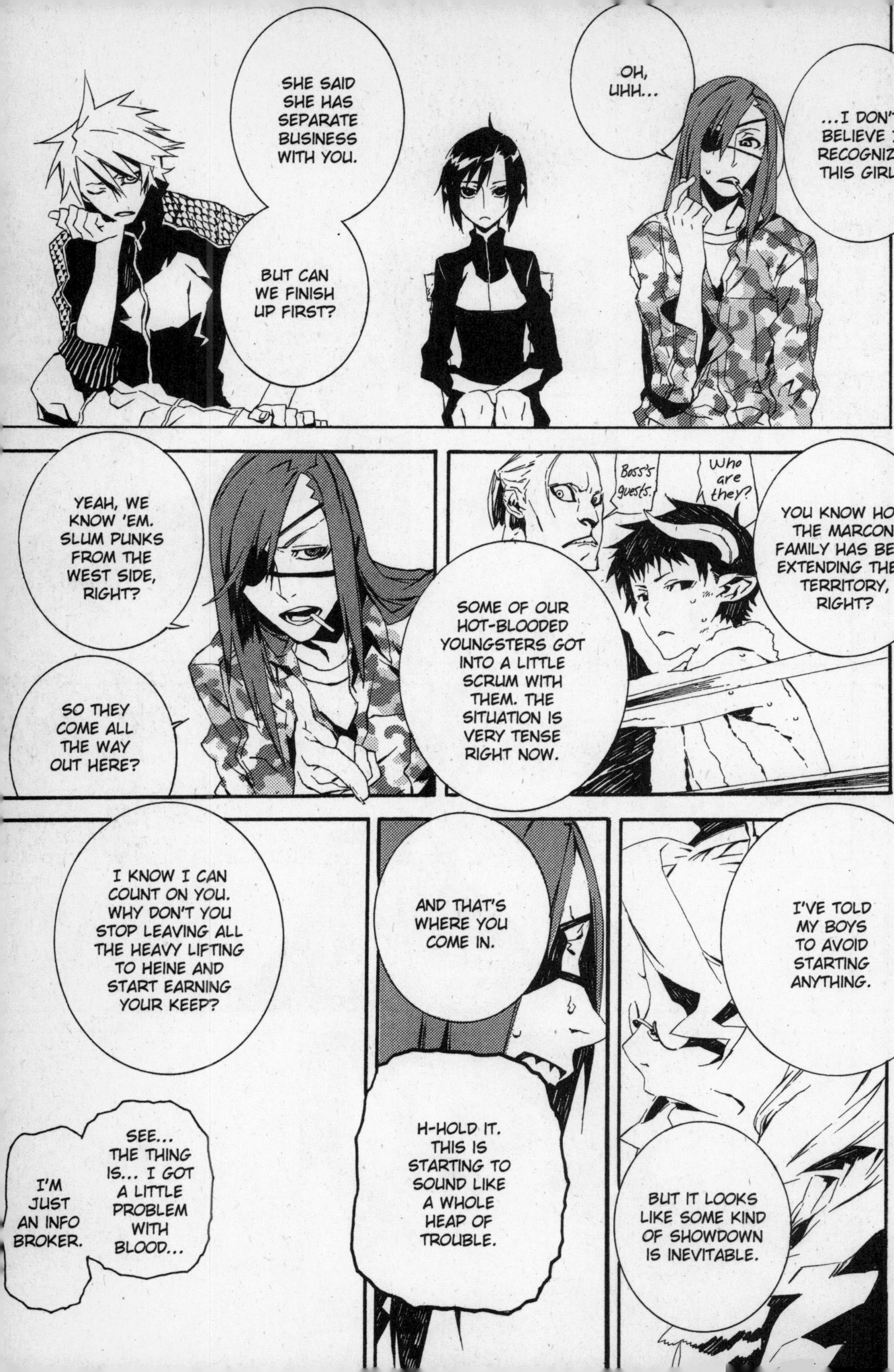
...I DON'T BELIEVE I RECOGNIZE THIS GIRL.
OH, UHH...
SHE SAID SHE HAS SEPARATE BUSINESS WITH YOU.
BUT CAN WE FINISH UP FIRST?
YOU KNOW HOW THE MARCONI FAMILY HAS BEEN EXTENDING THEIR TERRITORY, RIGHT?
Who are they?
Boss's guests.
SOME OF OUR HOT-BLOODED YOUNGSTERS GOT INTO A LITTLE SCRUM WITH THEM. THE SITUATION IS VERY TENSE RIGHT NOW.
YEAH, WE KNOW 'EM. SLUM PUNKS FROM THE WEST SIDE, RIGHT?
SO THEY COME ALL THE WAY OUT HERE?
I'VE TOLD MY BOYS TO AVOID STARTING ANYTHING.
BUT IT LOOKS LIKE SOME KIND OF SHOWDOWN IS INEVITABLE.
AND THAT'S WHERE YOU COME IN.
H-HOLD IT. THIS IS STARTING TO SOUND LIKE A WHOLE HEAP OF TROUBLE.
I KNOW I CAN COUNT ON YOU. WHY DON'T YOU STOP LEAVING ALL THE HEAVY LIFTING TO HEINE AND START EARNING YOUR KEEP?
SEE... THE THING IS... I GOT A LITTLE PROBLEM WITH BLOOD...
I'M JUST AN INFO BROKER.

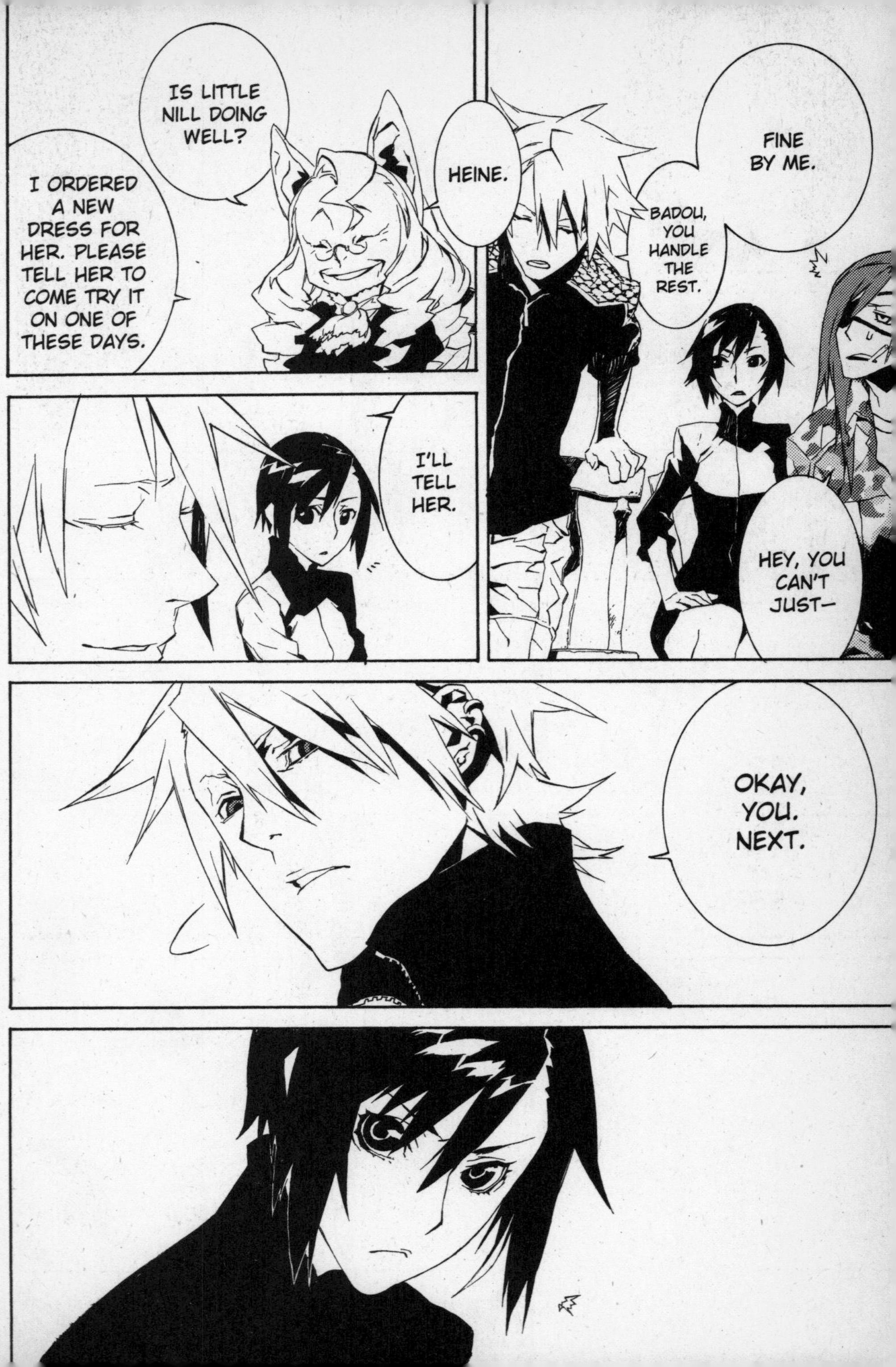
FINE BY ME.
BADOU, YOU HANDLE THE REST.
HEY, YOU CAN'T JUST—
HEINE.
IS LITTLE NILL DOING WELL?
I ORDERED A NEW DRESS FOR HER. PLEASE TELL HER TO COME TRY IT ON ONE OF THESE DAYS.
I'LL TELL HER.
OKAY, YOU. NEXT.

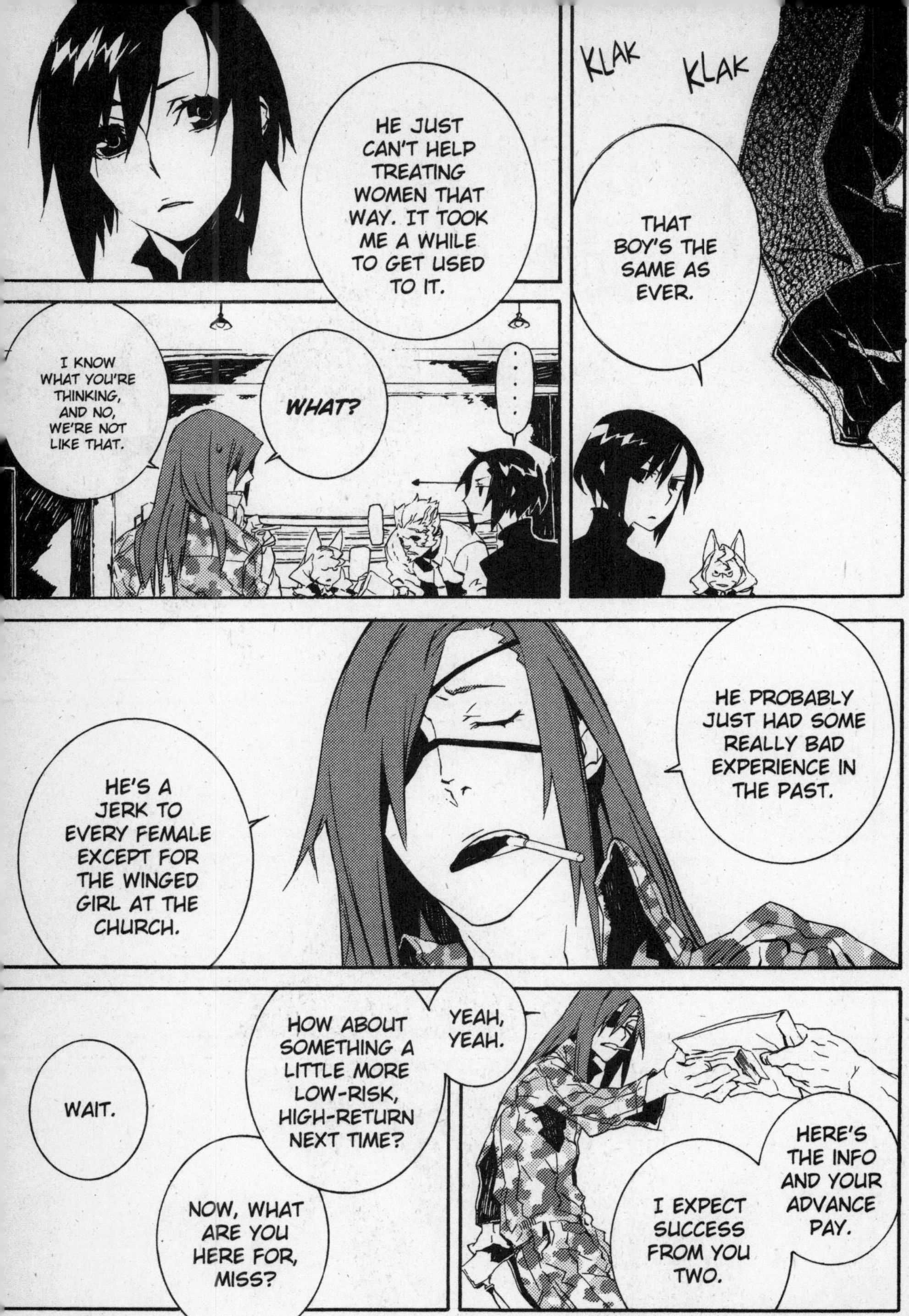
KLAK
KLAK
THAT BOY'S THE SAME AS EVER.
HE JUST CAN'T HELP TREATING WOMEN THAT WAY. IT TOOK ME A WHILE TO GET USED TO IT.
......
WHAT?
I KNOW WHAT YOU'RE THINKING, AND NO, WE'RE NOT LIKE THAT.
HE PROBABLY JUST HAD SOME REALLY BAD EXPERIENCE IN THE PAST.
HE'S A JERK TO EVERY FEMALE EXCEPT FOR THE WINGED GIRL AT THE CHURCH.
HERE'S THE INFO AND YOUR ADVANCE PAY.
I EXPECT SUCCESS FROM YOU TWO.
YEAH, YEAH.
HOW ABOUT SOMETHING A LITTLE MORE LOW-RISK, HIGH-RETURN NEXT TIME?
WAIT.
NOW, WHAT ARE YOU HERE FOR, MISS?

IF YOU'RE AN INFORMATION BROKER, I WANT TO TALK TO YOU AS WELL.

Oh, she speaks.

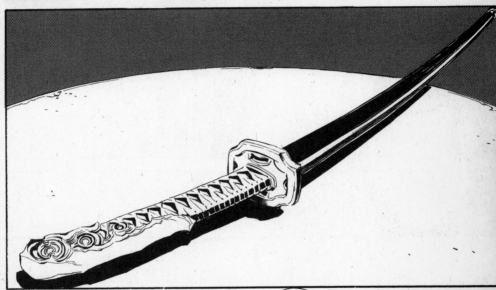

WHAT'S THIS? A KATANA?

#14 Silver & Steel Ⅱ

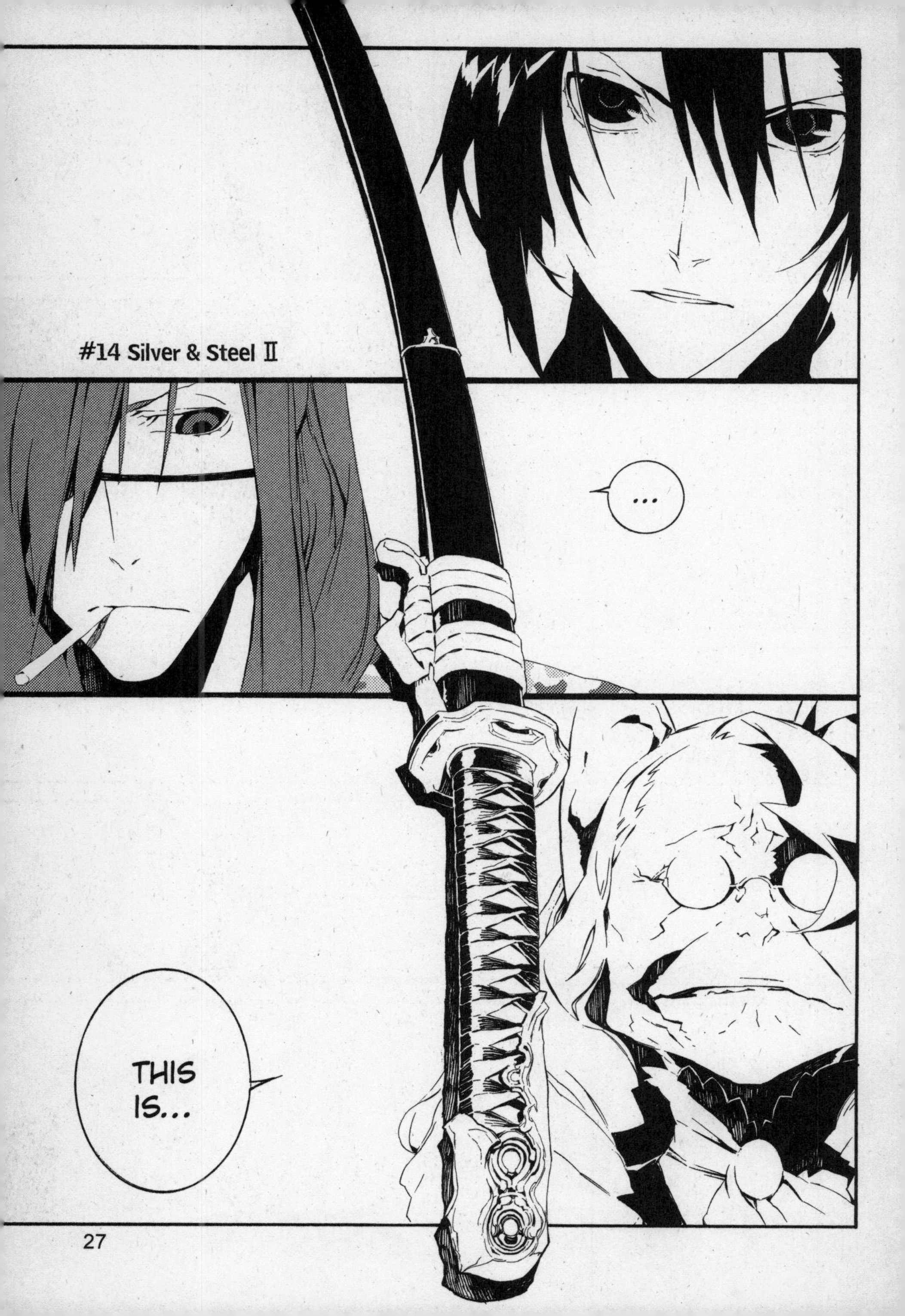
...
THIS IS...

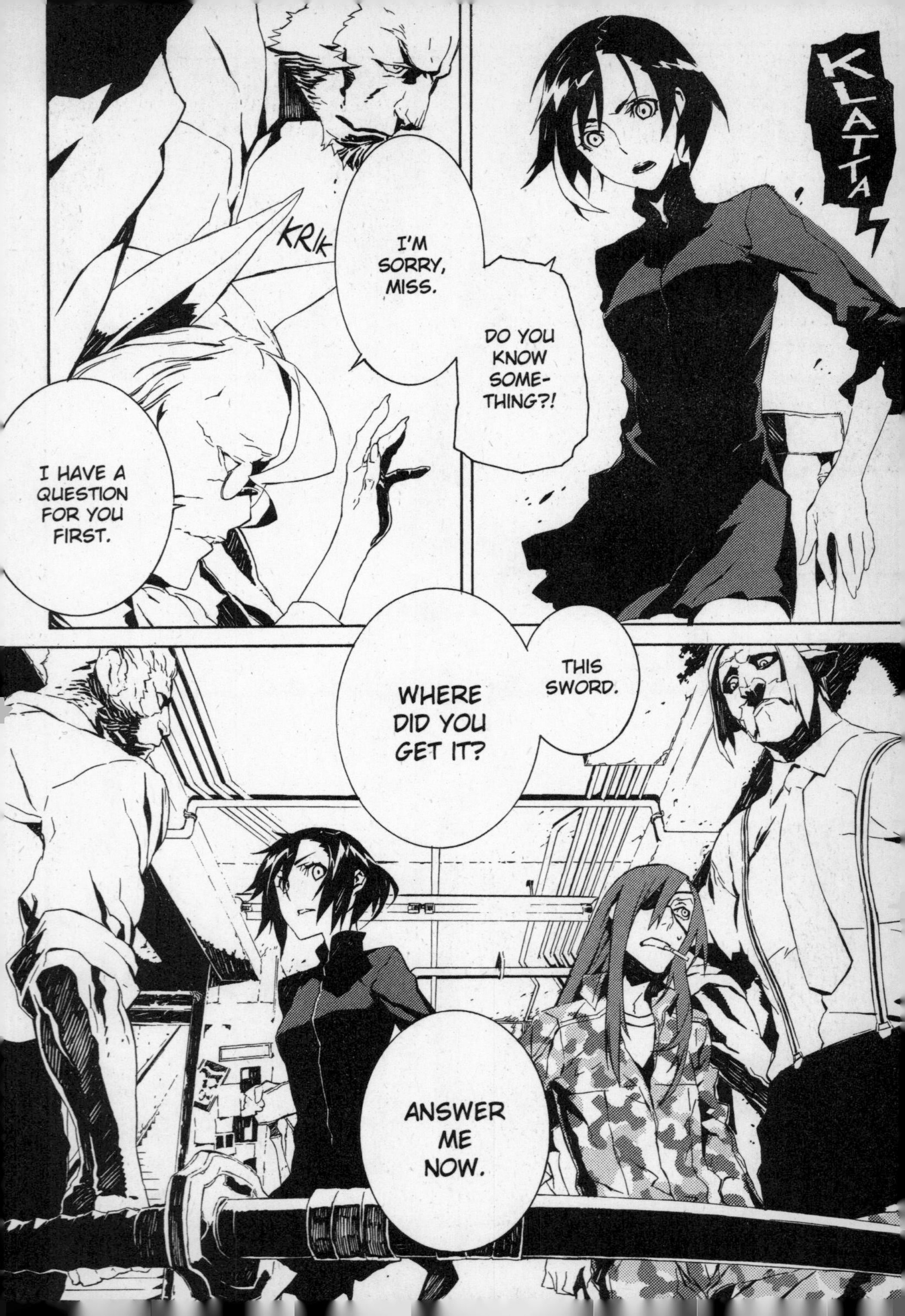
KLATTA
DO YOU KNOW SOME-THING?!
KRIK
I'M SORRY, MISS.
I HAVE A QUESTION FOR YOU FIRST.
THIS SWORD.
WHERE DID YOU GET IT?
ANSWER ME NOW.

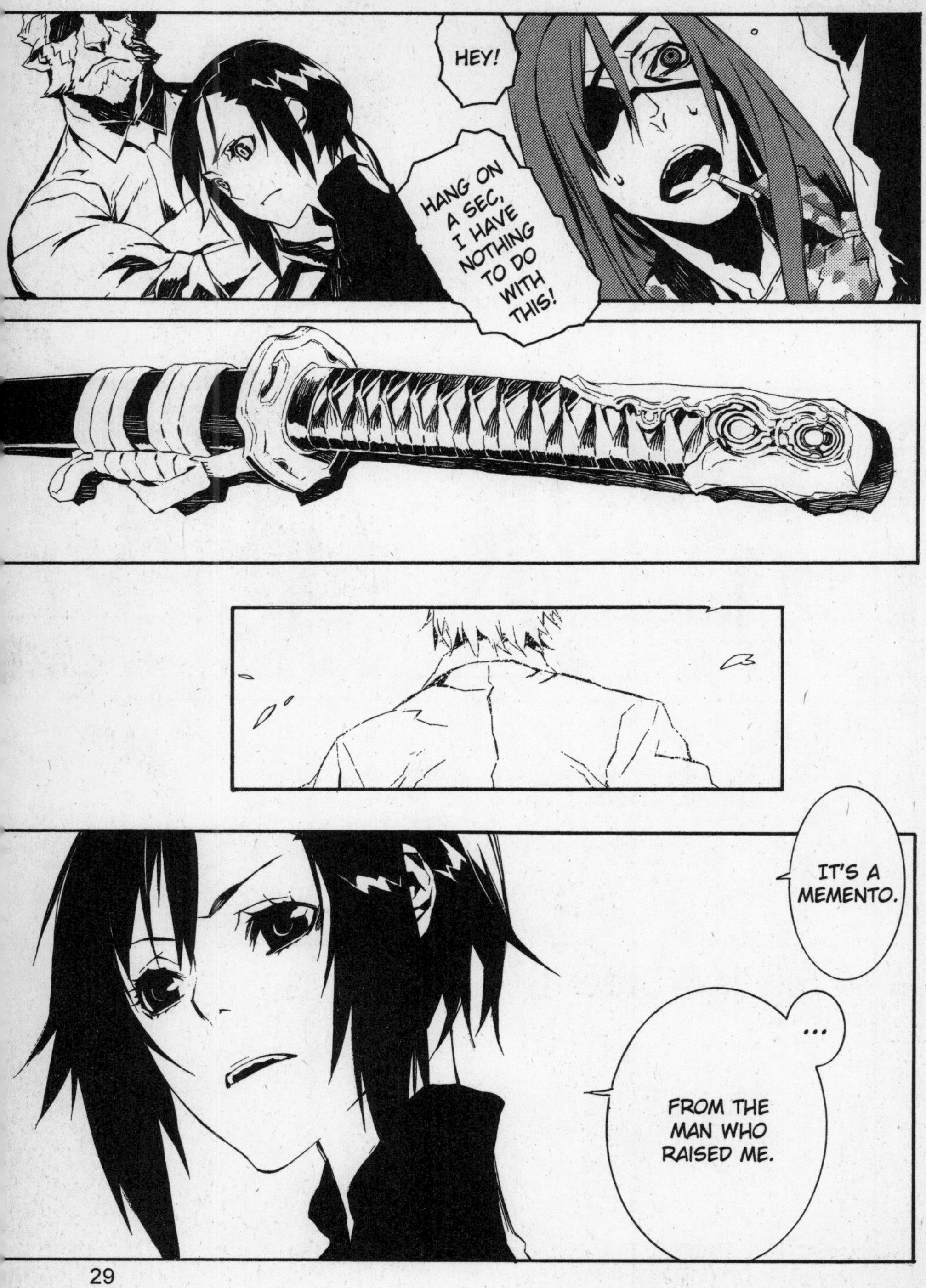
HEY!
HANG ON A SEC, I HAVE NOTHING TO DO WITH THIS!
IT'S A MEMENTO.
...
FROM THE MAN WHO RAISED ME.

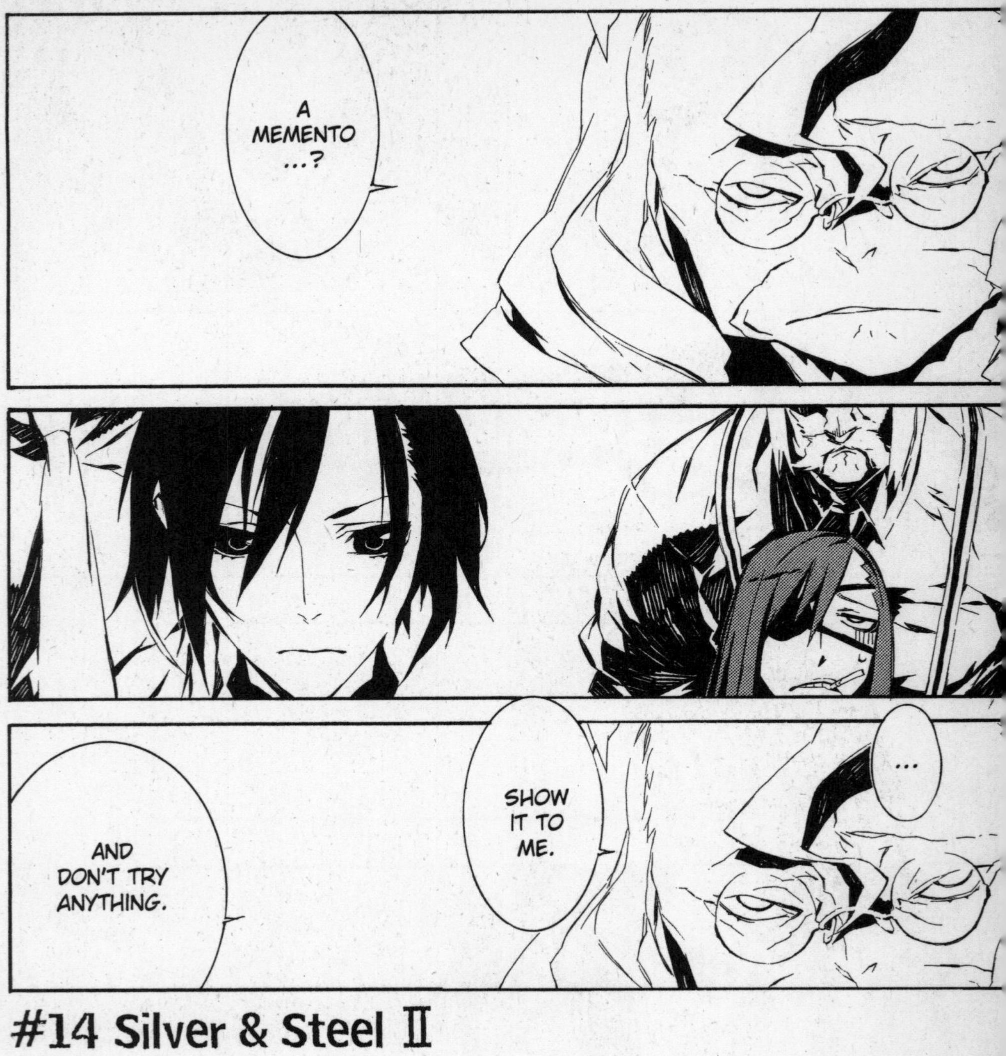
A MEMENTO ...?
...
SHOW IT TO ME.
AND DON'T TRY ANYTHING.

#14 Silver & Steel II

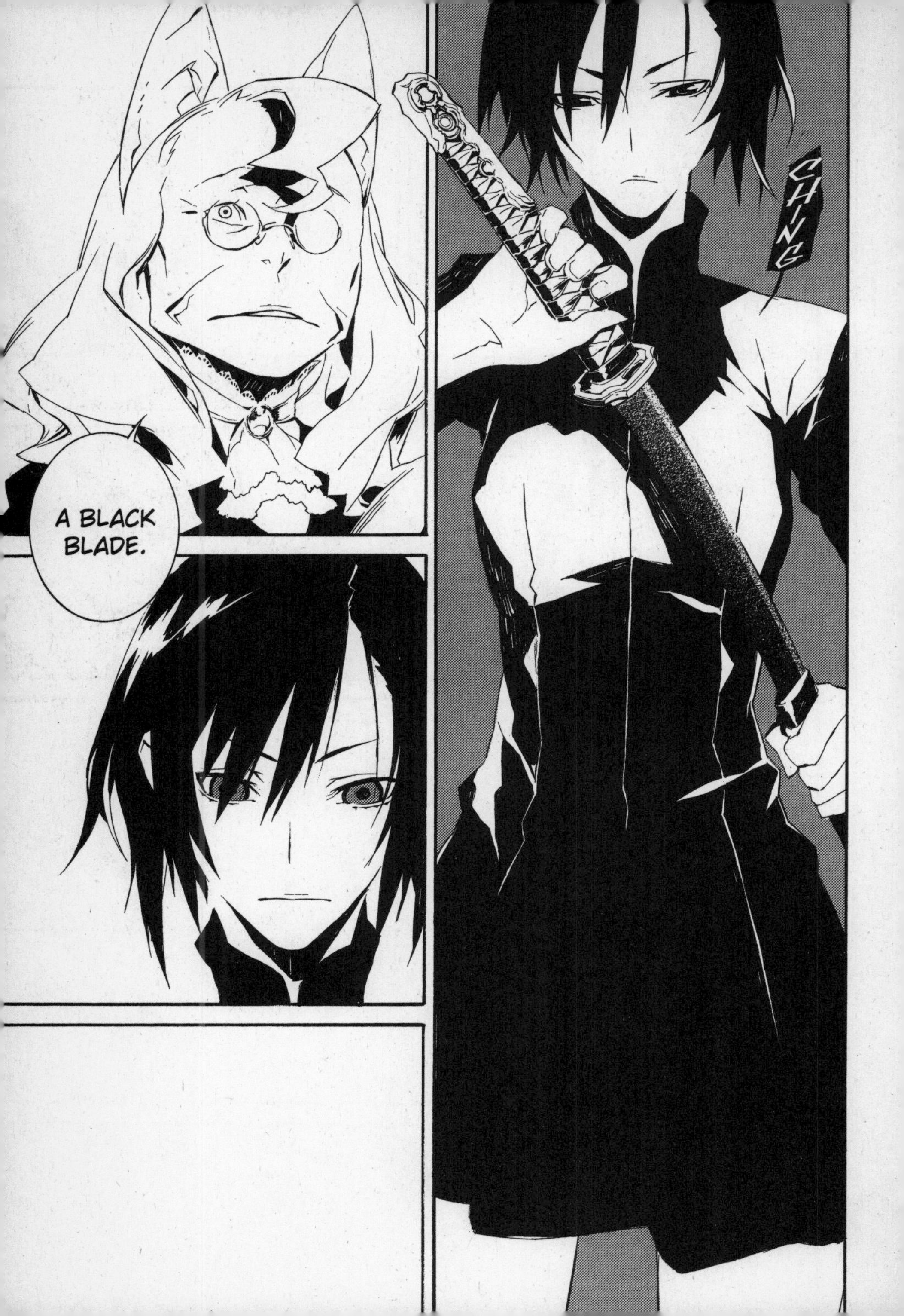
CHING
A BLACK BLADE.

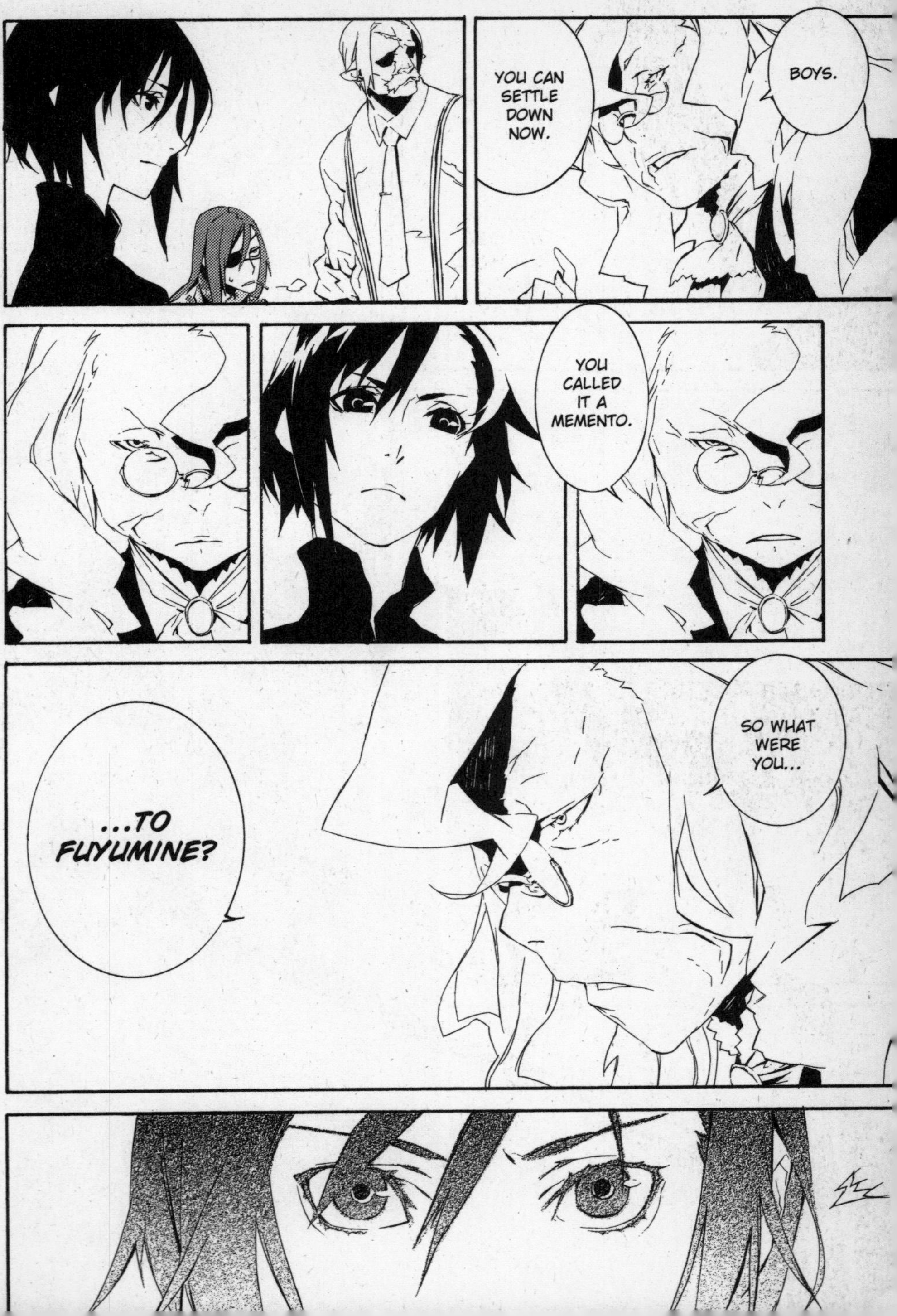
BOYS.
YOU CAN SETTLE DOWN NOW.
YOU CALLED IT A MEMENTO.
SO WHAT WERE YOU...
...TO FUYUMINE?

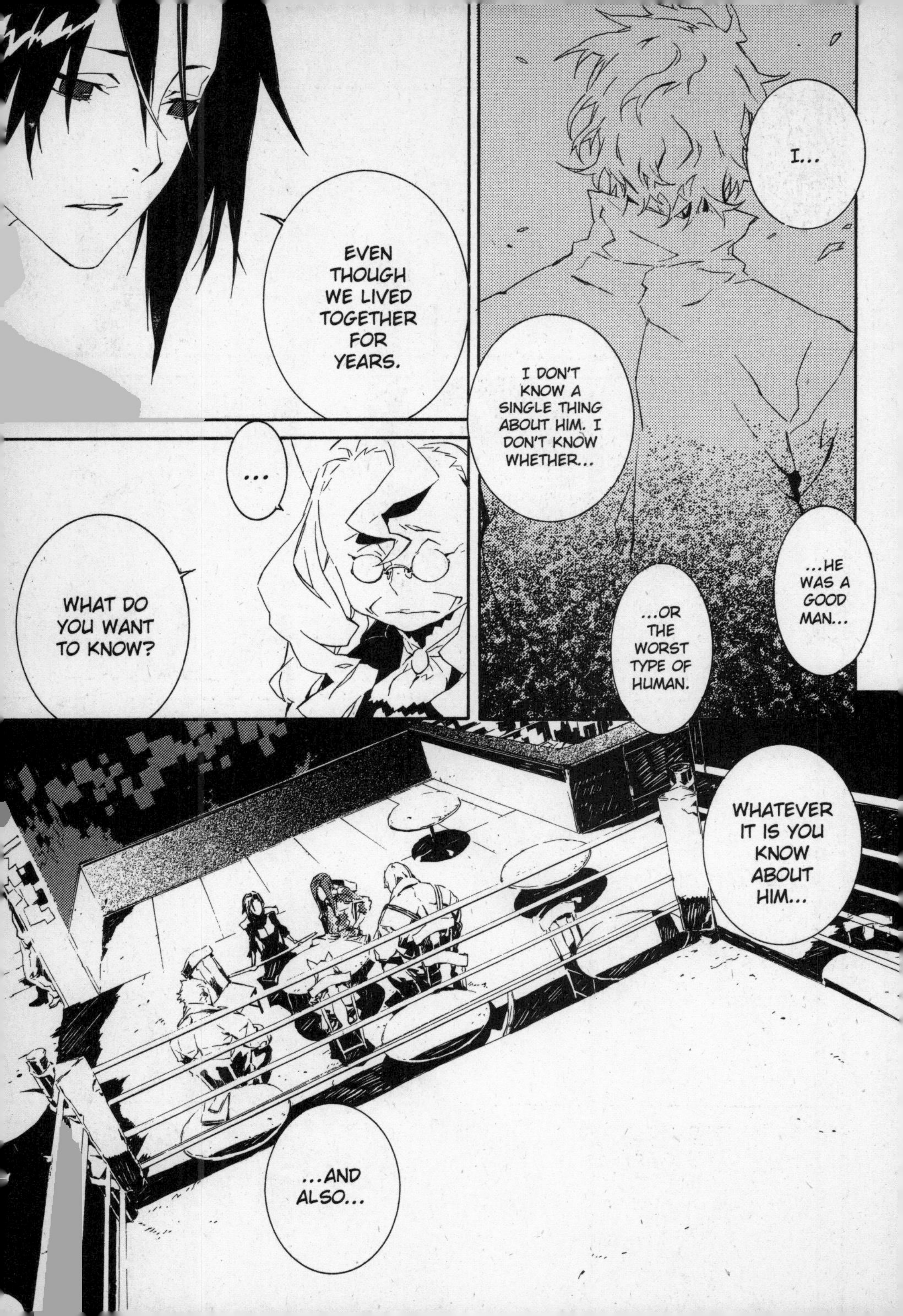
I...
I DON'T KNOW A SINGLE THING ABOUT HIM. I DON'T KNOW WHETHER...
...HE WAS A GOOD MAN...
...OR THE WORST TYPE OF HUMAN.
EVEN THOUGH WE LIVED TOGETHER FOR YEARS.
...
WHAT DO YOU WANT TO KNOW?
WHATEVER IT IS YOU KNOW ABOUT HIM...
...AND ALSO...

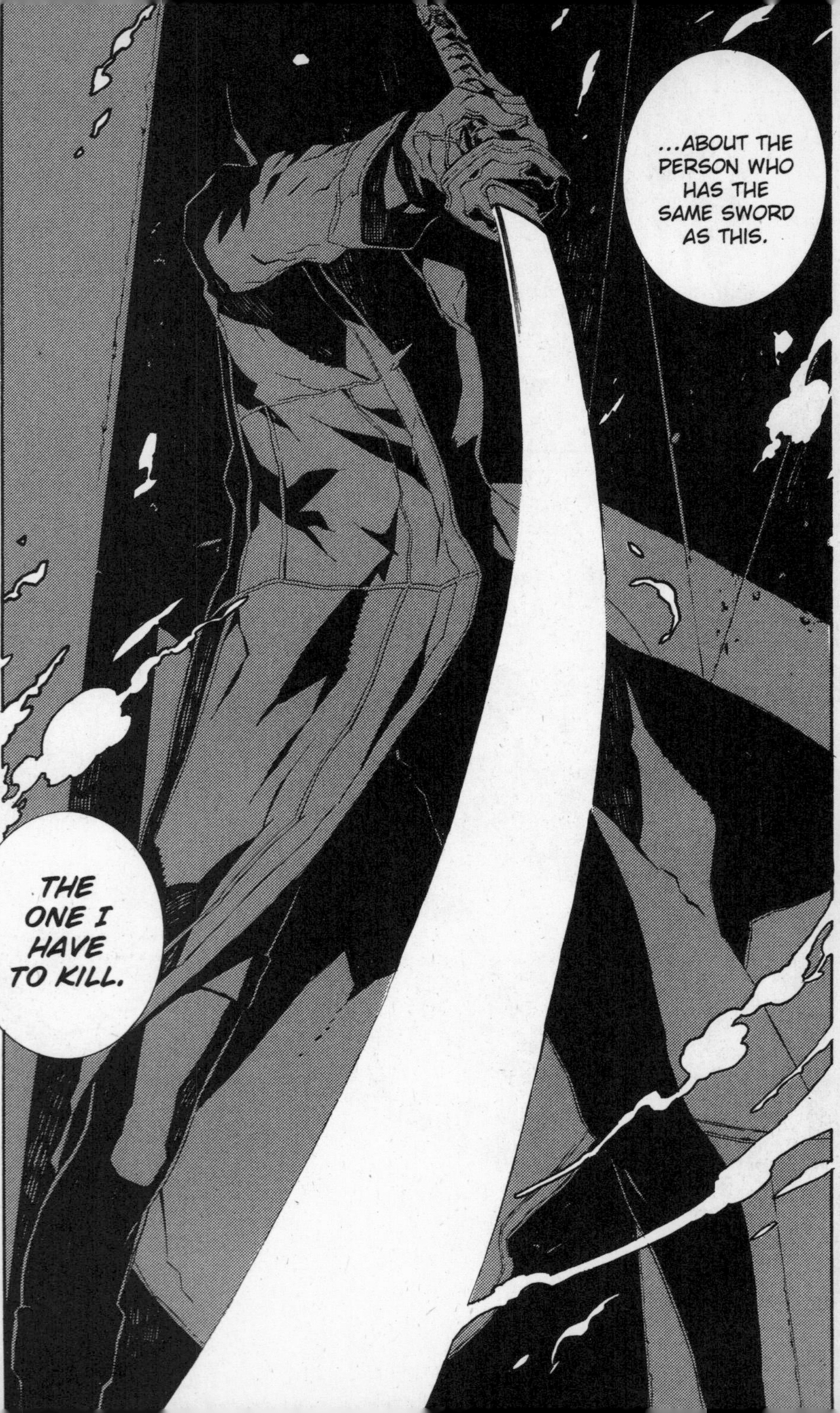
...ABOUT THE PERSON WHO HAS THE SAME SWORD AS THIS.
THE ONE I HAVE TO KILL.

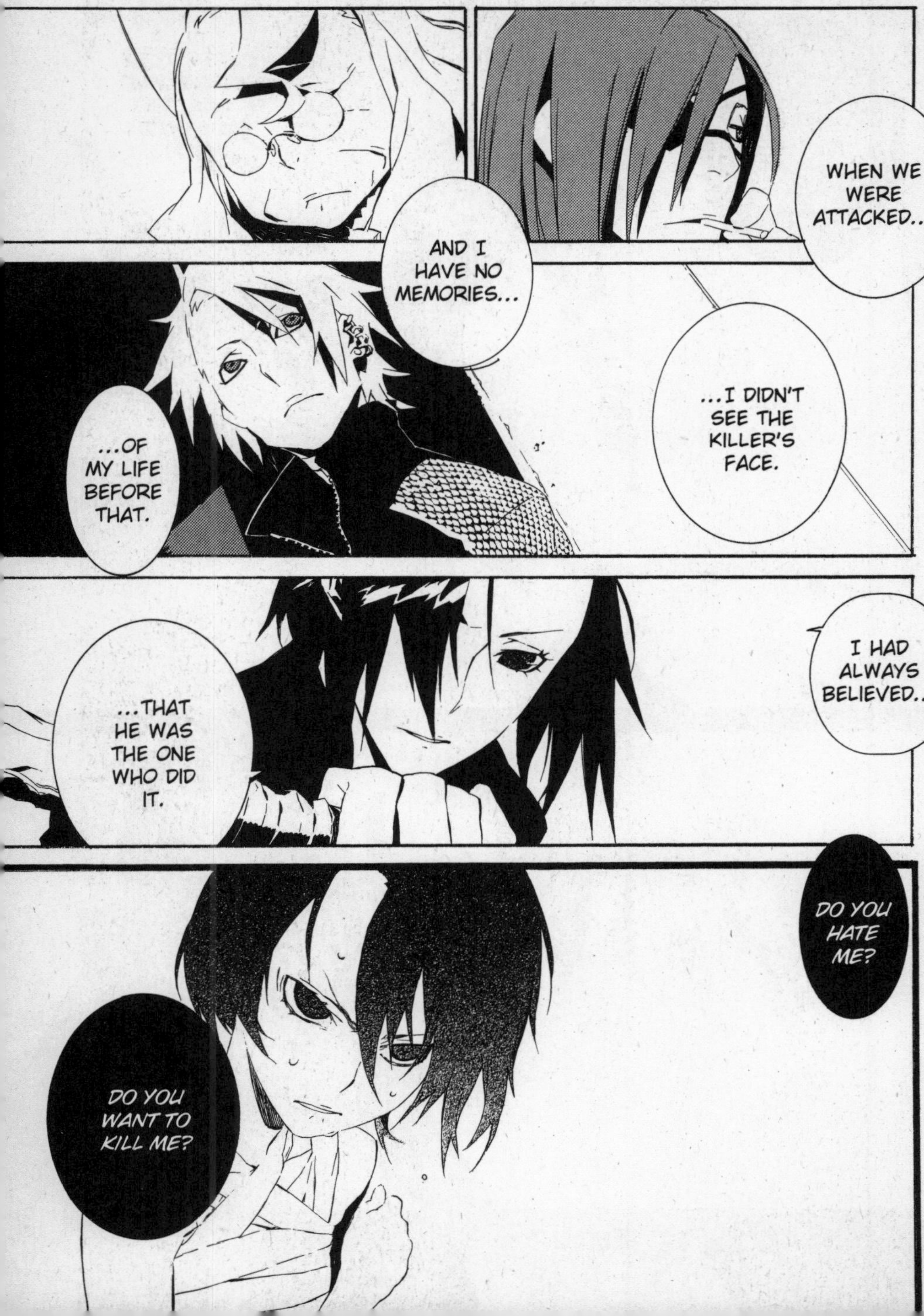
WHEN WE WERE ATTACKED...
...I DIDN'T SEE THE KILLER'S FACE.
AND I HAVE NO MEMORIES...
...OF MY LIFE BEFORE THAT.
I HAD ALWAYS BELIEVED...
...THAT HE WAS THE ONE WHO DID IT.
DO YOU HATE ME?
DO YOU WANT TO KILL ME?

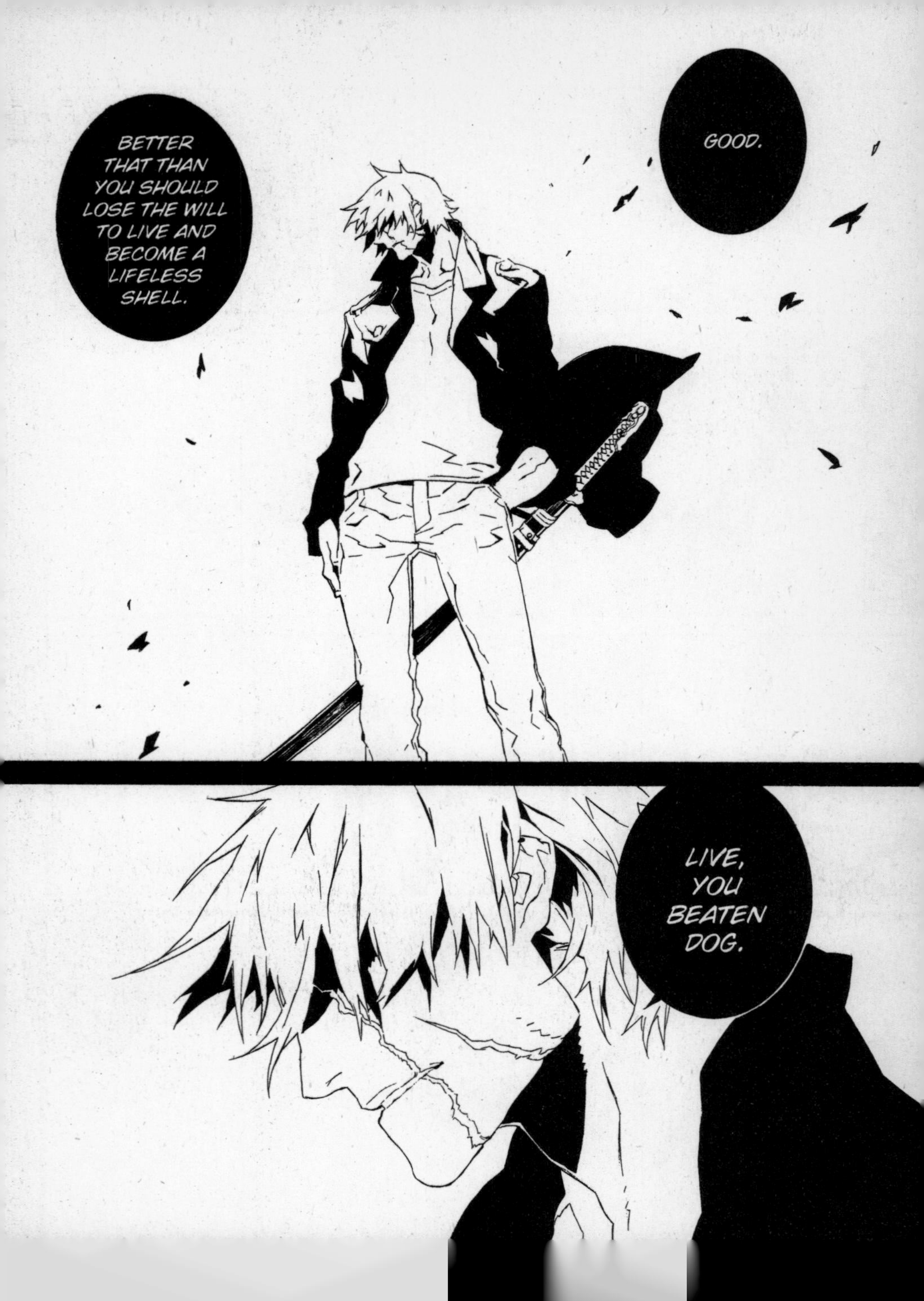
GOOD.
BETTER THAT THAN YOU SHOULD LOSE THE WILL TO LIVE AND BECOME A LIFELESS SHELL.
LIVE, YOU BEATEN DOG.

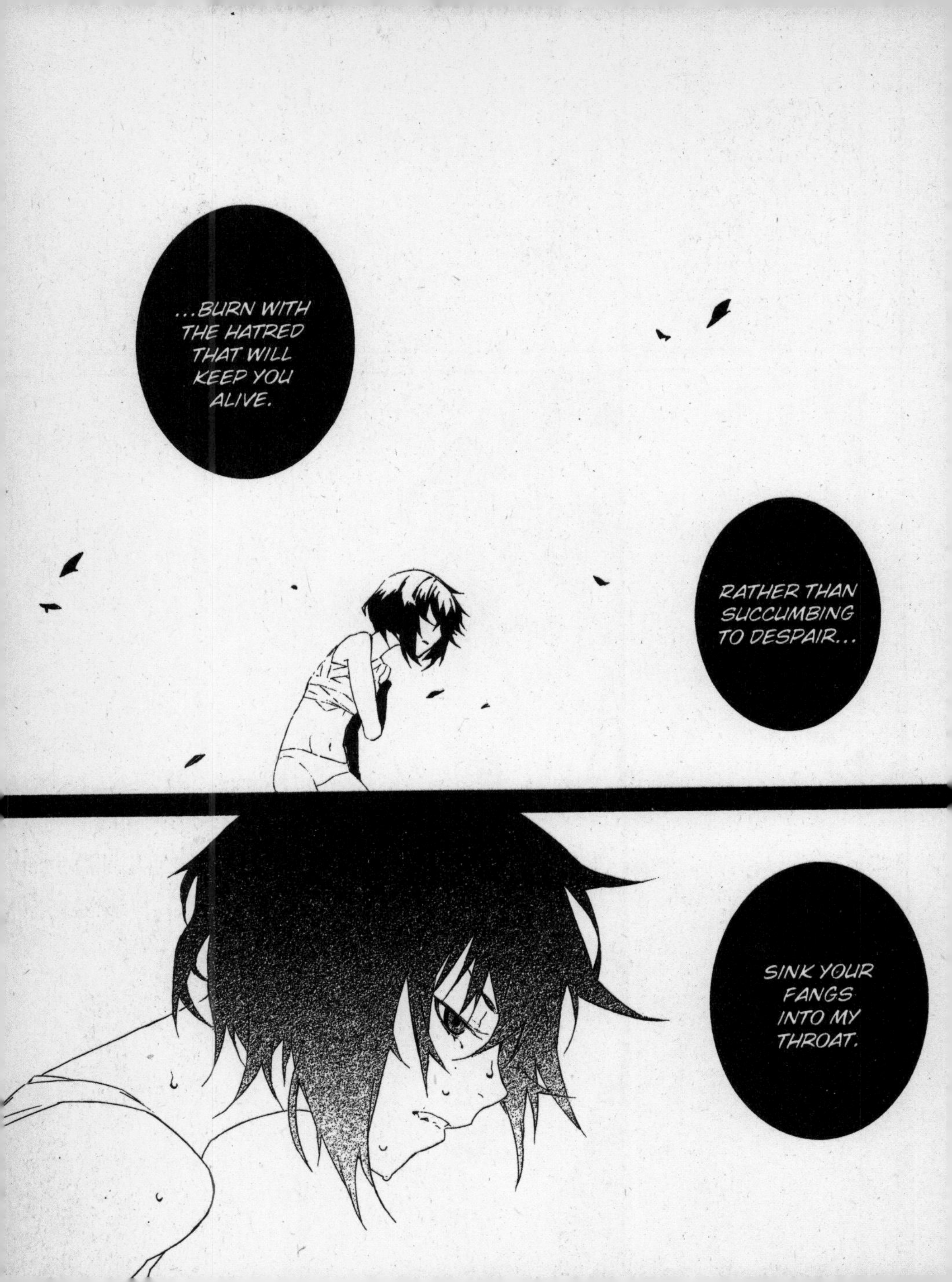
RATHER THAN SUCCUMBING TO DESPAIR...
...BURN WITH THE HATRED THAT WILL KEEP YOU ALIVE.
SINK YOUR FANGS INTO MY THROAT.

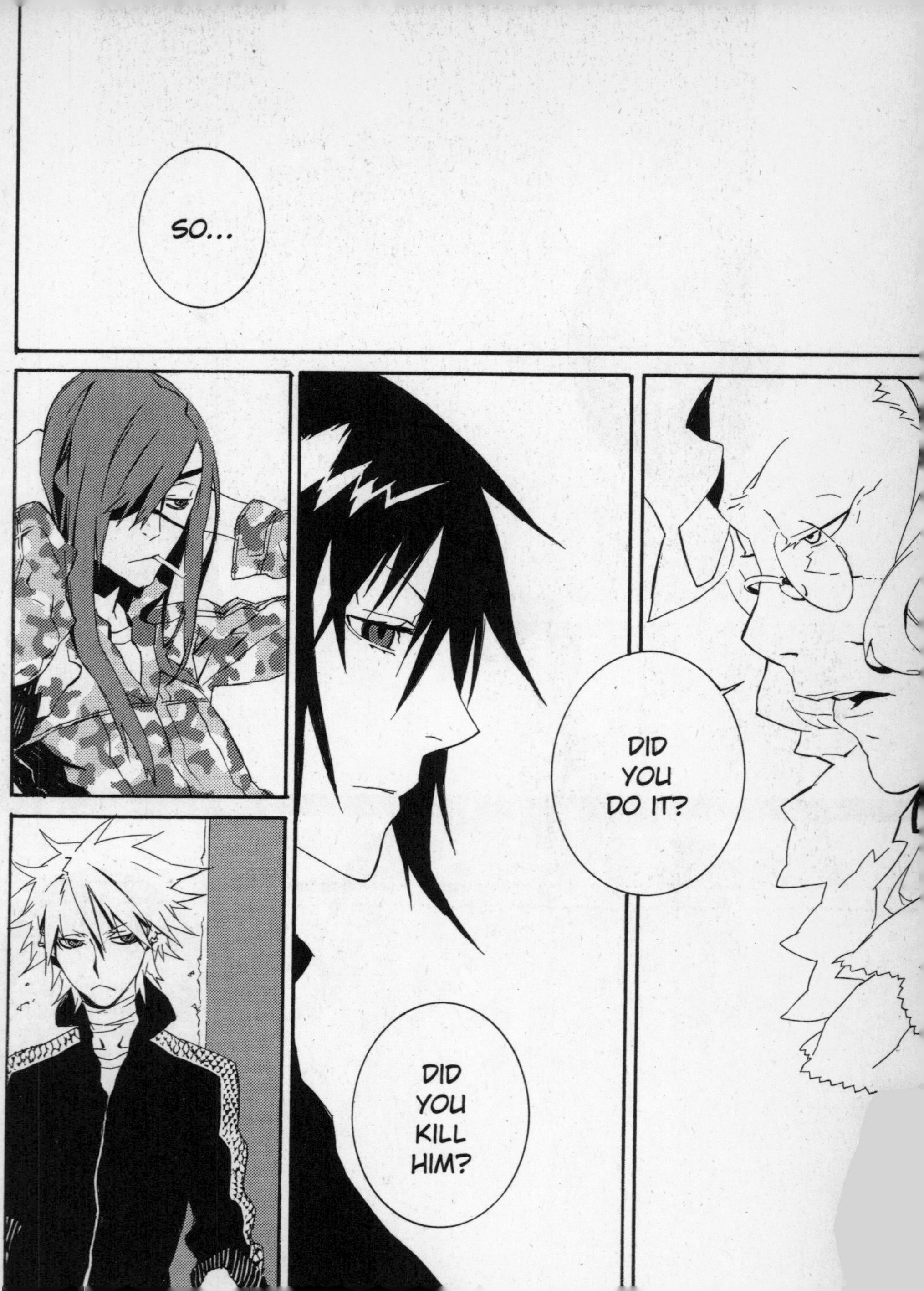
SO...
DID YOU DO IT?
DID YOU KILL HIM?

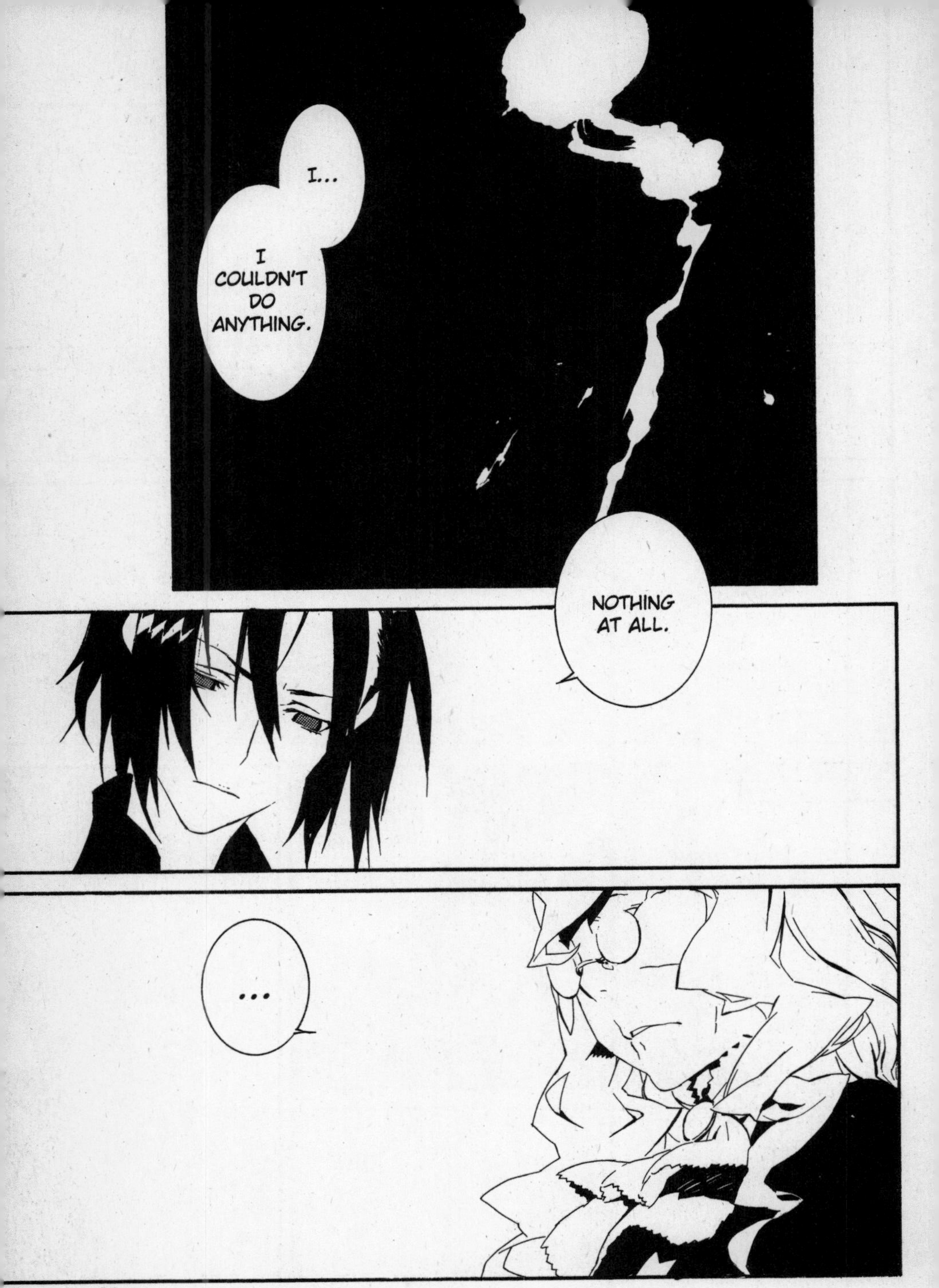

I...
I COULDN'T DO ANYTHING.
NOTHING AT ALL.
...

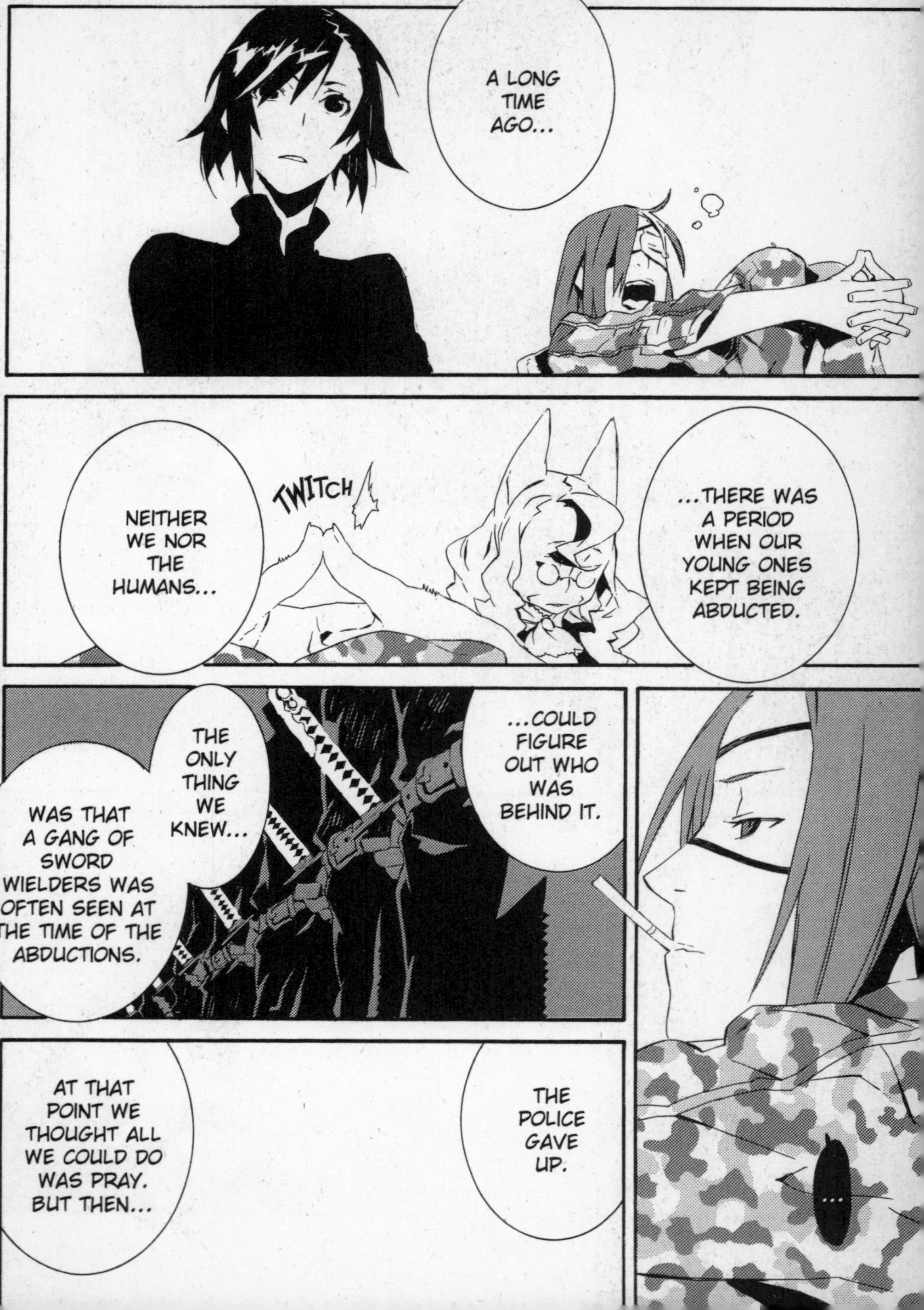
A LONG TIME AGO...
...THERE WAS A PERIOD WHEN OUR YOUNG ONES KEPT BEING ABDUCTED.
TWITCH
NEITHER WE NOR THE HUMANS...
...
...COULD FIGURE OUT WHO WAS BEHIND IT.
THE ONLY THING WE KNEW...
WAS THAT A GANG OF SWORD WIELDERS WAS OFTEN SEEN AT THE TIME OF THE ABDUCTIONS.
THE POLICE GAVE UP.
AT THAT POINT WE THOUGHT ALL WE COULD DO WAS PRAY. BUT THEN...

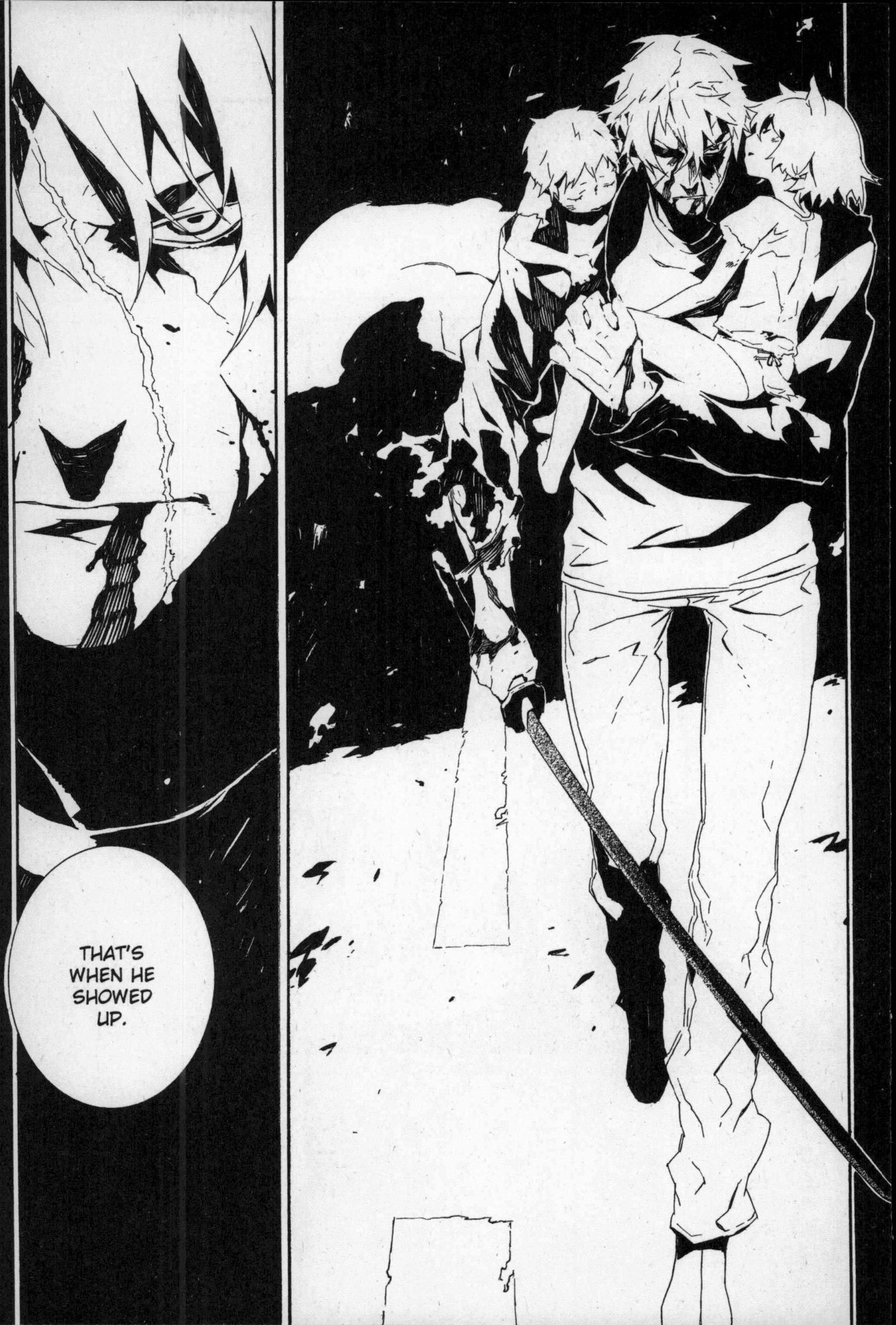
THAT'S WHEN HE SHOWED UP.

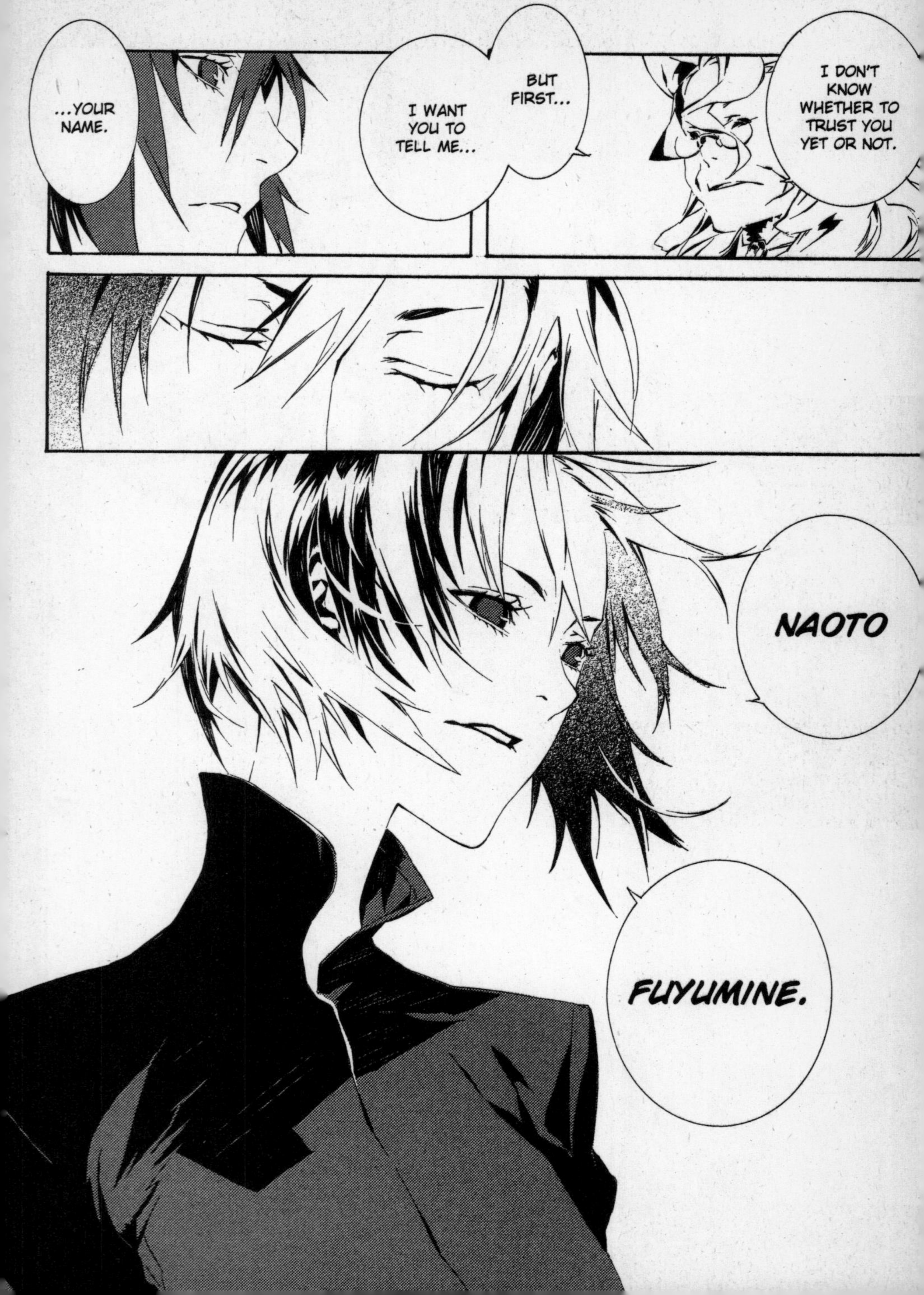
I DON'T KNOW WHETHER TO TRUST YOU YET OR NOT.
BUT FIRST...
I WANT YOU TO TELL ME...
...YOUR NAME.
NAOTO
FUYUMINE.

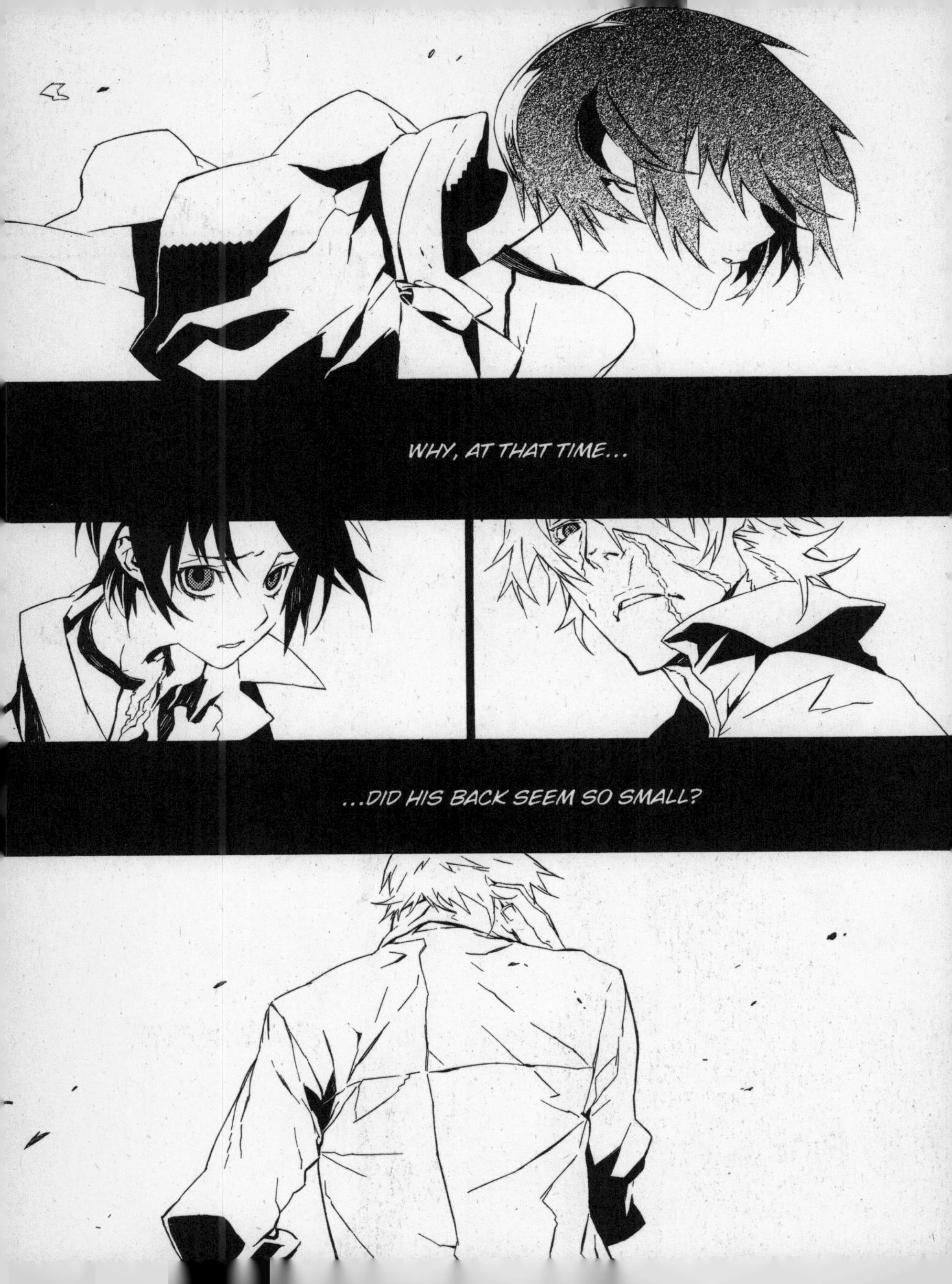
WHY, AT THAT TIME...
...DID HIS BACK SEEM SO SMALL?

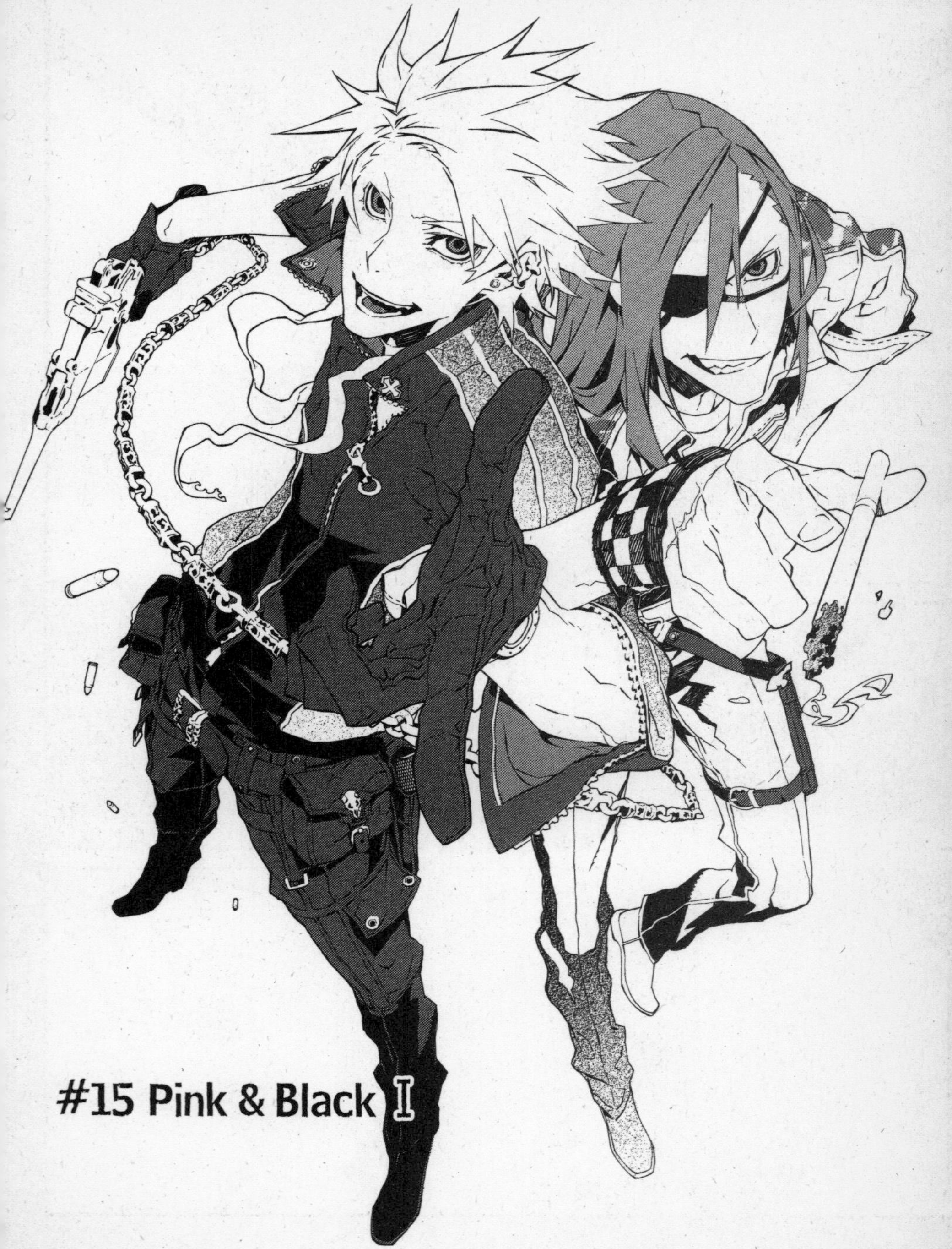

#15 Pink & Black I

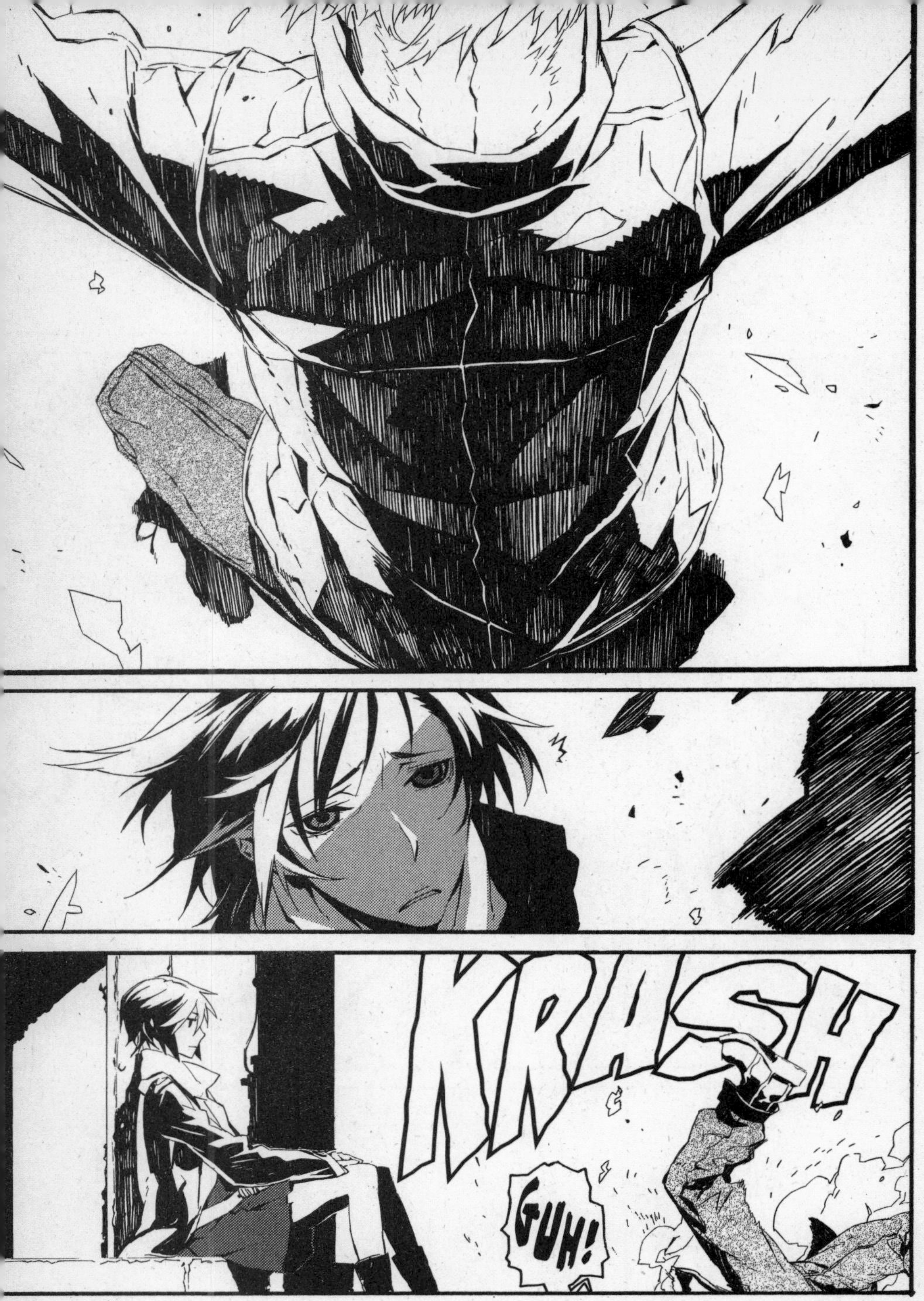
KRASH
GUH!

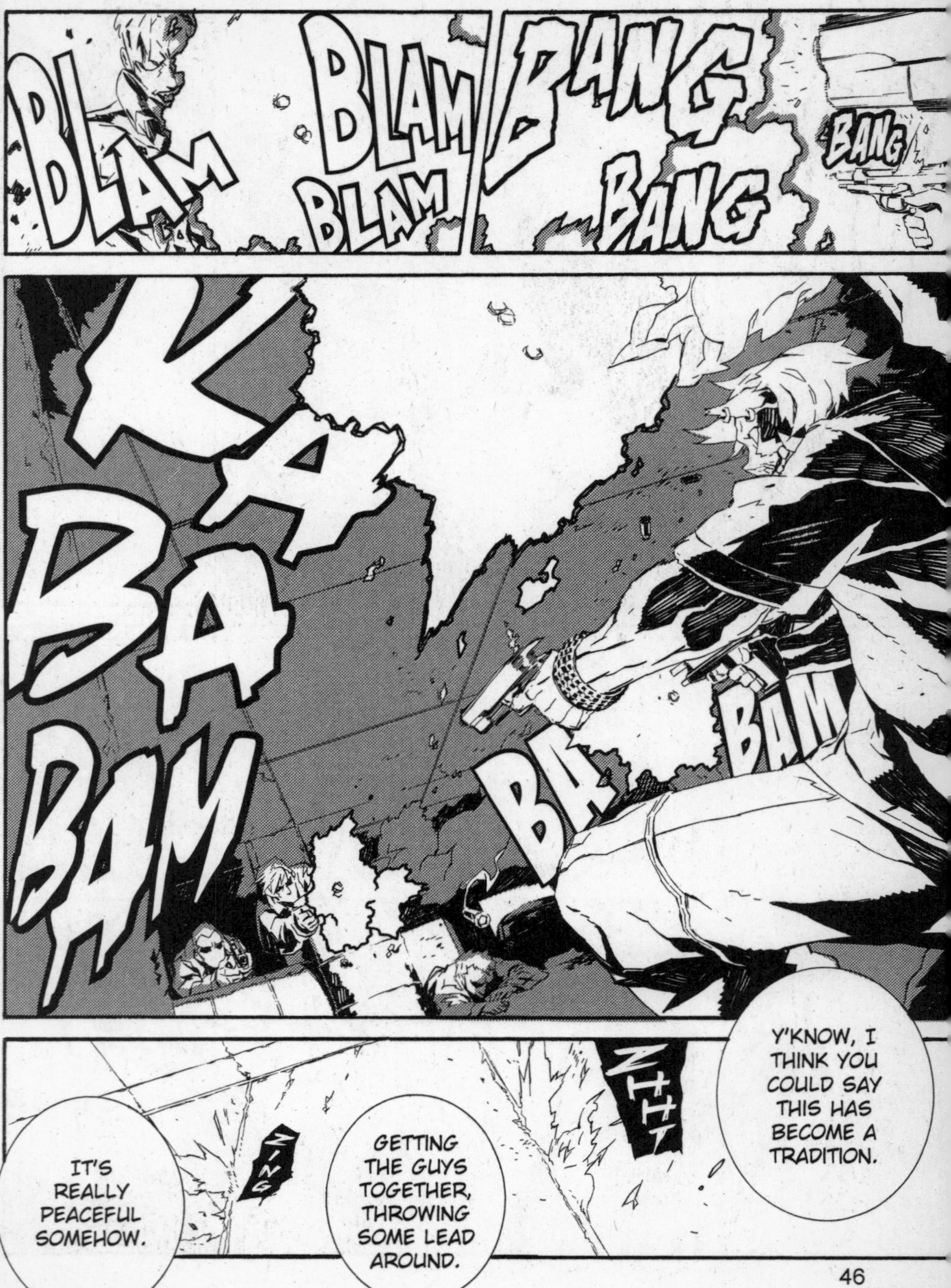
BANG
BANG
BANG
BLAM
BLAM
BLAM
BA BAM
BA BAM
Y'KNOW, I THINK YOU COULD SAY THIS HAS BECOME A TRADITION.
ZHHT
GETTING THE GUYS TOGETHER, THROWING SOME LEAD AROUND.
ZING
IT'S REALLY PEACEFUL SOMEHOW.

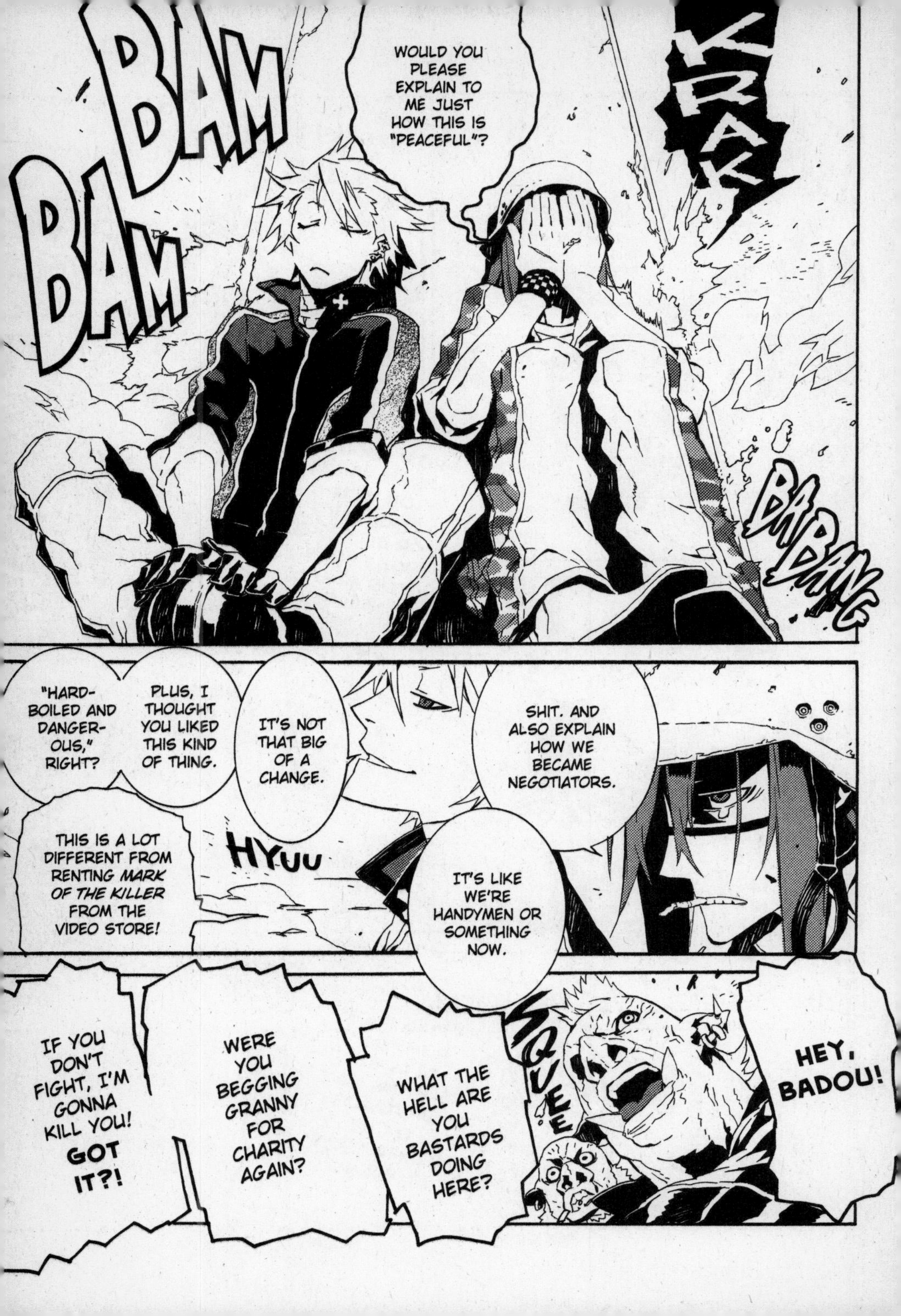
KRAK
WOULD YOU PLEASE EXPLAIN TO ME JUST HOW THIS IS "PEACEFUL"?
BAM BAM
BAM BAM
BABANG
SHIT. AND ALSO EXPLAIN HOW WE BECAME NEGOTIATORS.
IT'S LIKE WE'RE HANDYMEN OR SOMETHING NOW.
IT'S NOT THAT BIG OF A CHANGE.
PLUS, I THOUGHT YOU LIKED THIS KIND OF THING.
"HARD-BOILED AND DANGER-OUS," RIGHT?
HYUU
THIS IS A LOT DIFFERENT FROM RENTING *MARK OF THE KILLER* FROM THE VIDEO STORE!
HEY, BADOU!
MQUEE
WHAT THE HELL ARE YOU BASTARDS DOING HERE?
WERE YOU BEGGING GRANNY FOR CHARITY AGAIN?
IF YOU DON'T FIGHT, I'M GONNA KILL YOU! GOT IT?!

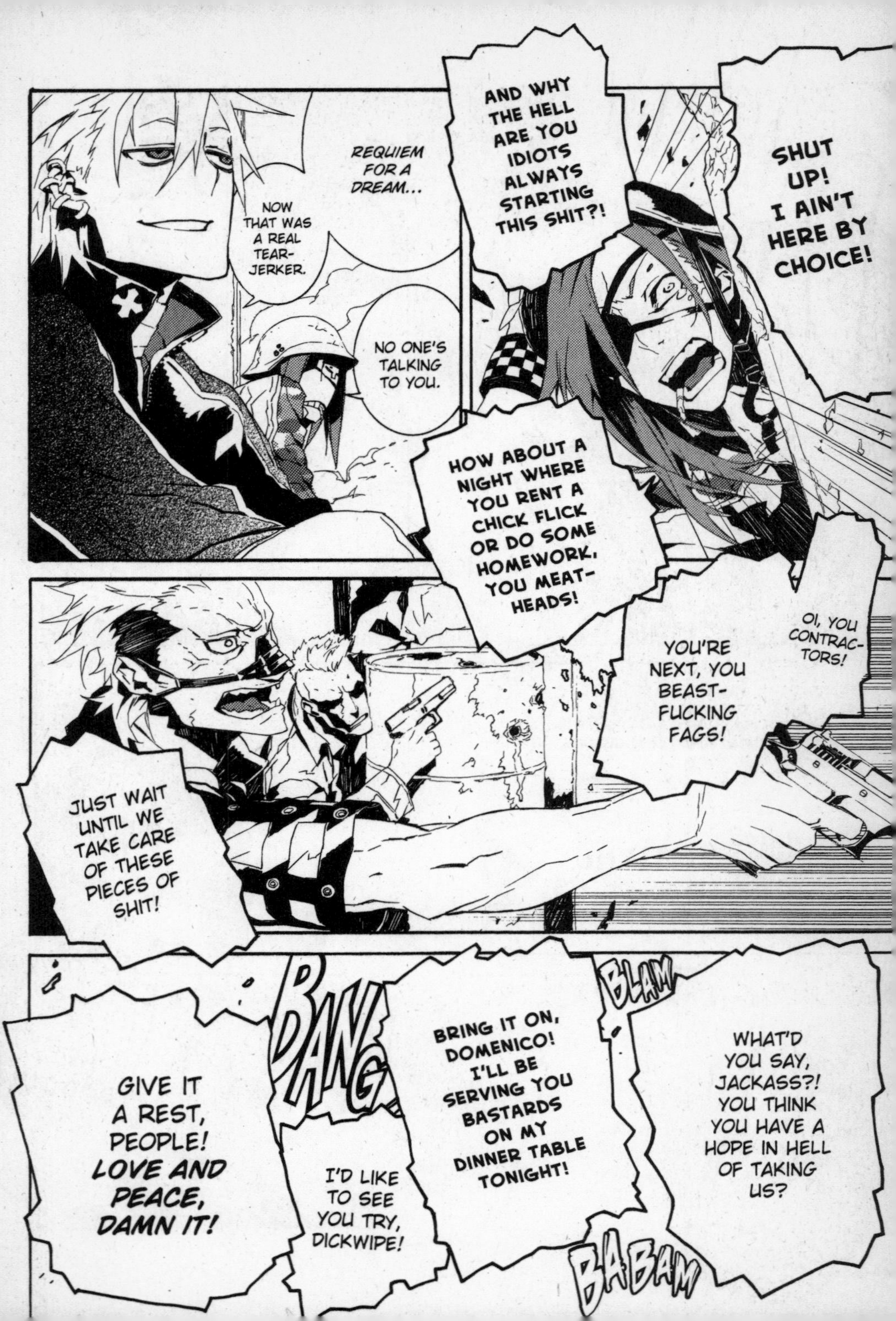
AND WHY THE HELL ARE YOU IDIOTS ALWAYS STARTING THIS SHIT?!
SHUT UP! I AIN'T HERE BY CHOICE!
REQUIEM FOR A DREAM...
NOW THAT WAS A REAL TEAR-JERKER.
NO ONE'S TALKING TO YOU.
HOW ABOUT A NIGHT WHERE YOU RENT A CHICK FLICK OR DO SOME HOMEWORK, YOU MEAT-HEADS!
OI, YOU CONTRAC-TORS!
YOU'RE NEXT, YOU BEAST-FUCKING FAGS!
JUST WAIT UNTIL WE TAKE CARE OF THESE PIECES OF SHIT!
WHAT'D YOU SAY, JACKASS?! YOU THINK YOU HAVE A HOPE IN HELL OF TAKING US?
BLAM
BRING IT ON, DOMENICO! I'LL BE SERVING YOU BASTARDS ON MY DINNER TABLE TONIGHT!
BABAM
I'D LIKE TO SEE YOU TRY, DICKWIPE!
BANG
GIVE IT A REST, PEOPLE! LOVE AND PEACE, DAMN IT!

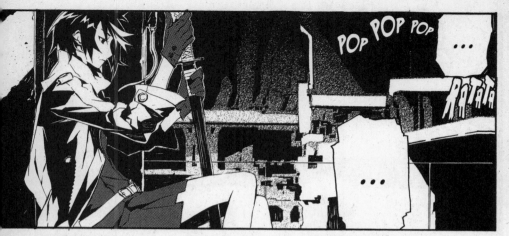

POP POP POP ...

RATATA

...

YOU WANT TO KILL ME, RIGHT? YOU WANT TO SURPASS ME?

THEN GO AHEAD AND TRY.

ATTACK ME IN MY SLEEP, STEAL MY MOVES, DO WHATEVER IT TAKES.

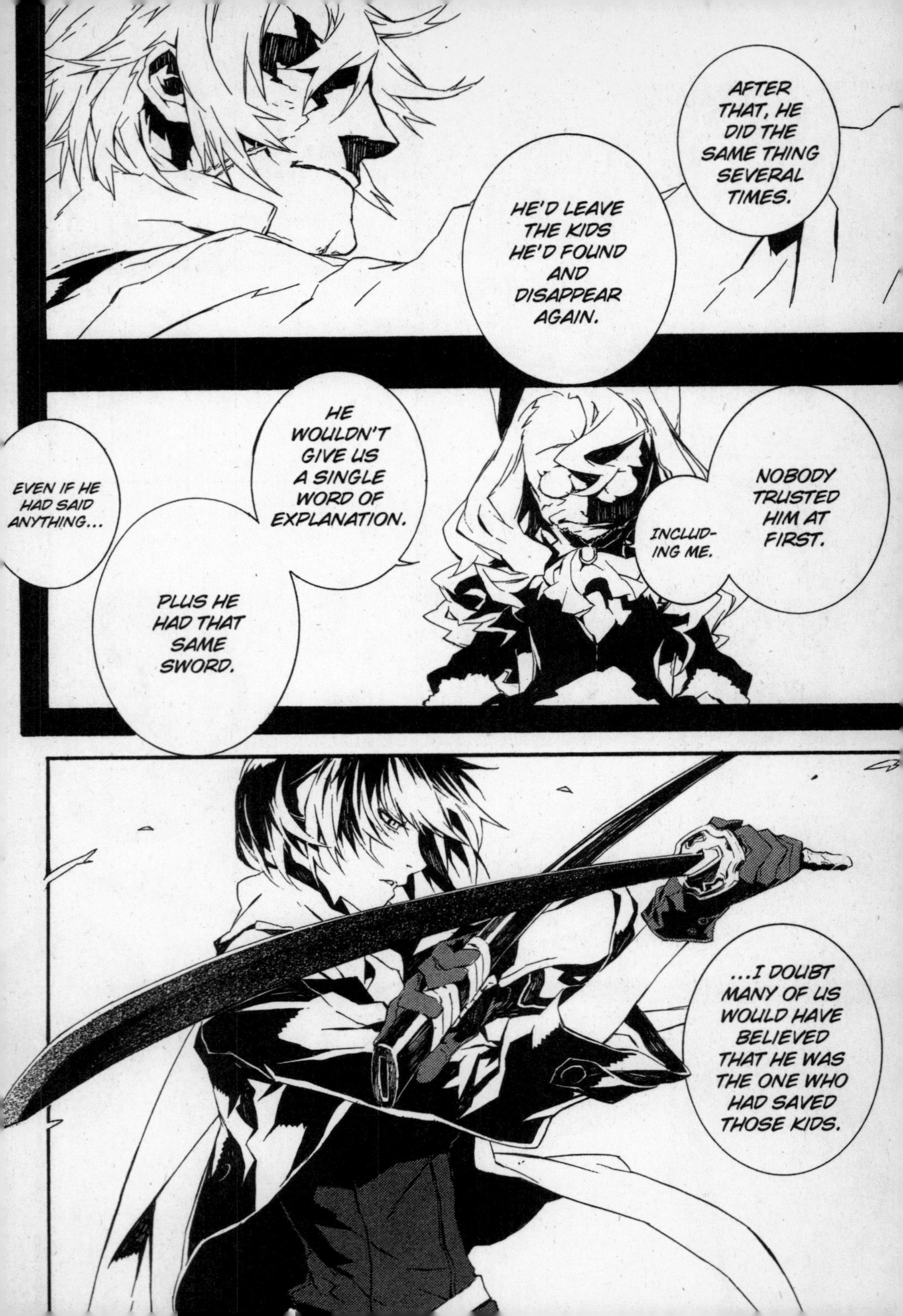
AFTER THAT, HE DID THE SAME THING SEVERAL TIMES.
HE'D LEAVE THE KIDS HE'D FOUND AND DISAPPEAR AGAIN.
NOBODY TRUSTED HIM AT FIRST.
INCLUD-ING ME.
HE WOULDN'T GIVE US A SINGLE WORD OF EXPLANATION.
PLUS HE HAD THAT SAME SWORD.
EVEN IF HE HAD SAID ANYTHING...
...I DOUBT MANY OF US WOULD HAVE BELIEVED THAT HE WAS THE ONE WHO HAD SAVED THOSE KIDS.

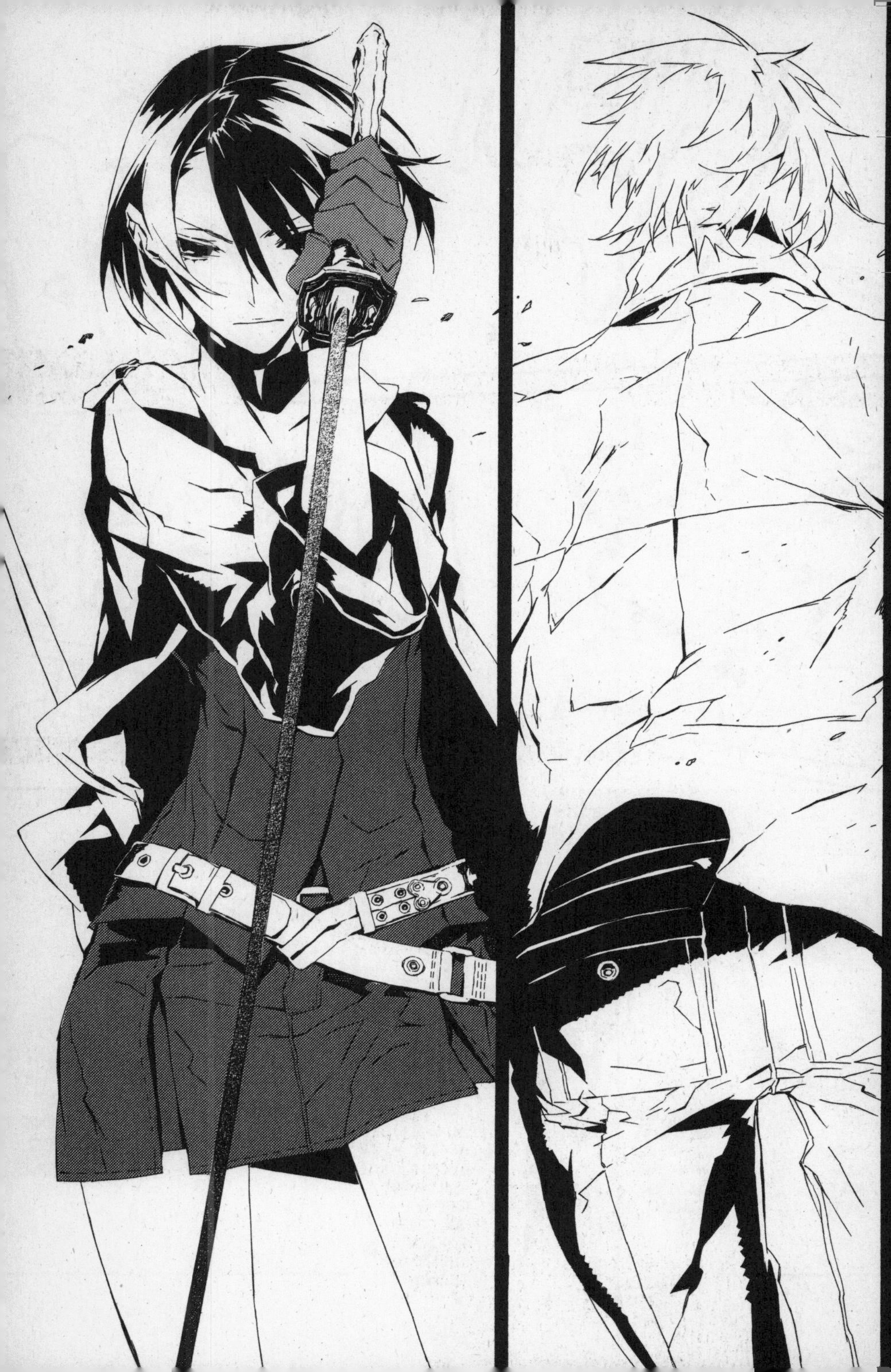

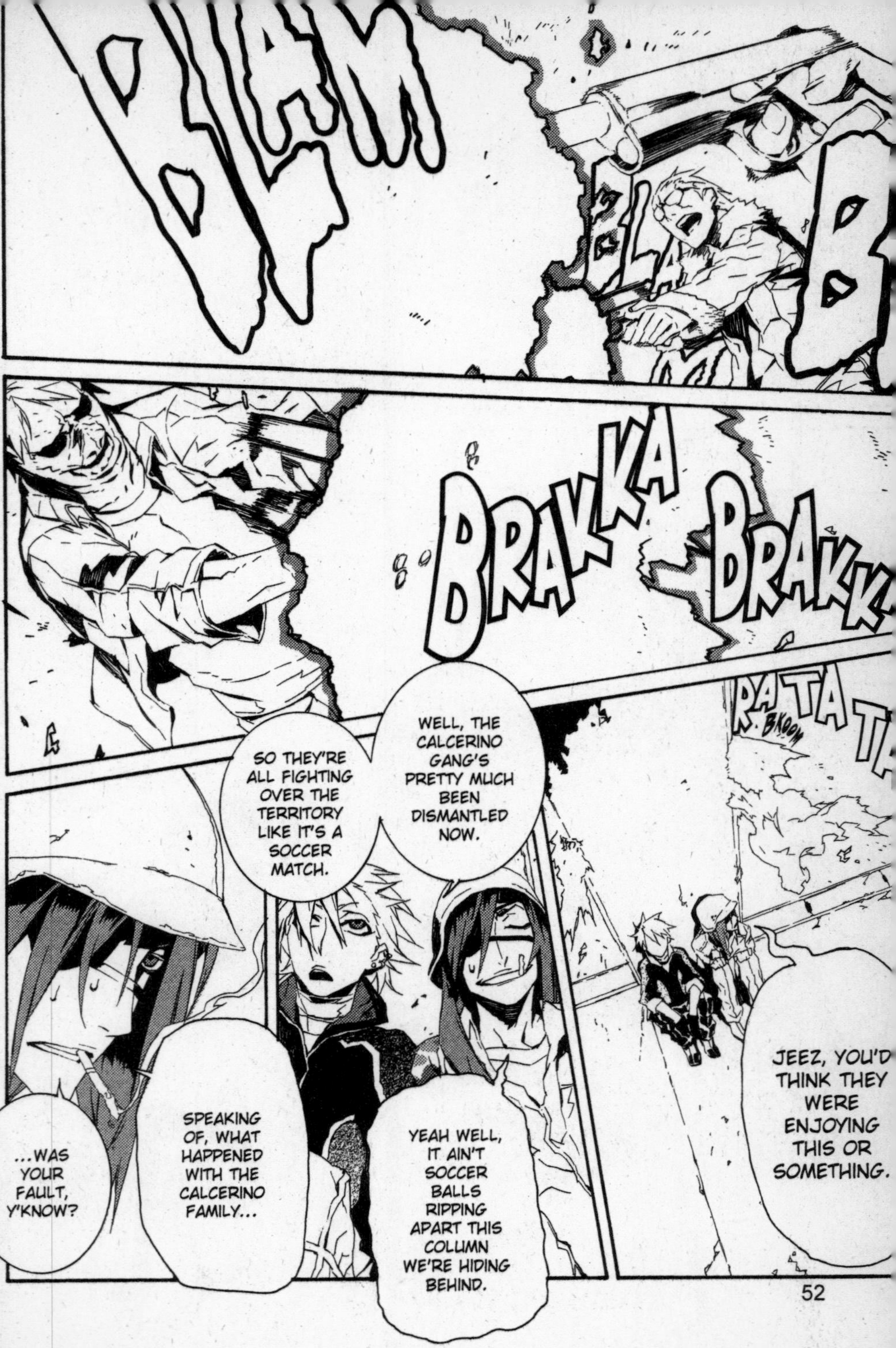
BLAM
BRAKKA
RATATA
BKOOM
JEEZ, YOU'D THINK THEY WERE ENJOYING THIS OR SOMETHING.
WELL, THE CALCERINO GANG'S PRETTY MUCH BEEN DISMANTLED NOW.
SO THEY'RE ALL FIGHTING OVER THE TERRITORY LIKE IT'S A SOCCER MATCH.
YEAH WELL, IT AIN'T SOCCER BALLS RIPPING APART THIS COLUMN WE'RE HIDING BEHIND.
SPEAKING OF, WHAT HAPPENED WITH THE CALCERINO FAMILY...
...WAS YOUR FAULT, Y'KNOW?

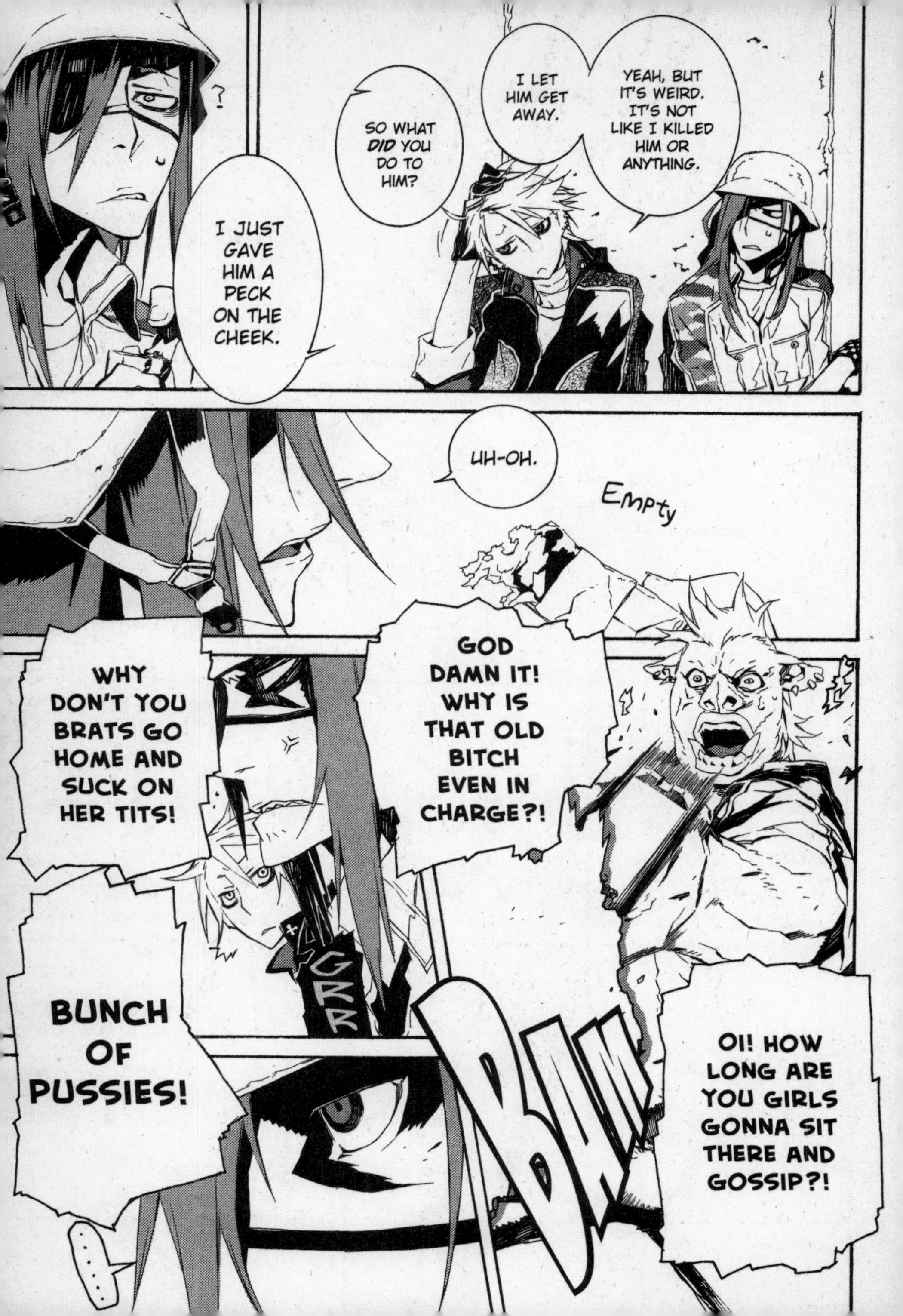
I LET HIM GET AWAY.
YEAH, BUT IT'S WEIRD. IT'S NOT LIKE I KILLED HIM OR ANYTHING.
SO WHAT DID YOU DO TO HIM?
?
I JUST GAVE HIM A PECK ON THE CHEEK.
UH-OH.
Empty
GOD DAMN IT! WHY IS THAT OLD BITCH EVEN IN CHARGE?!
WHY DON'T YOU BRATS GO HOME AND SUCK ON HER TITS!
GRR
OI! HOW LONG ARE YOU GIRLS GONNA SIT THERE AND GOSSIP?!
BAM
BUNCH OF PUSSIES!
.....

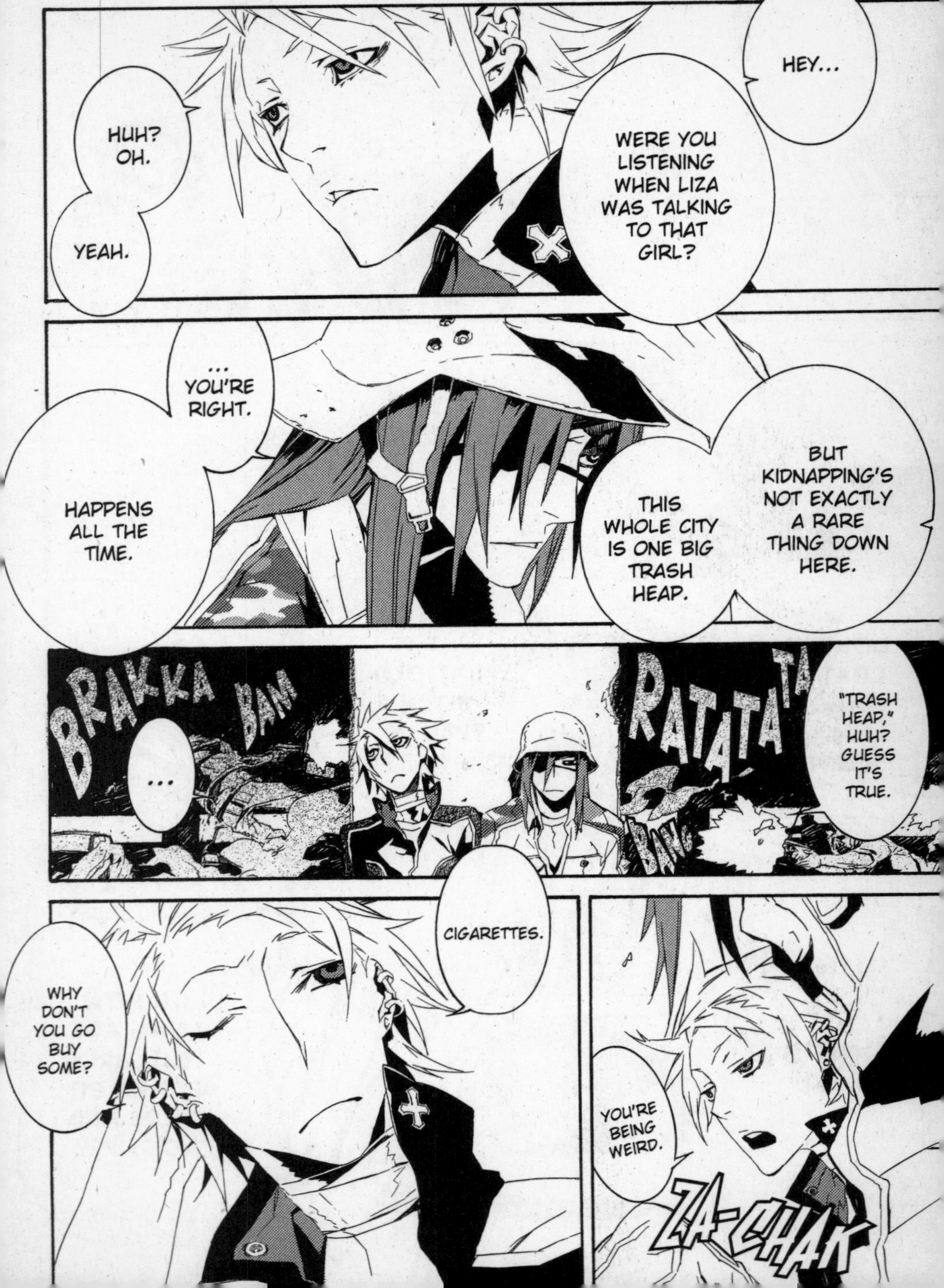

HEY...
WERE YOU LISTENING WHEN LIZA WAS TALKING TO THAT GIRL?
HUH? OH.
YEAH.
BUT KIDNAPPING'S NOT EXACTLY A RARE THING DOWN HERE.
THIS WHOLE CITY IS ONE BIG TRASH HEAP.
... YOU'RE RIGHT.
HAPPENS ALL THE TIME.
RATATATA
"TRASH HEAP," HUH? GUESS IT'S TRUE.
BANG
BRAKKA
BAM
...
YOU'RE BEING WEIRD.
ZA-CHAK
CIGARETTES.
WHY DON'T YOU GO BUY SOME?

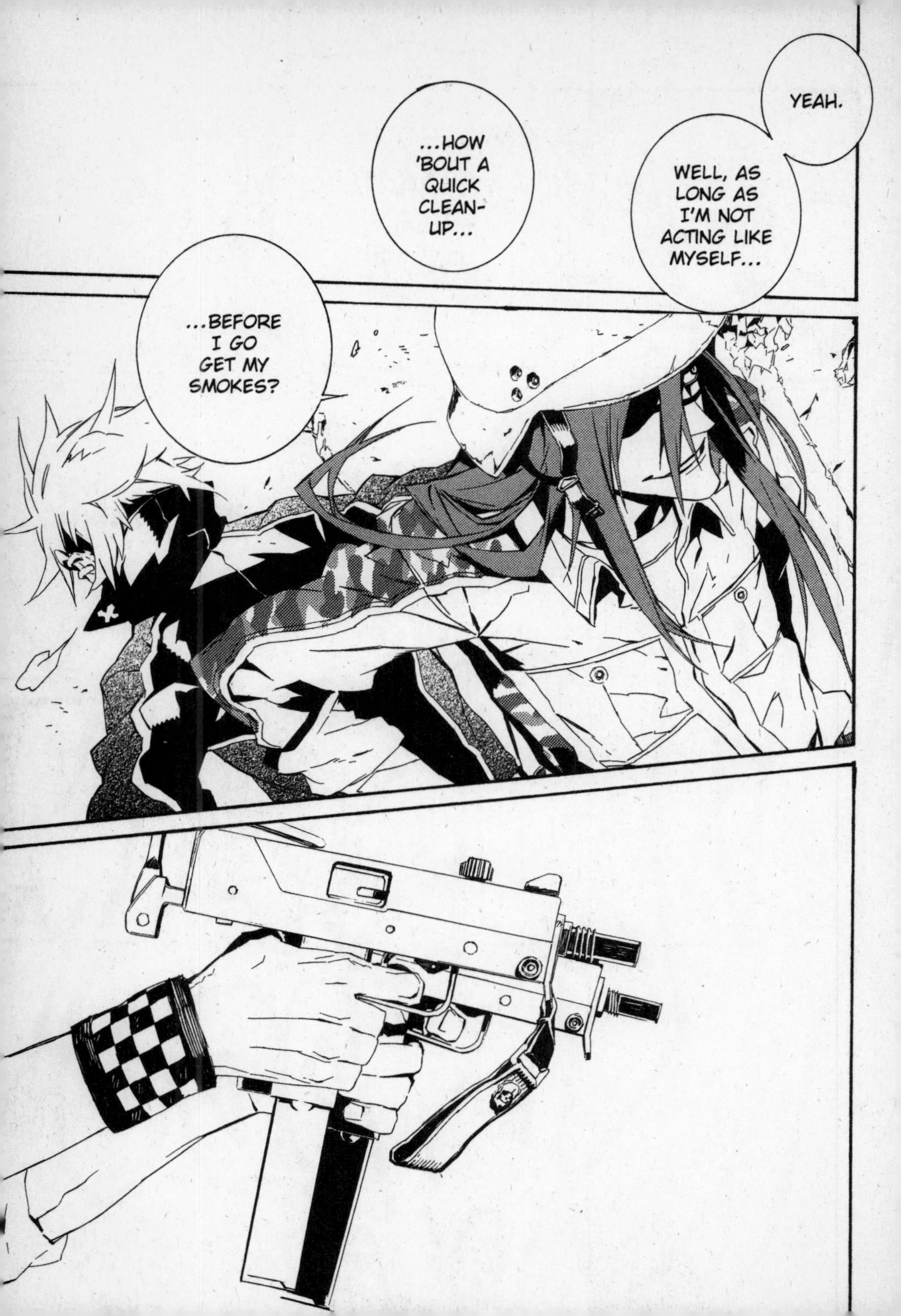
YEAH.
WELL, AS LONG AS I'M NOT ACTING LIKE MYSELF...
...HOW 'BOUT A QUICK CLEAN-UP...
...BEFORE I GO GET MY SMOKES?

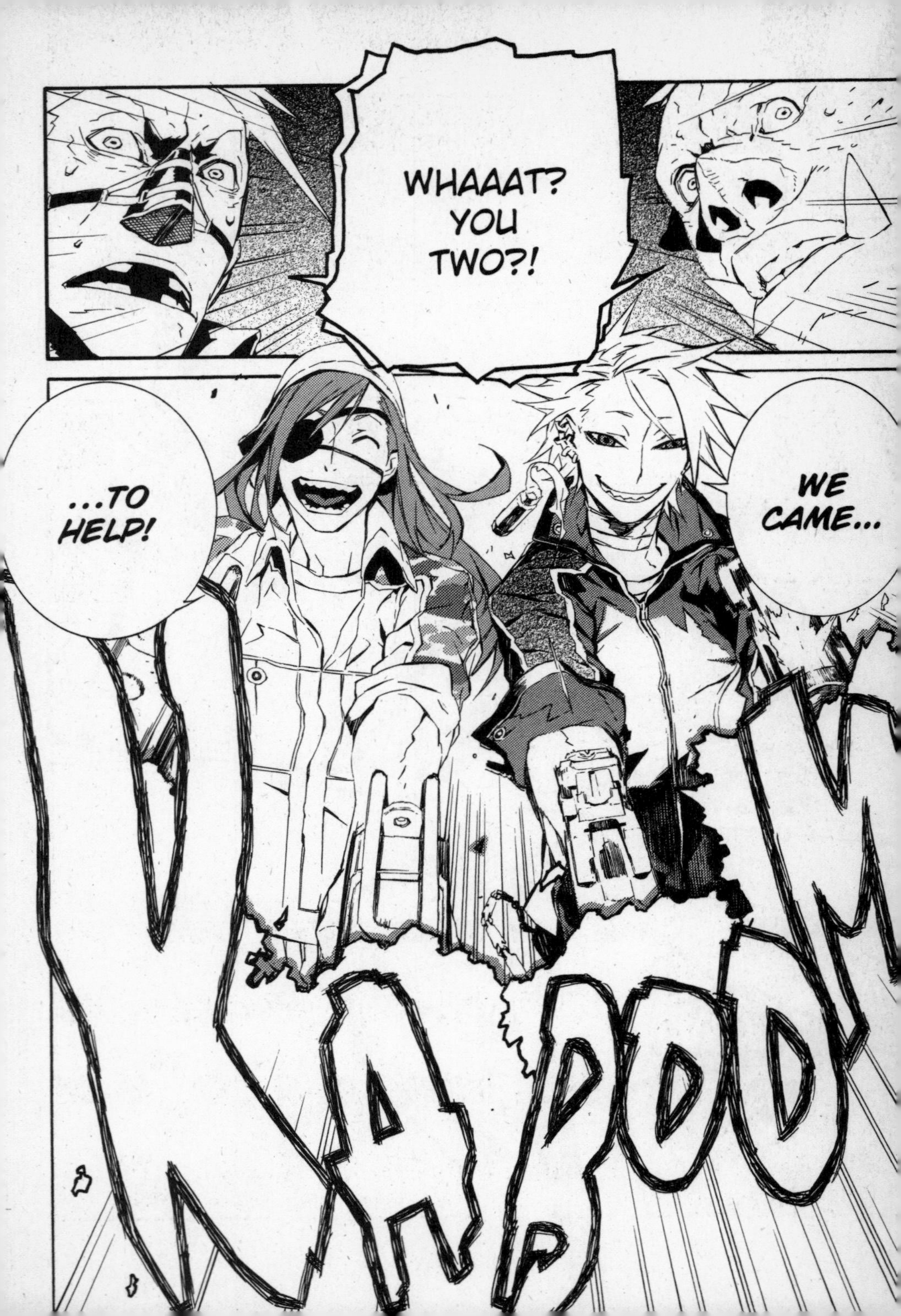
WHAAAT? YOU TWO?!
WE CAME...
...TO HELP!

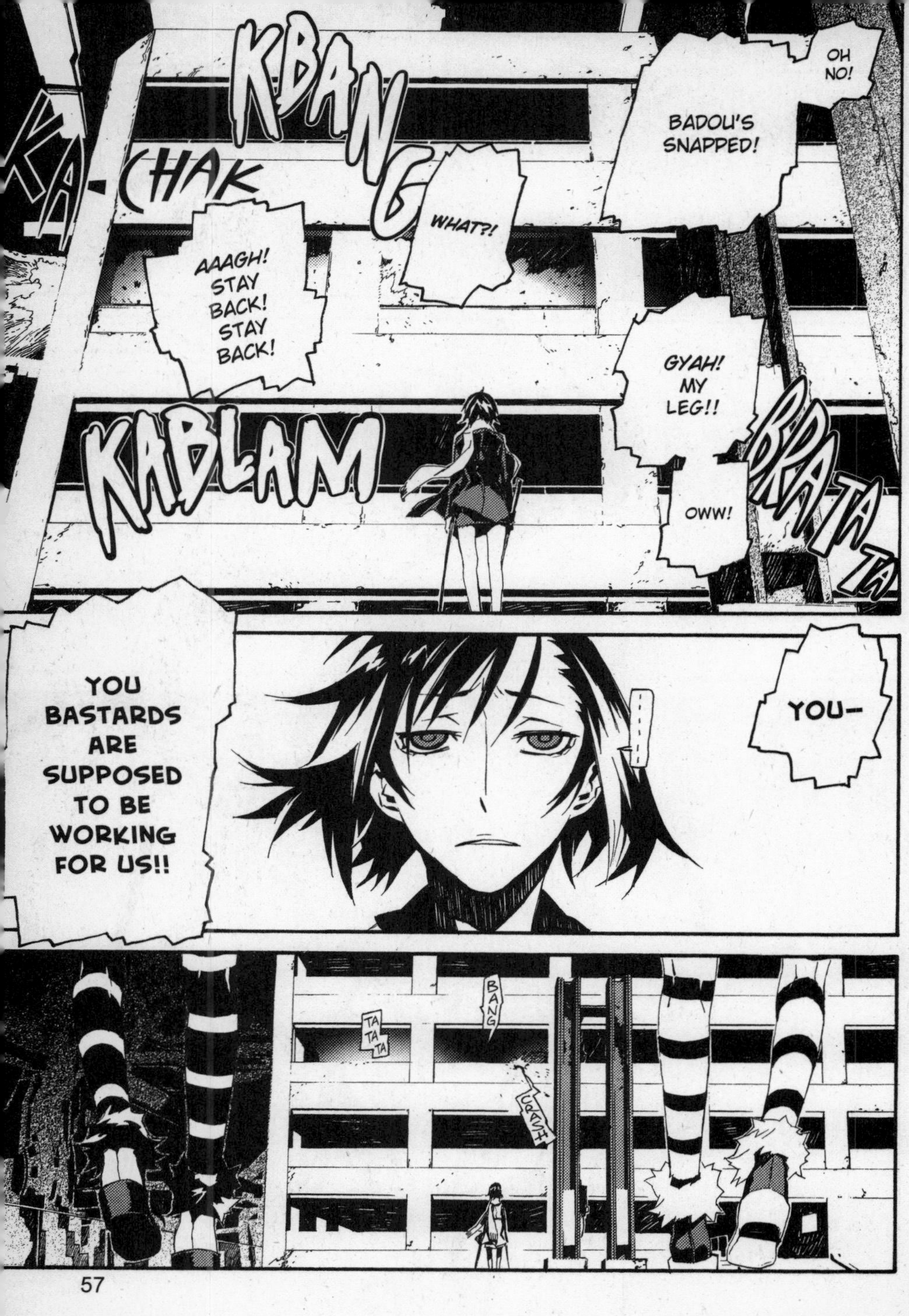
OH NO!
BADOU'S SNAPPED!
KBANG
WHAT?!
KA-CHAK
AAAGH! STAY BACK! STAY BACK!
GYAH! MY LEG!!
BRATATATA
OWW!
KABLAM
YOU-
YOU BASTARDS ARE SUPPOSED TO BE WORKING FOR US!!
BANG
TATATATA
CRASH

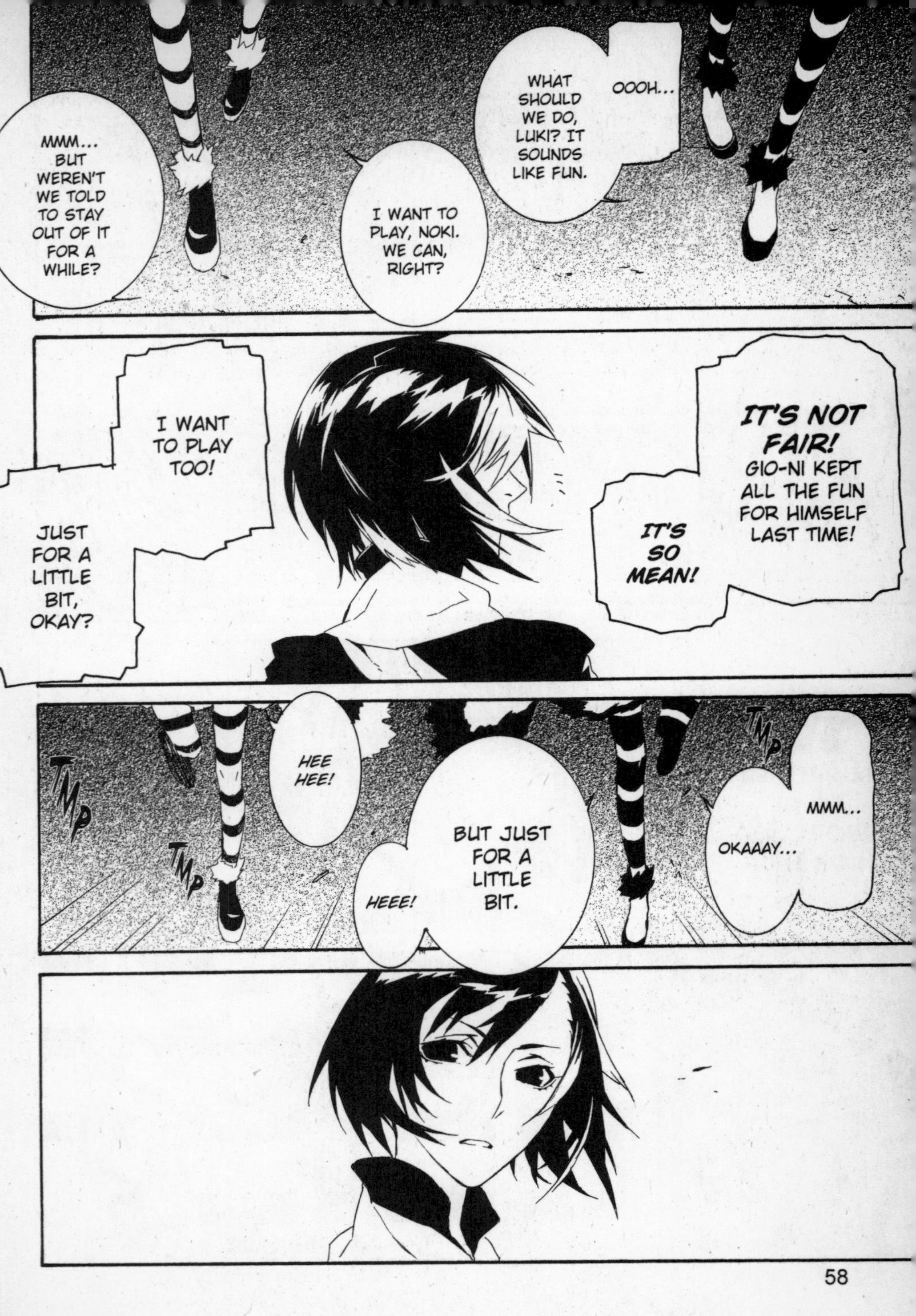
OOOH...
WHAT SHOULD WE DO, LUKI? IT SOUNDS LIKE FUN.
I WANT TO PLAY, NOKI. WE CAN, RIGHT?
MMM... BUT WEREN'T WE TOLD TO STAY OUT OF IT FOR A WHILE?
IT'S NOT FAIR! GIO-NI KEPT ALL THE FUN FOR HIMSELF LAST TIME!
IT'S SO MEAN!
I WANT TO PLAY TOO!
JUST FOR A LITTLE BIT, OKAY?
TMP
MMM...
OKAAAY...
BUT JUST FOR A LITTLE BIT.
HEEE!
HEE HEE!
TMP
TMP

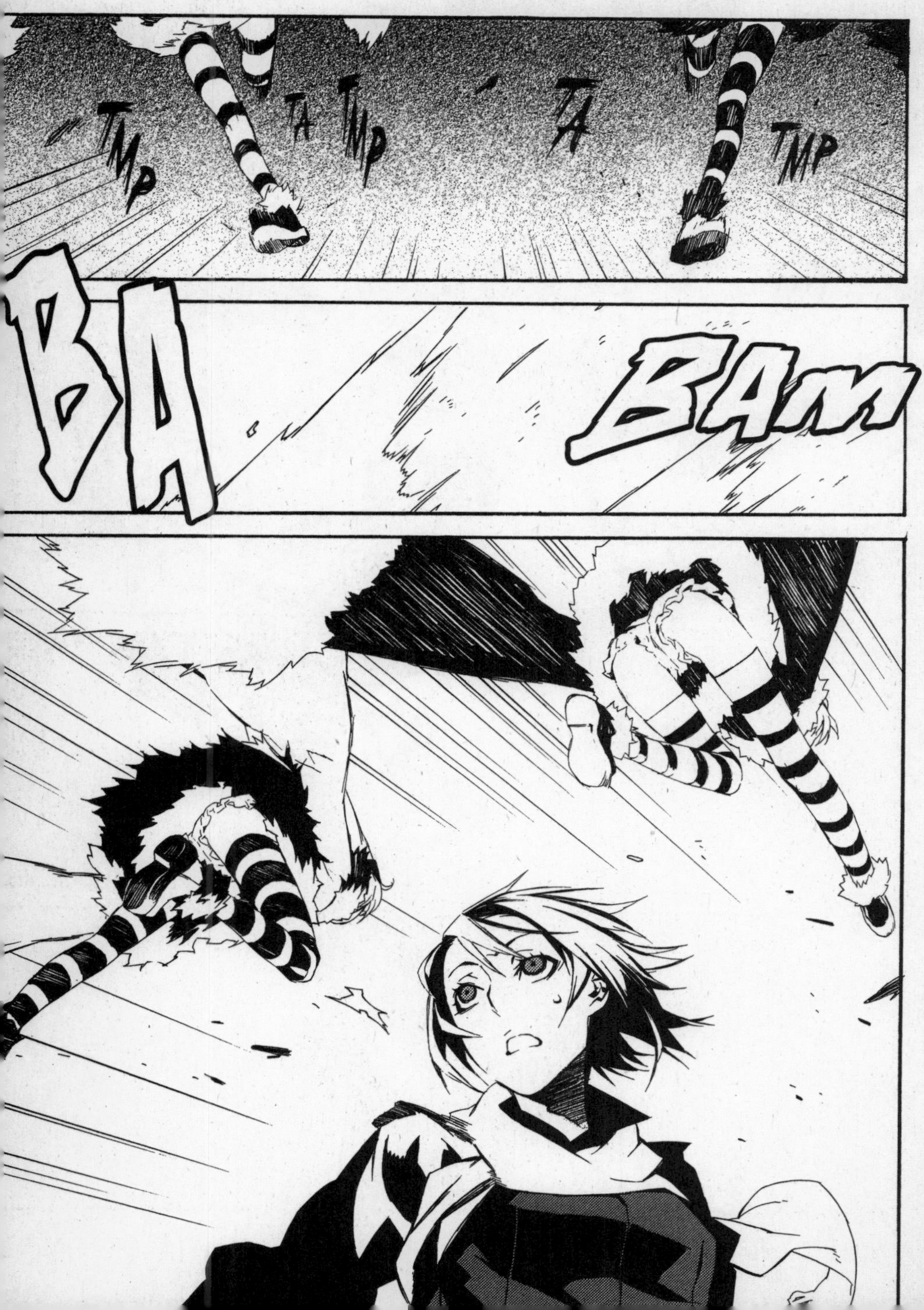
TMP
TA
TMP
TA
TMP
BAM
BA

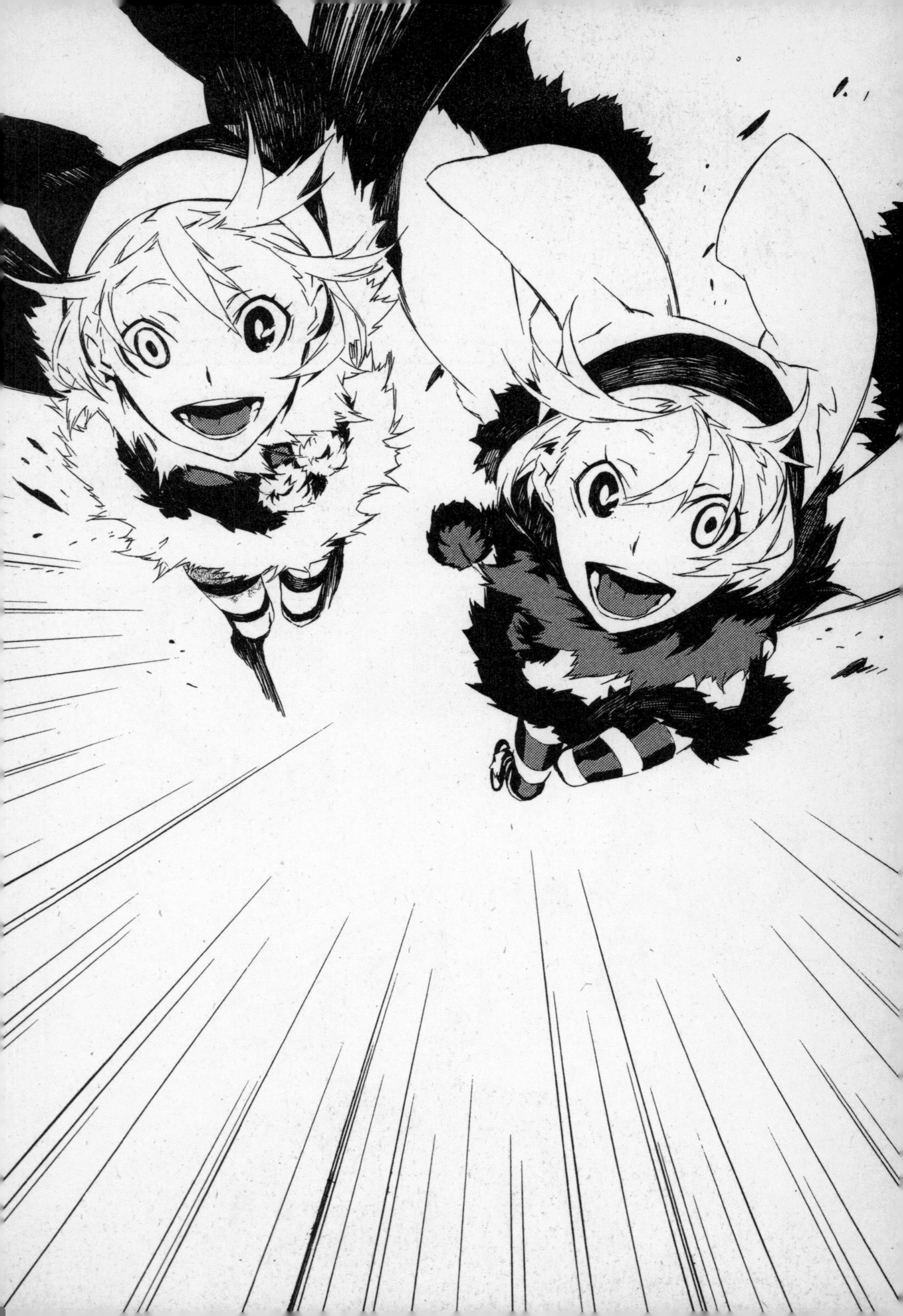

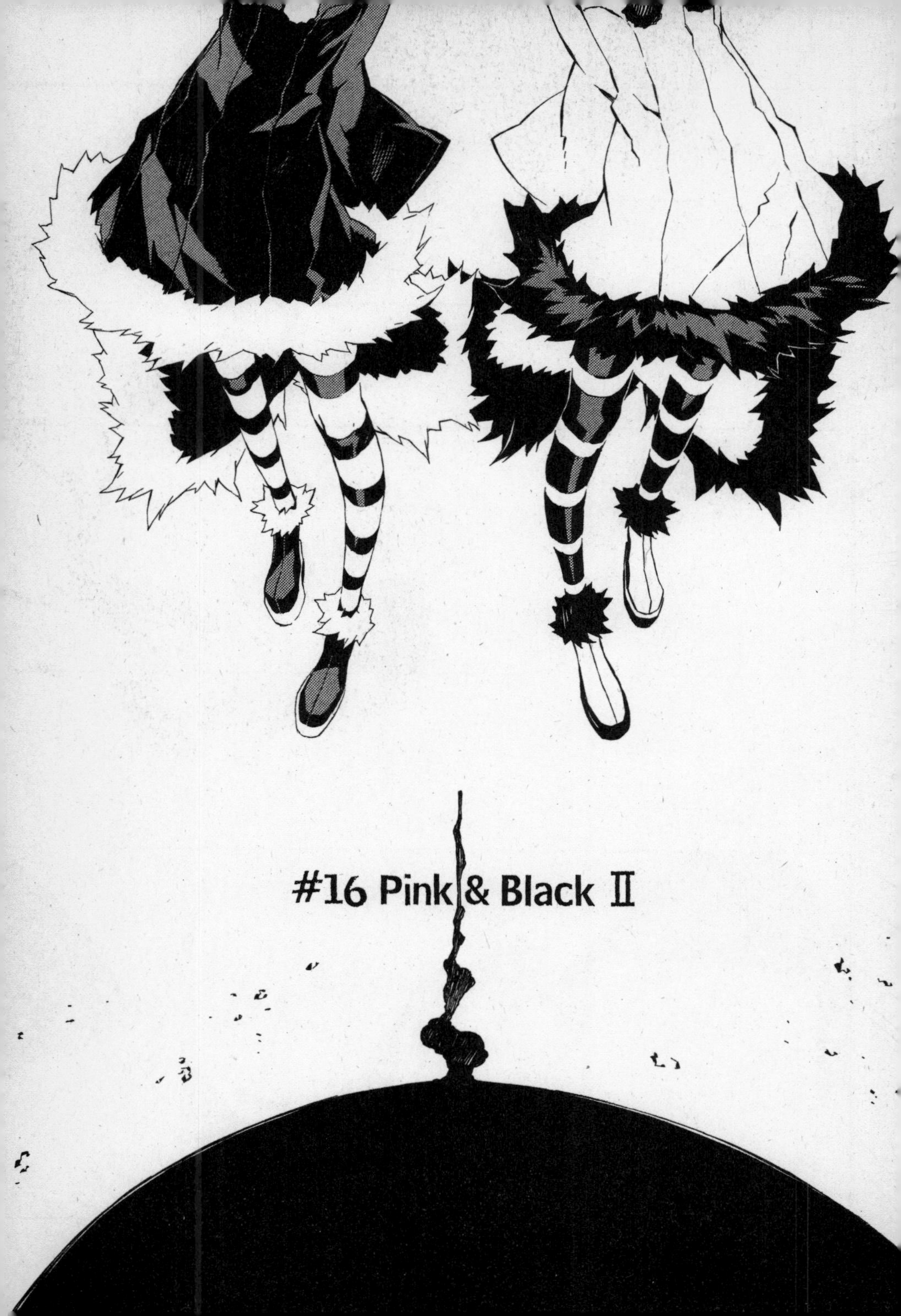
#16 Pink & Black Ⅱ

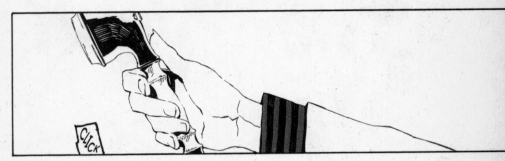

YES?

GIOVANNI,
WHAT IS
GOING
ON?

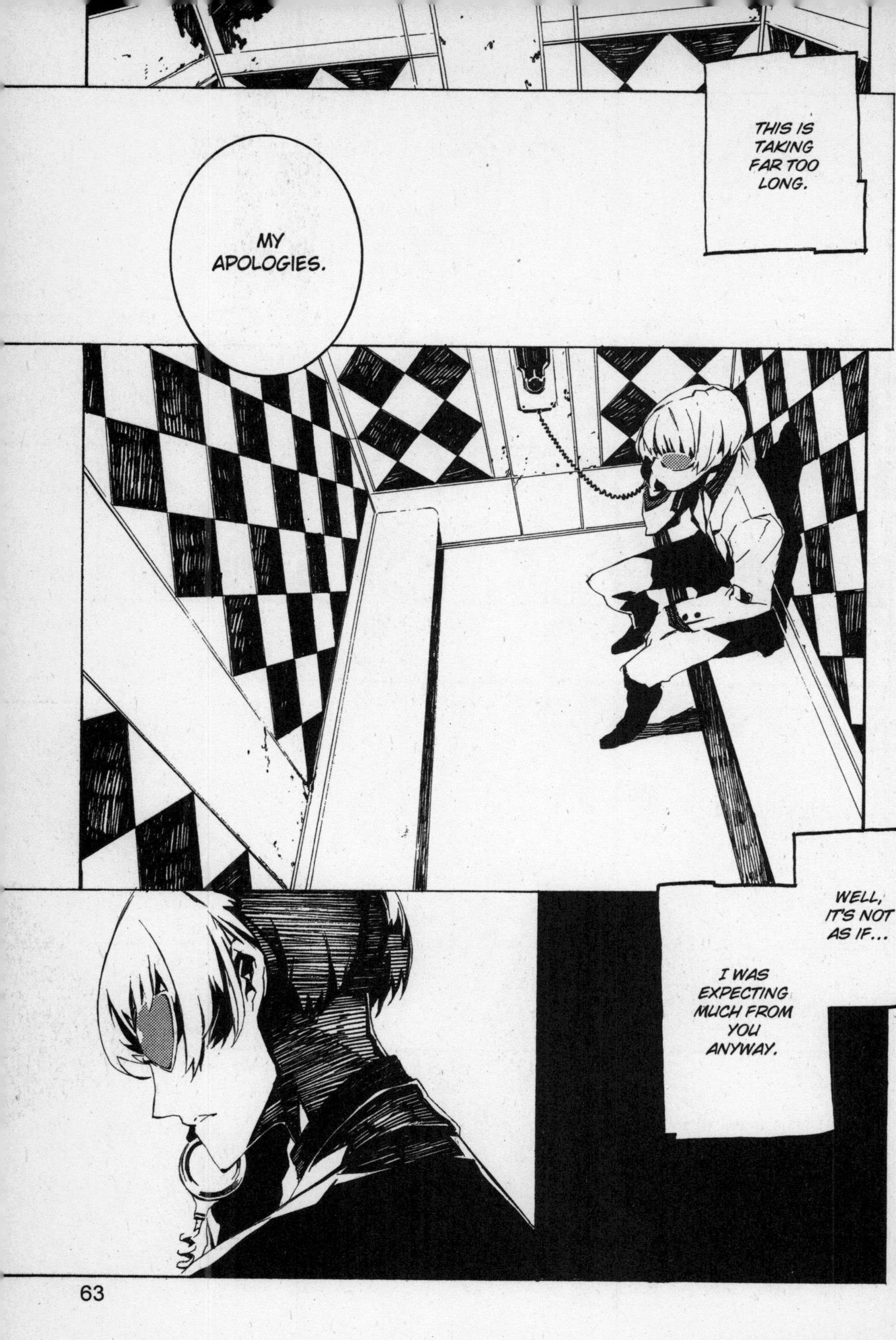
THIS IS TAKING FAR TOO LONG.
MY APOLOGIES.
WELL, IT'S NOT AS IF...
I WAS EXPECTING MUCH FROM YOU ANYWAY.

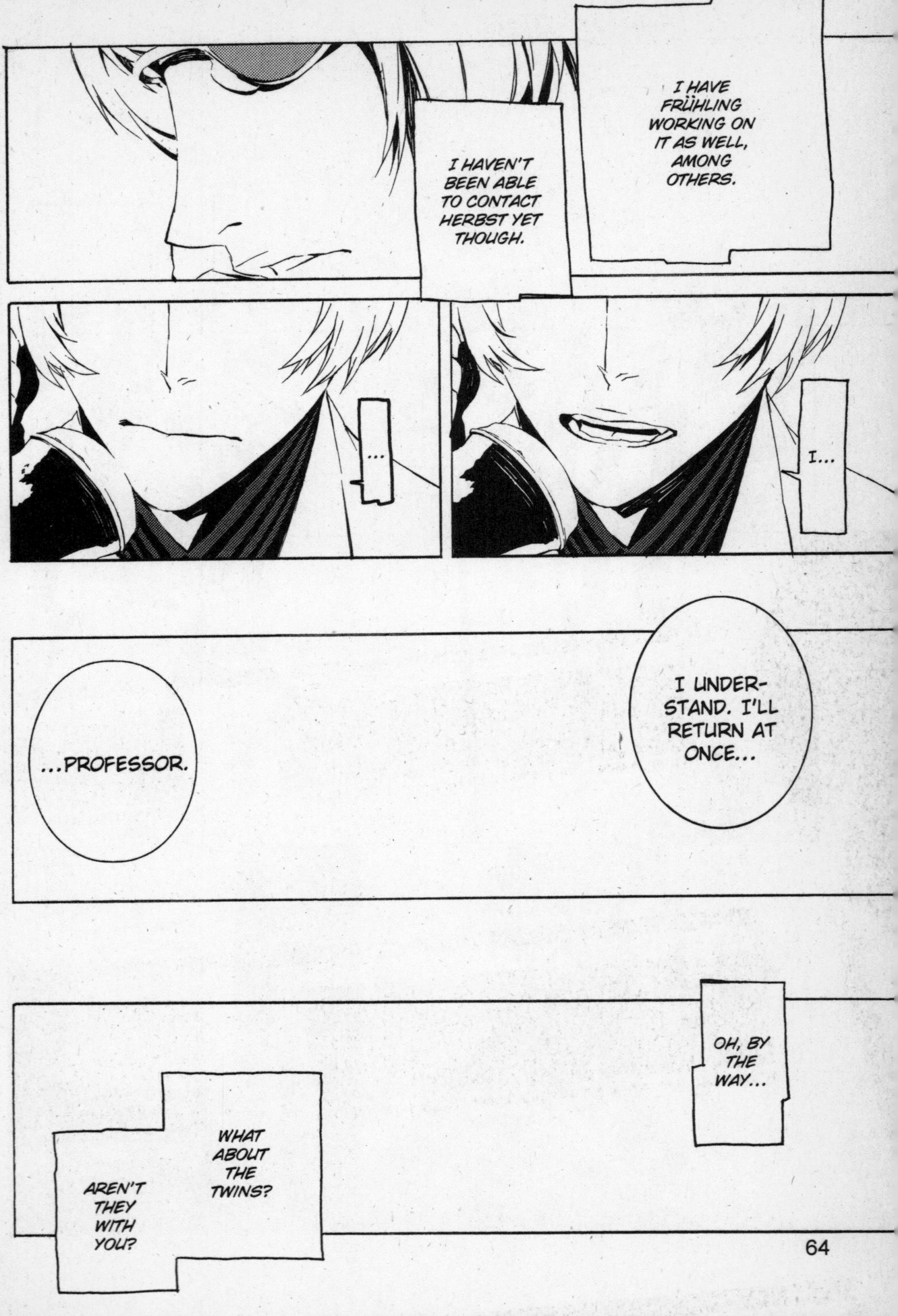
I HAVE FRÜHLING WORKING ON IT AS WELL, AMONG OTHERS.
I HAVEN'T BEEN ABLE TO CONTACT HERBST YET THOUGH.
I...
...
I UNDER-STAND. I'LL RETURN AT ONCE...
...PROFESSOR.
OH, BY THE WAY...
WHAT ABOUT THE TWINS?
AREN'T THEY WITH YOU?

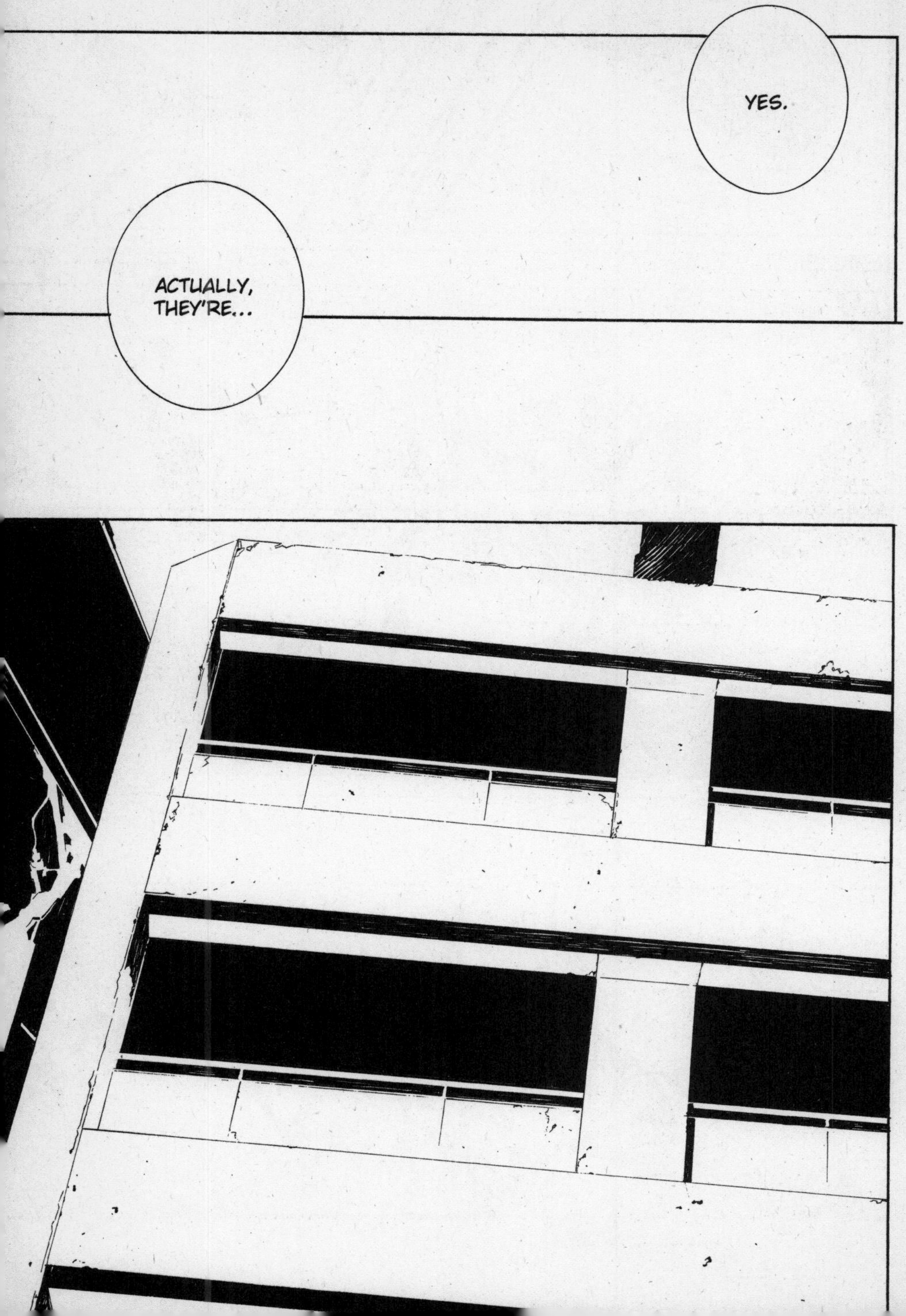
YES.
ACTUALLY, THEY'RE...

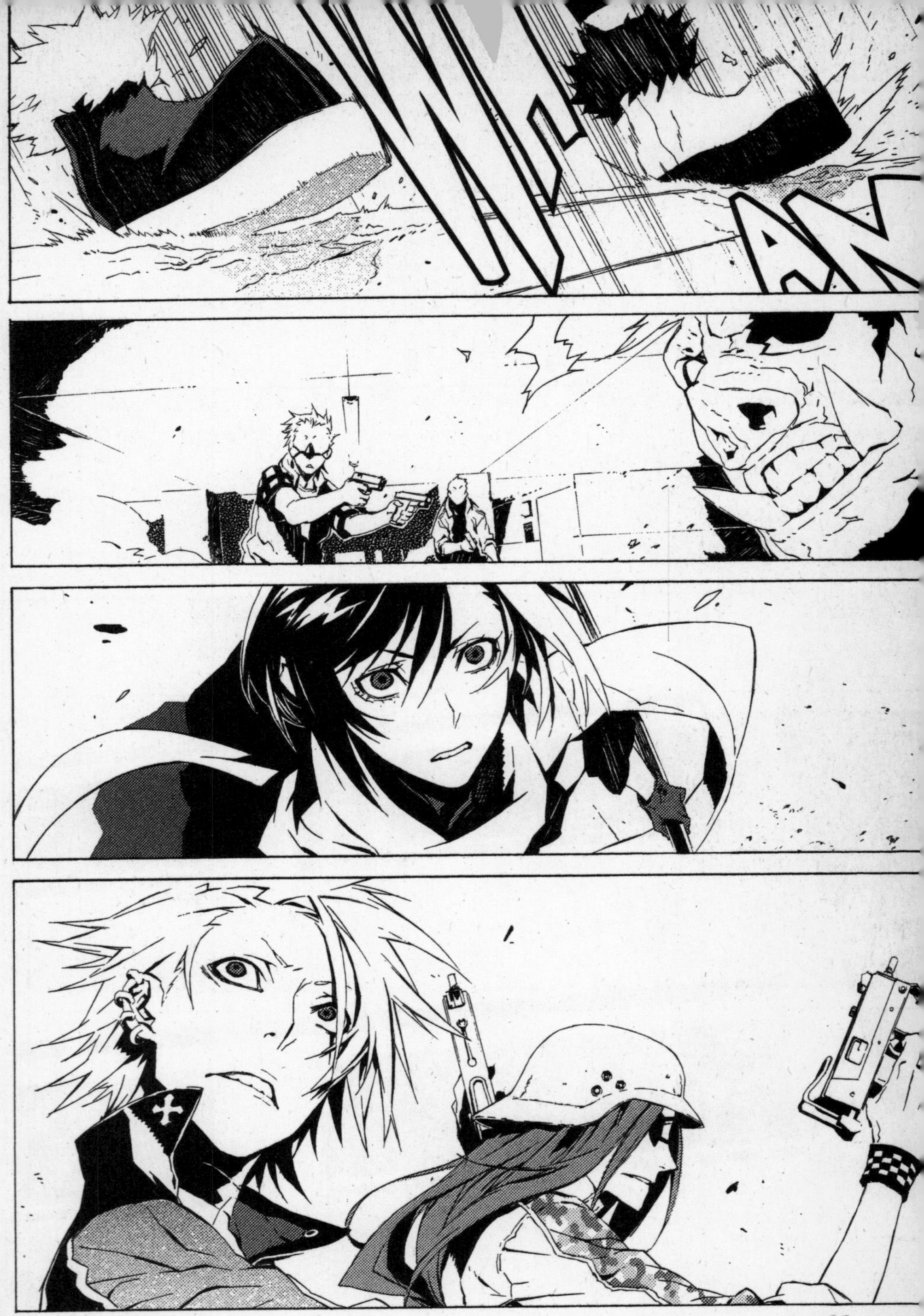

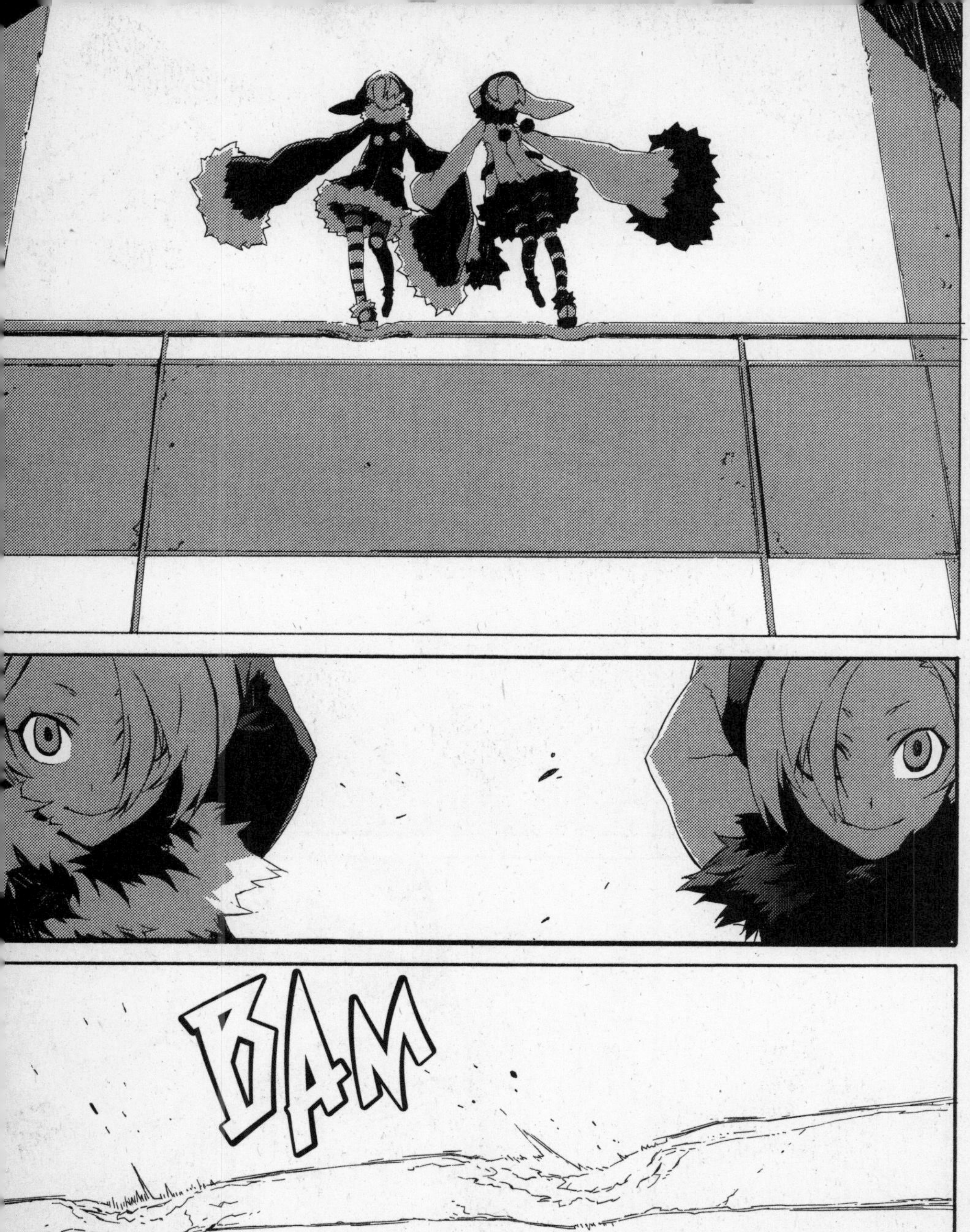
BAM

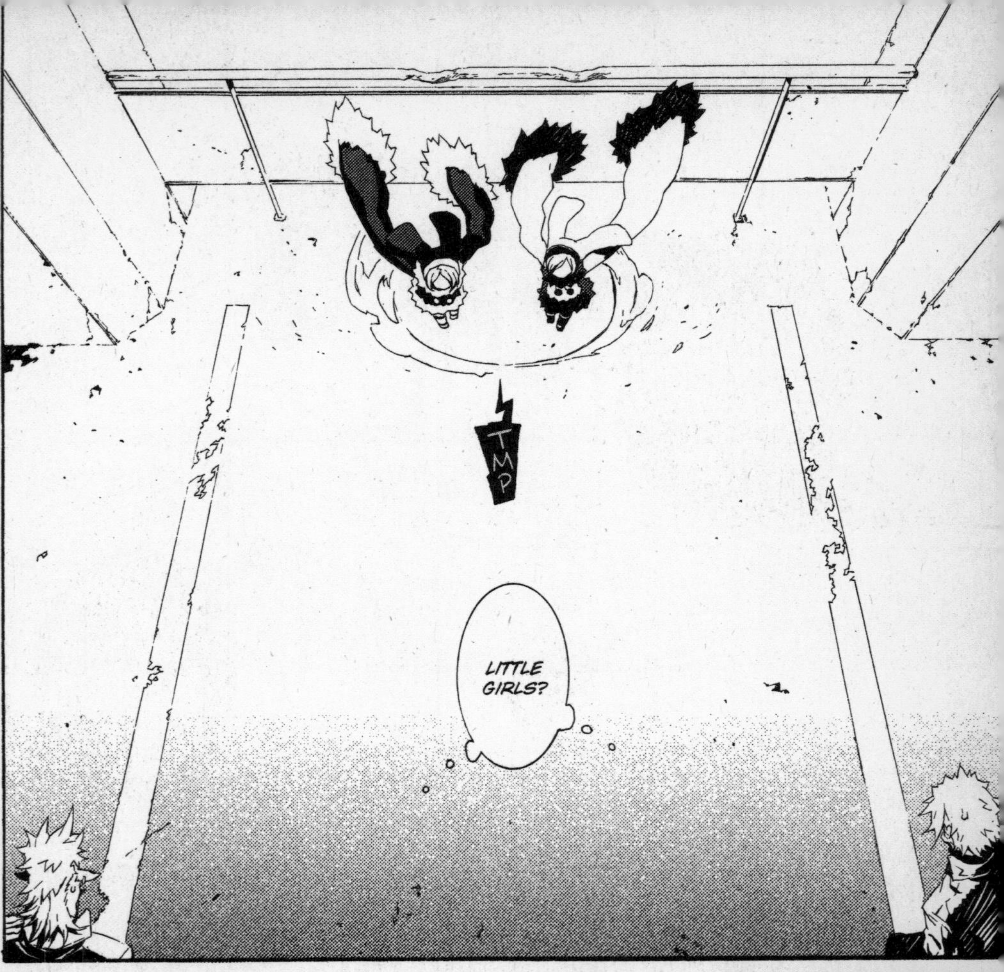
TMP
LITTLE GIRLS?
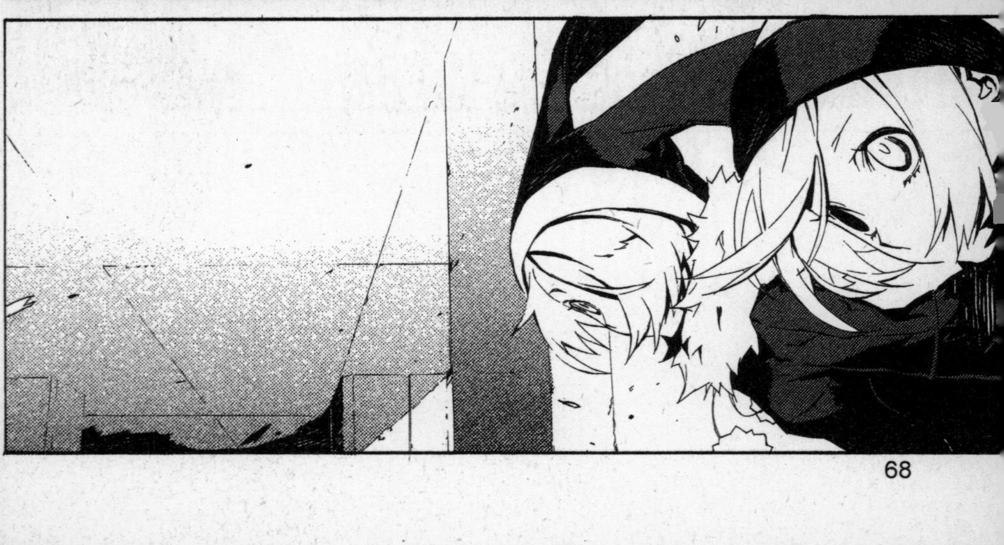

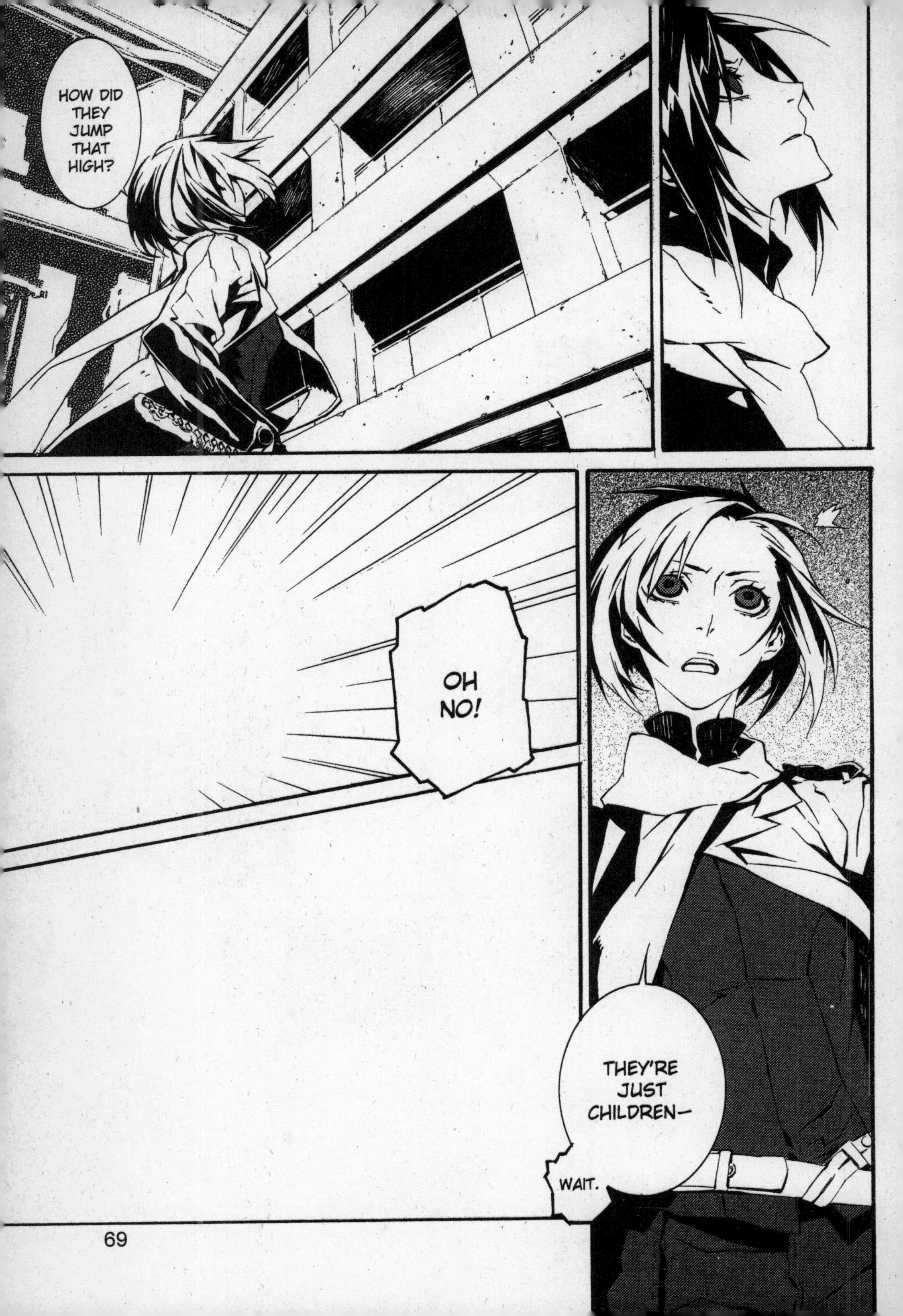
HOW DID THEY JUMP THAT HIGH?
THEY'RE JUST CHILDREN—
WAIT.
OH NO!

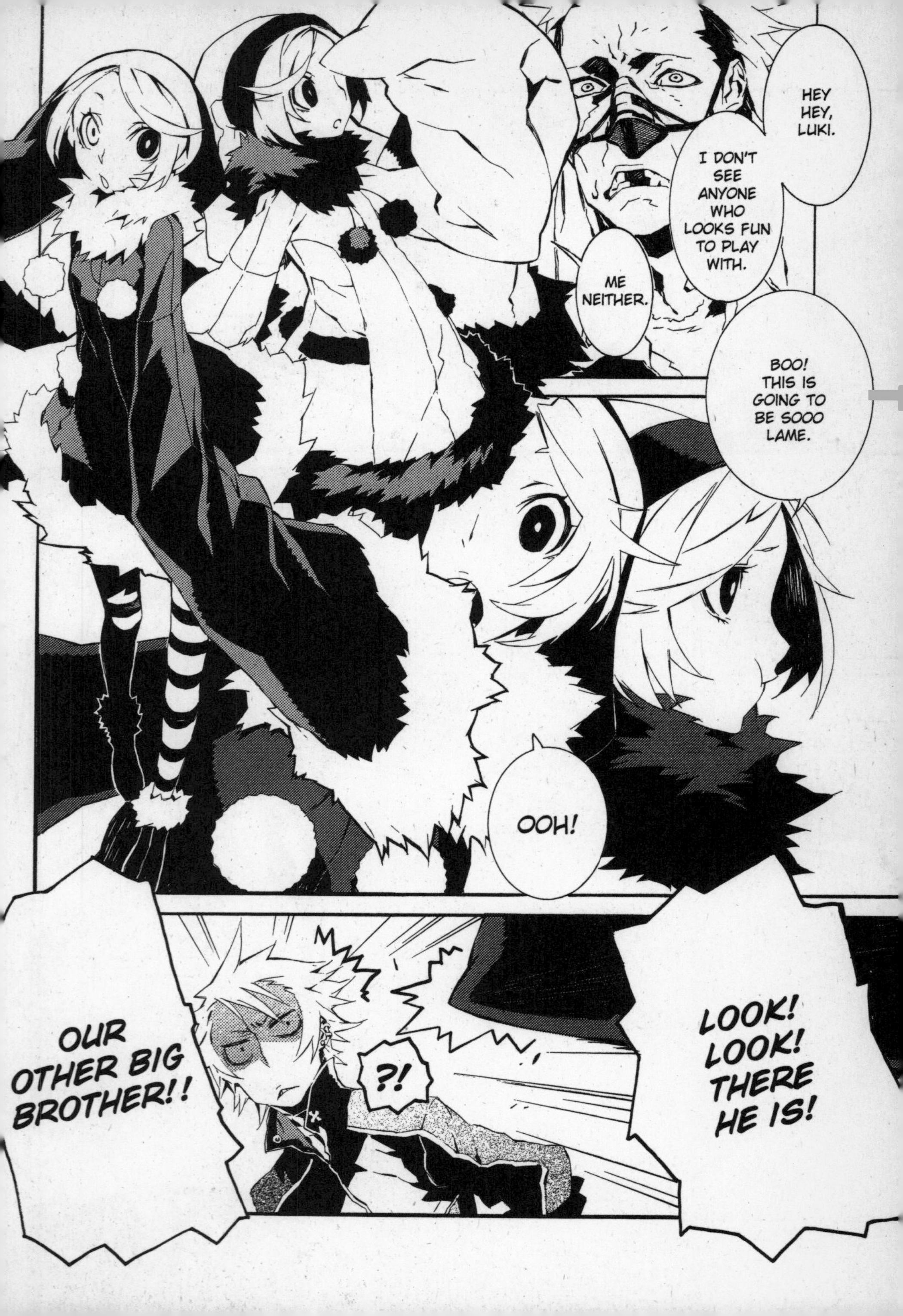
HEY HEY, LUKI.
I DON'T SEE ANYONE WHO LOOKS FUN TO PLAY WITH.
ME NEITHER.
BOO! THIS IS GOING TO BE SOOO LAME.
OOH!
LOOK! LOOK! THERE HE IS!
?!
OUR OTHER BIG BROTHER!!

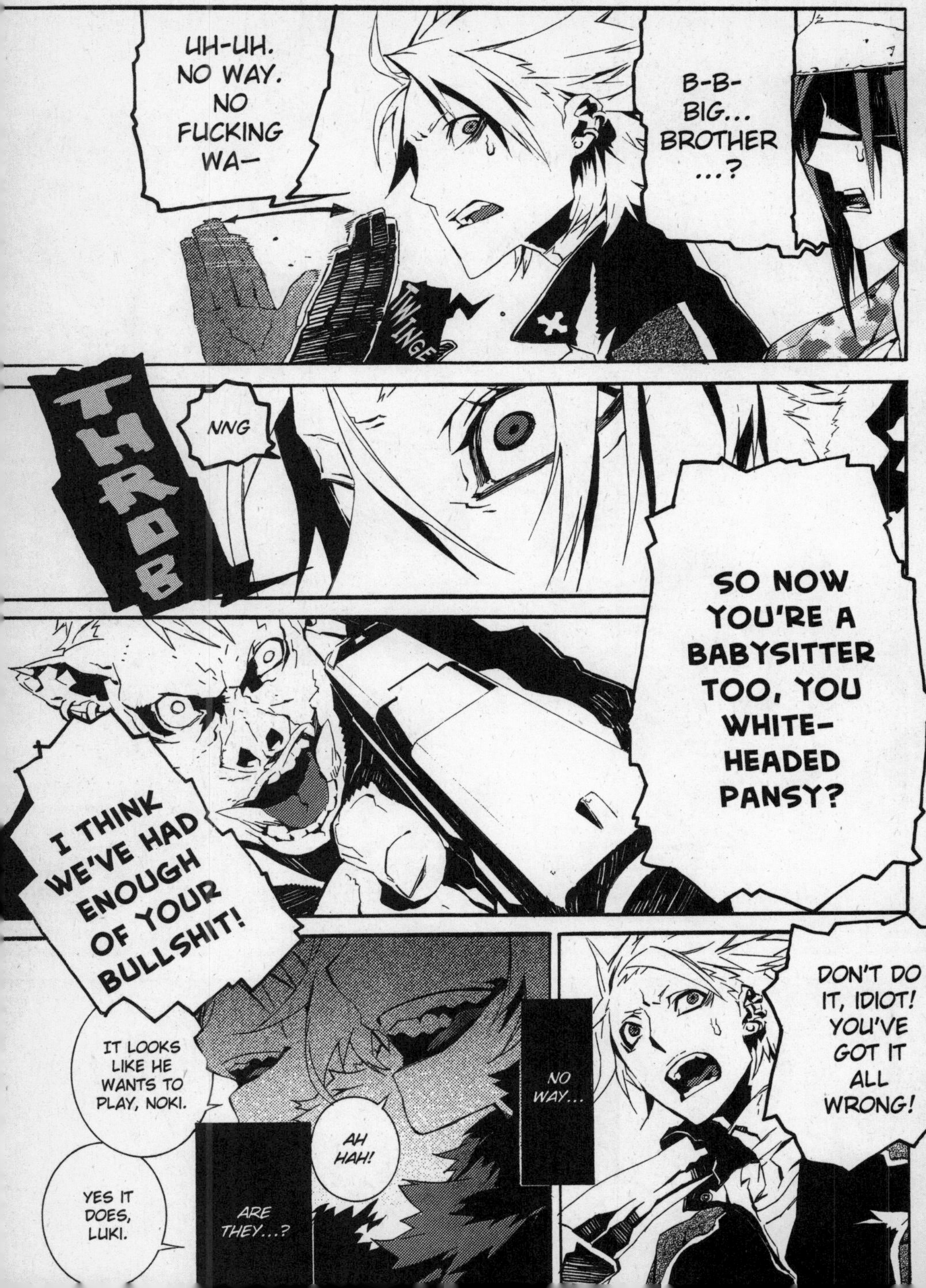
B-B-BIG... BROTHER ...?
UH-UH. NO WAY. NO FUCKING WA—
TWINGE
NNG
THROB
SO NOW YOU'RE A BABYSITTER TOO, YOU WHITE-HEADED PANSY?
I THINK WE'VE HAD ENOUGH OF YOUR BULLSHIT!
DON'T DO IT, IDIOT! YOU'VE GOT IT ALL WRONG!
NO WAY...
IT LOOKS LIKE HE WANTS TO PLAY, NOKI.
AH HAH!
ARE THEY...?
YES IT DOES, LUKI.

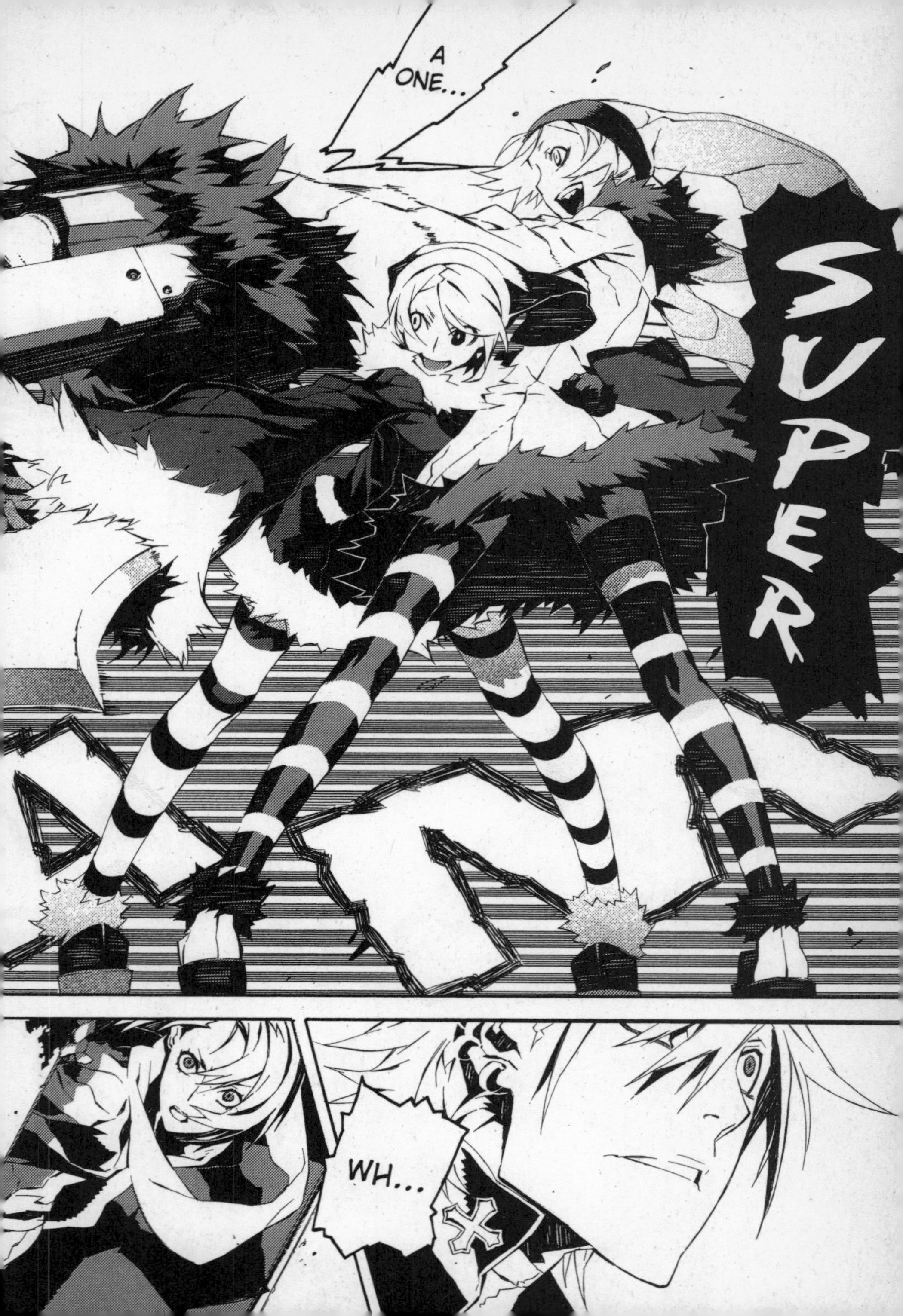
!
A ONE...
SUPER
WH...

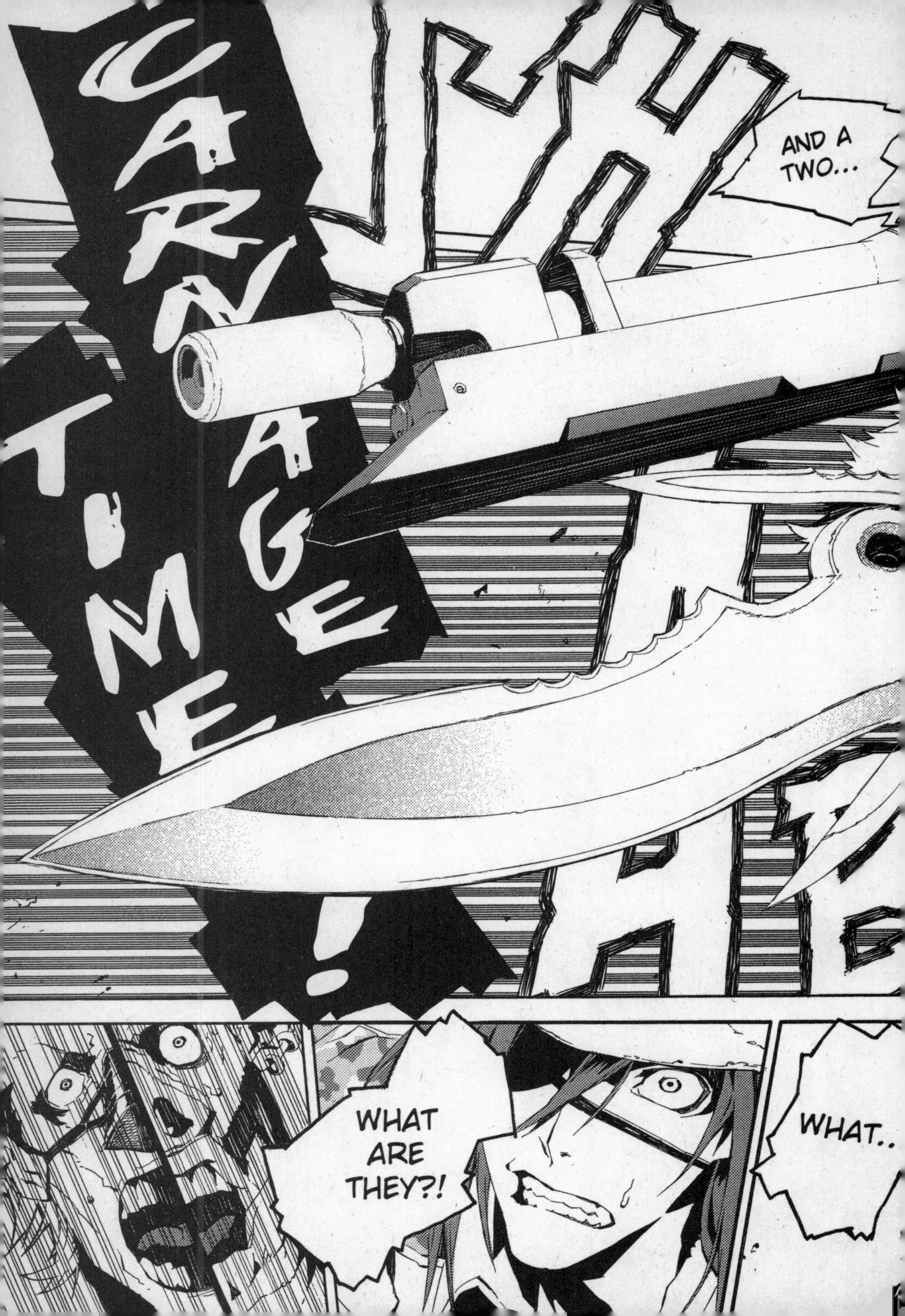
AND A TWO...
CARNAGE TIME!
WHAT..
WHAT ARE THEY?!

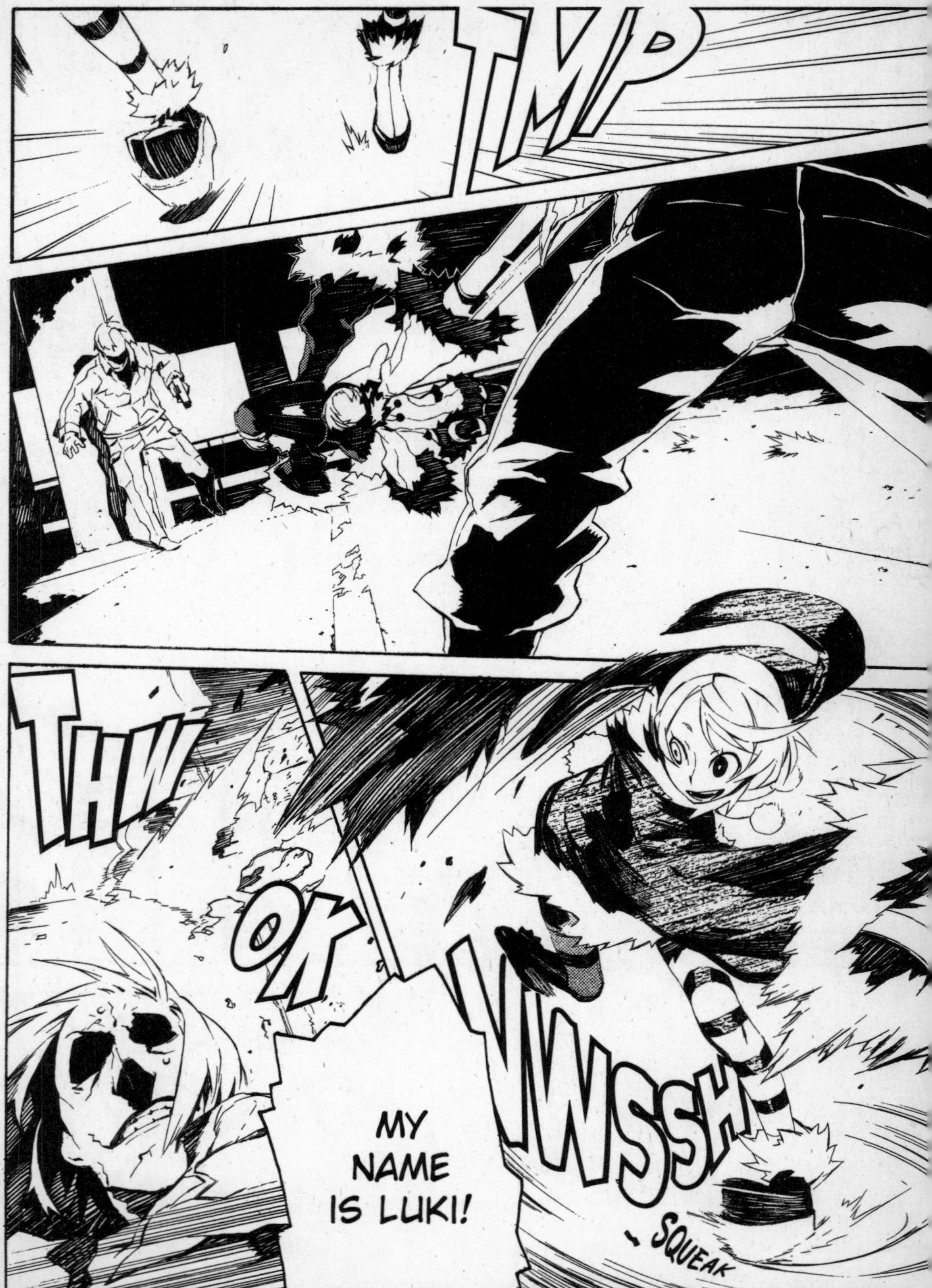
TMP
VWSSH
SQUEAK
MY NAME IS LUKI!
THWOK

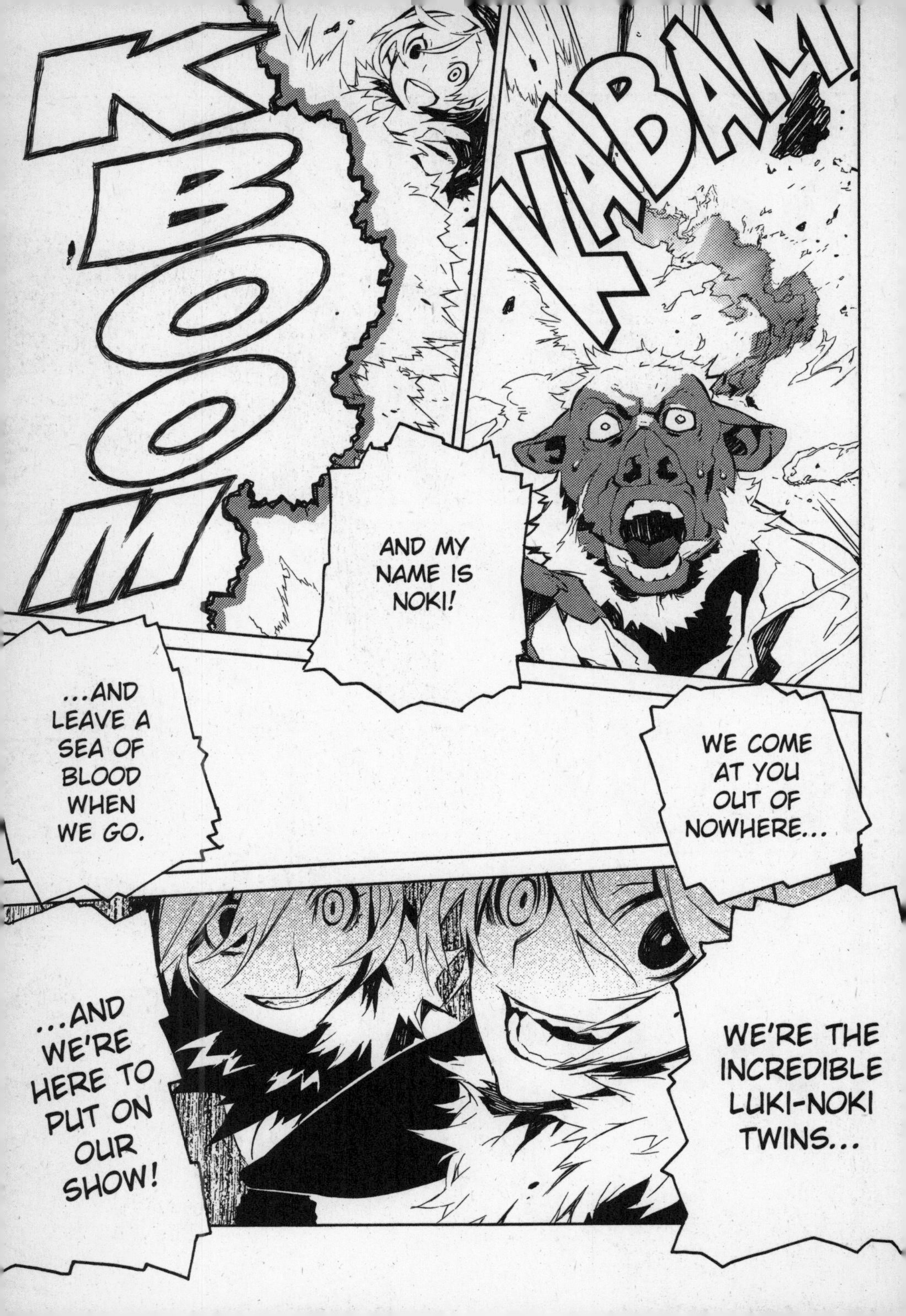
KABAM!
AND MY NAME IS NOKI!
KBOOM
WE COME AT YOU OUT OF NOWHERE...
...AND LEAVE A SEA OF BLOOD WHEN WE GO.
WE'RE THE INCREDIBLE LUKI-NOKI TWINS...
...AND WE'RE HERE TO PUT ON OUR SHOW!

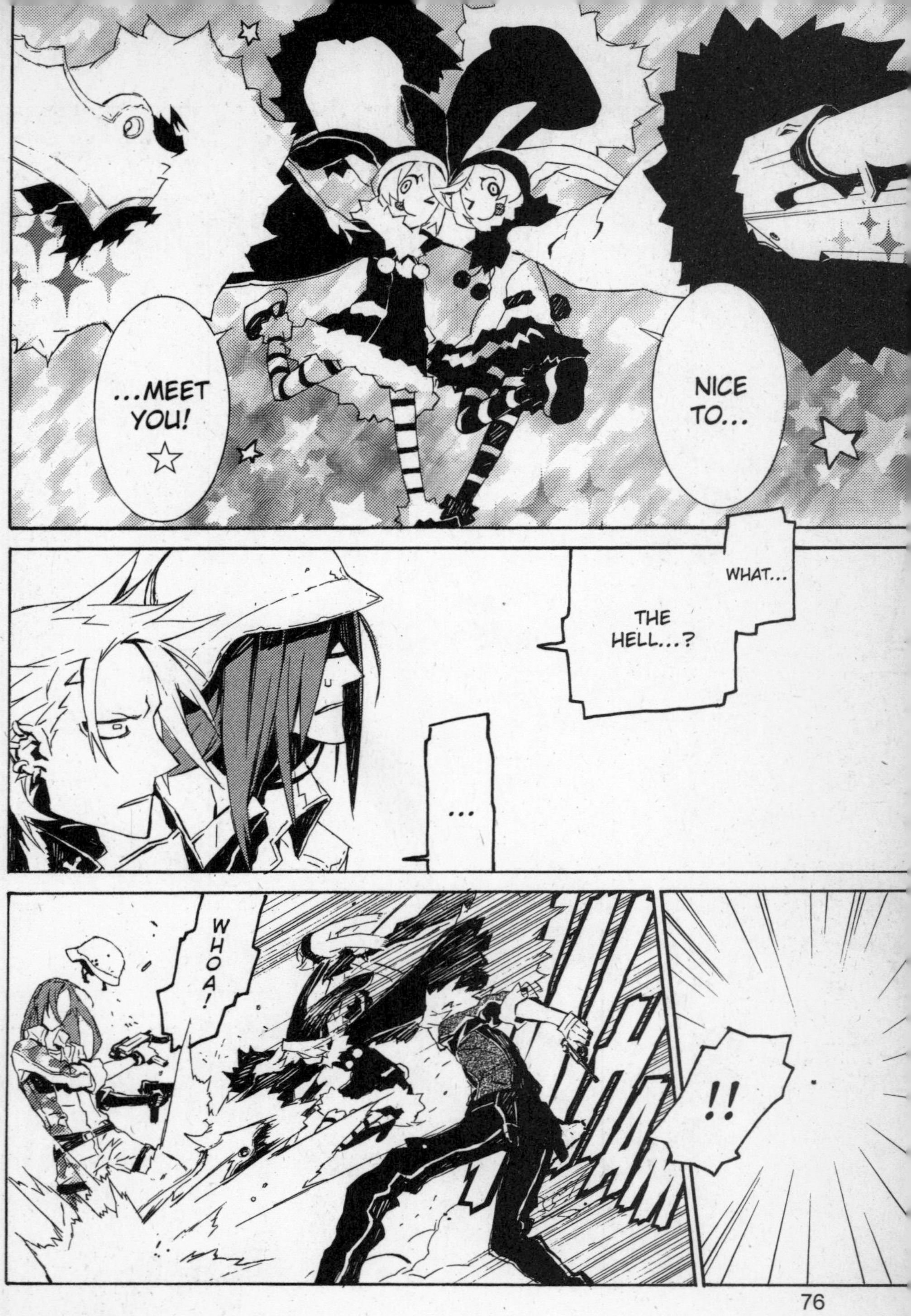
NICE TO...
...MEET YOU! ☆
WHAT... THE HELL...?
...
!!
WHOA!

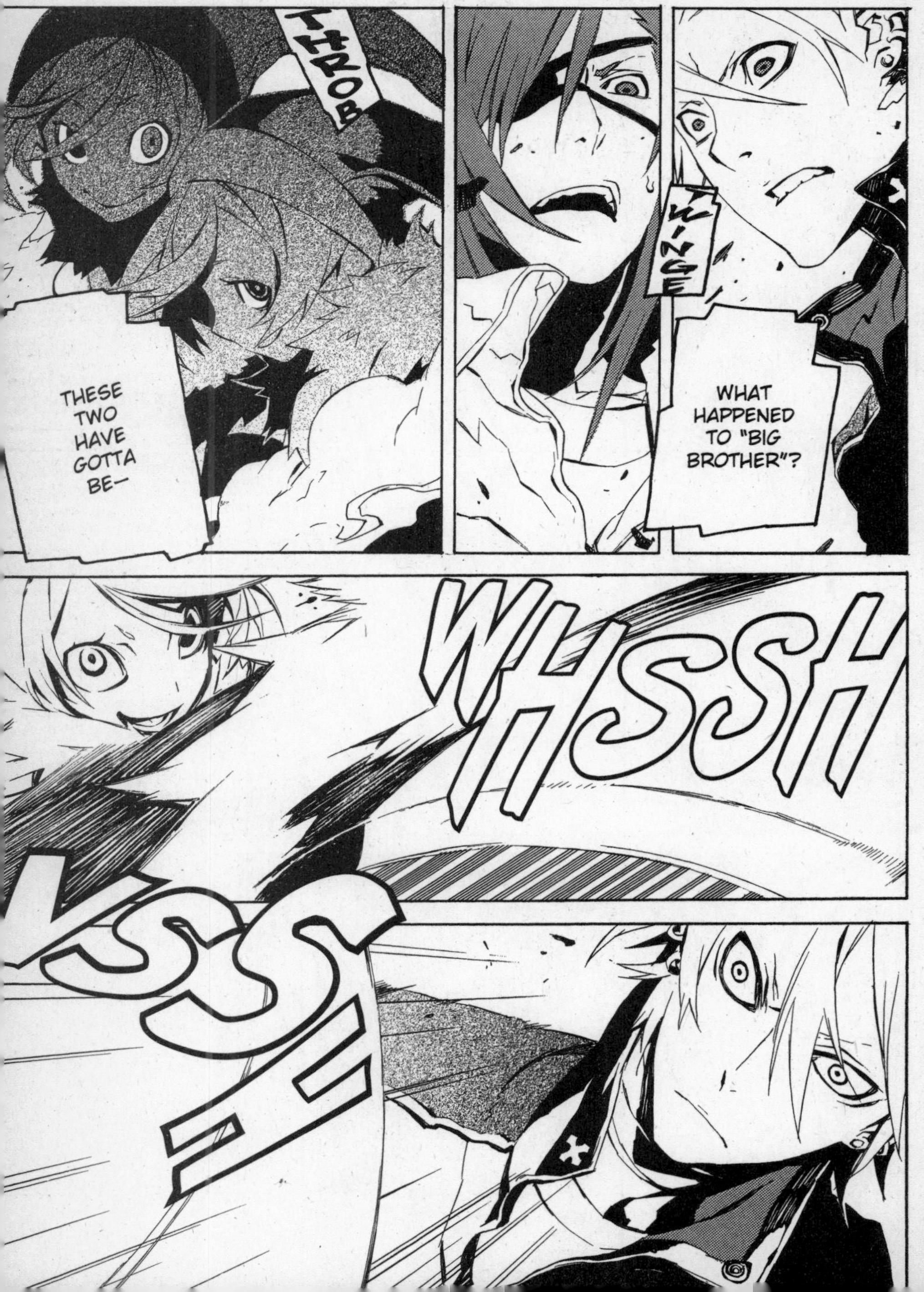
WHAT HAPPENED TO "BIG BROTHER"?
TWINGE
THROB
THESE TWO HAVE GOTTA BE—
WHSSH

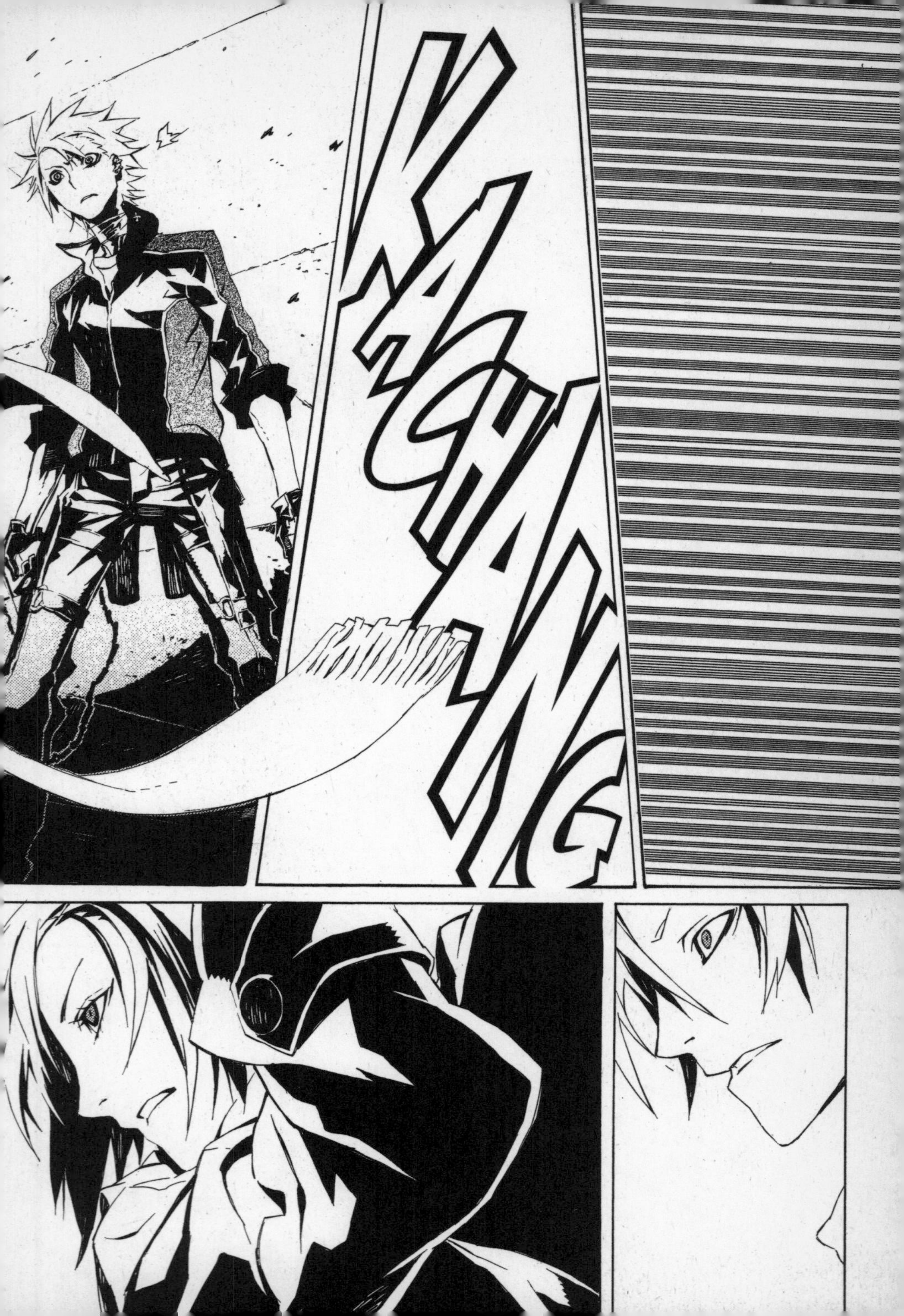
KACHANG

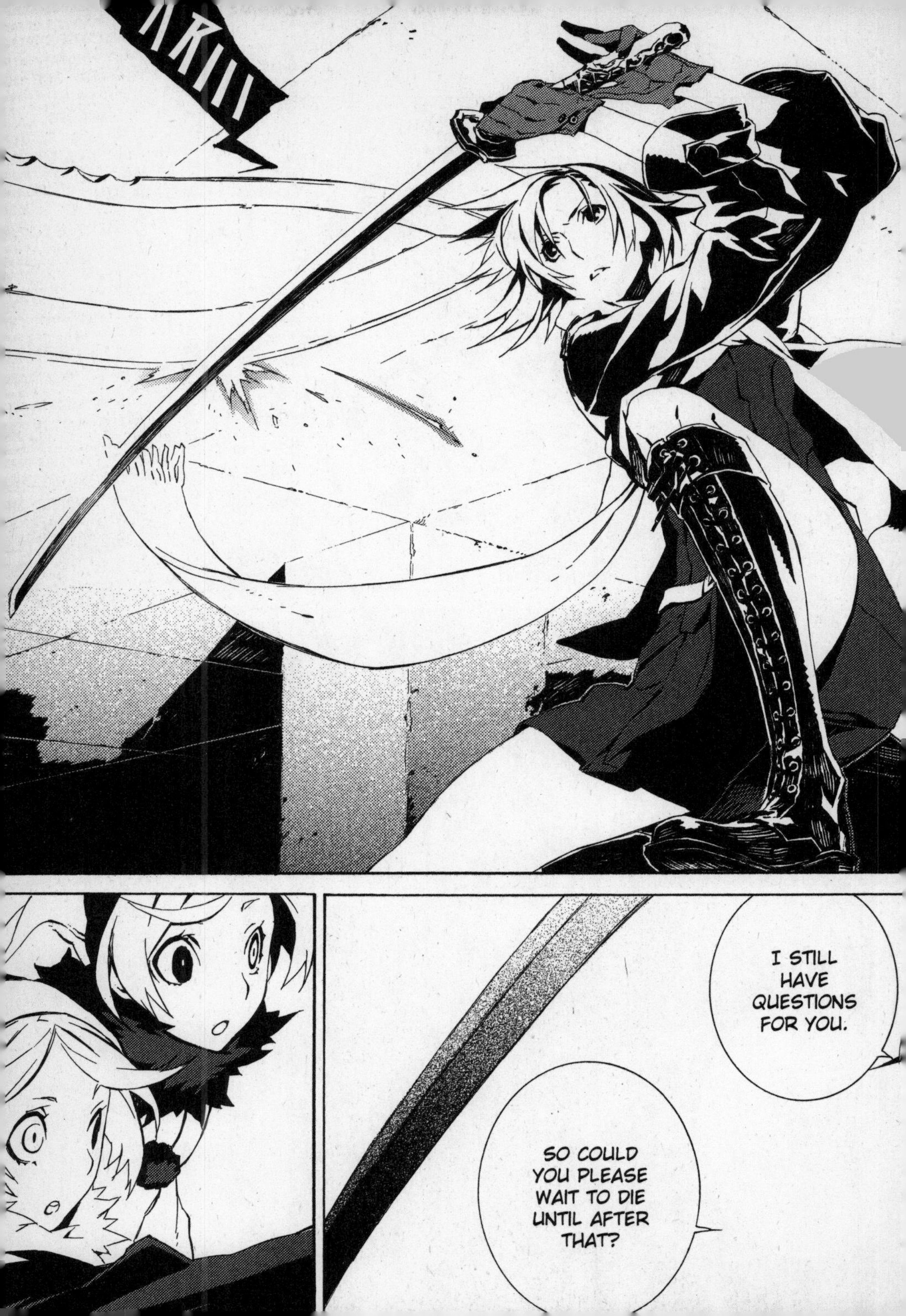
KRIII
I STILL HAVE QUESTIONS FOR YOU.
SO COULD YOU PLEASE WAIT TO DIE UNTIL AFTER THAT?

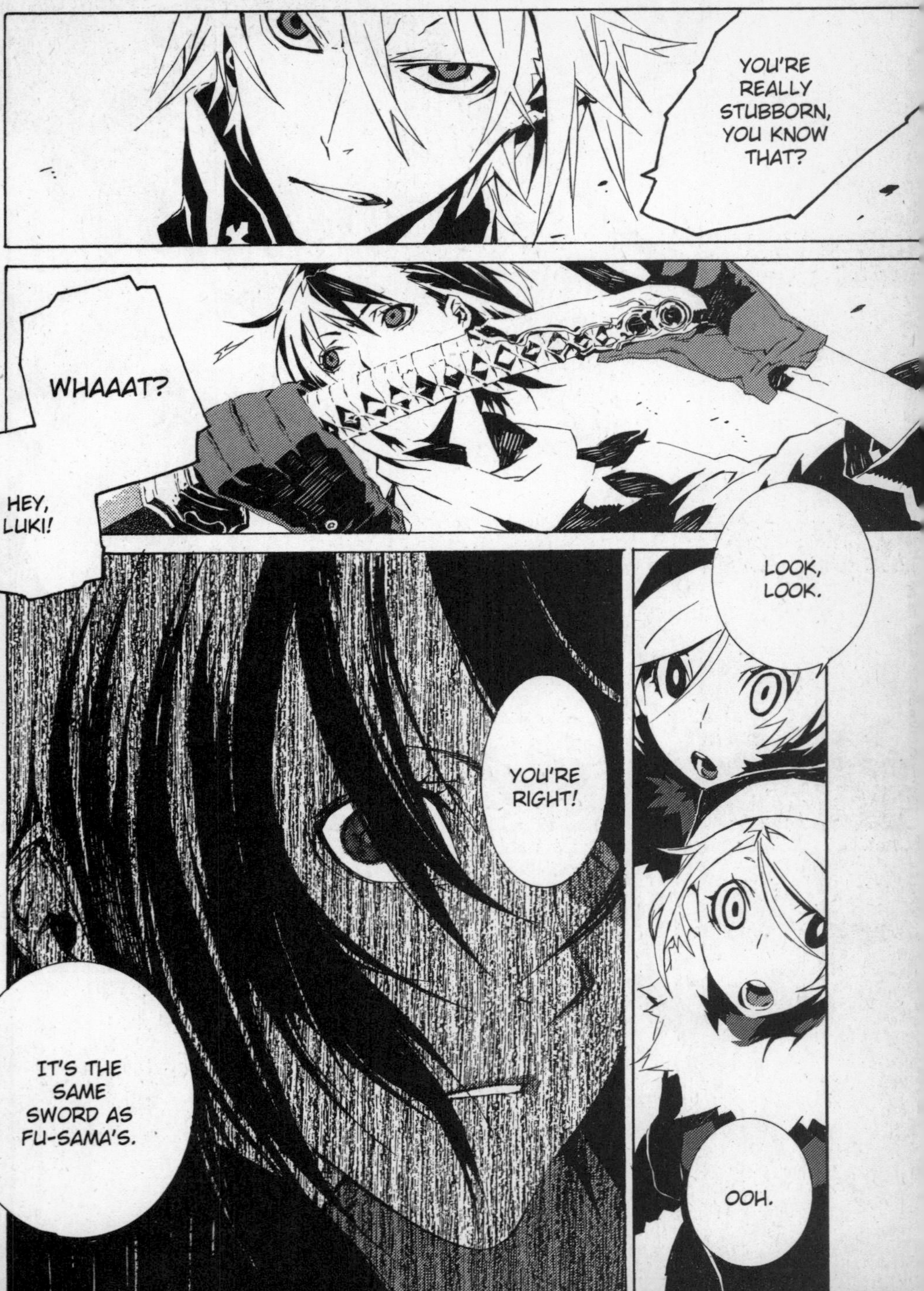
YOU'RE REALLY STUBBORN, YOU KNOW THAT?
WHAAAT?
HEY, LUKI!
LOOK, LOOK.
OOH.
YOU'RE RIGHT!
IT'S THE SAME SWORD AS FU-SAMA'S.

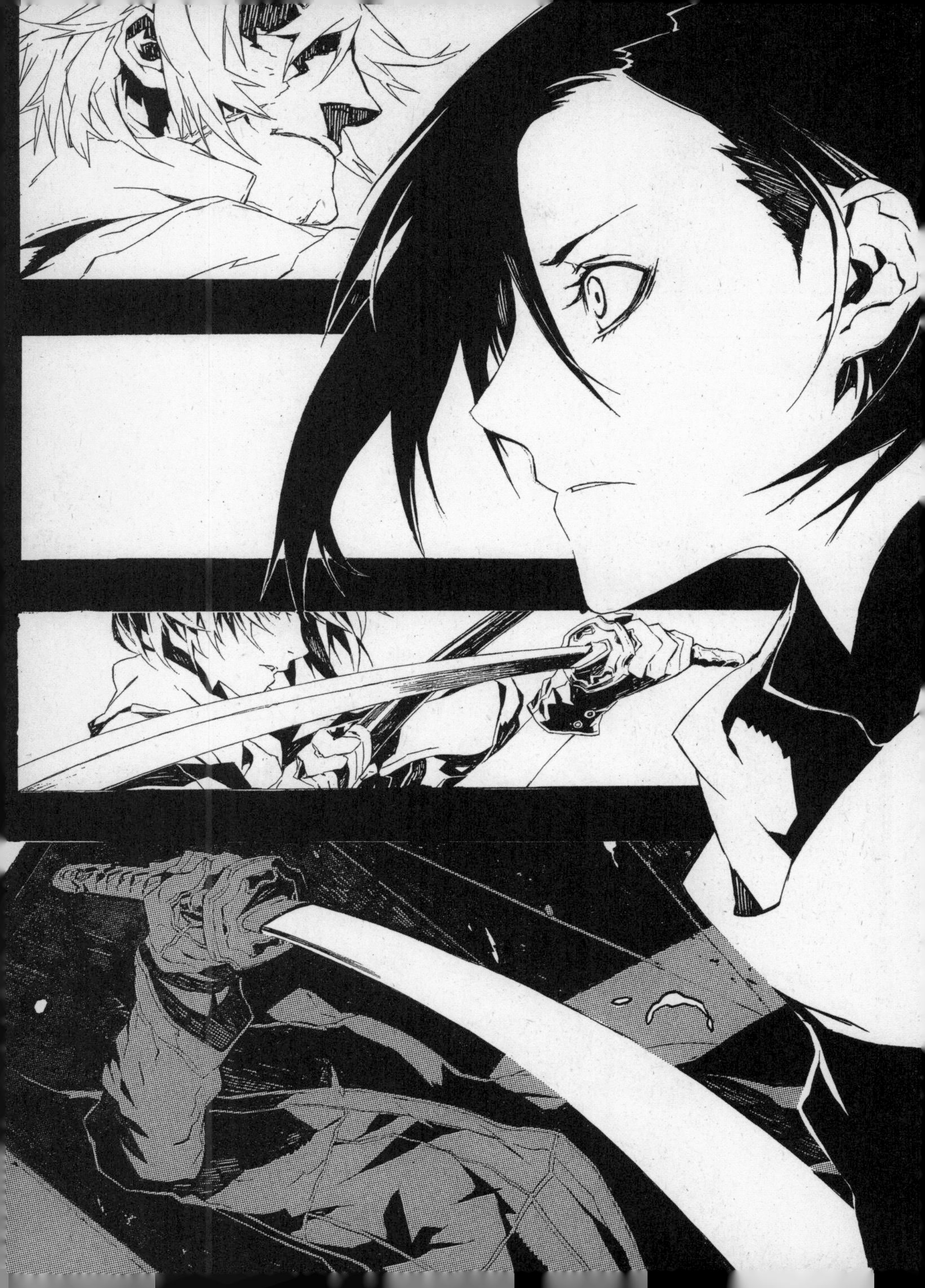

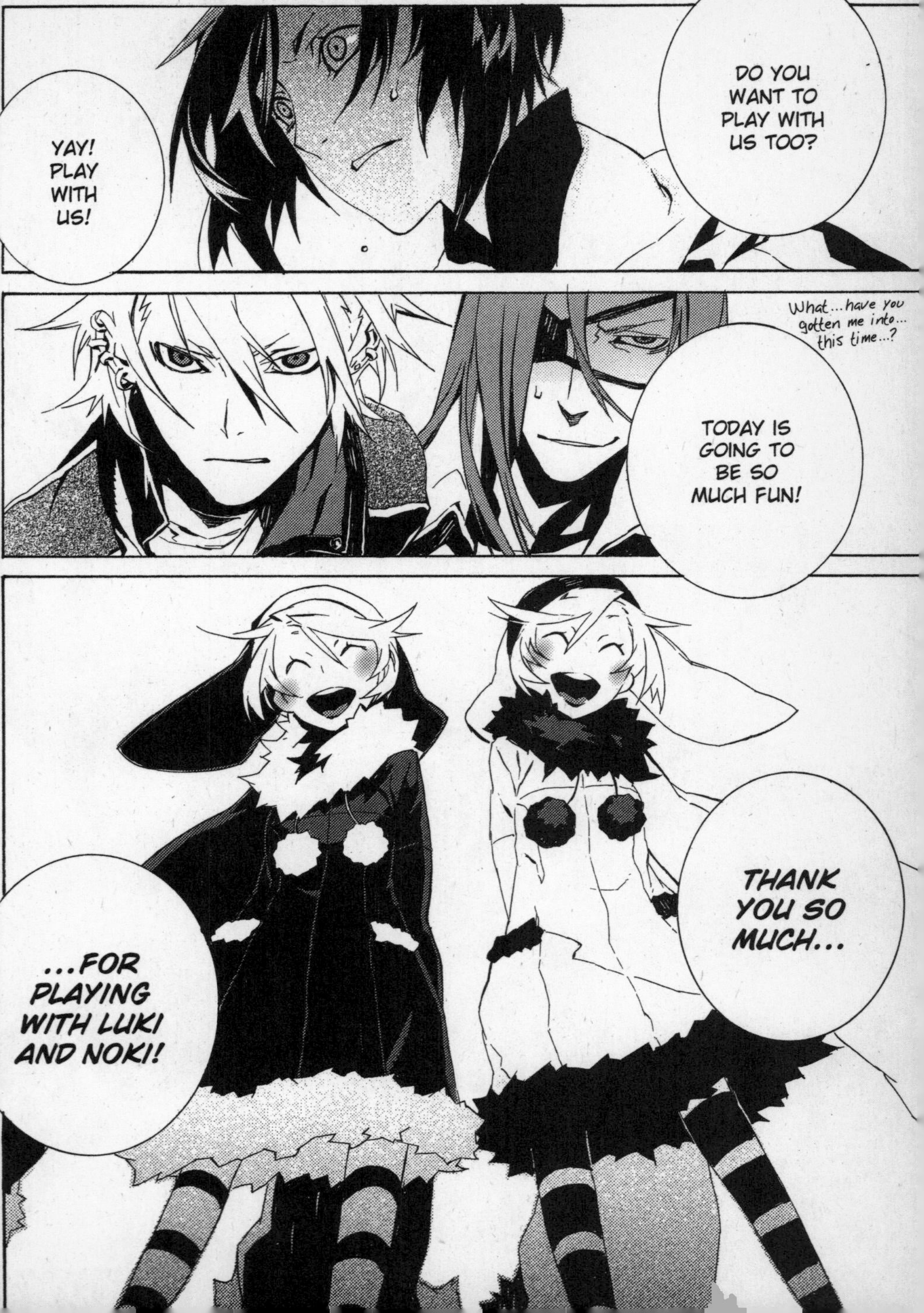
DO YOU WANT TO PLAY WITH US TOO?
YAY! PLAY WITH US!
What... have you gotten me into... this time...?
TODAY IS GOING TO BE SO MUCH FUN!
THANK YOU SO MUCH...
...FOR PLAYING WITH LUKI AND NOKI!

#17 Pink & Black Ⅲ

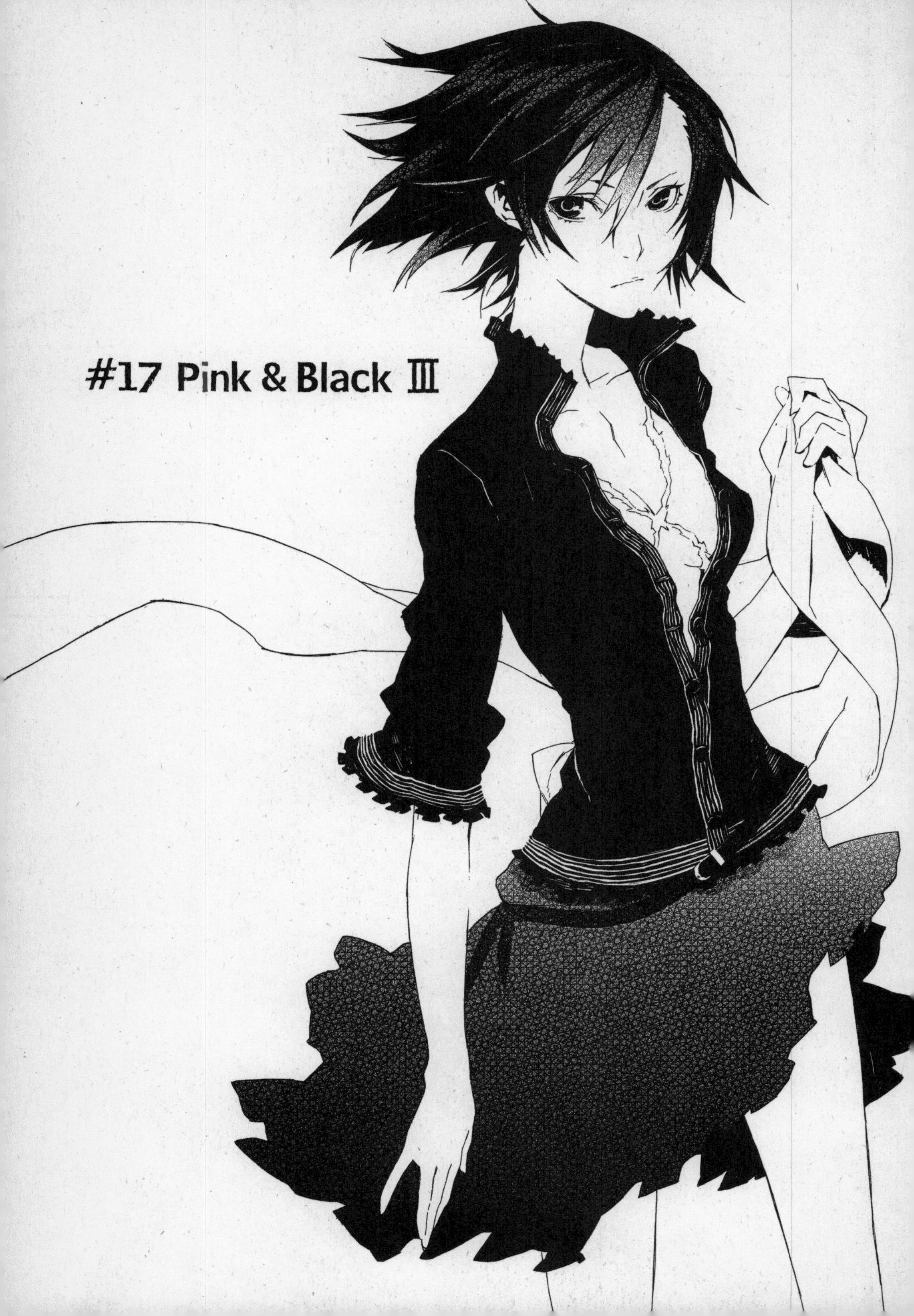

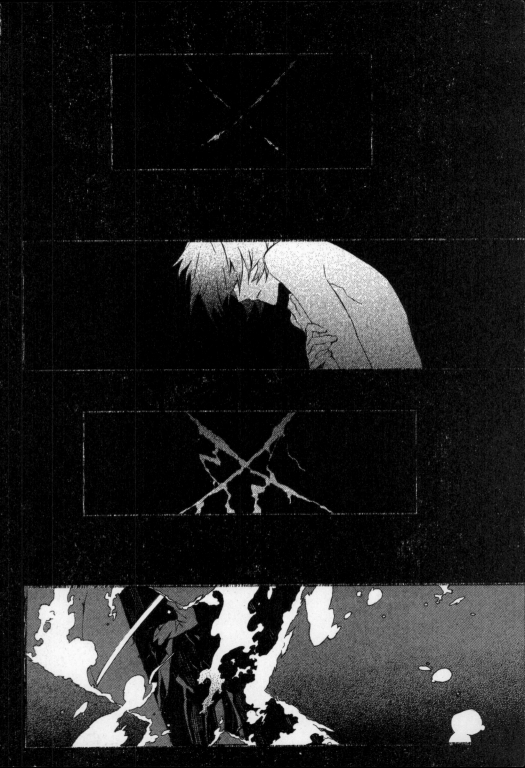

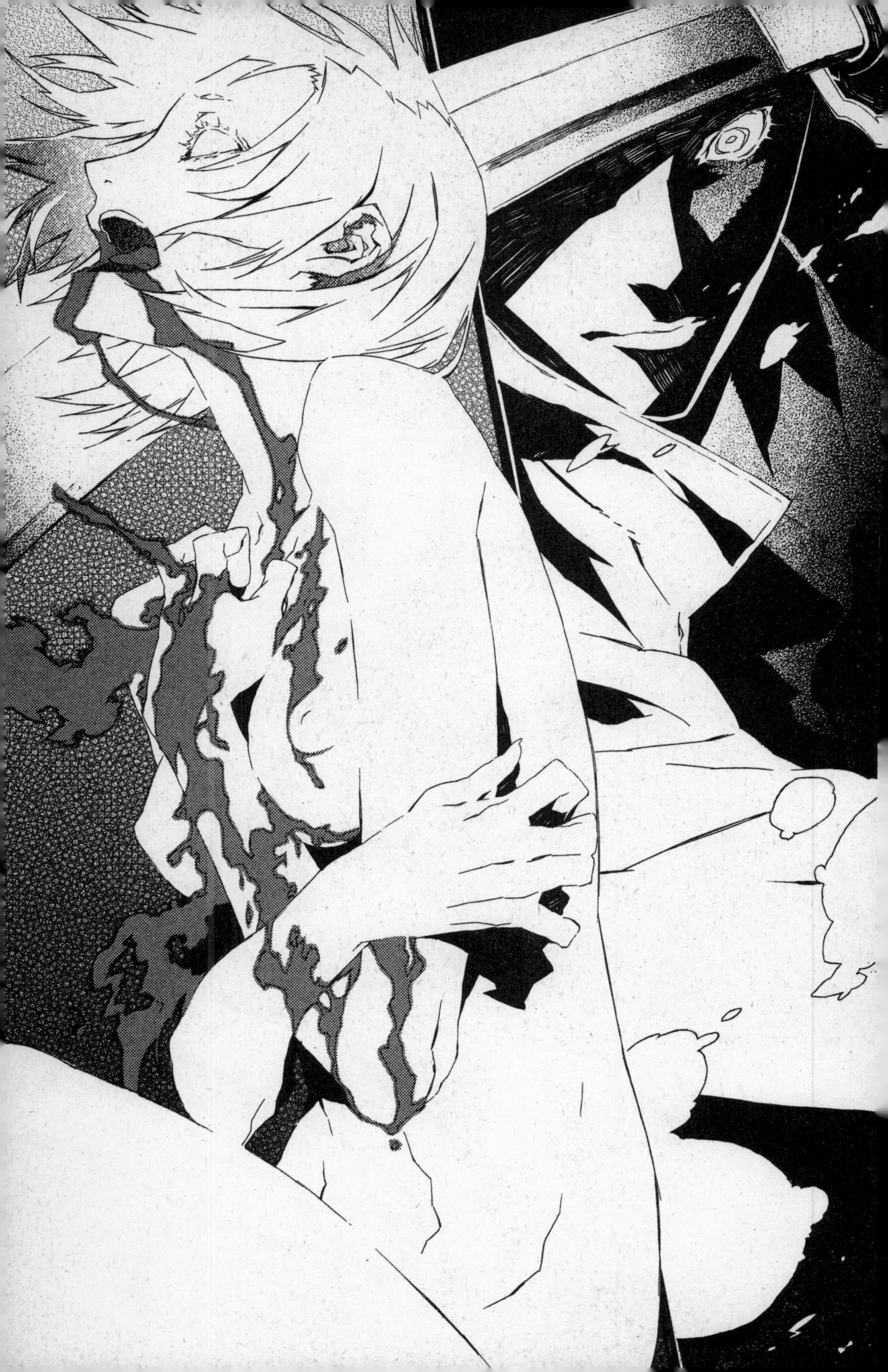

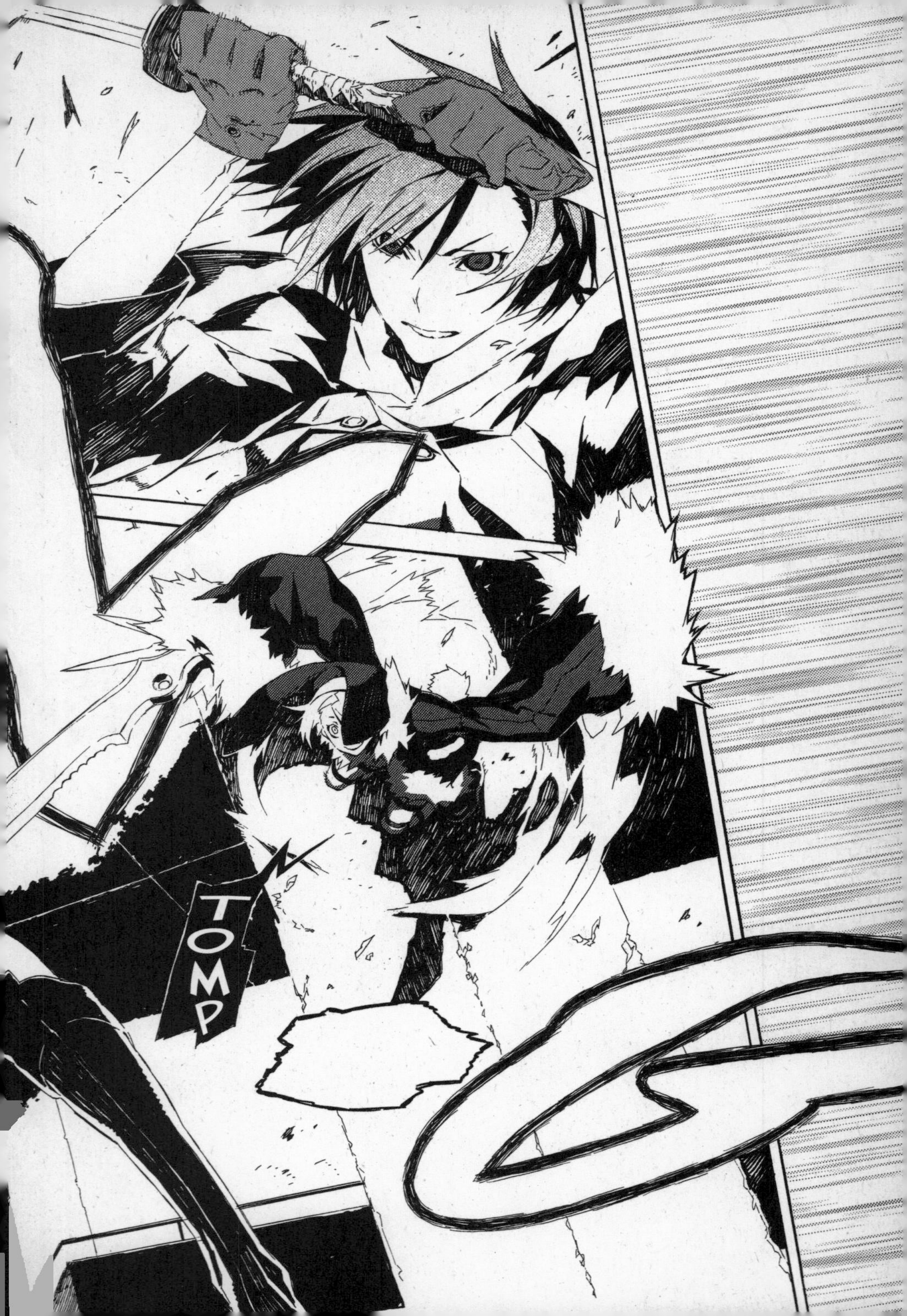
TOMP

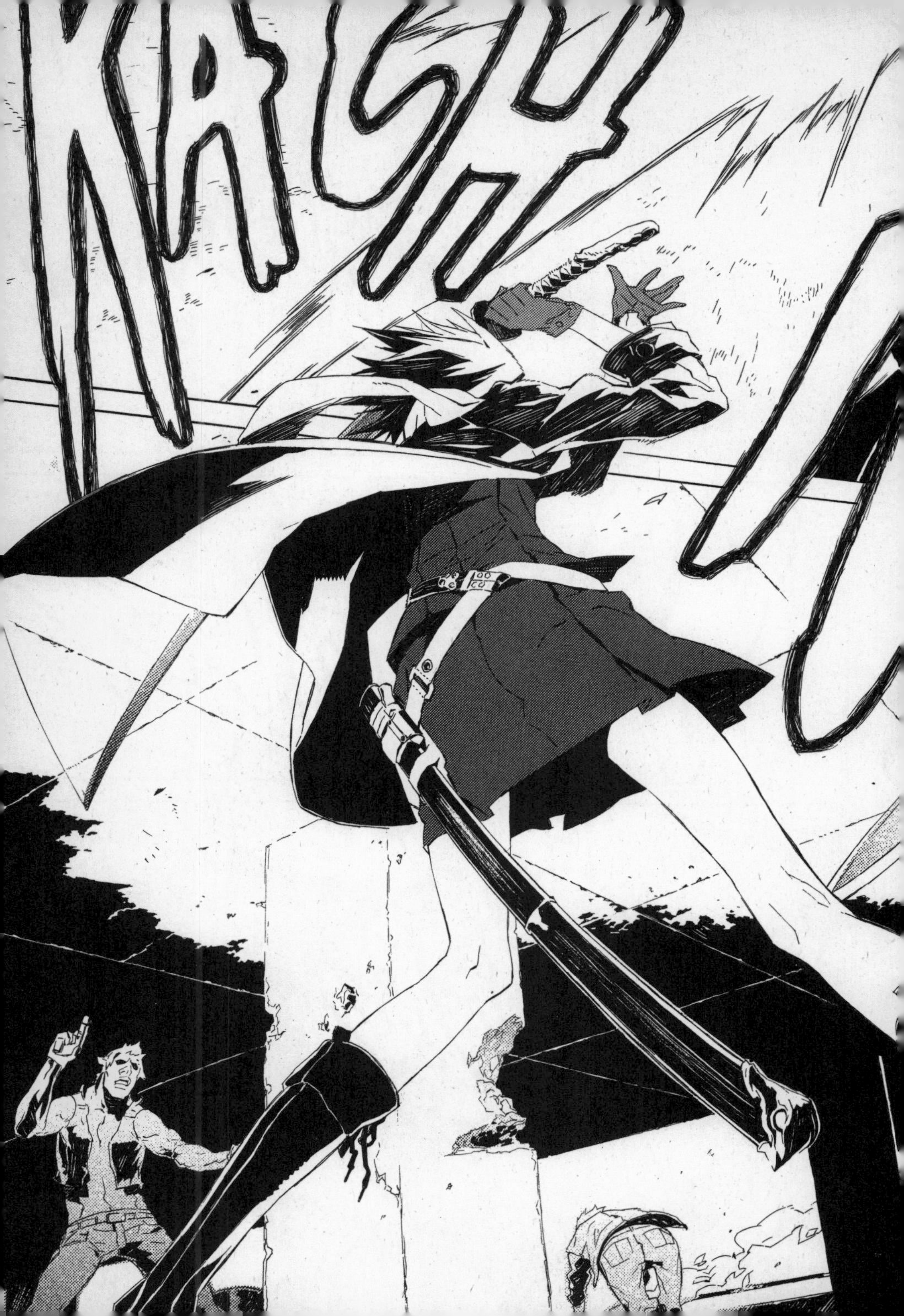

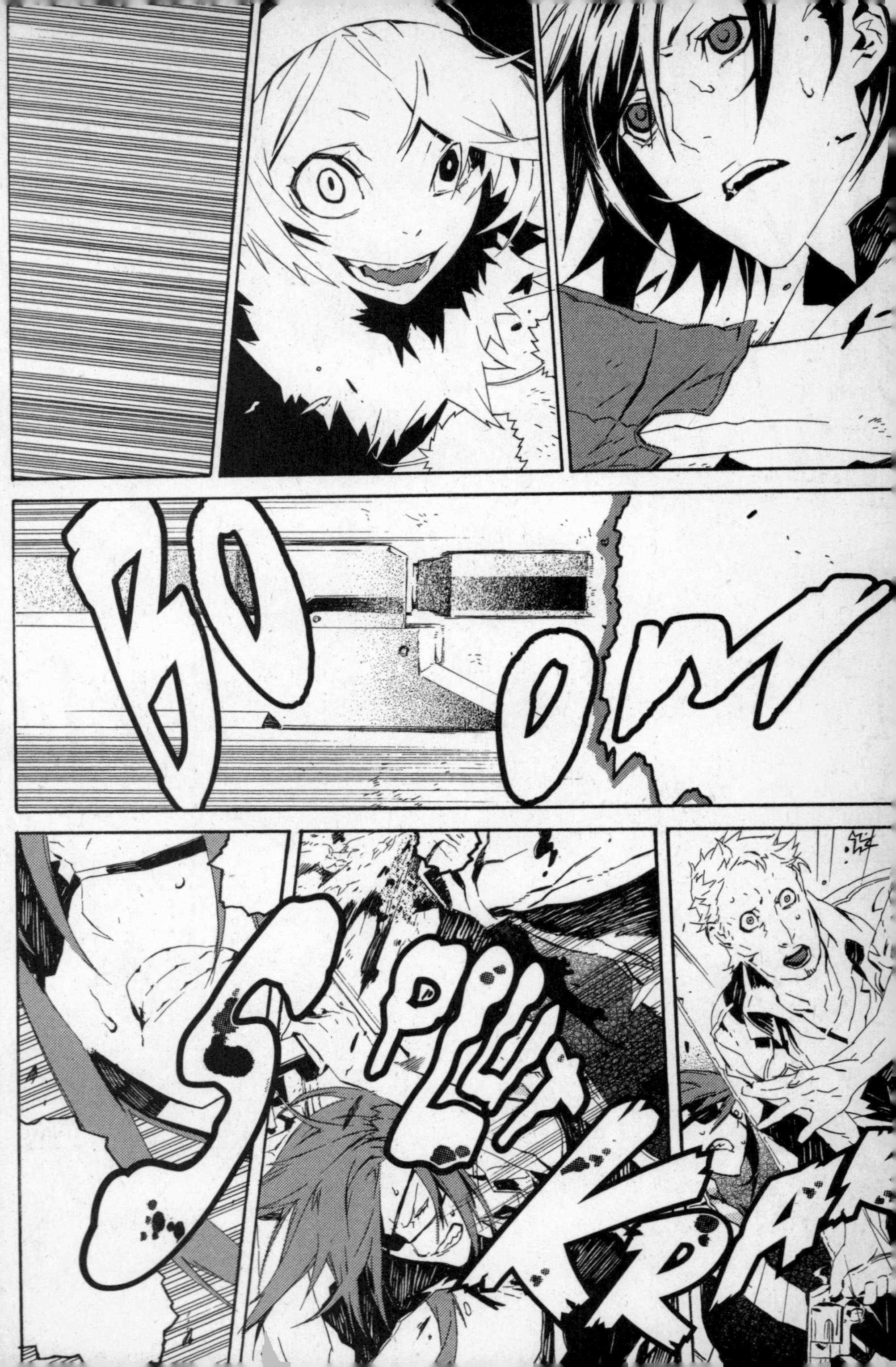
BOOM
SPLUT
KRA

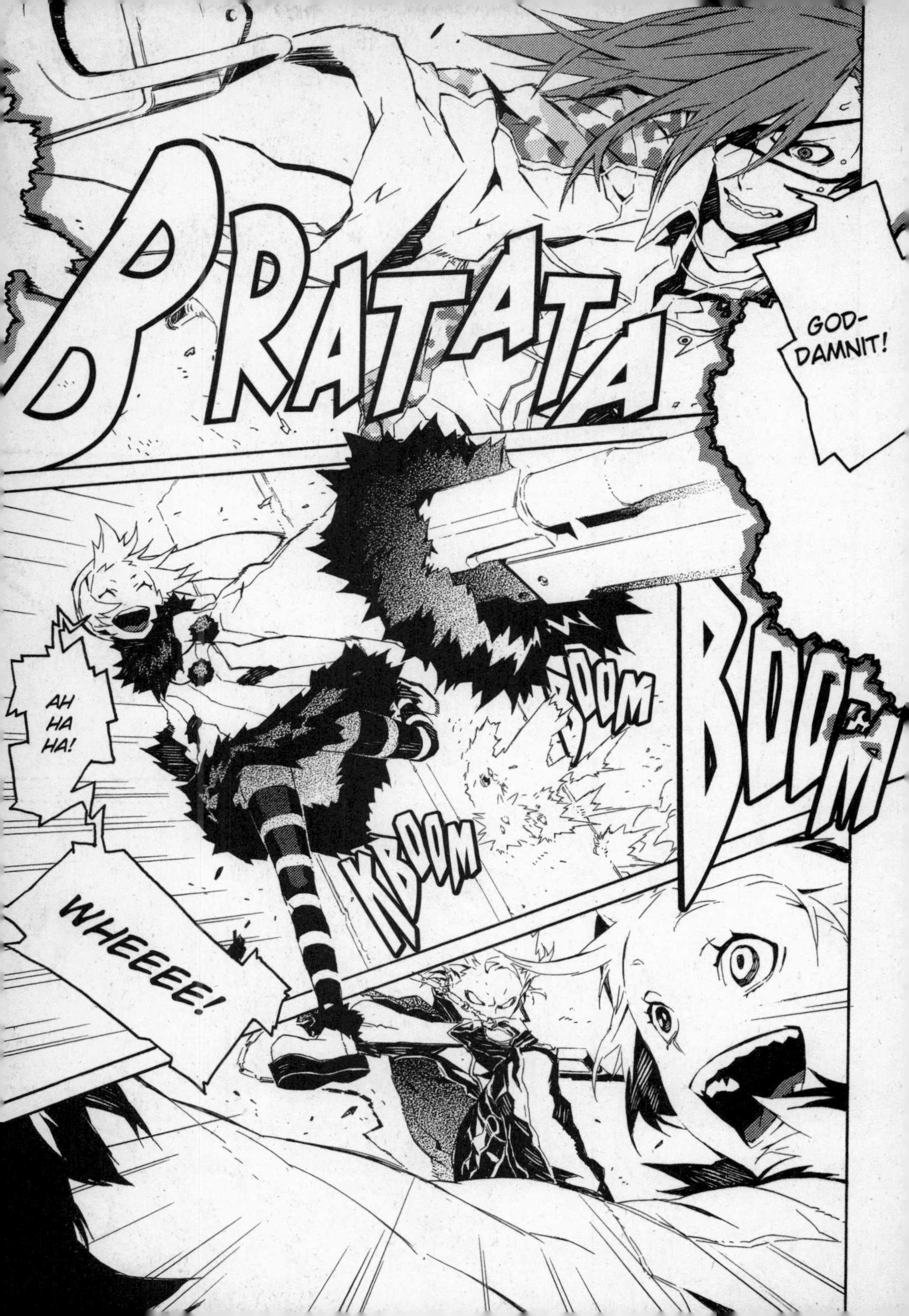
GOD-DAMNIT!
PRATATA
BOOM
BOOM
KBOOM
AH HA HA!
WHEEEEE!

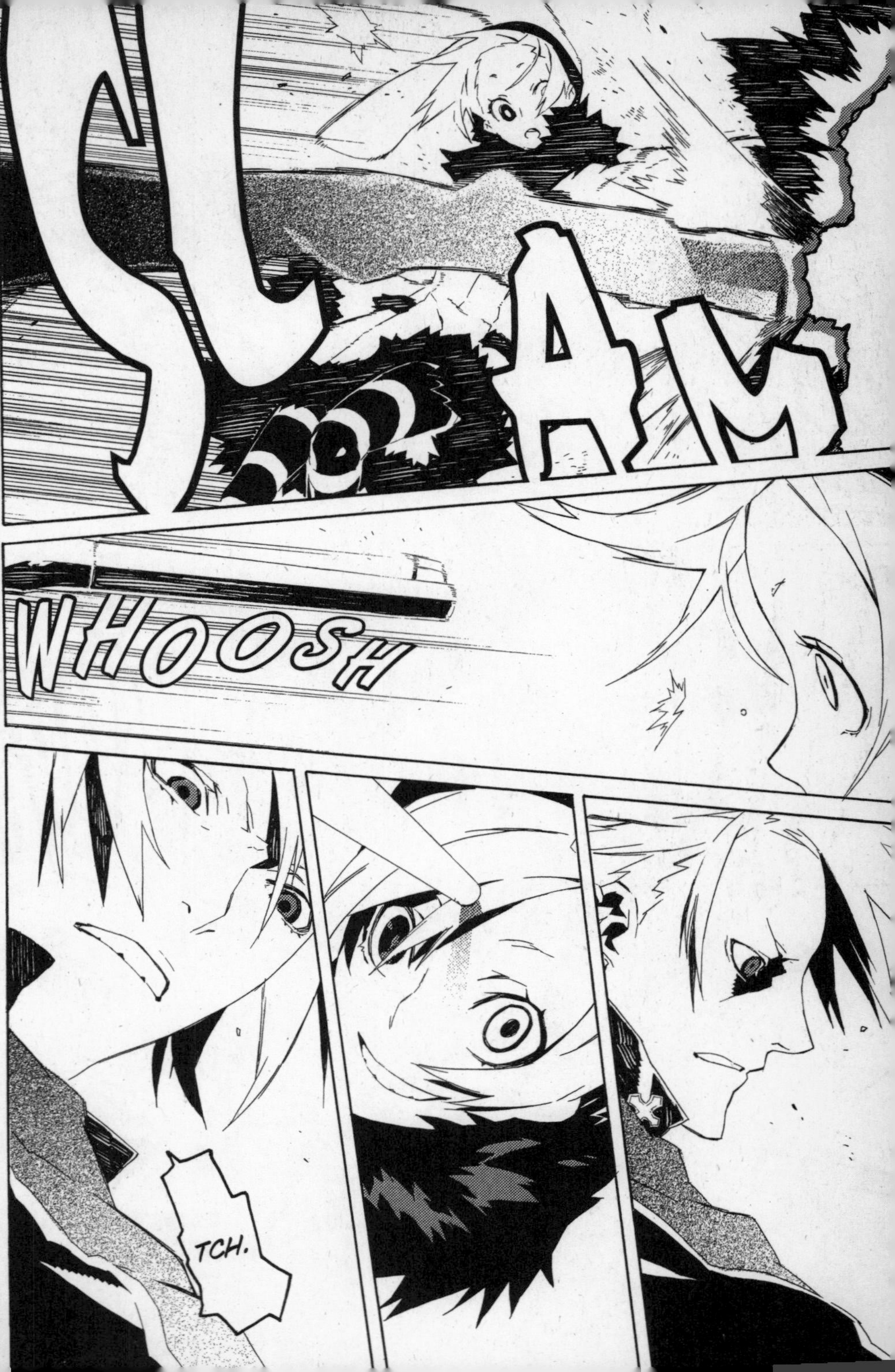
SLAM
WHOOSH
TCH.

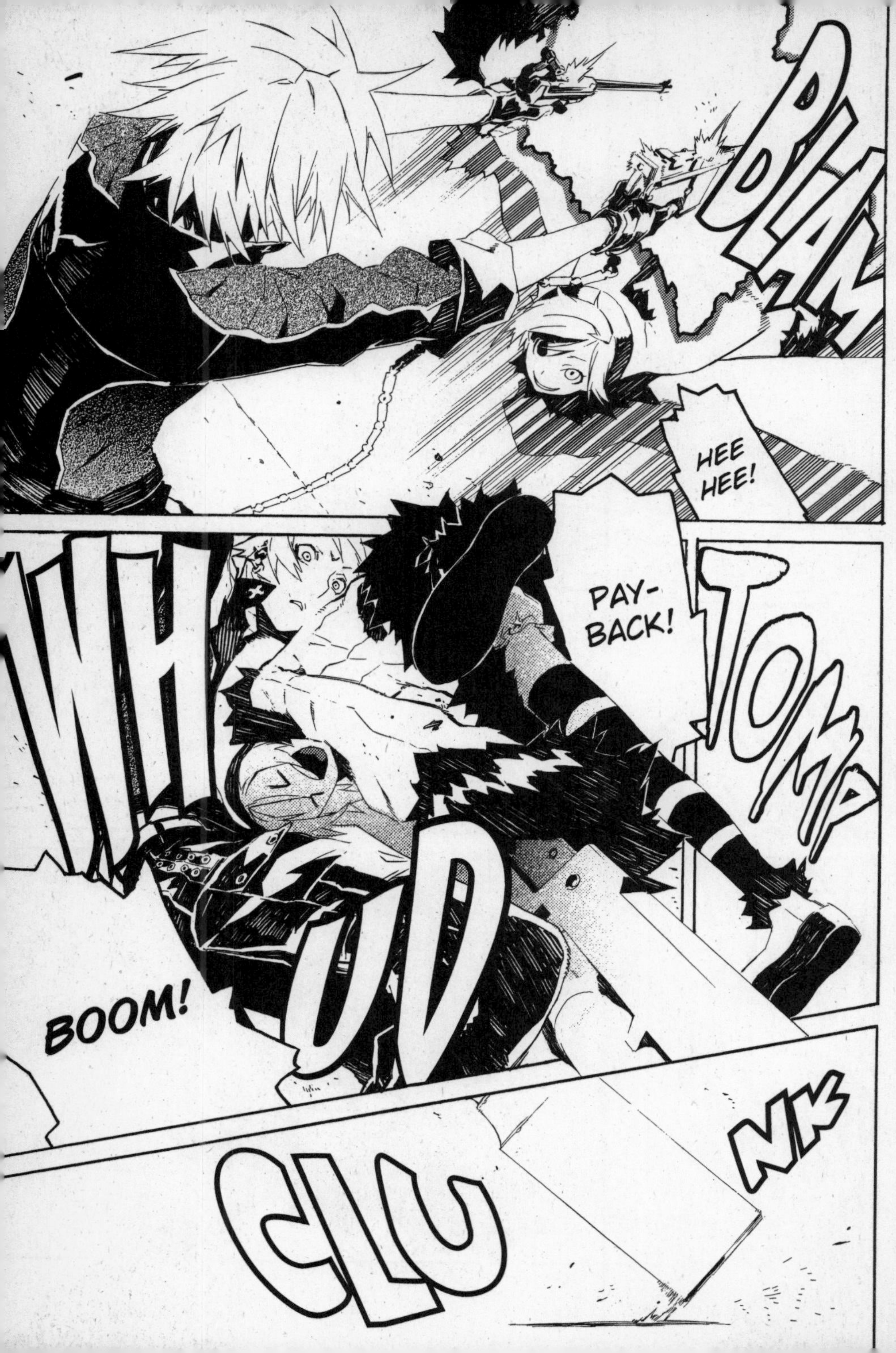
BLAM
HEE HEE!
TOMP
PAY-BACK!
BOOM!
CLUNK

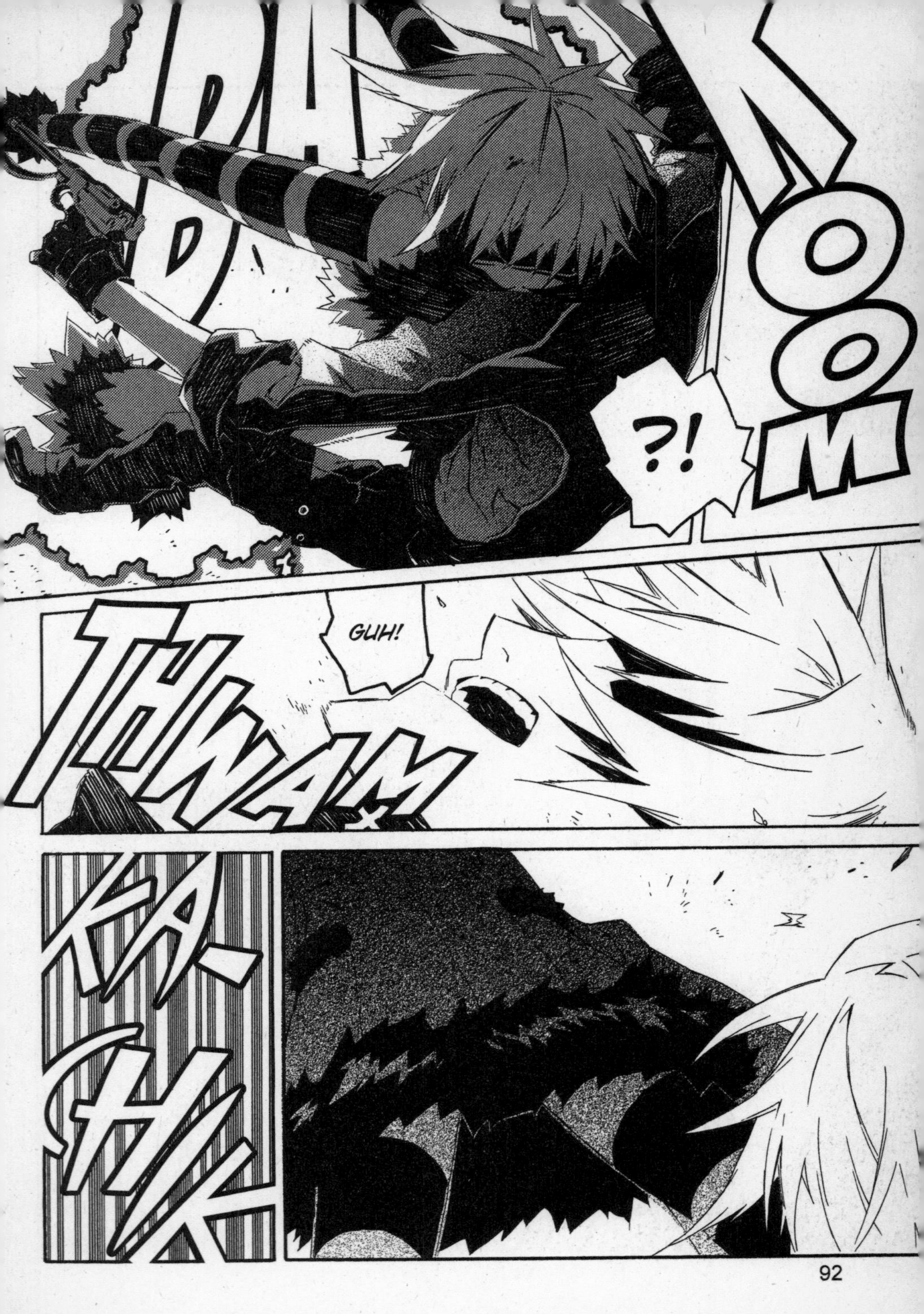
?!
GUH!
THWAM

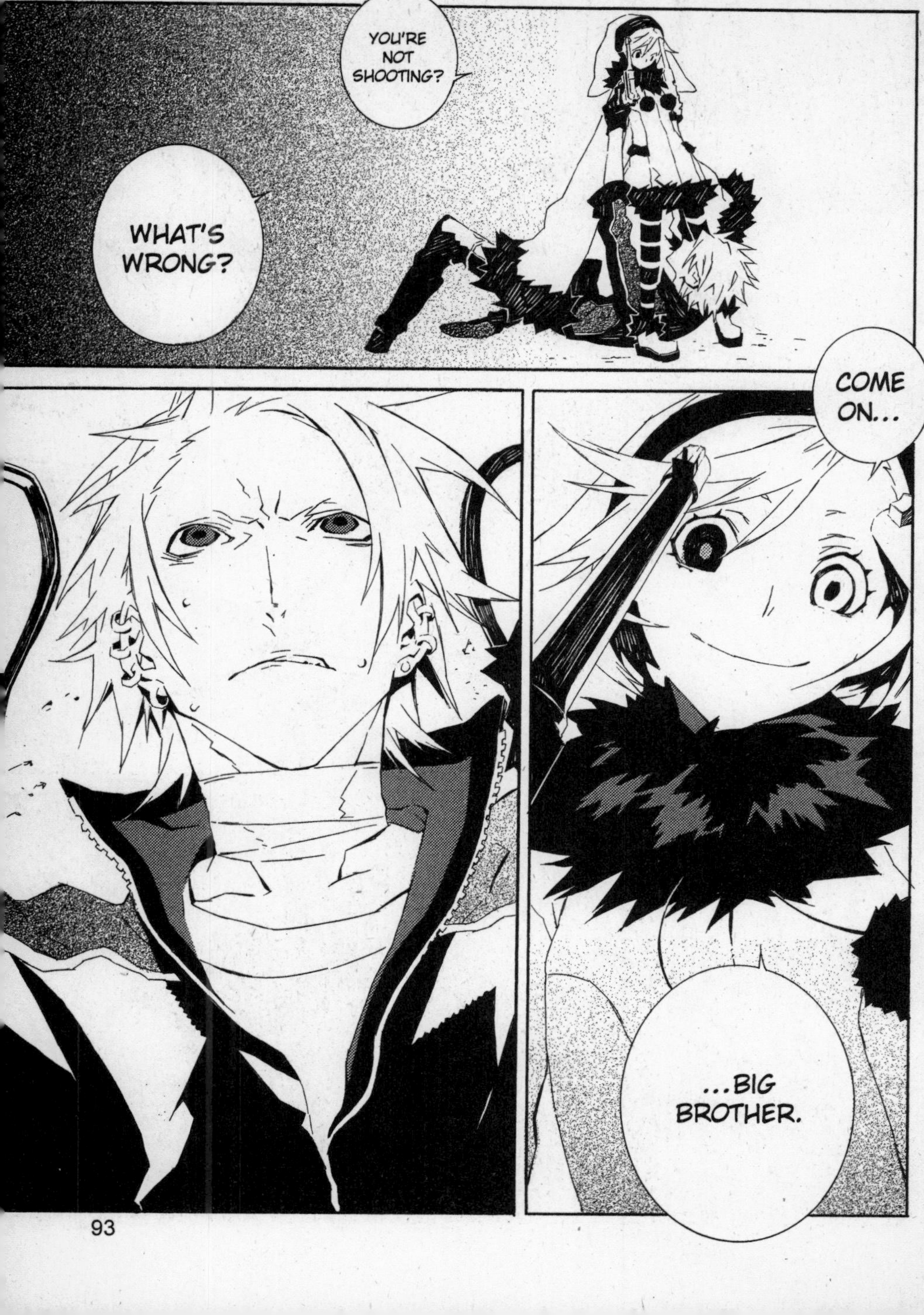
YOU'RE NOT SHOOTING?
WHAT'S WRONG?
COME ON...
...BIG BROTHER.

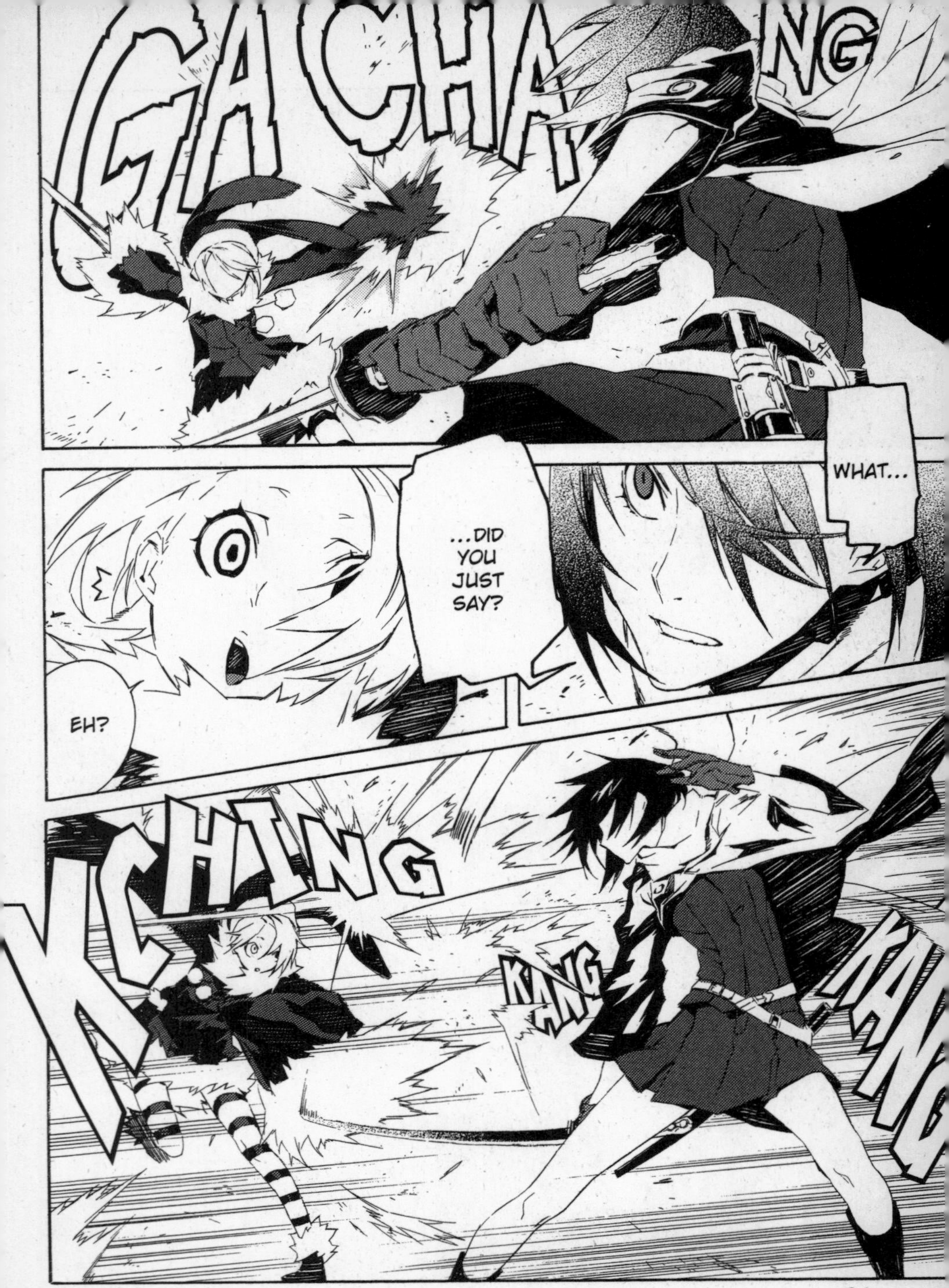
GACHANG
WHAT...
...DID YOU JUST SAY?
EH?
KANG
KANG
KCHING

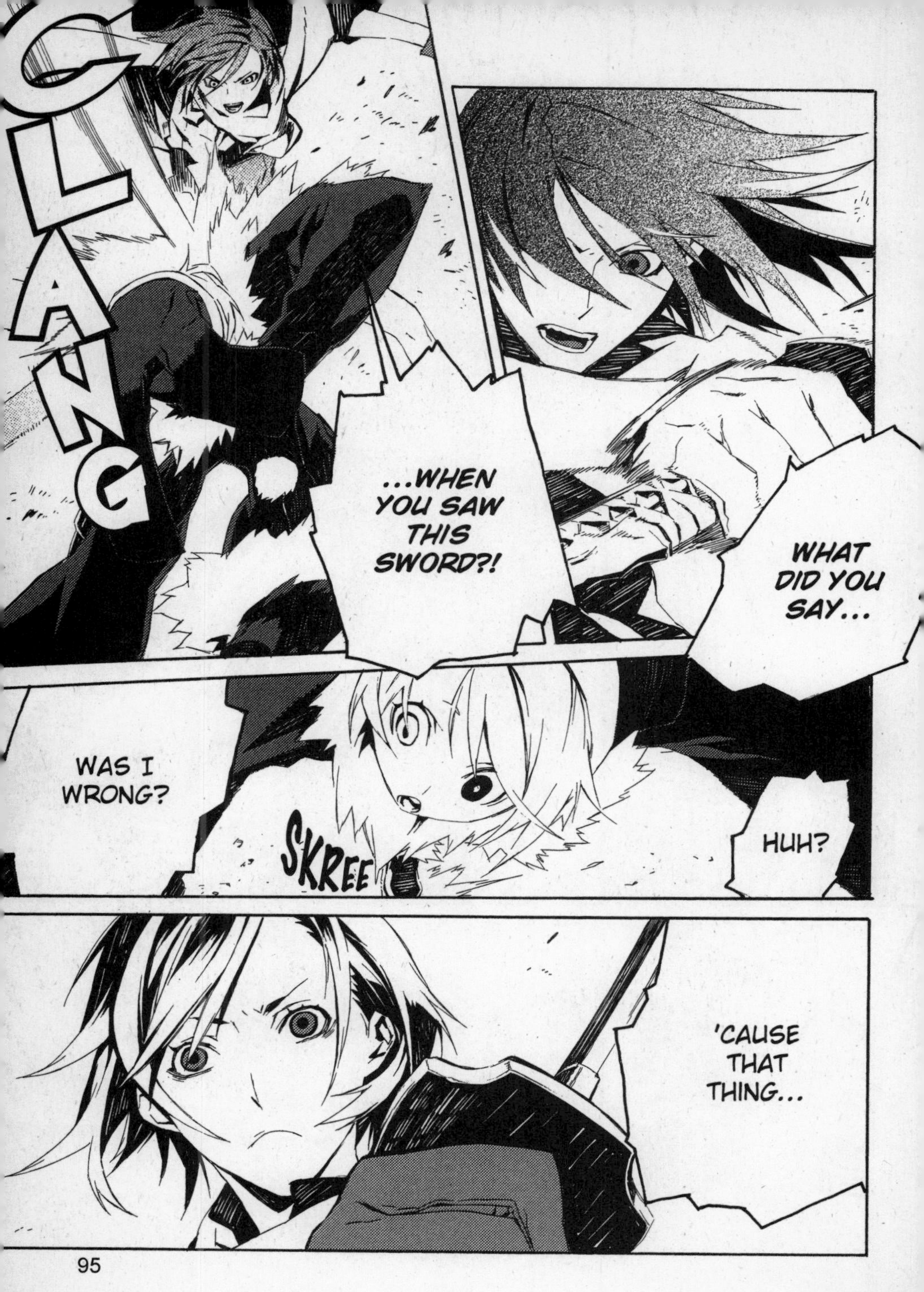
WHAT DID YOU SAY...
...WHEN YOU SAW THIS SWORD?!
CLANG
HUH?
SKREE
WAS I WRONG?
'CAUSE THAT THING...

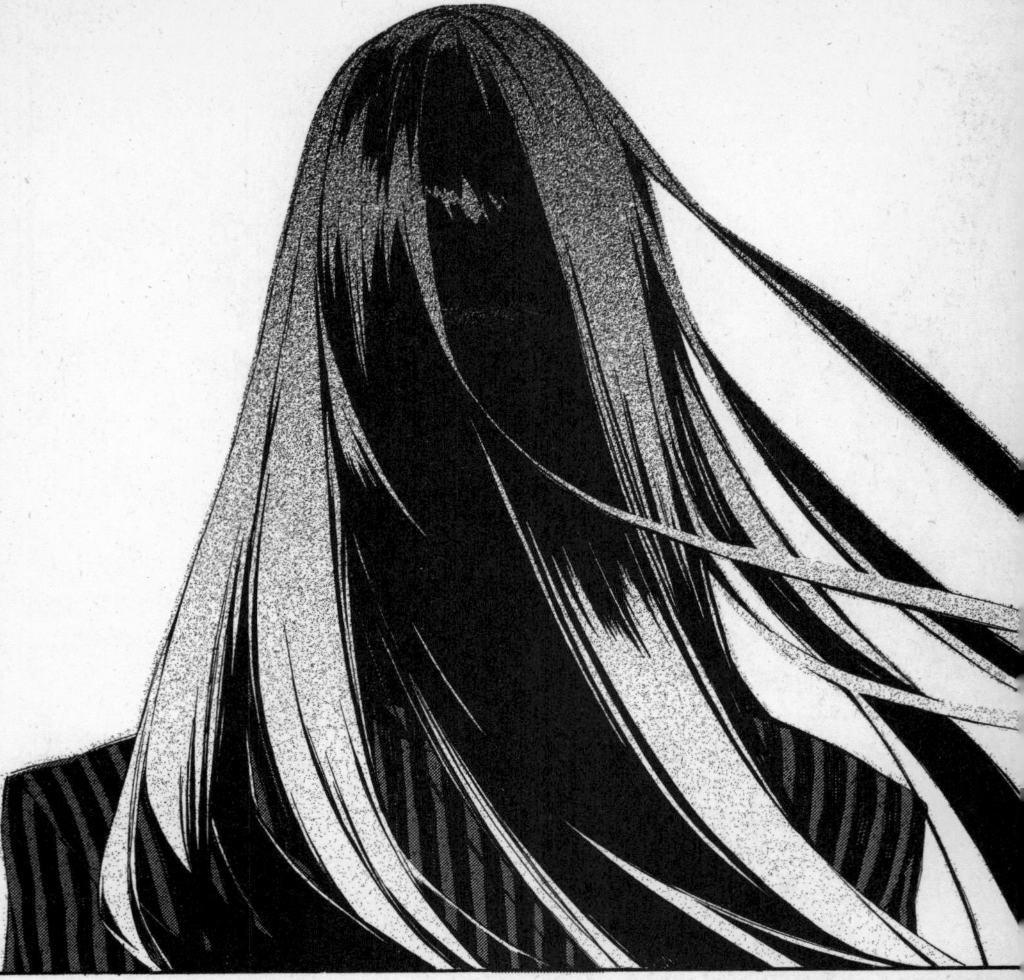
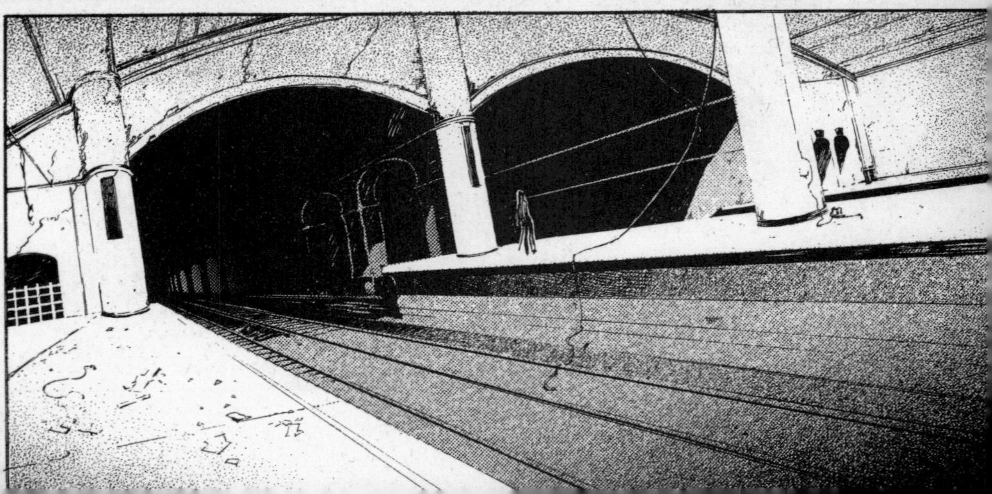

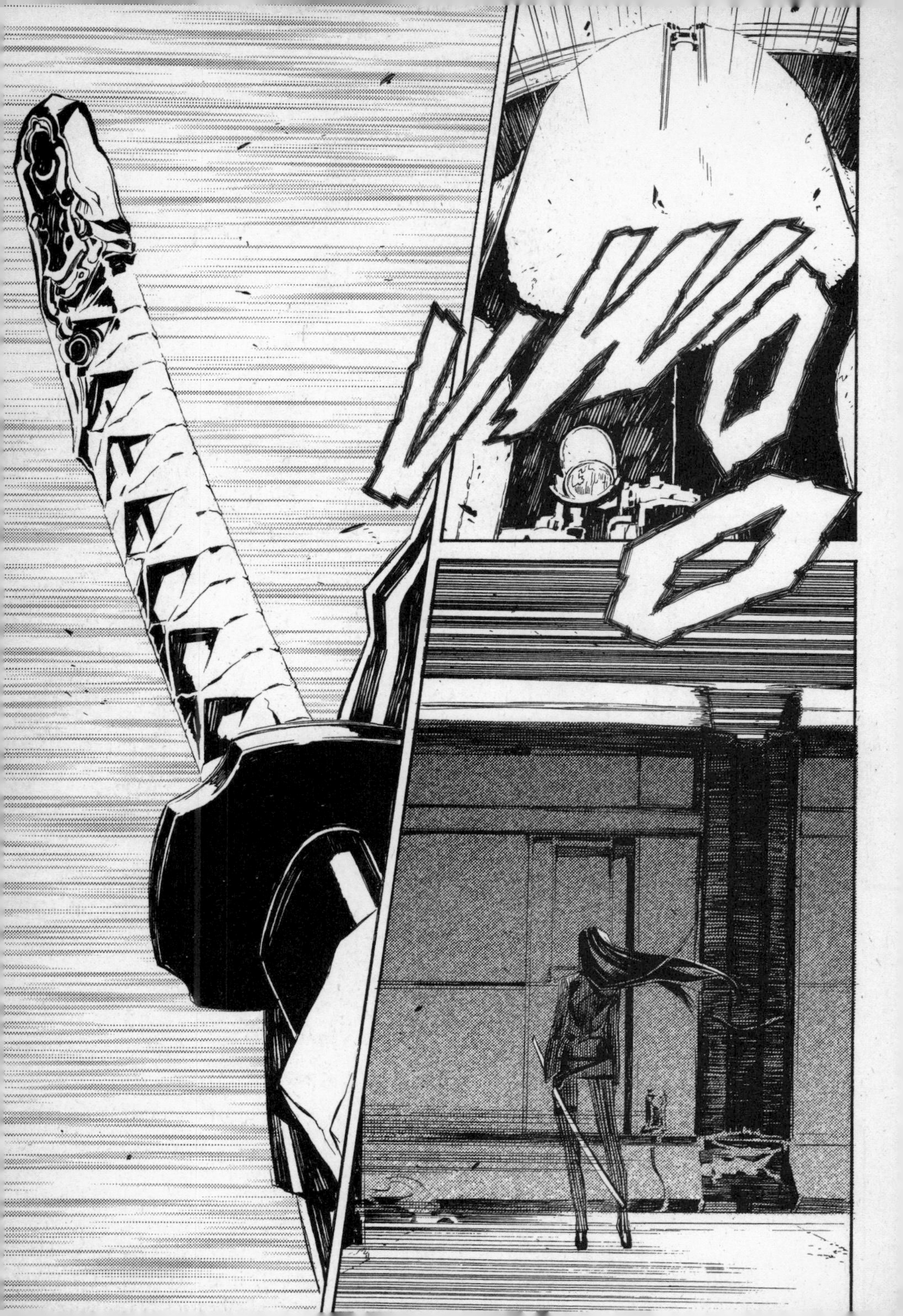
VWOO

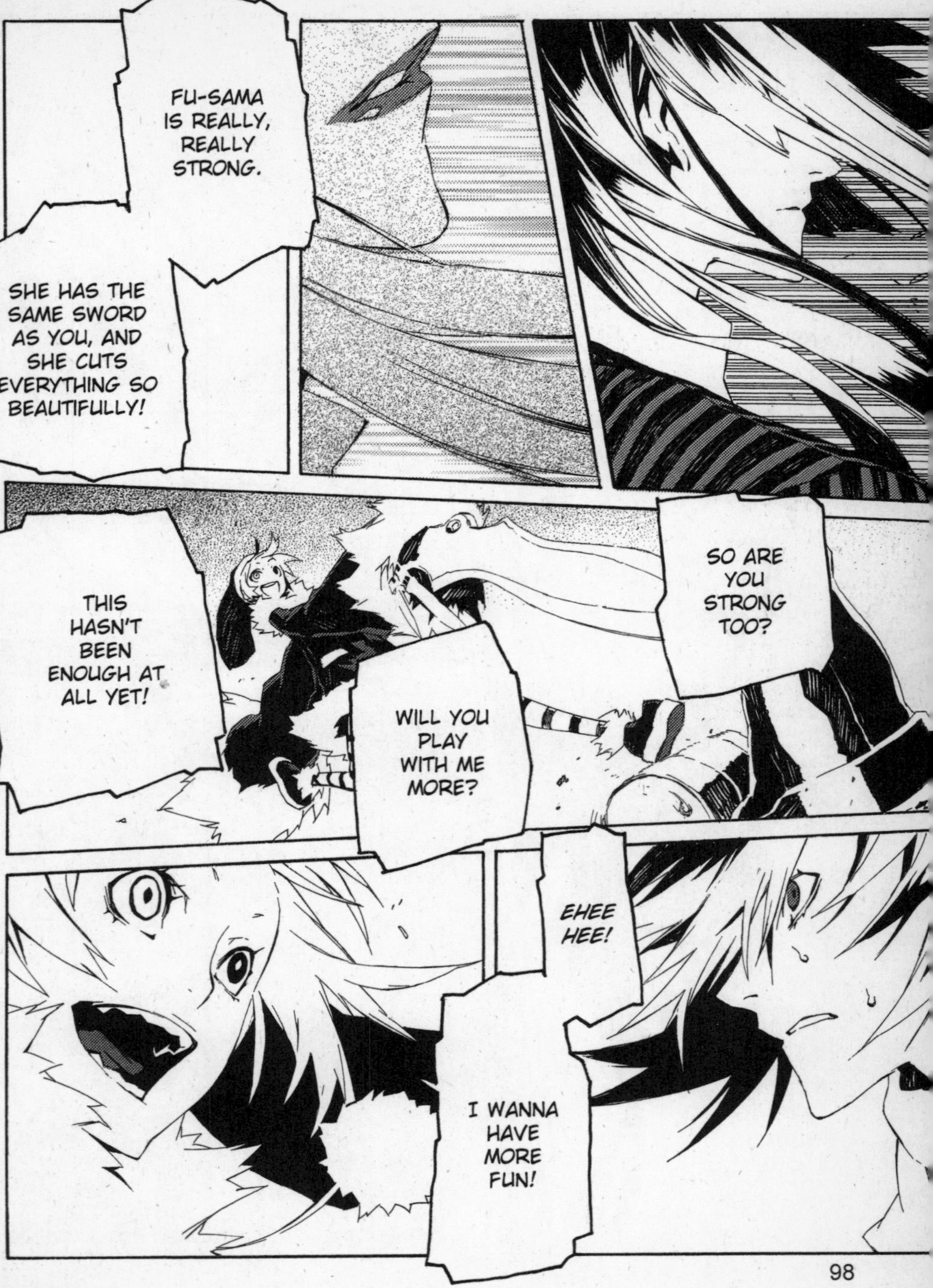
FU-SAMA IS REALLY, REALLY STRONG.
SHE HAS THE SAME SWORD AS YOU, AND SHE CUTS EVERYTHING SO BEAUTIFULLY!
SO ARE YOU STRONG TOO?
WILL YOU PLAY WITH ME MORE?
THIS HASN'T BEEN ENOUGH AT ALL YET!
EHEE HEE!
I WANNA HAVE MORE FUN!

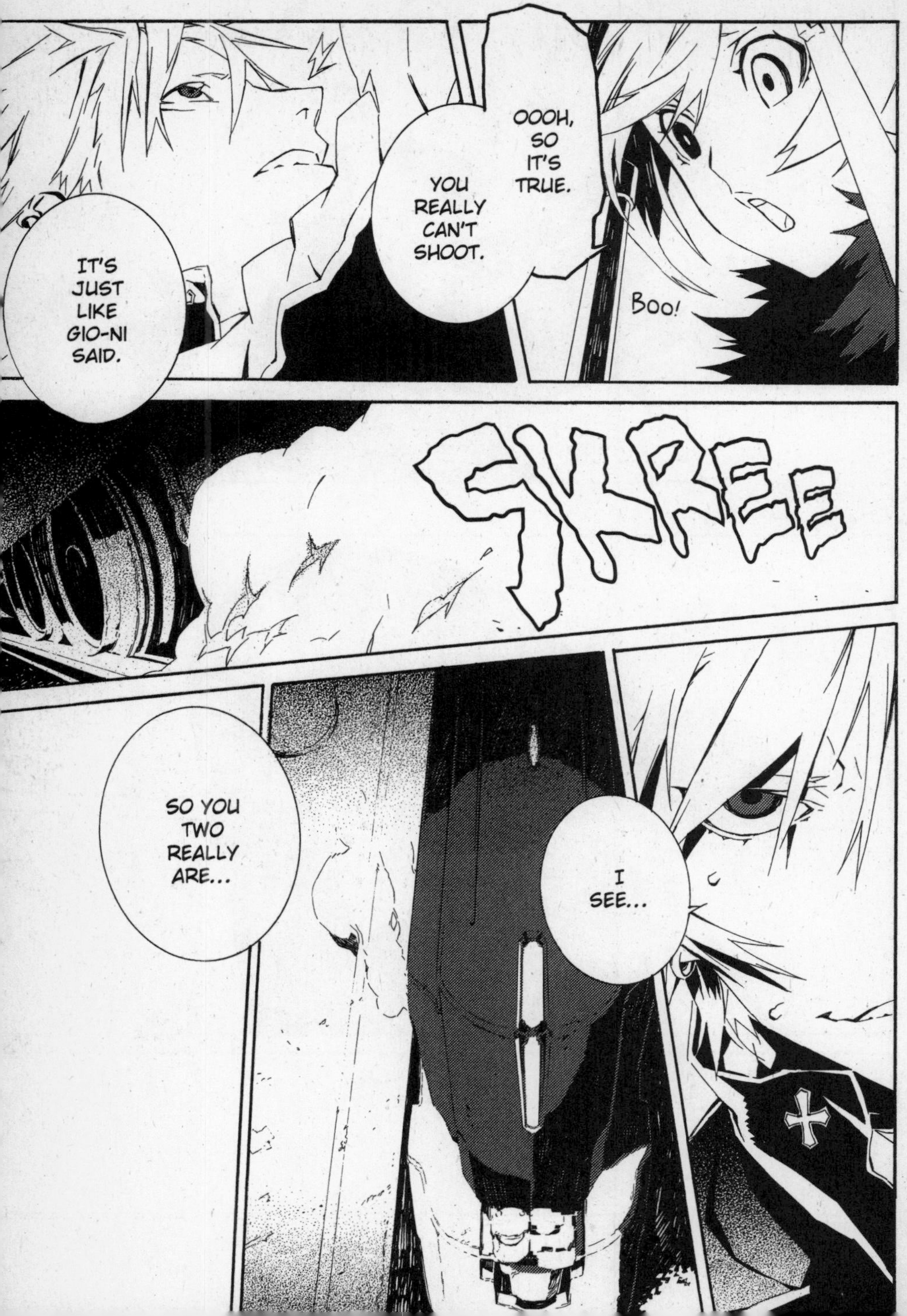
OOOH, SO IT'S TRUE.
YOU REALLY CAN'T SHOOT.
BOO!
IT'S JUST LIKE GIO-NI SAID.
SKREE
I SEE...
SO YOU TWO REALLY ARE...

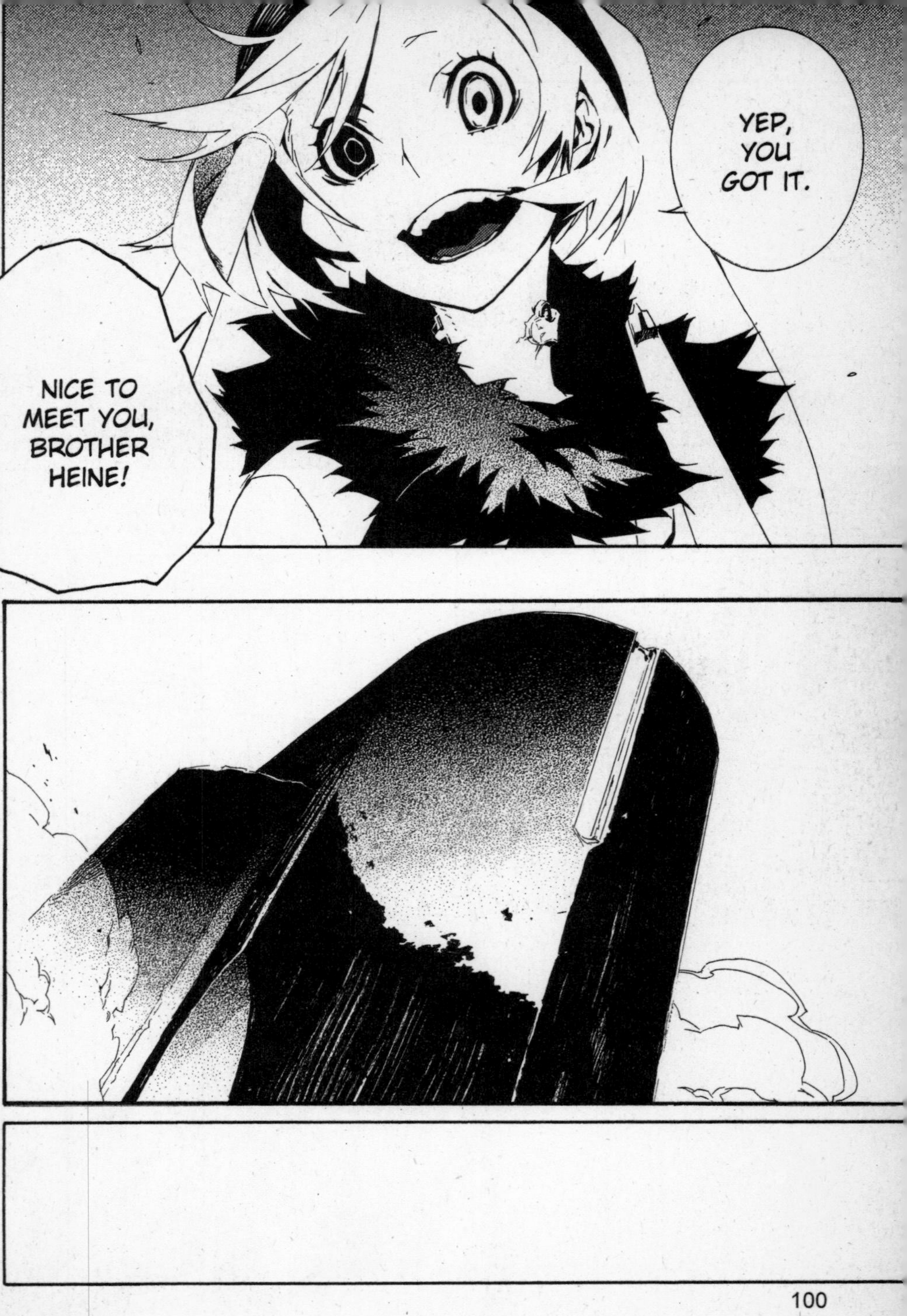
YEP, YOU GOT IT.
NICE TO MEET YOU, BROTHER HEINE!

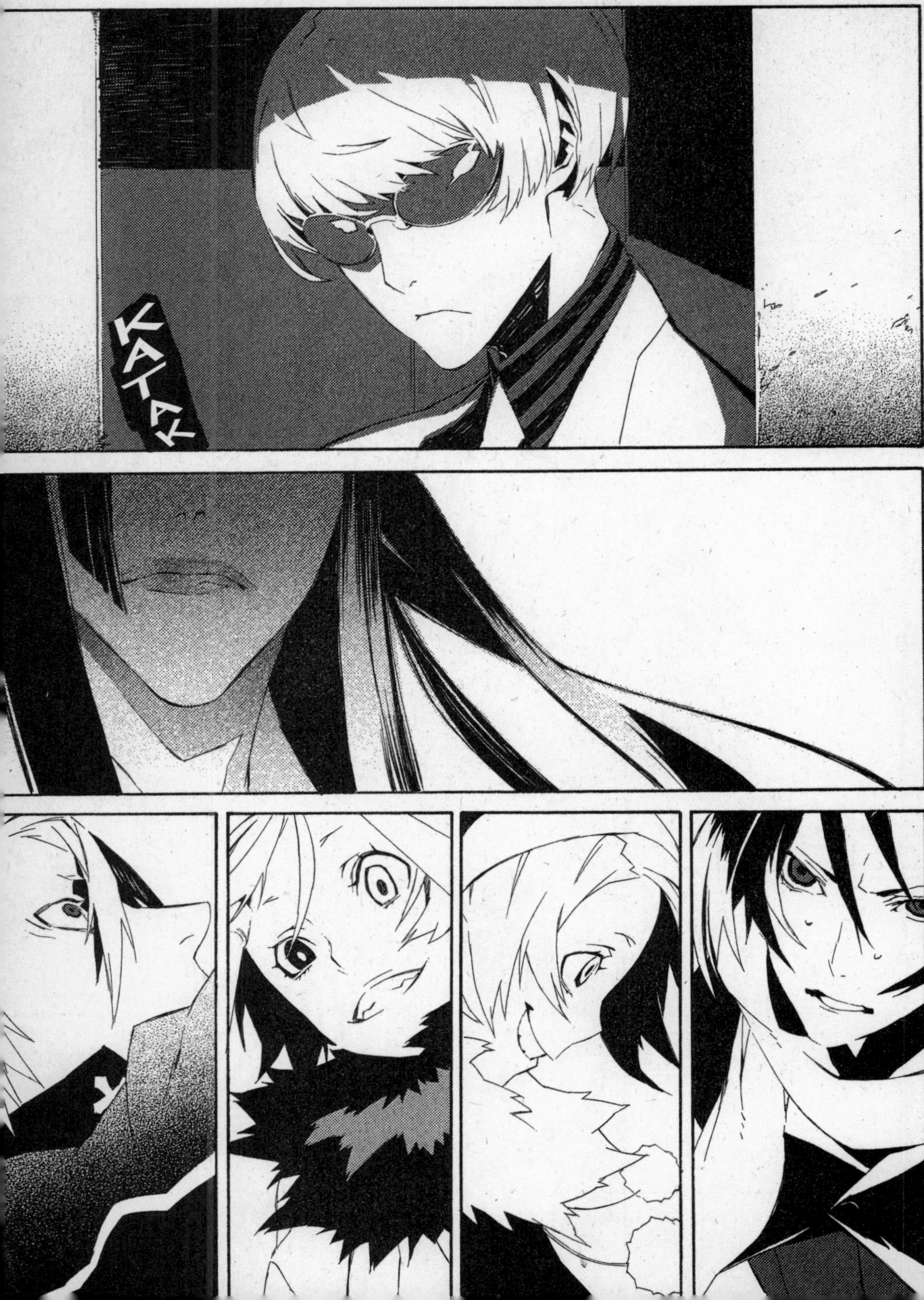
KATAK

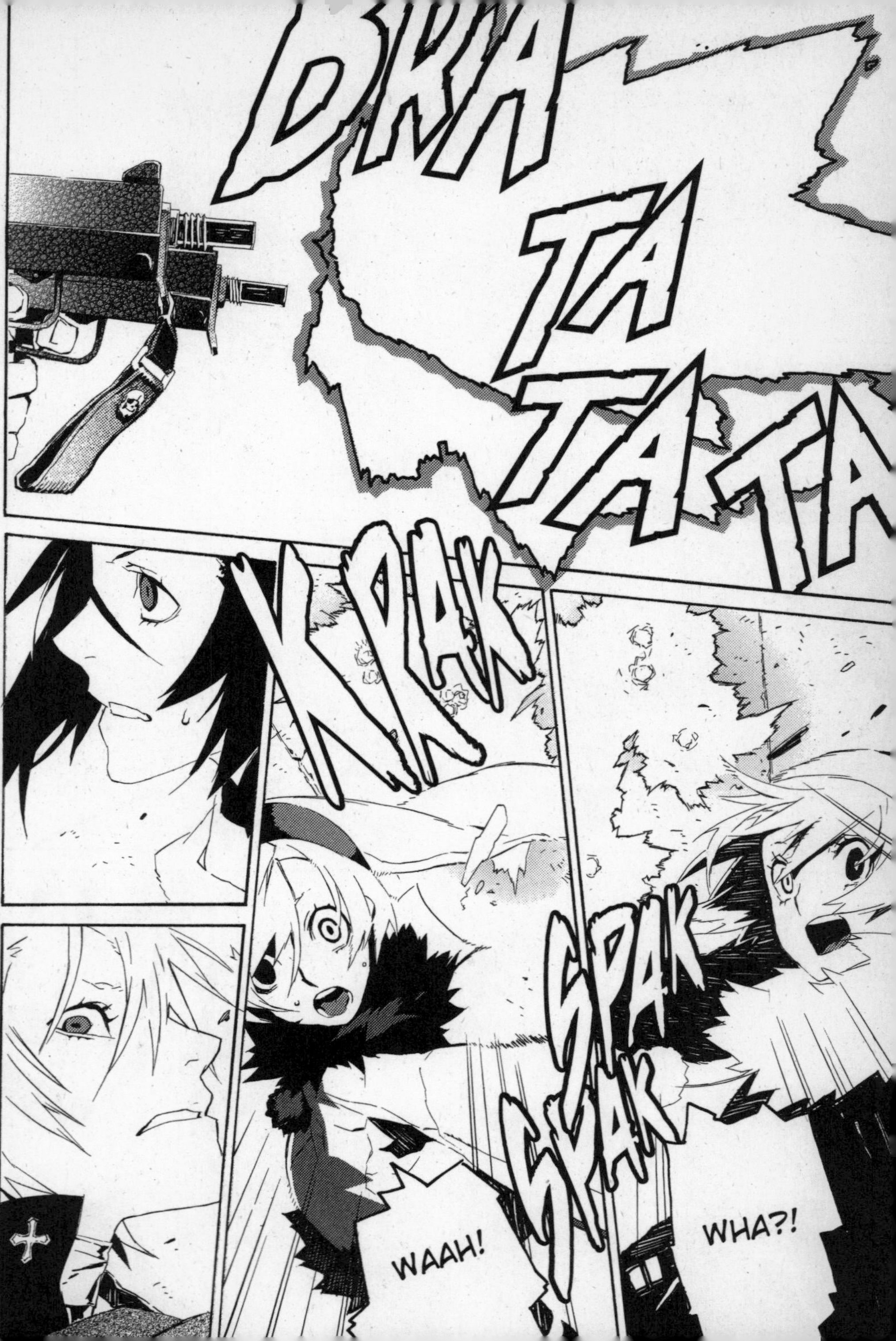
DKA TA TA TA
SPAK
SPAK
WHA?!
KPAK
WAAH!

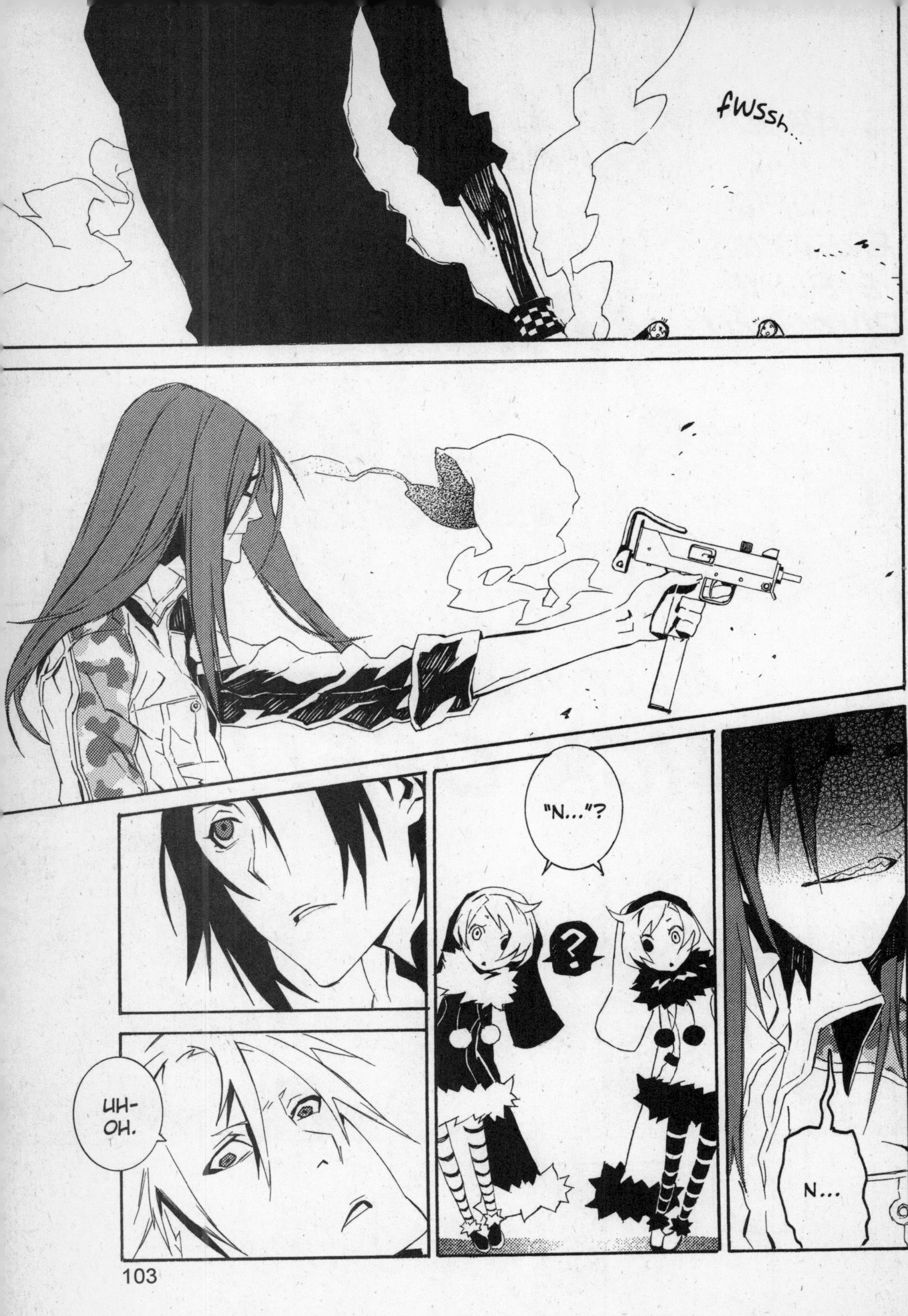
fWSsh...
N...
"N..."?
?
UH-OH.

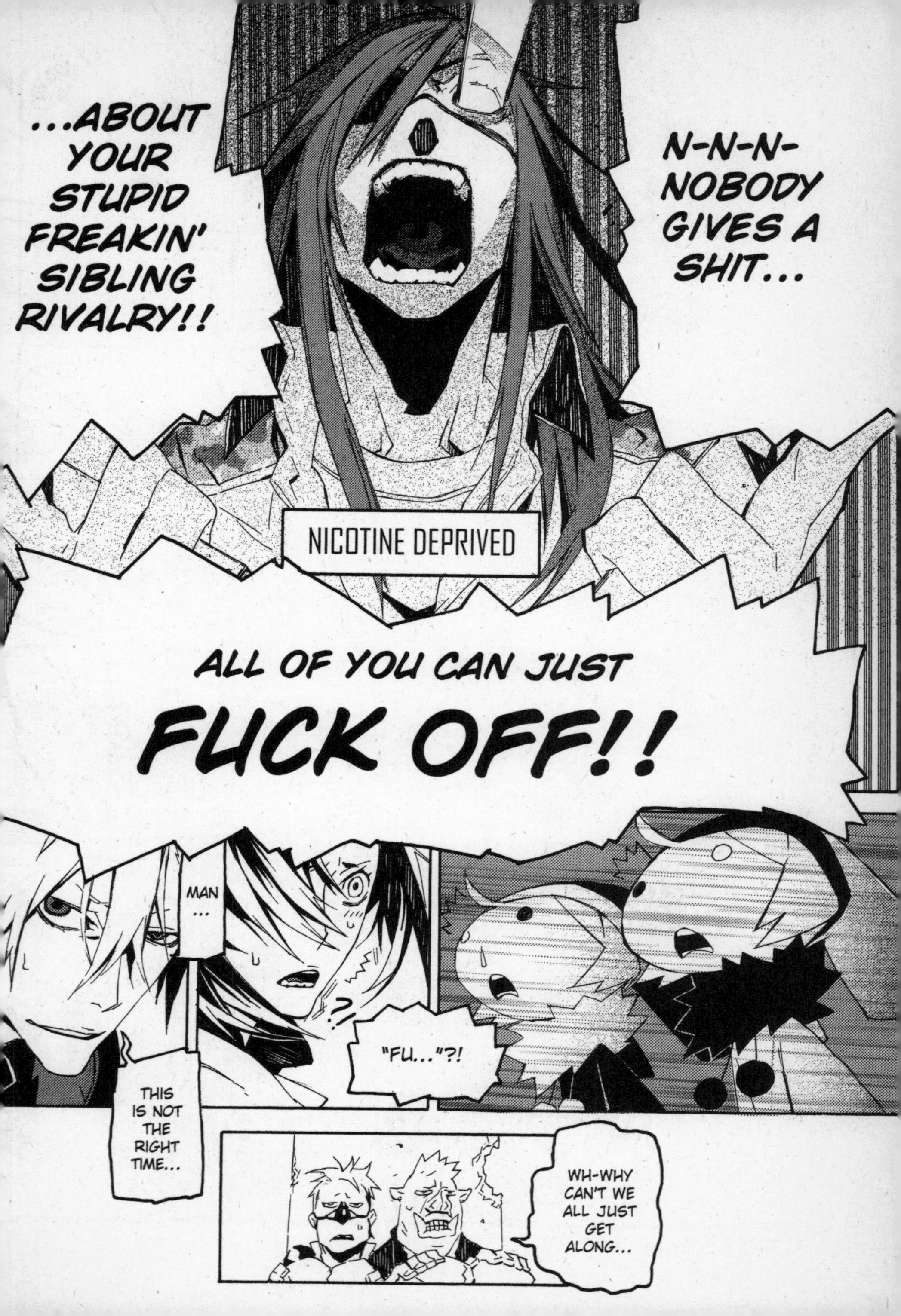
N-N-N-NOBODY GIVES A SHIT...
...ABOUT YOUR STUPID FREAKIN' SIBLING RIVALRY!!
NICOTINE DEPRIVED
ALL OF YOU CAN JUST FUCK OFF!!
MAN ...
?!
"FU..."?!
THIS IS NOT THE RIGHT TIME...
WH-WHY CAN'T WE ALL JUST GET ALONG...

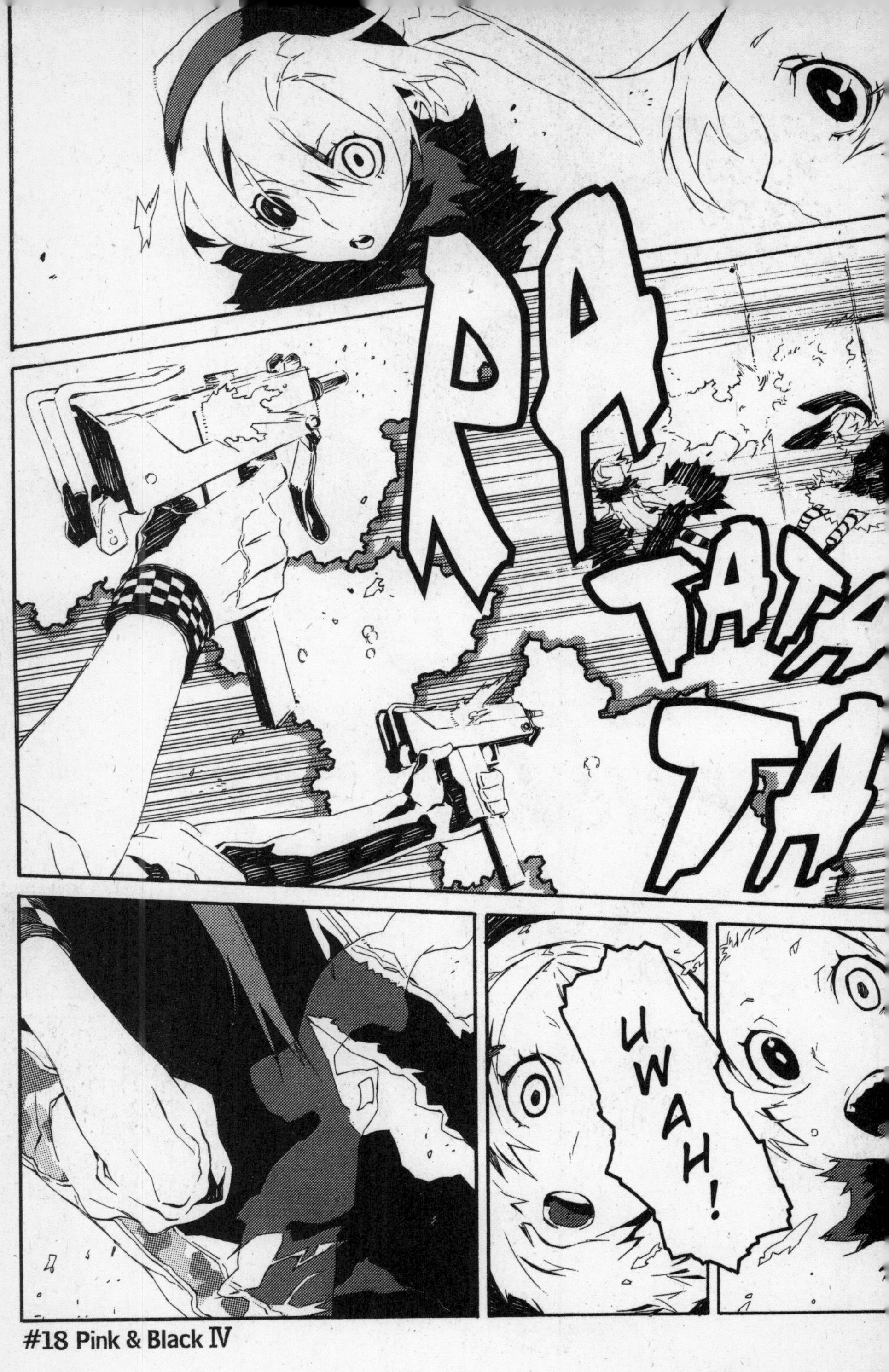
RA
TATA
TA
UWAH!

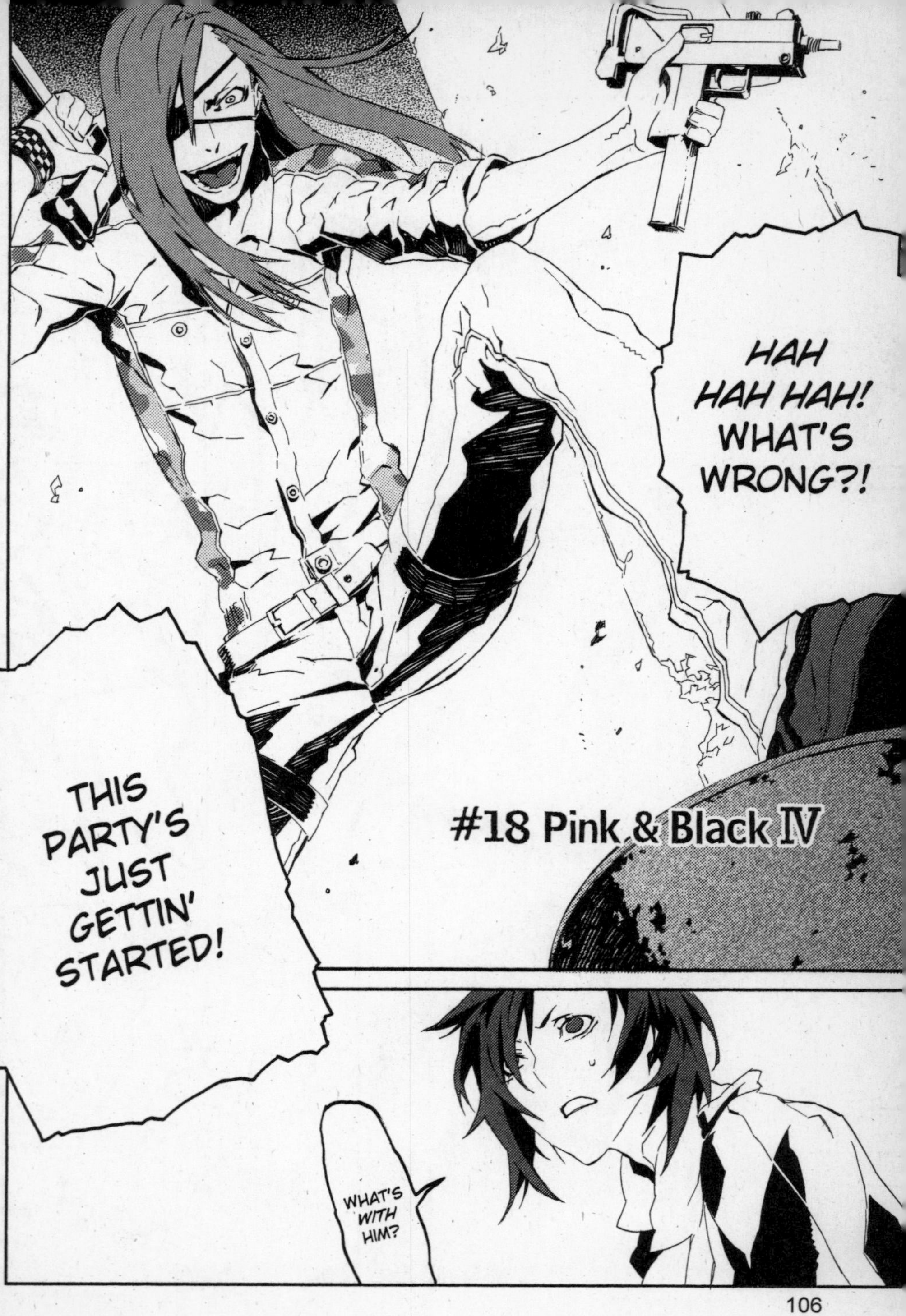
HAH HAH HAH! WHAT'S WRONG?!
THIS PARTY'S JUST GETTIN' STARTED!
#18 Pink & Black IV
WHAT'S WITH HIM?

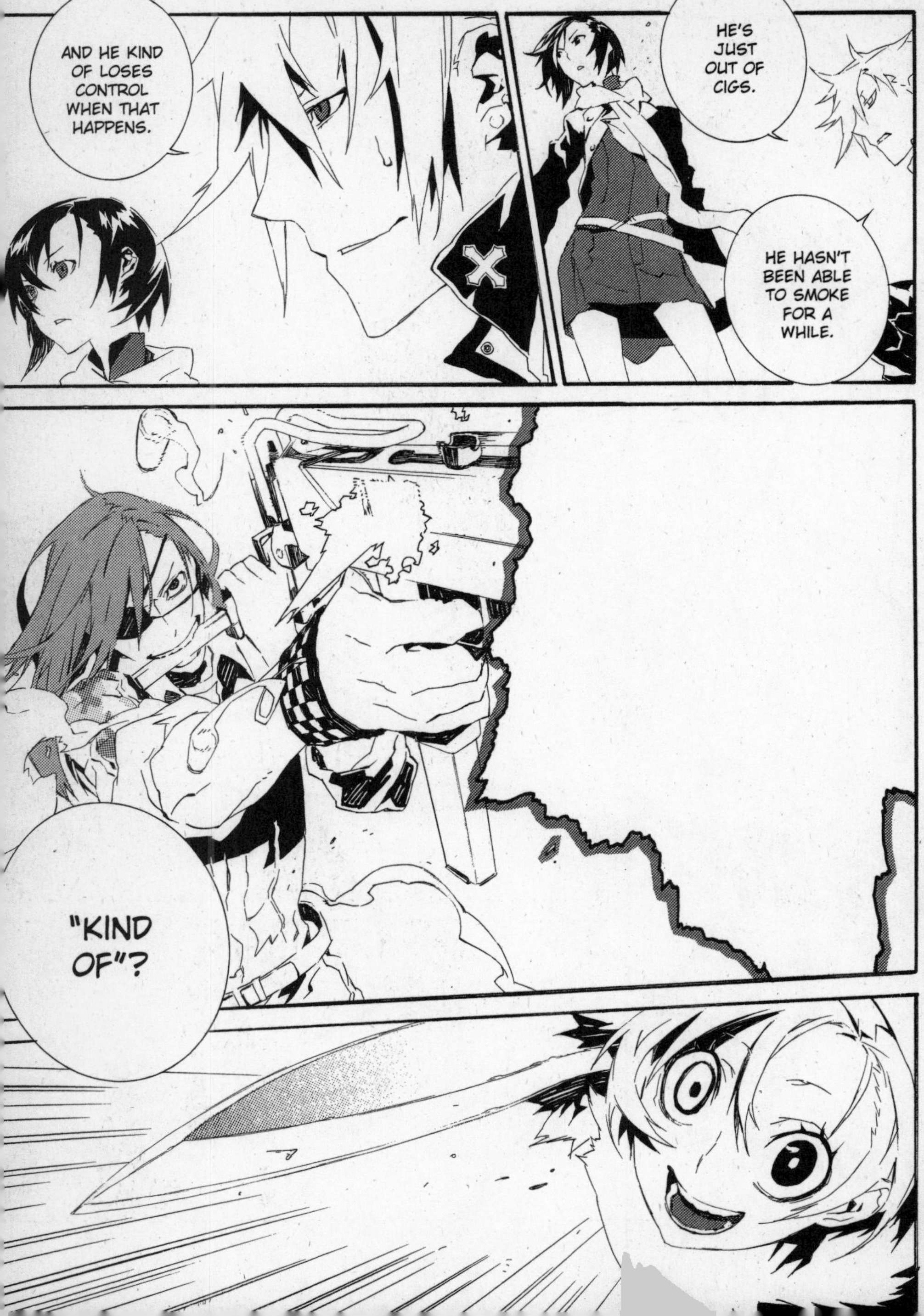
HE'S JUST OUT OF CIGS.
HE HASN'T BEEN ABLE TO SMOKE FOR A WHILE.
AND HE KIND OF LOSES CONTROL WHEN THAT HAPPENS.
"KIND OF"?

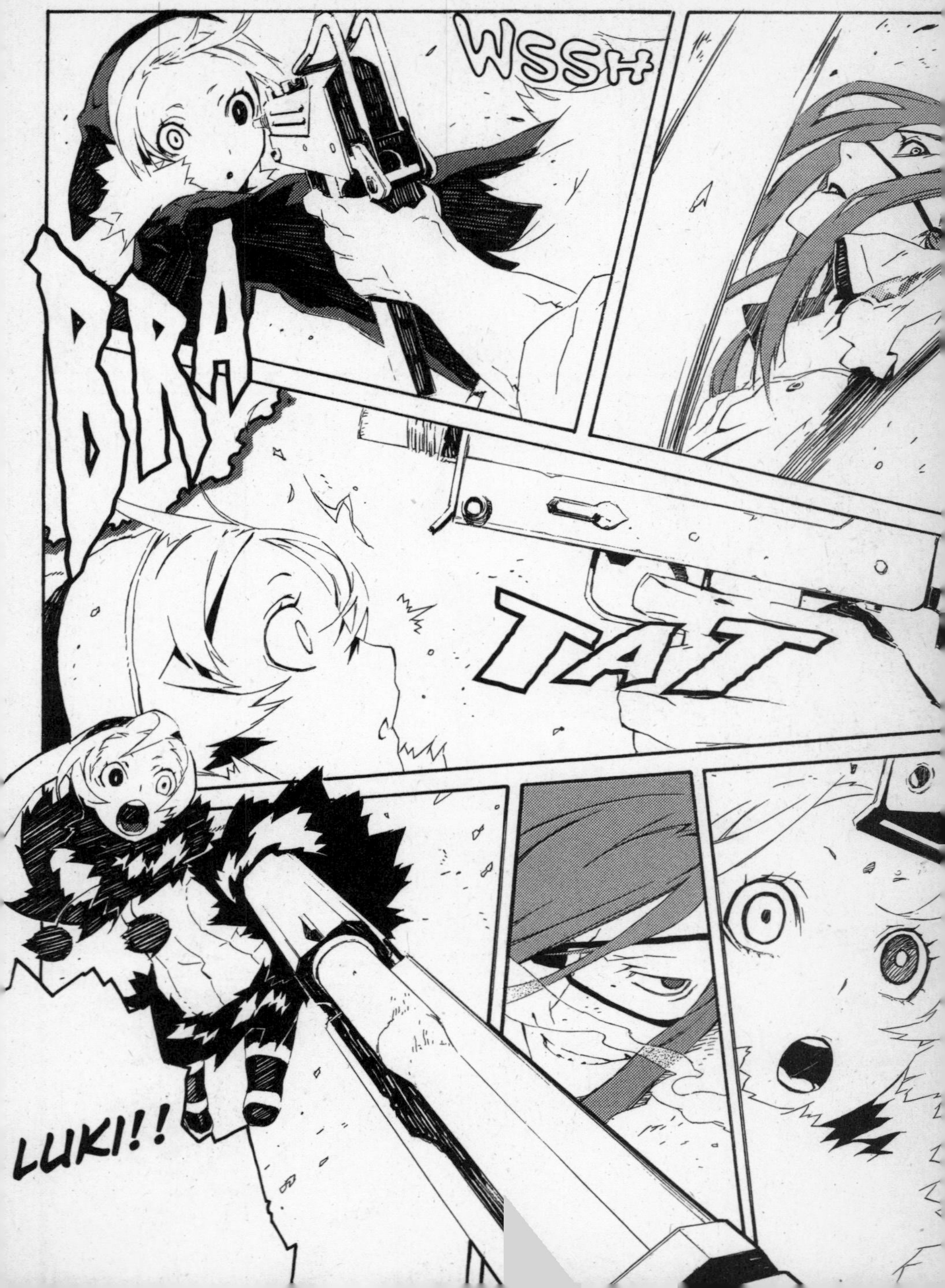
WSSH
BRA
TAT
LUKI!!

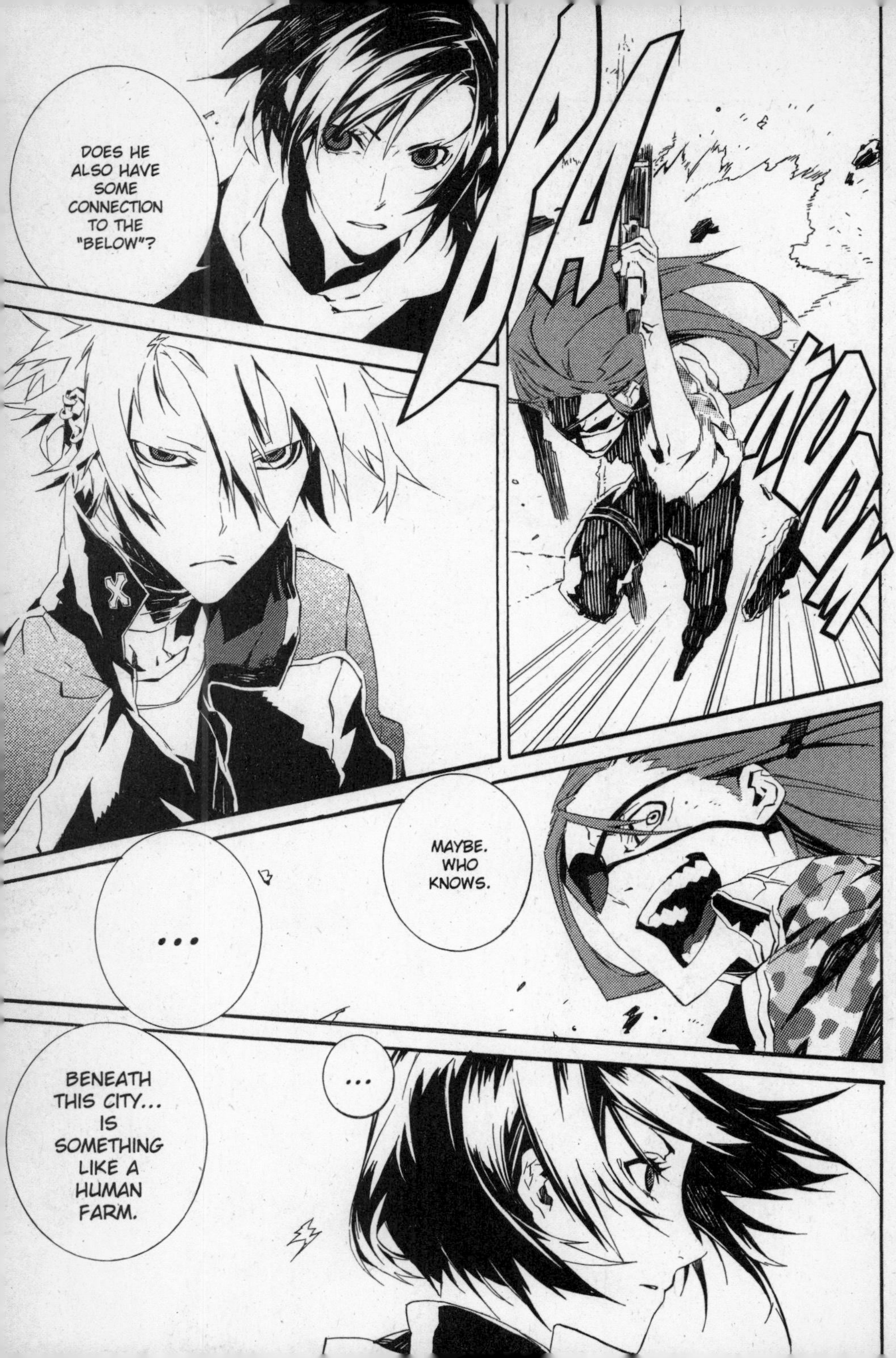
DOES HE ALSO HAVE SOME CONNECTION TO THE "BELOW"?
MAYBE. WHO KNOWS.
...
...
BENEATH THIS CITY... IS SOMETHING LIKE A HUMAN FARM.

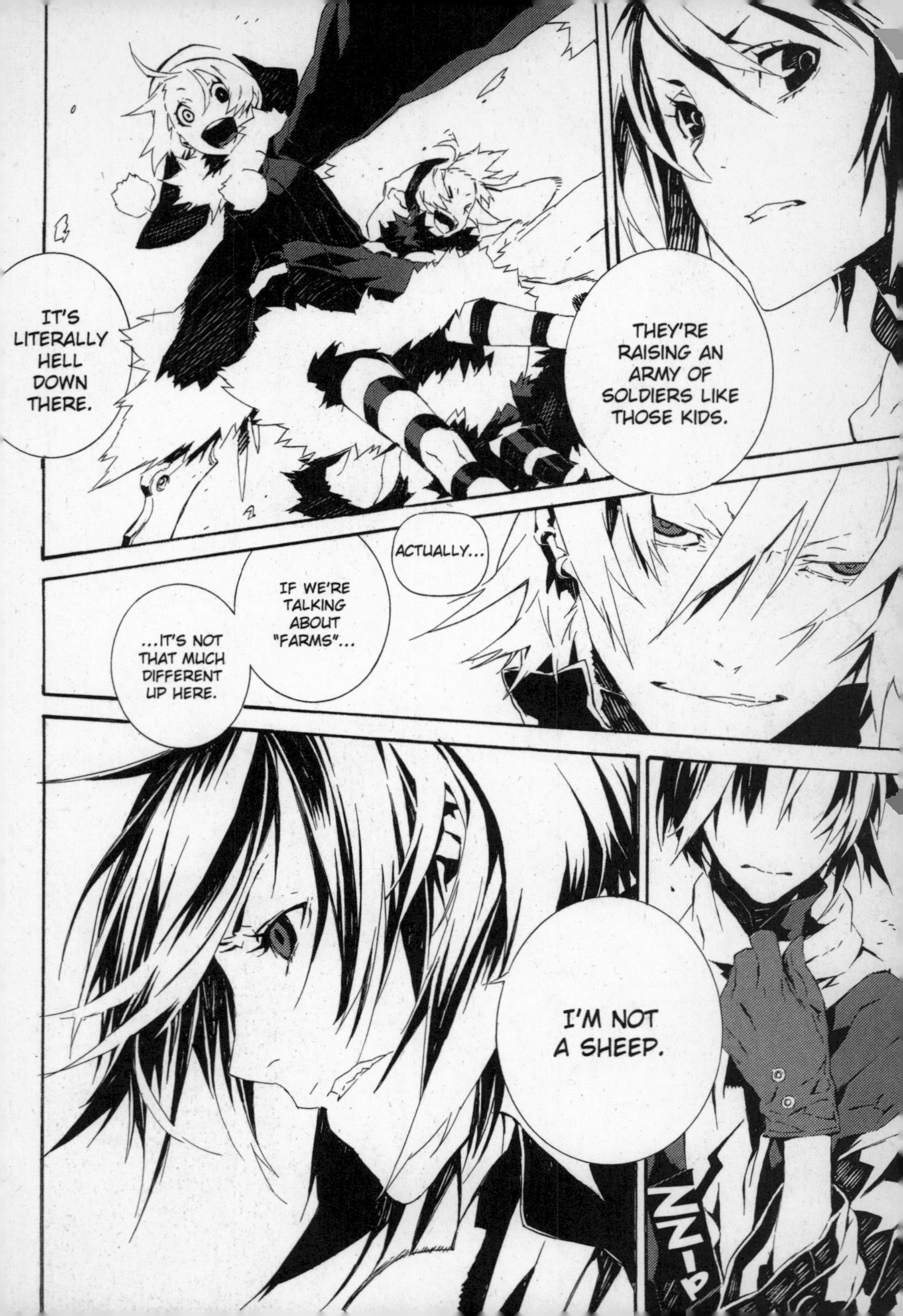
THEY'RE RAISING AN ARMY OF SOLDIERS LIKE THOSE KIDS.
IT'S LITERALLY HELL DOWN THERE.
ACTUALLY...
IF WE'RE TALKING ABOUT "FARMS"...
...IT'S NOT THAT MUCH DIFFERENT UP HERE.
I'M NOT A SHEEP.
ZZIP

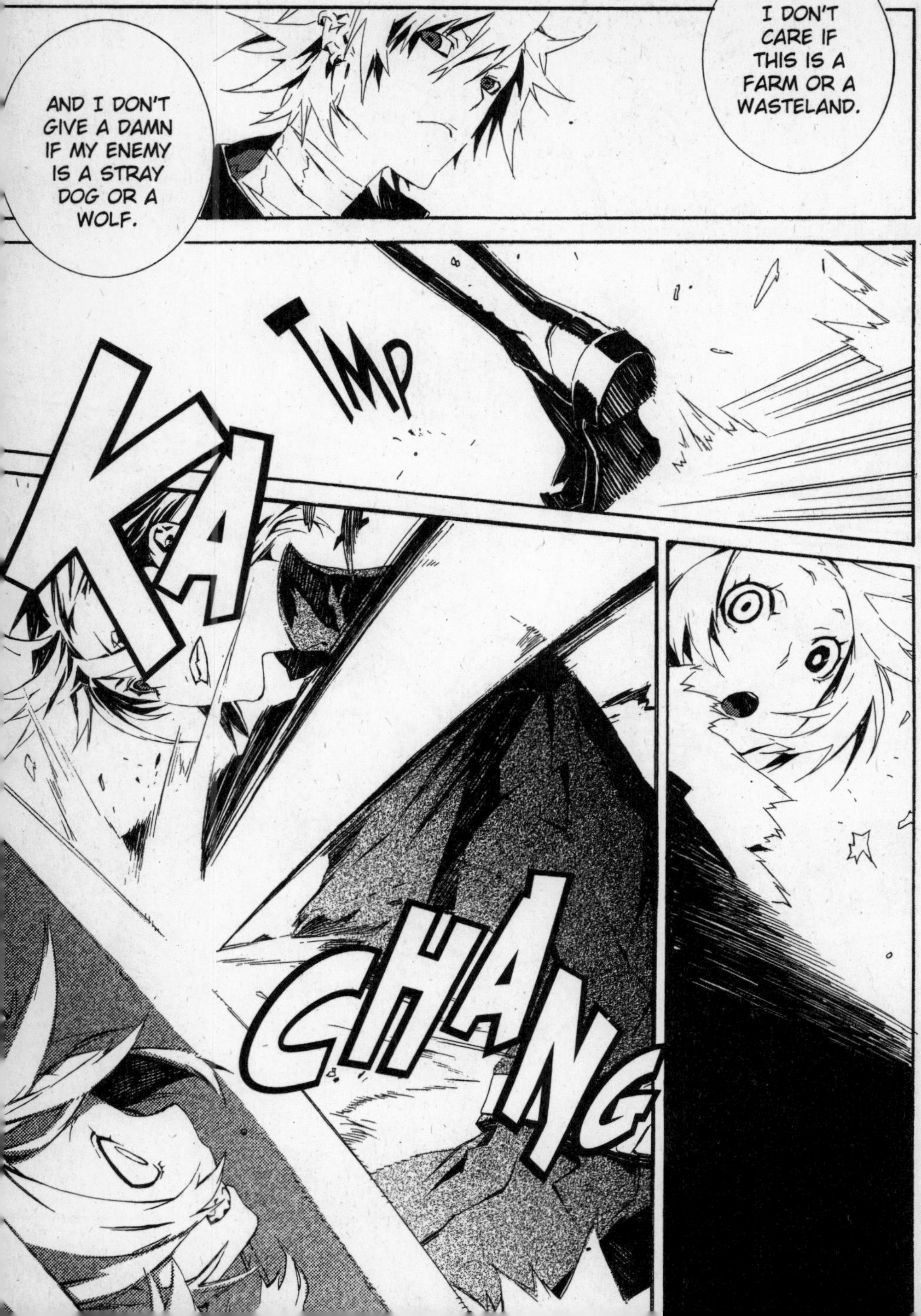
I DON'T CARE IF THIS IS A FARM OR A WASTELAND.
AND I DON'T GIVE A DAMN IF MY ENEMY IS A STRAY DOG OR A WOLF.
TMP
KA
CHANG

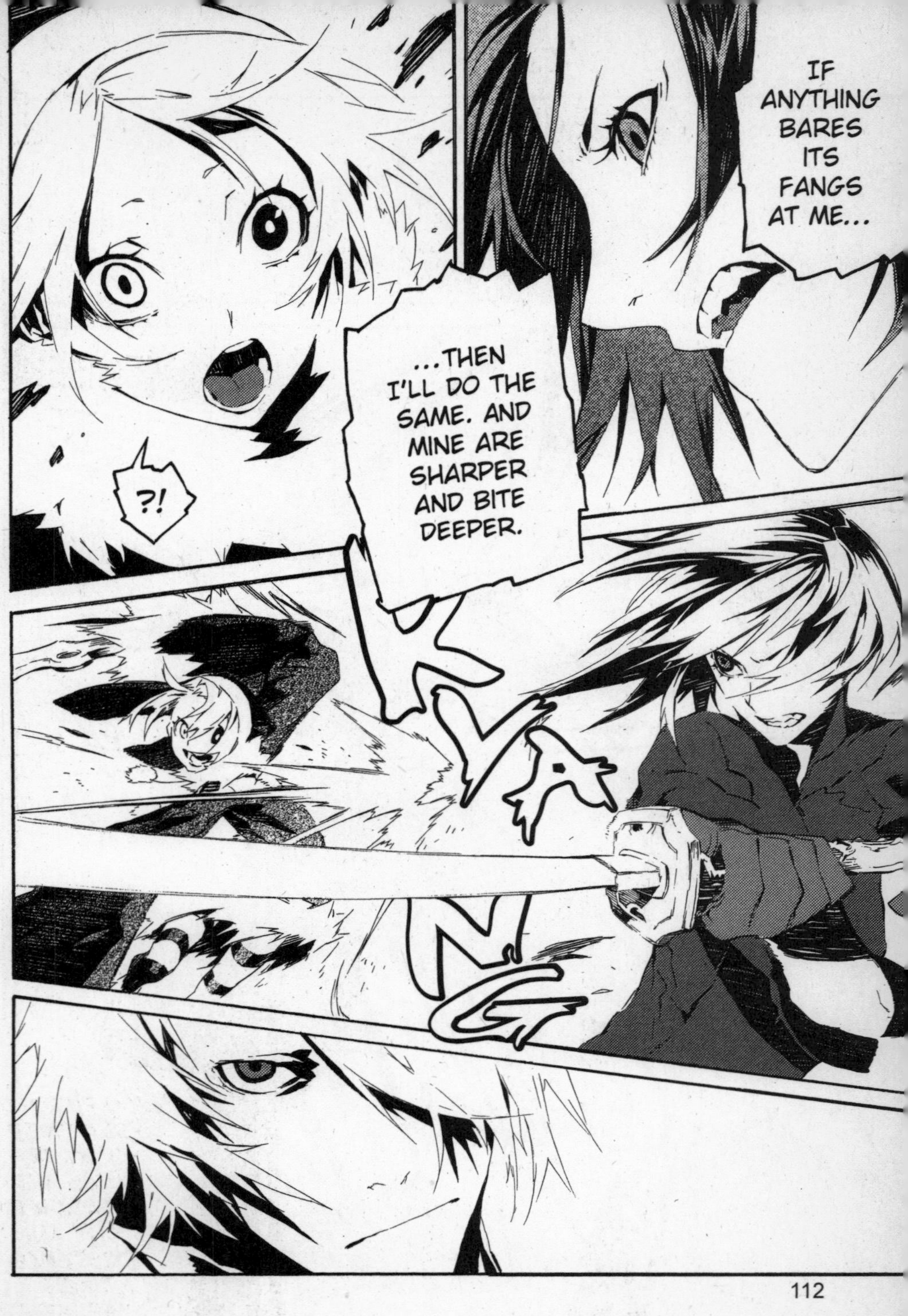
IF ANYTHING BARES ITS FANGS AT ME...
...THEN I'LL DO THE SAME. AND MINE ARE SHARPER AND BITE DEEPER.
?!
KANG

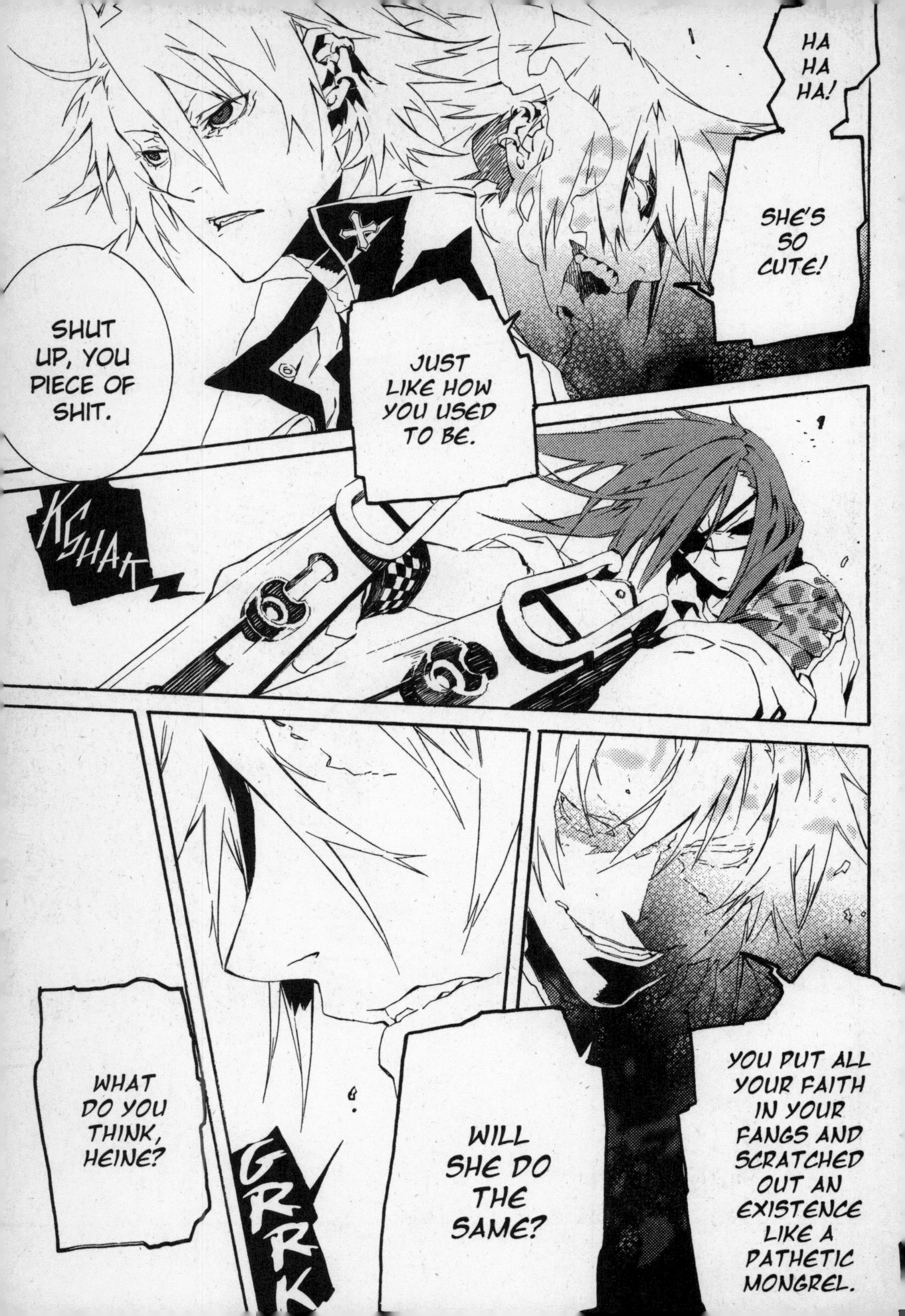
HA HA HA!
SHE'S SO CUTE!
JUST LIKE HOW YOU USED TO BE.
SHUT UP, YOU PIECE OF SHIT.
KSHAK
YOU PUT ALL YOUR FAITH IN YOUR FANGS AND SCRATCHED OUT AN EXISTENCE LIKE A PATHETIC MONGREL.
WILL SHE DO THE SAME?
GRRK
WHAT DO YOU THINK, HEINE?

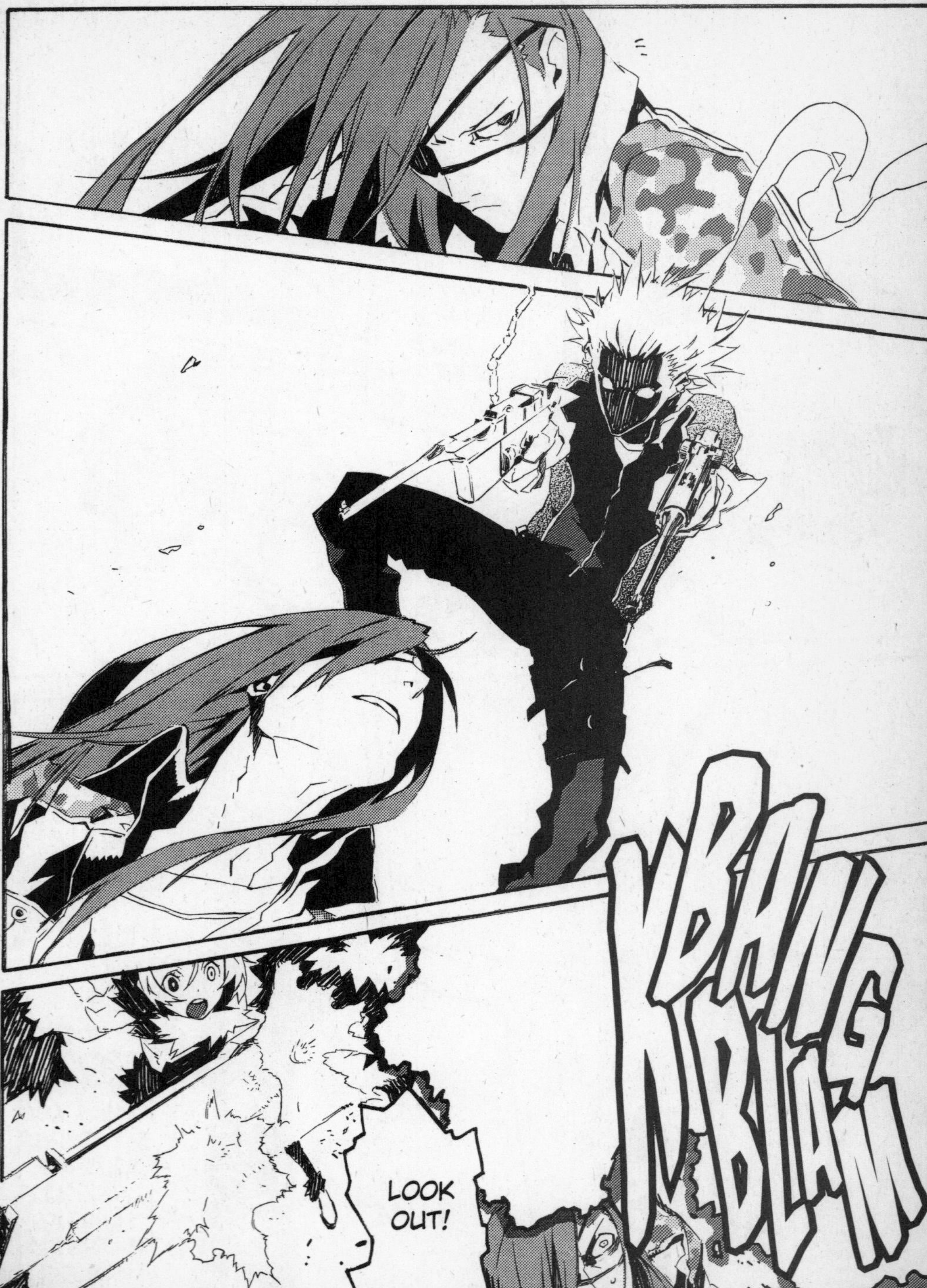
BANG
BLAM
LOOK OUT!

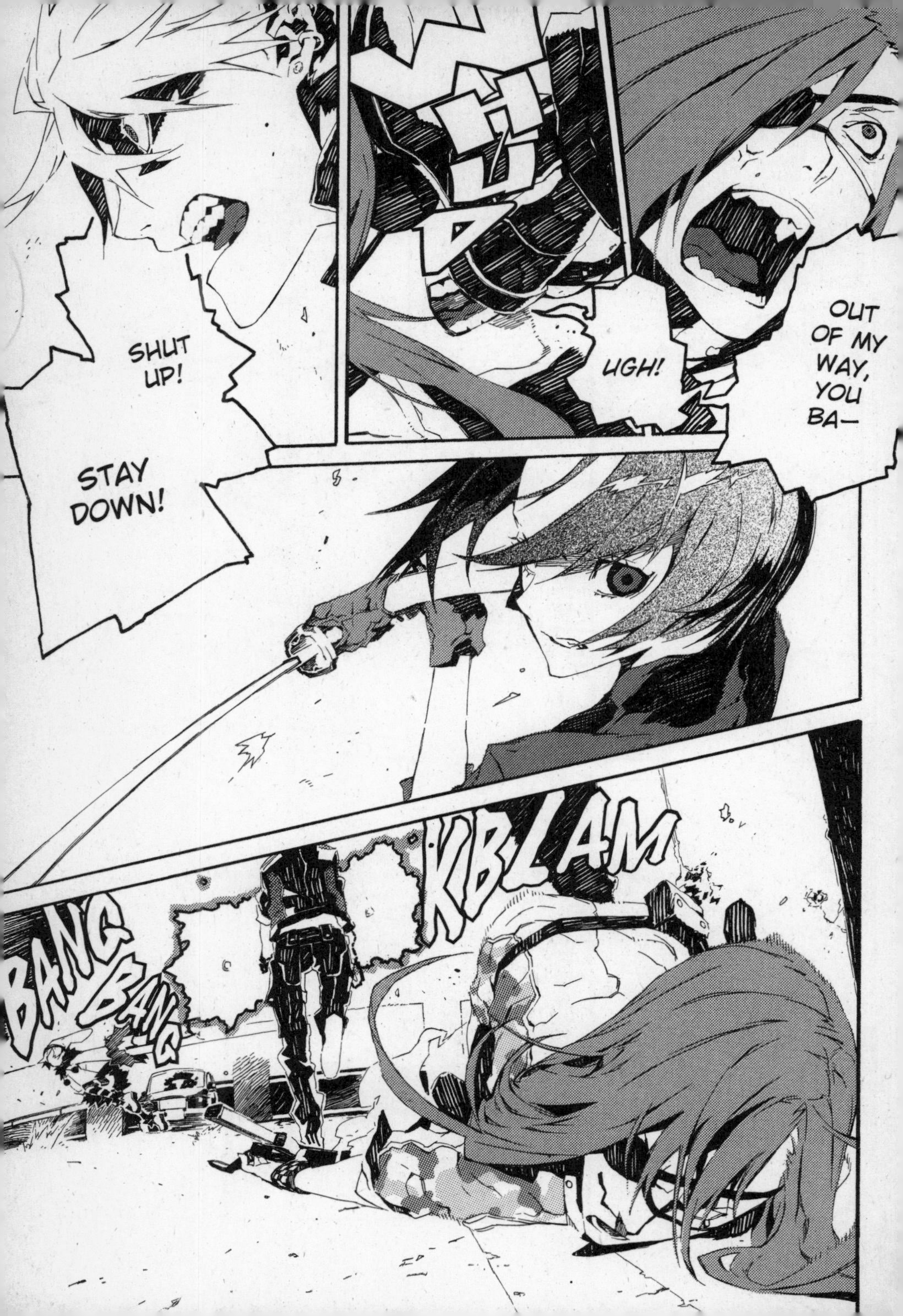
OUT OF MY WAY, YOU BA—
UGH!
SHUT UP!
STAY DOWN!
KBLAM
BANG BANG BANG

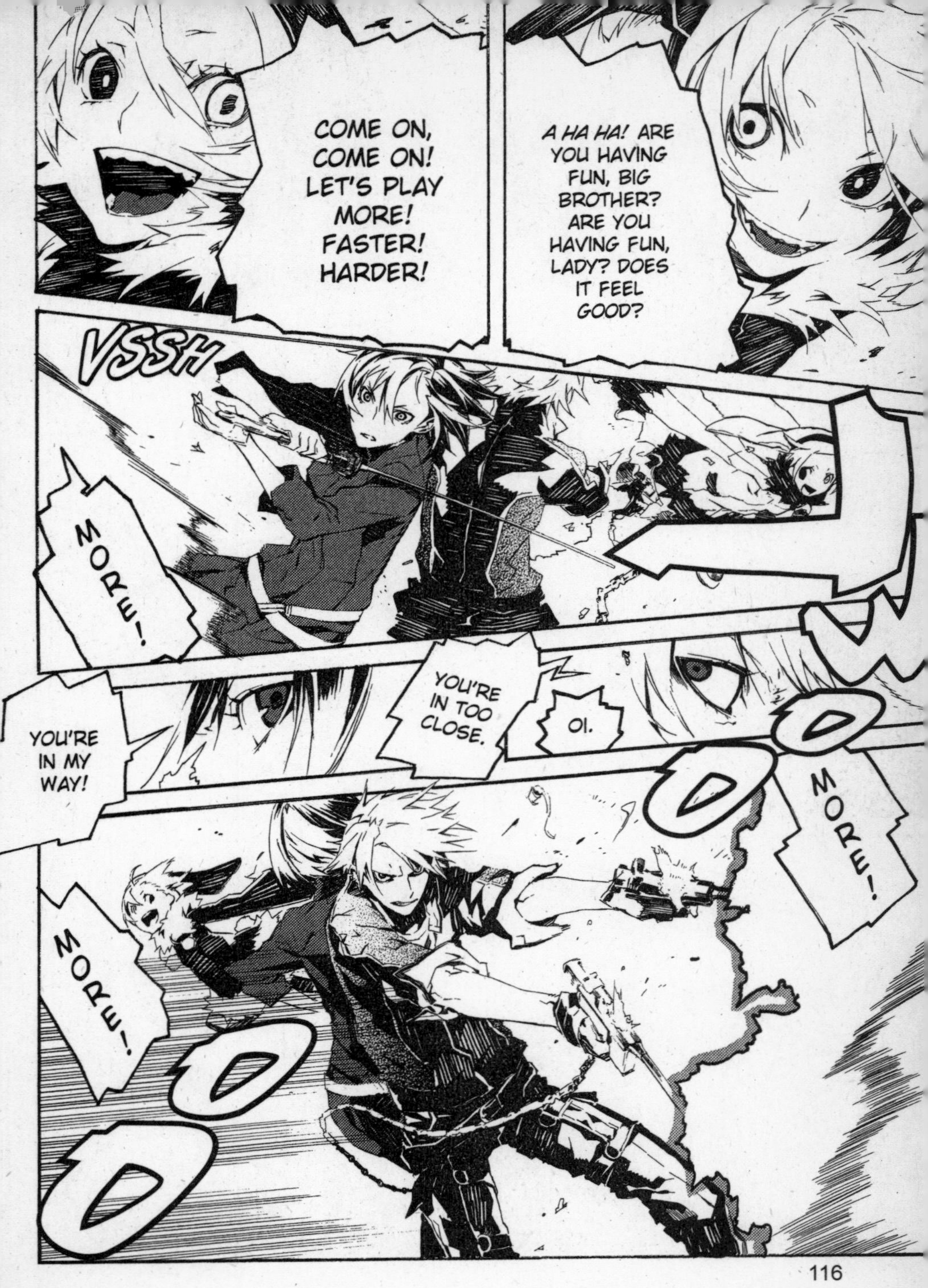
A HA HA! ARE YOU HAVING FUN, BIG BROTHER? ARE YOU HAVING FUN, LADY? DOES IT FEEL GOOD?
COME ON, COME ON! LET'S PLAY MORE! FASTER! HARDER!
VSSH
MORE!
OI.
YOU'RE IN TOO CLOSE.
YOU'RE IN MY WAY!
MORE!
MORE!

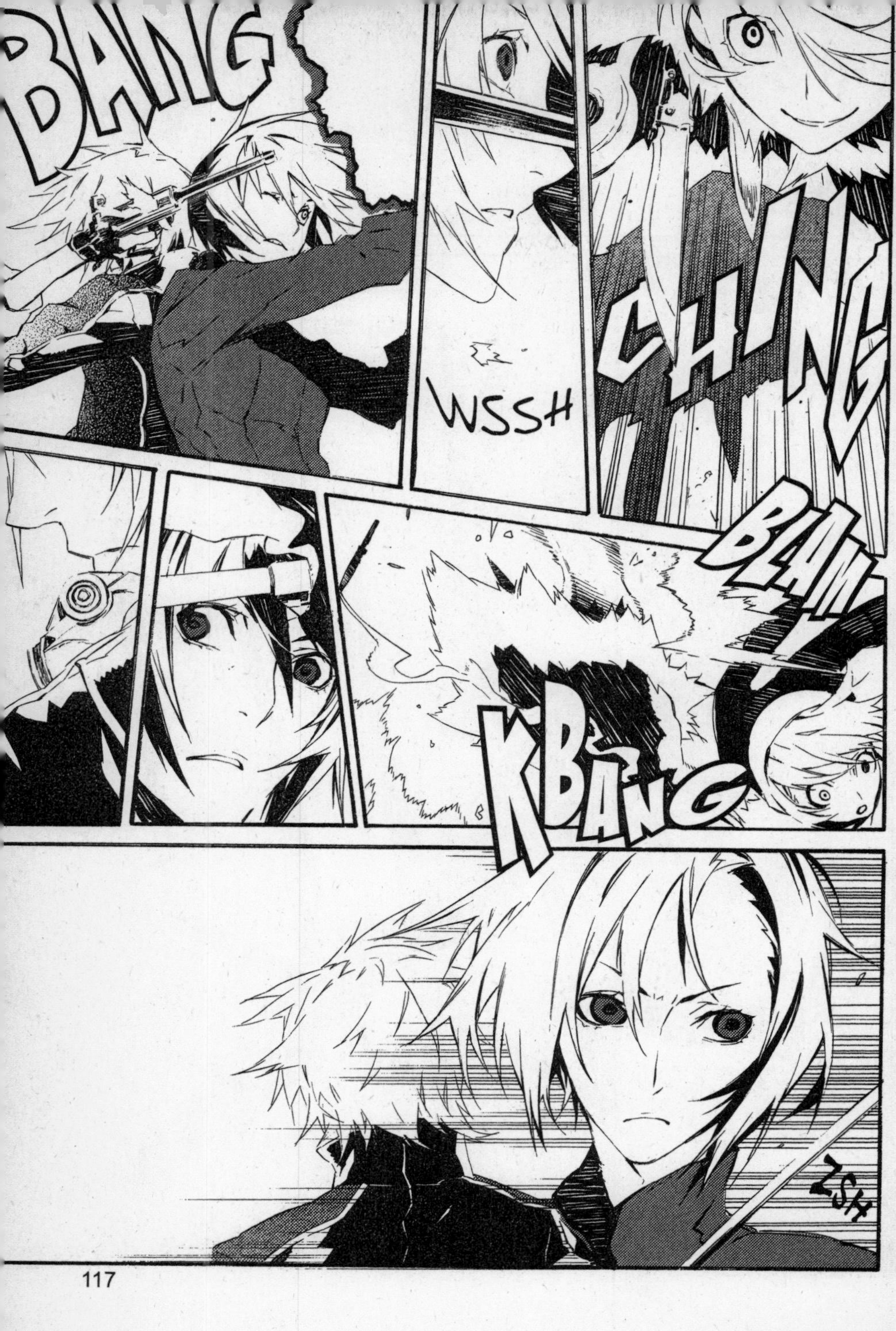
CHING
WSSH
BANG
BLAM
KBANG
ZSH

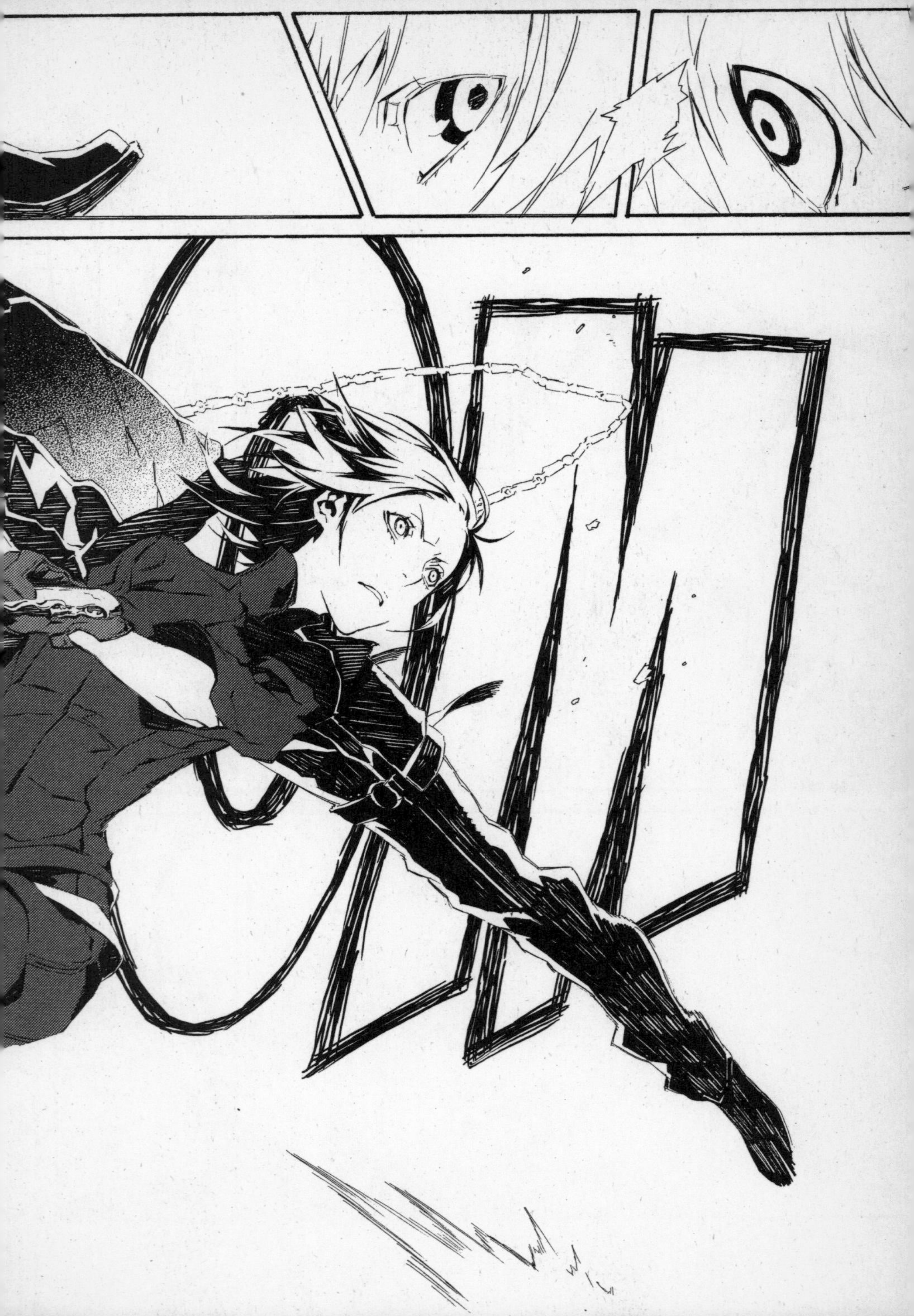

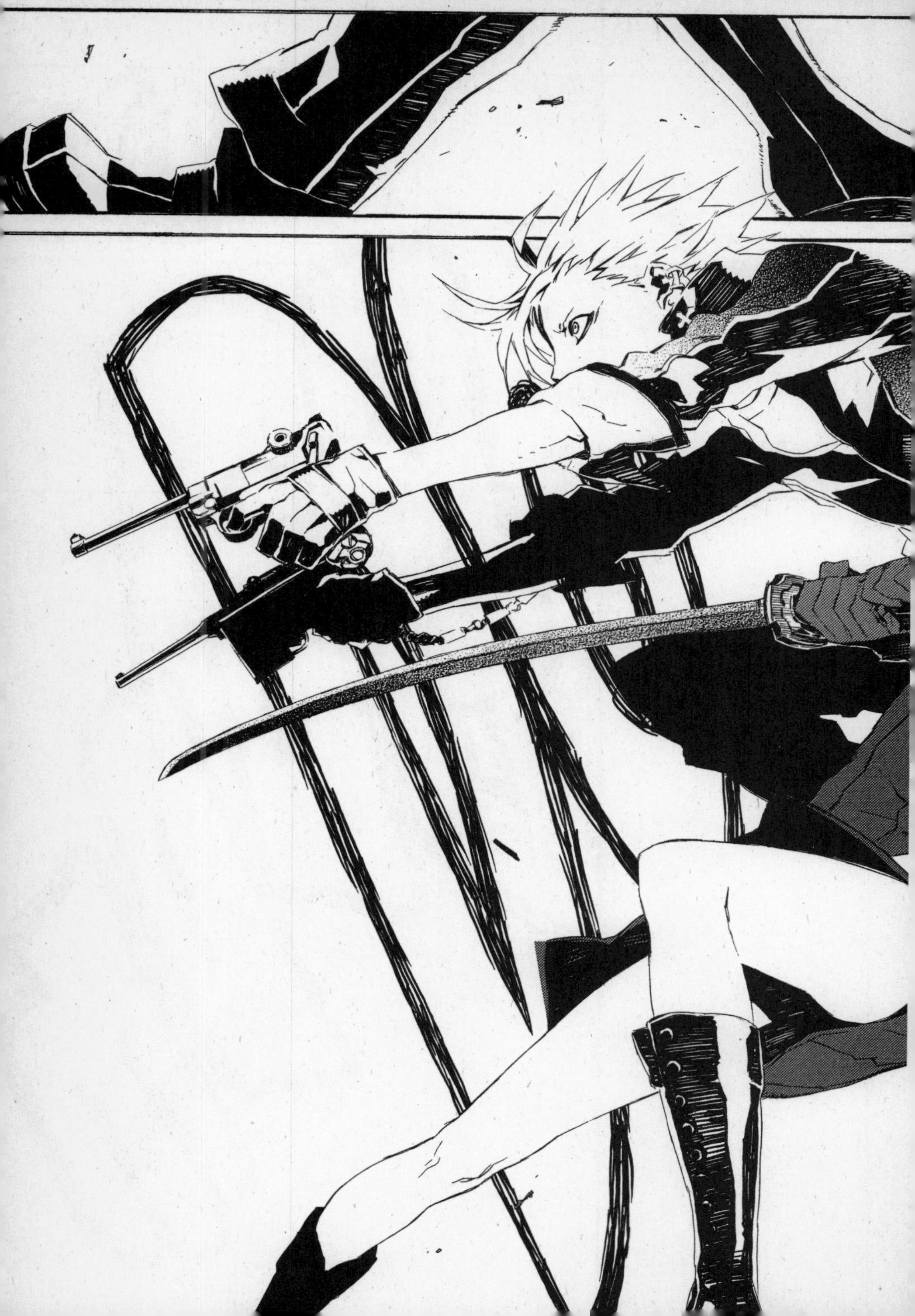

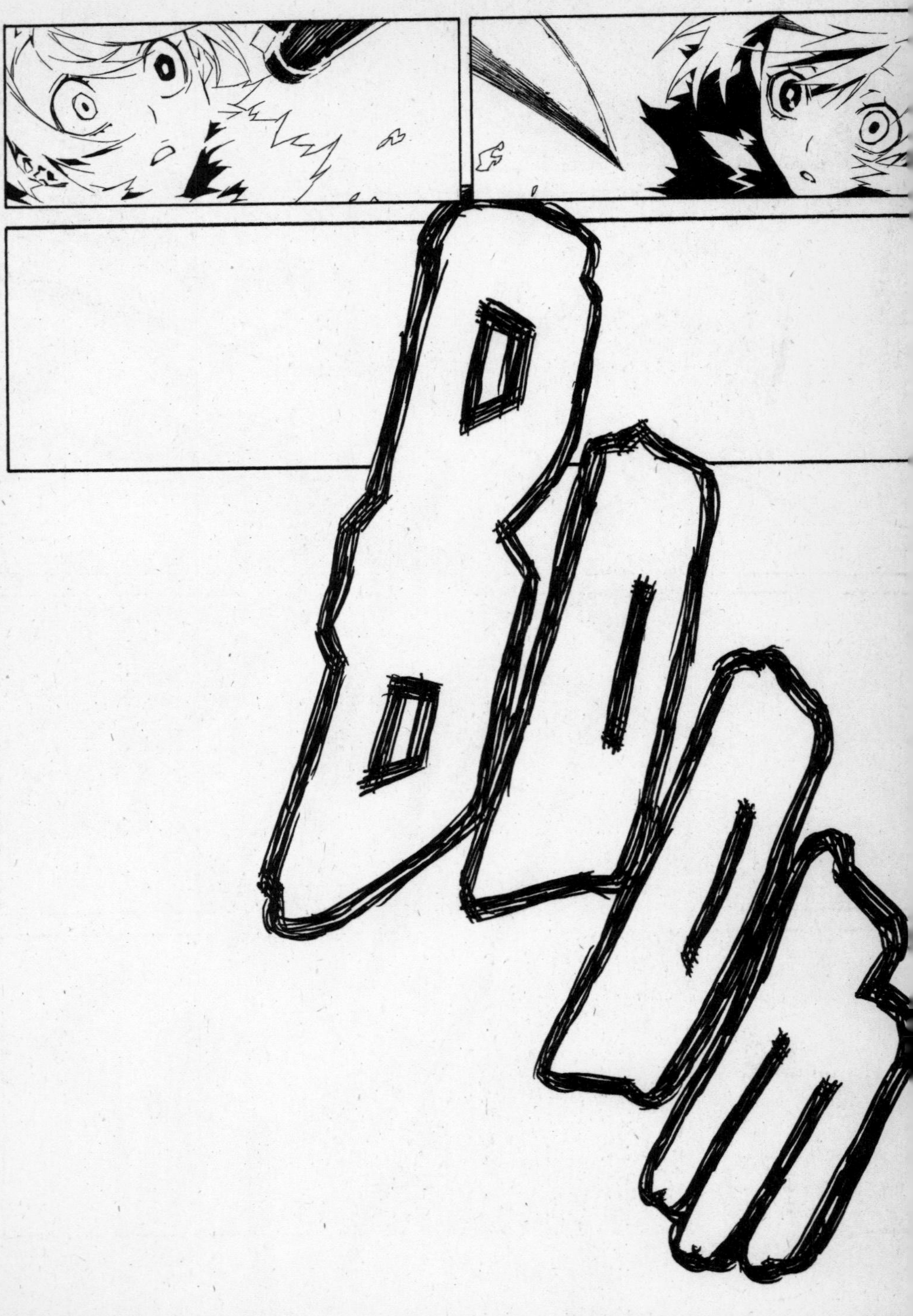

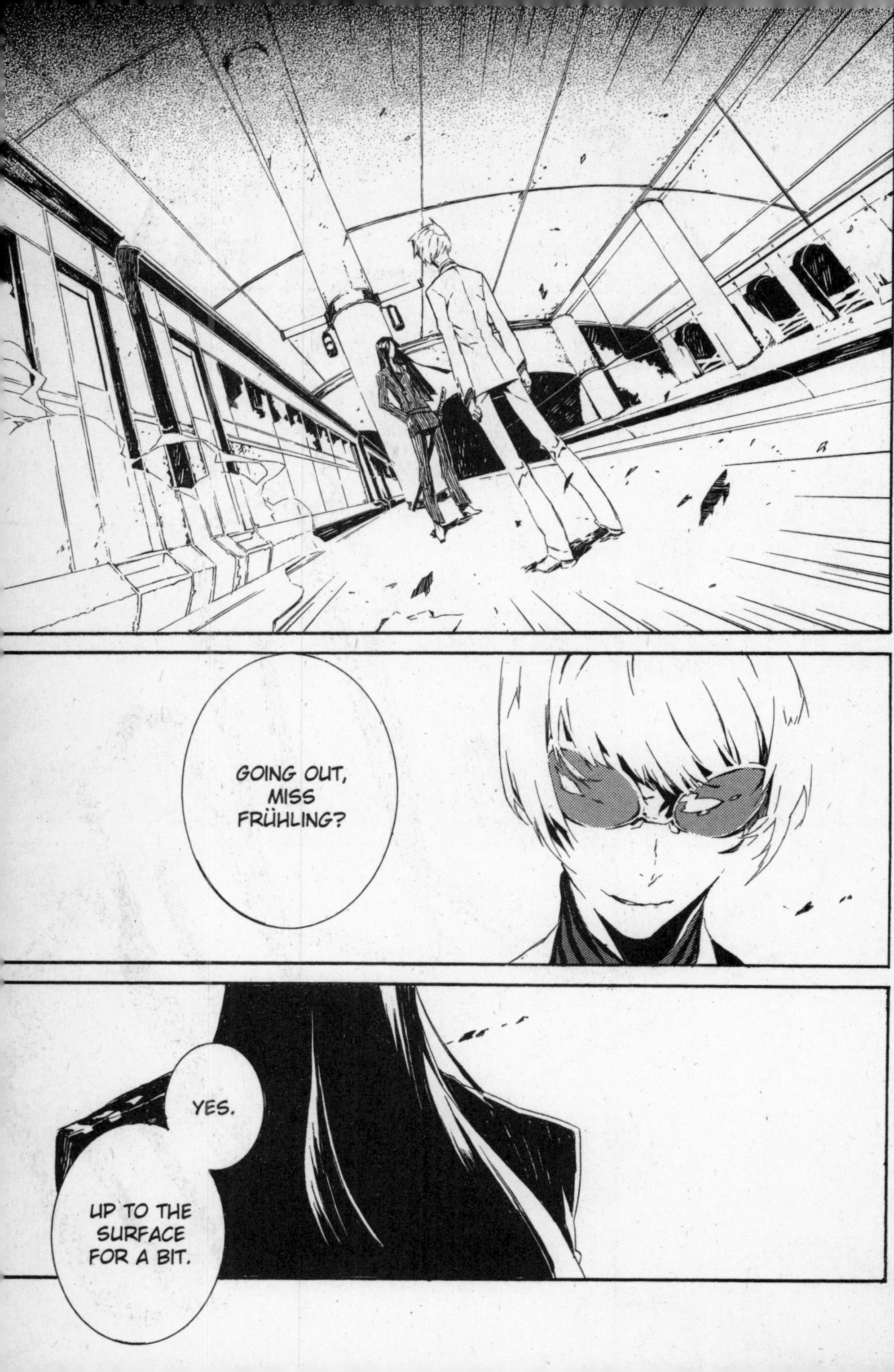
GOING OUT, MISS FRÜHLING?
YES.
UP TO THE SURFACE FOR A BIT.

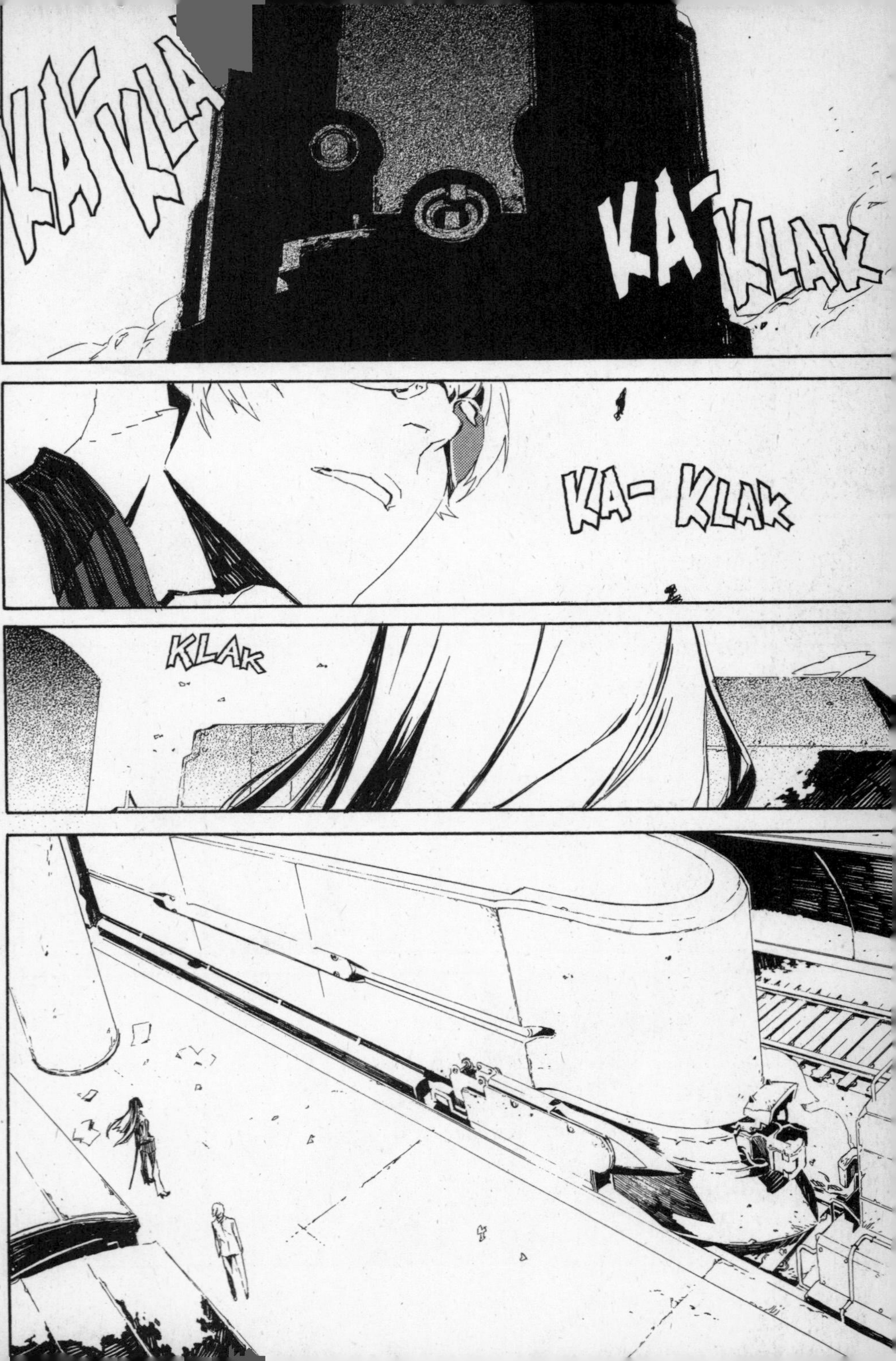
KA-KLAK
KA-KLA
KA- KLAK
KLAK

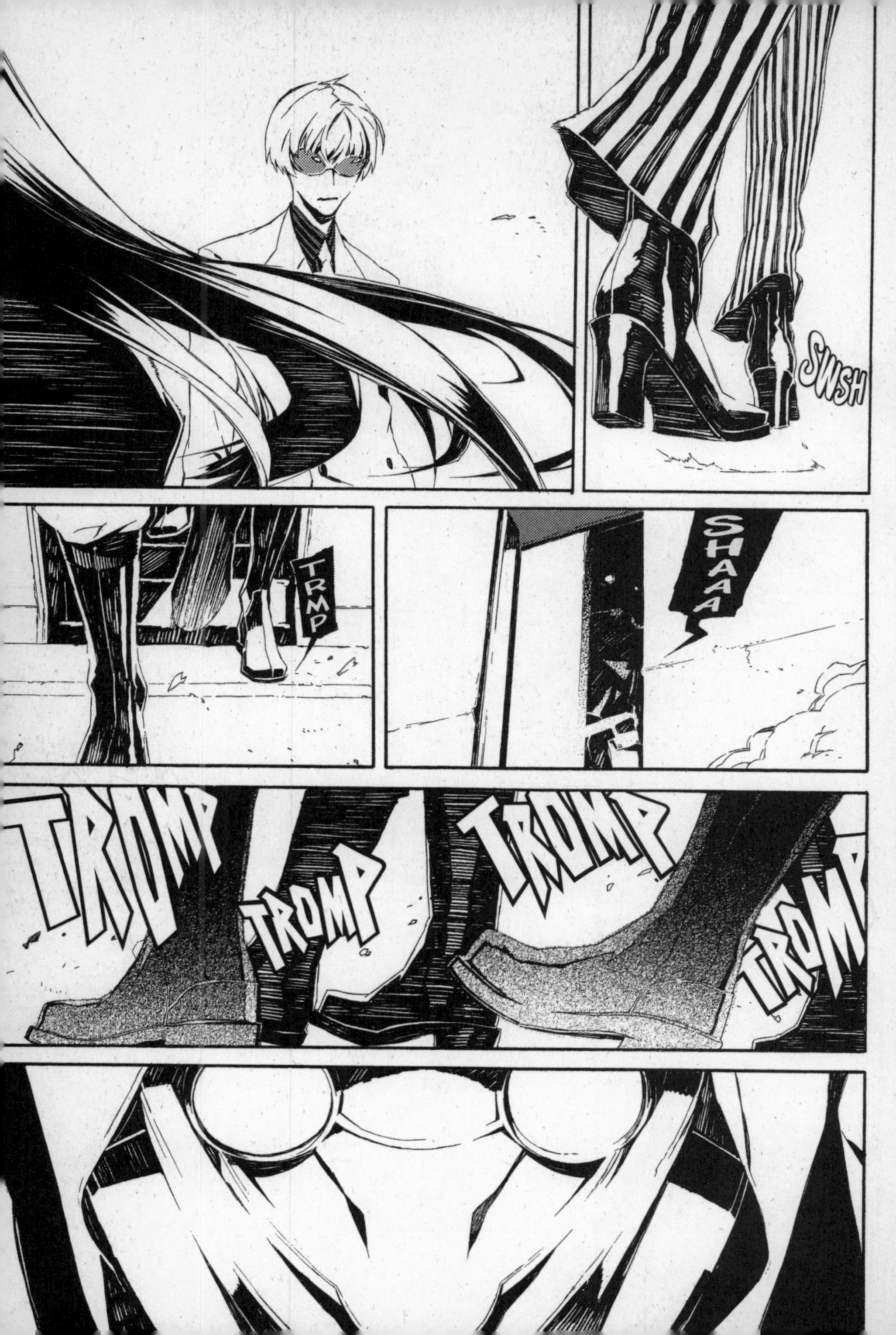
SWSH
SHAAA
TRMP
TROMP
TROMP
TROMP
TROMP

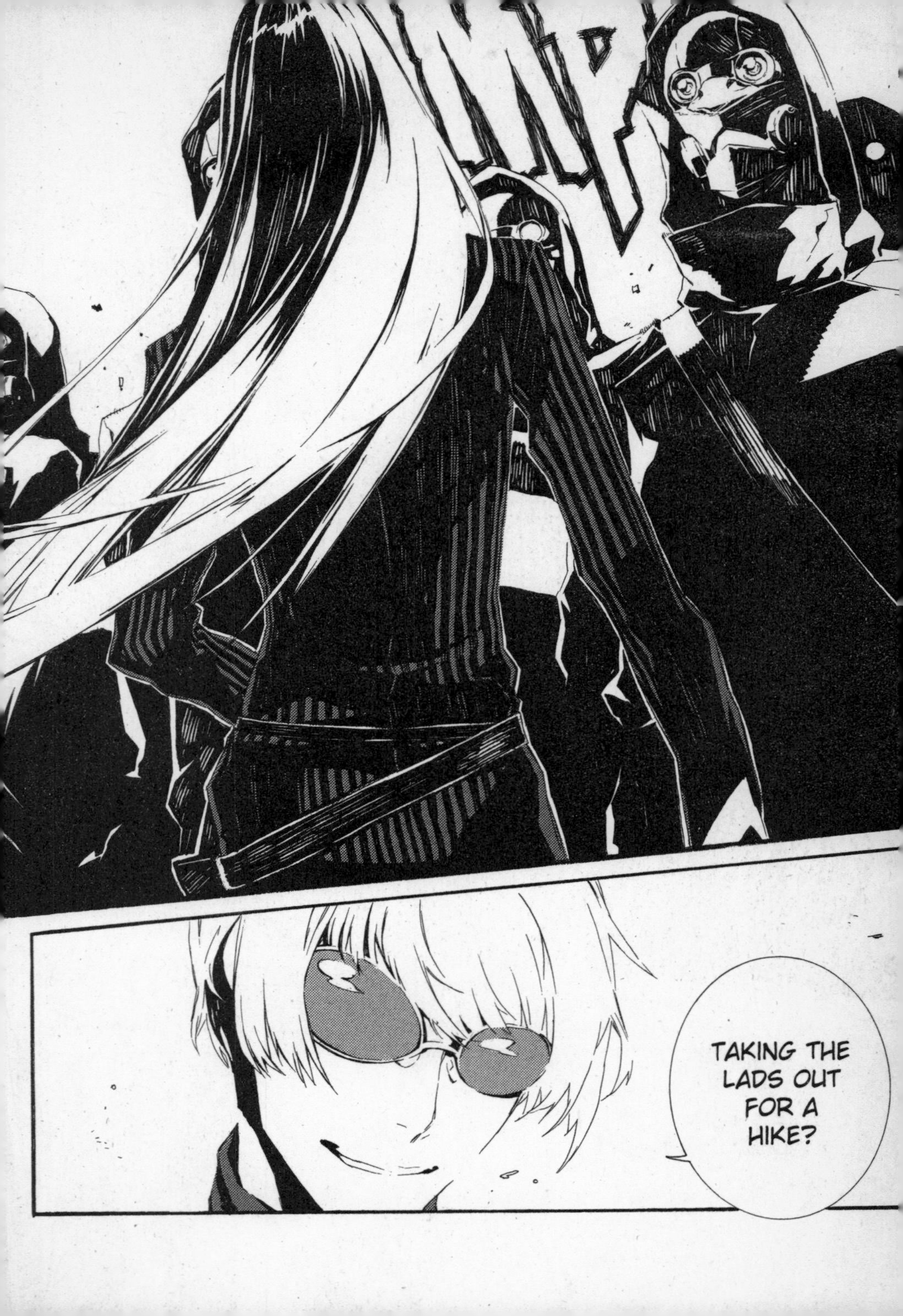
TAKING THE LADS OUT FOR A HIKE?

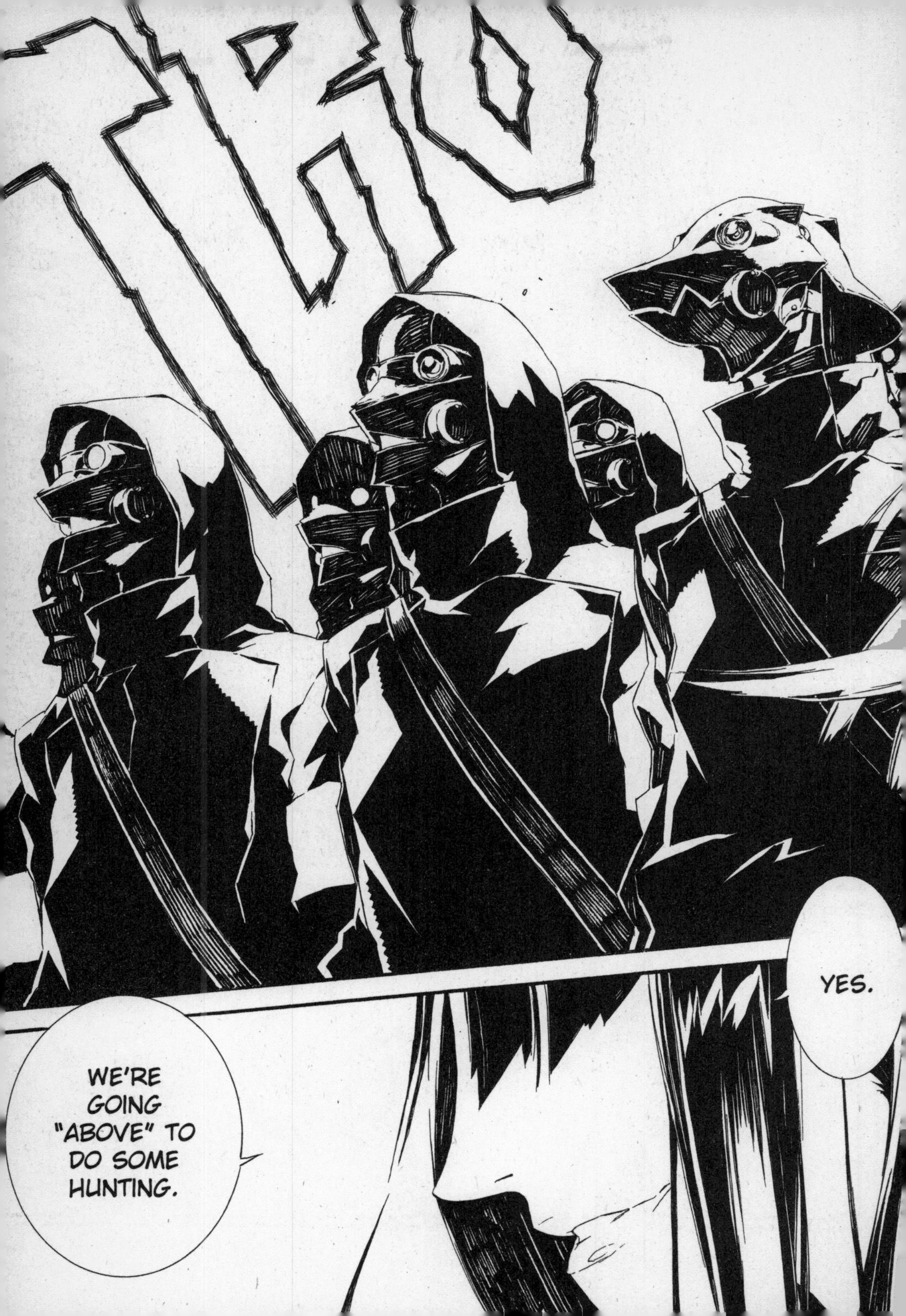
YES.
WE'RE GOING "ABOVE" TO DO SOME HUNTING.

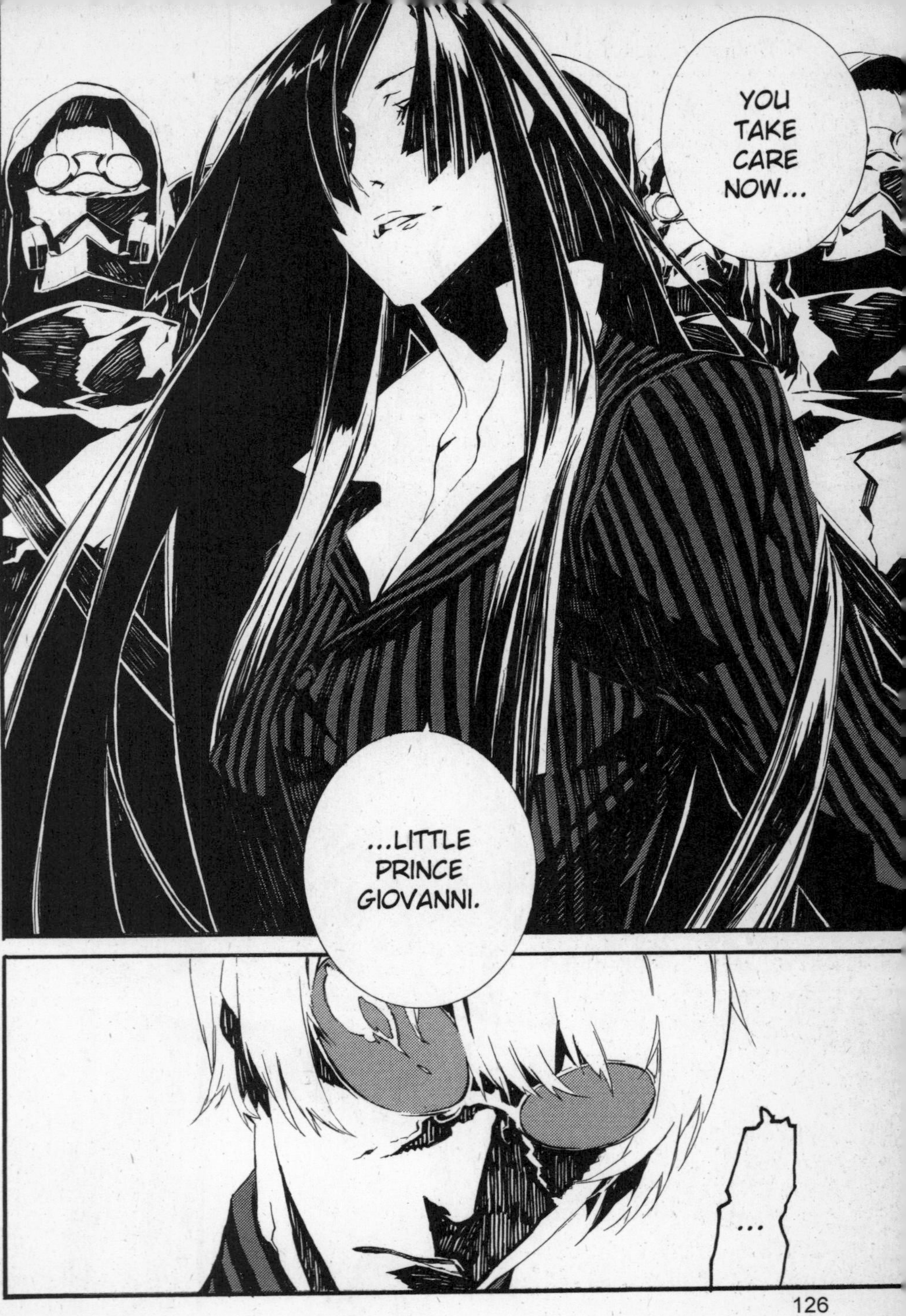
YOU TAKE CARE NOW...
...LITTLE PRINCE GIOVANNI.
...

#19 Pink & Black V

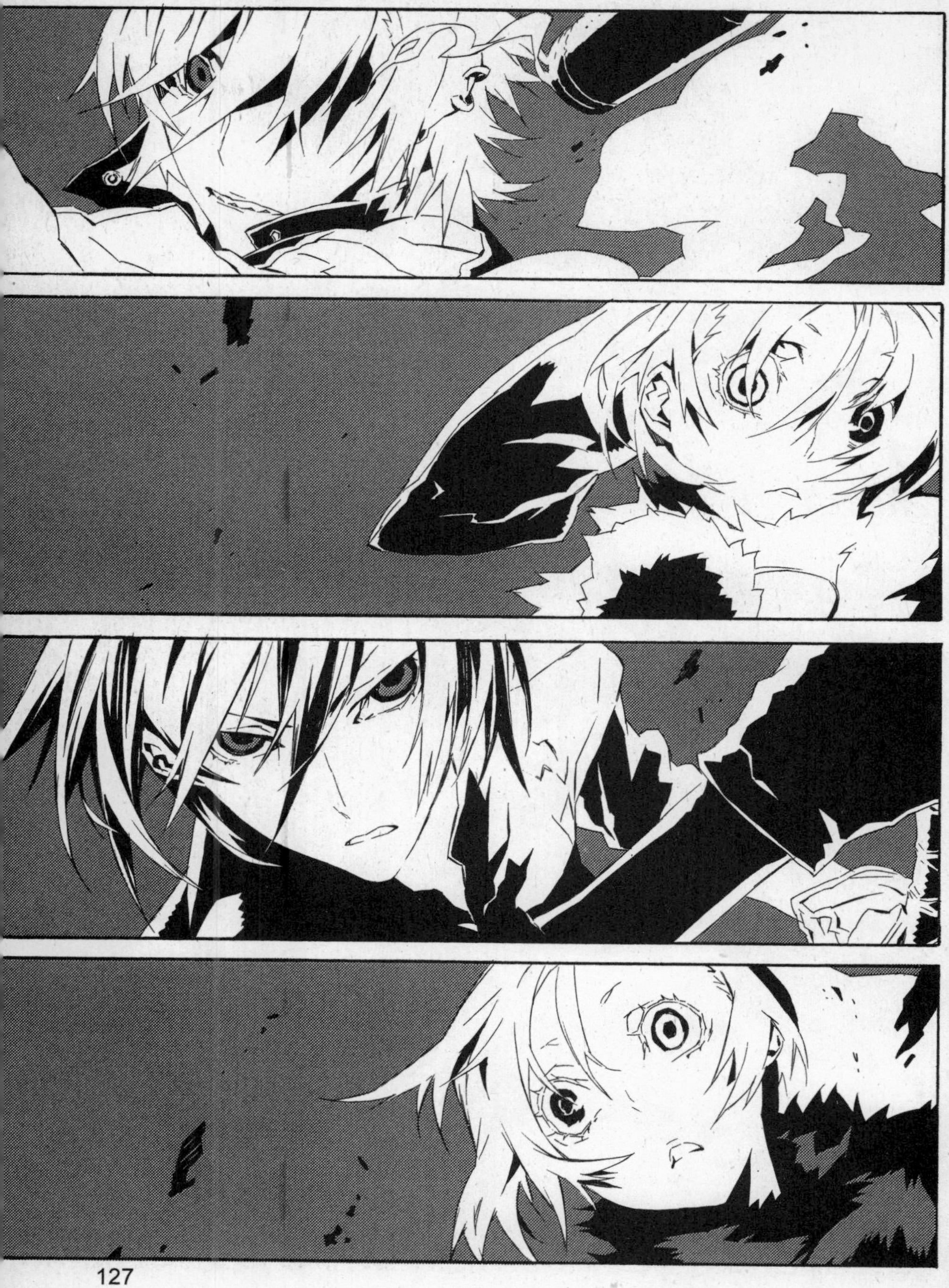

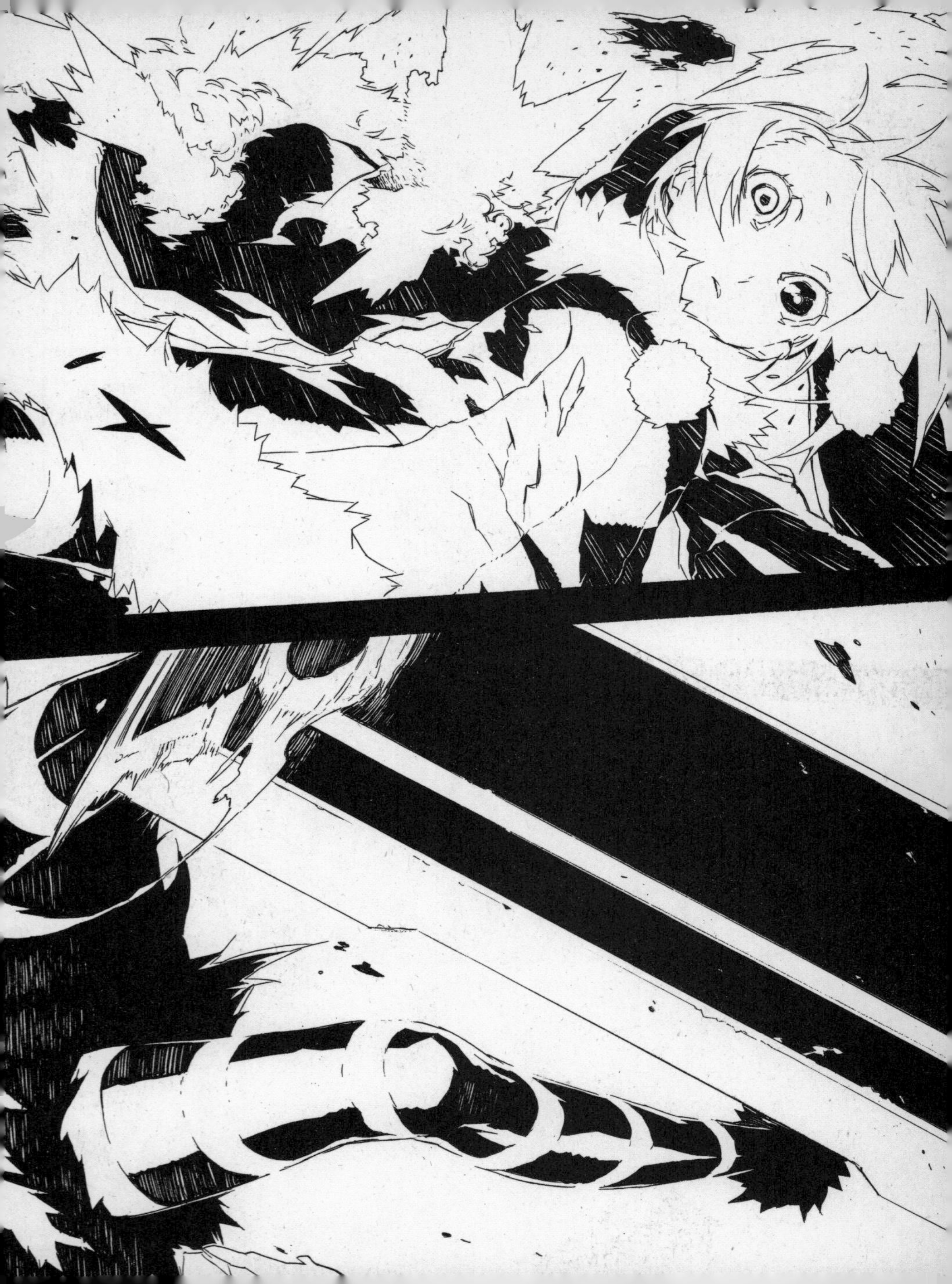

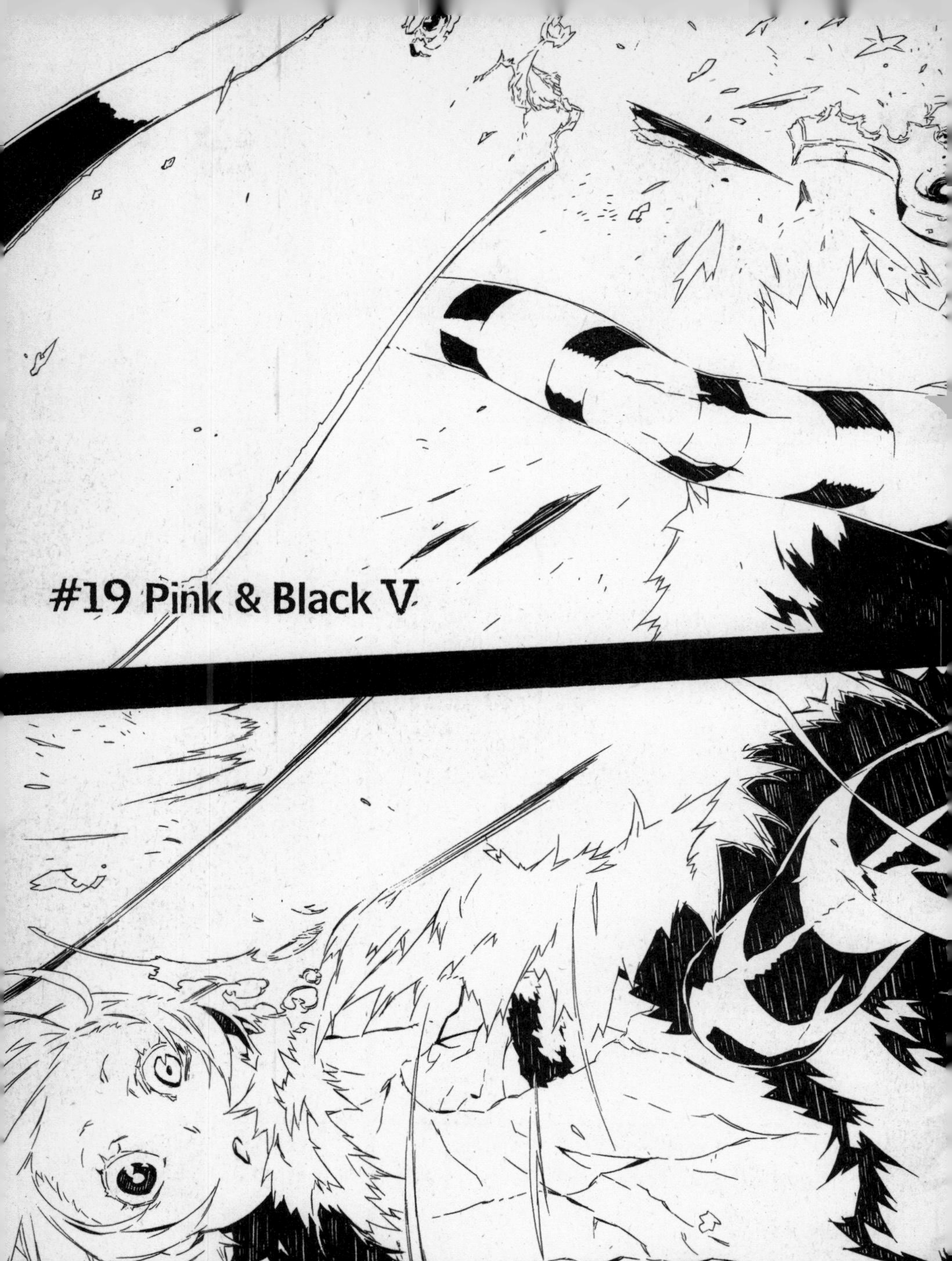
#19 Pink & Black V

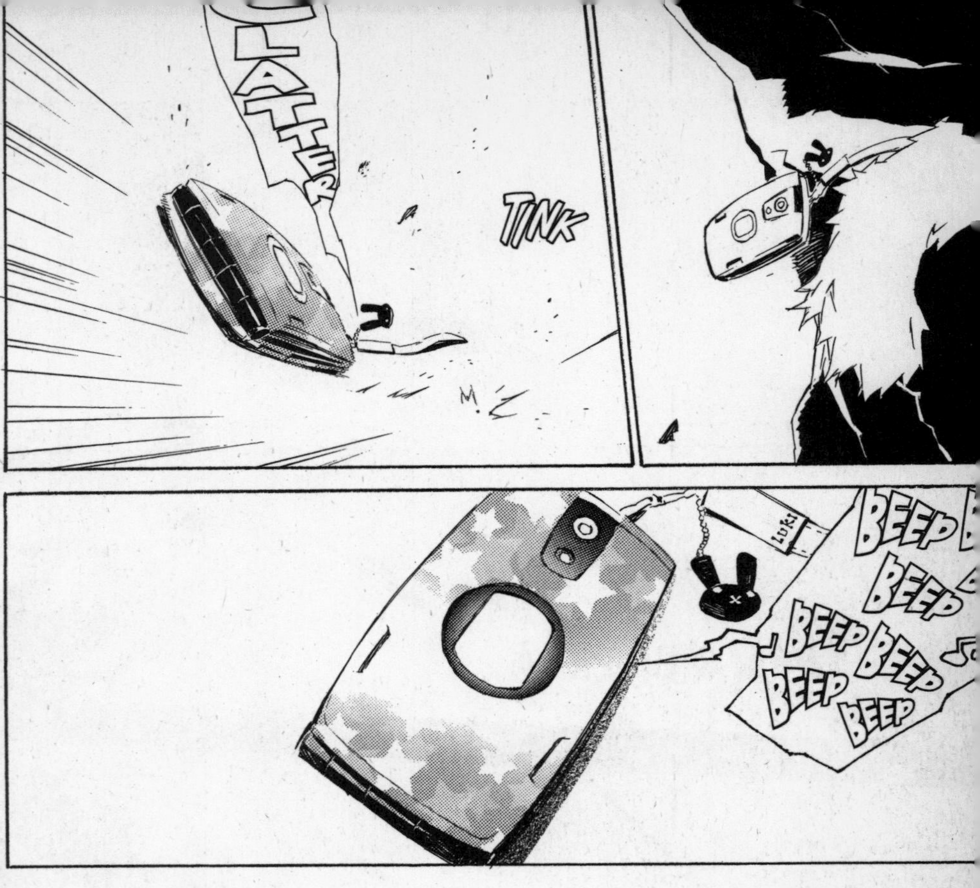
CLATTER
TINK
Luki
BEEP
BEEP
BEEP
BEEP
BEEP
BEEP

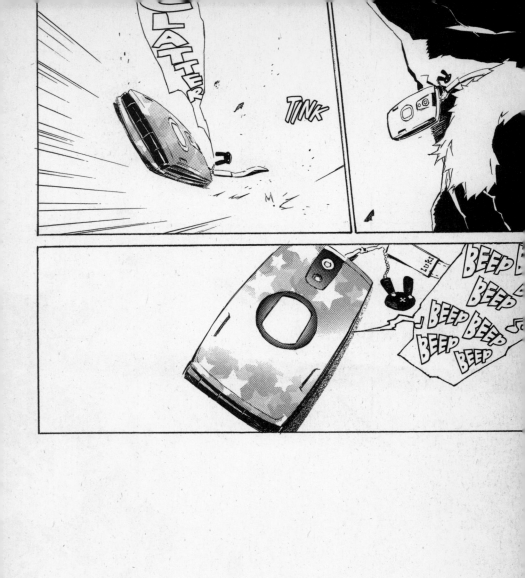

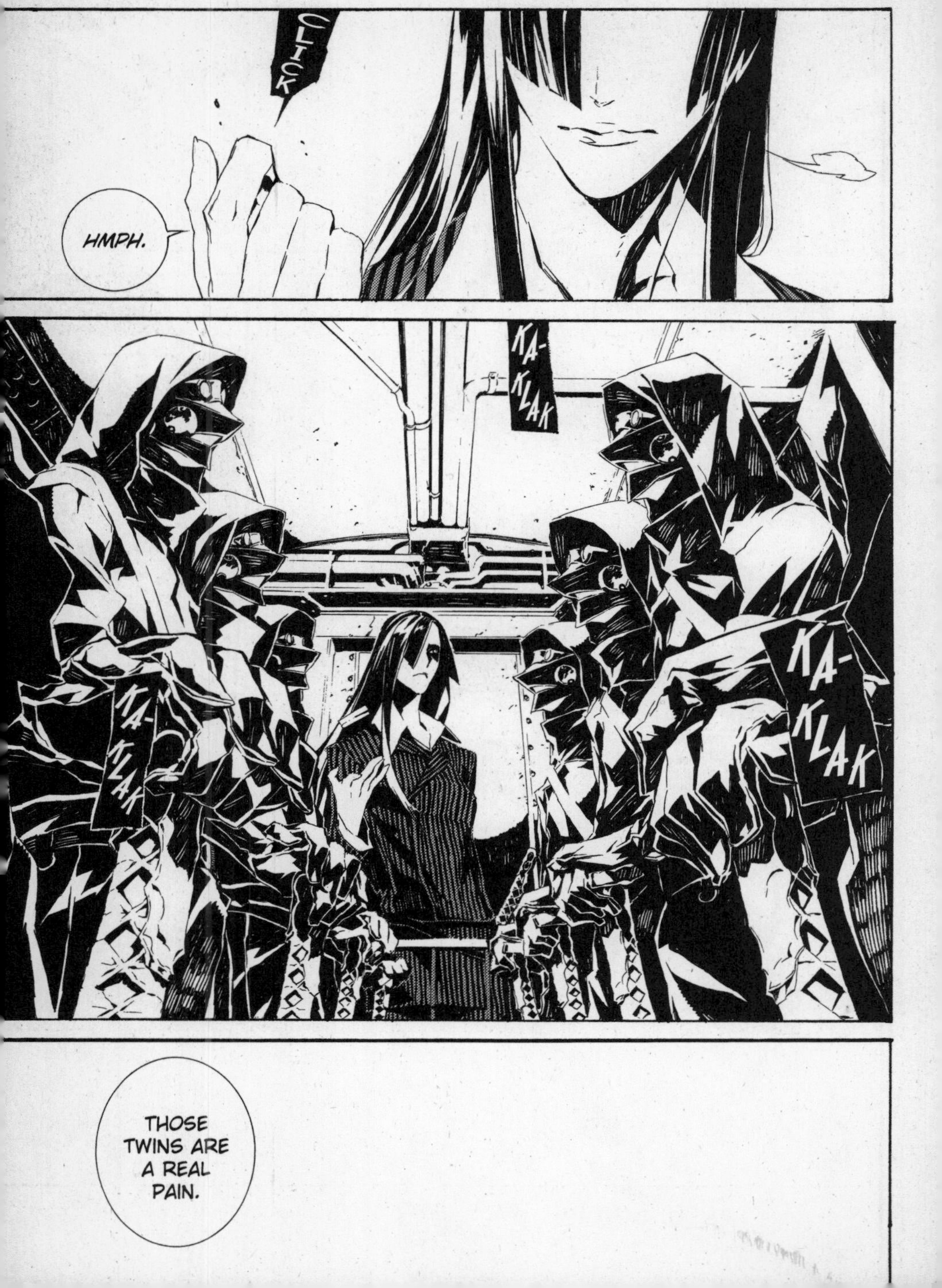
CLICK
HMPH.
KA-KLAK
KA-KLAK
KA-KLAK
THOSE TWINS ARE A REAL PAIN.

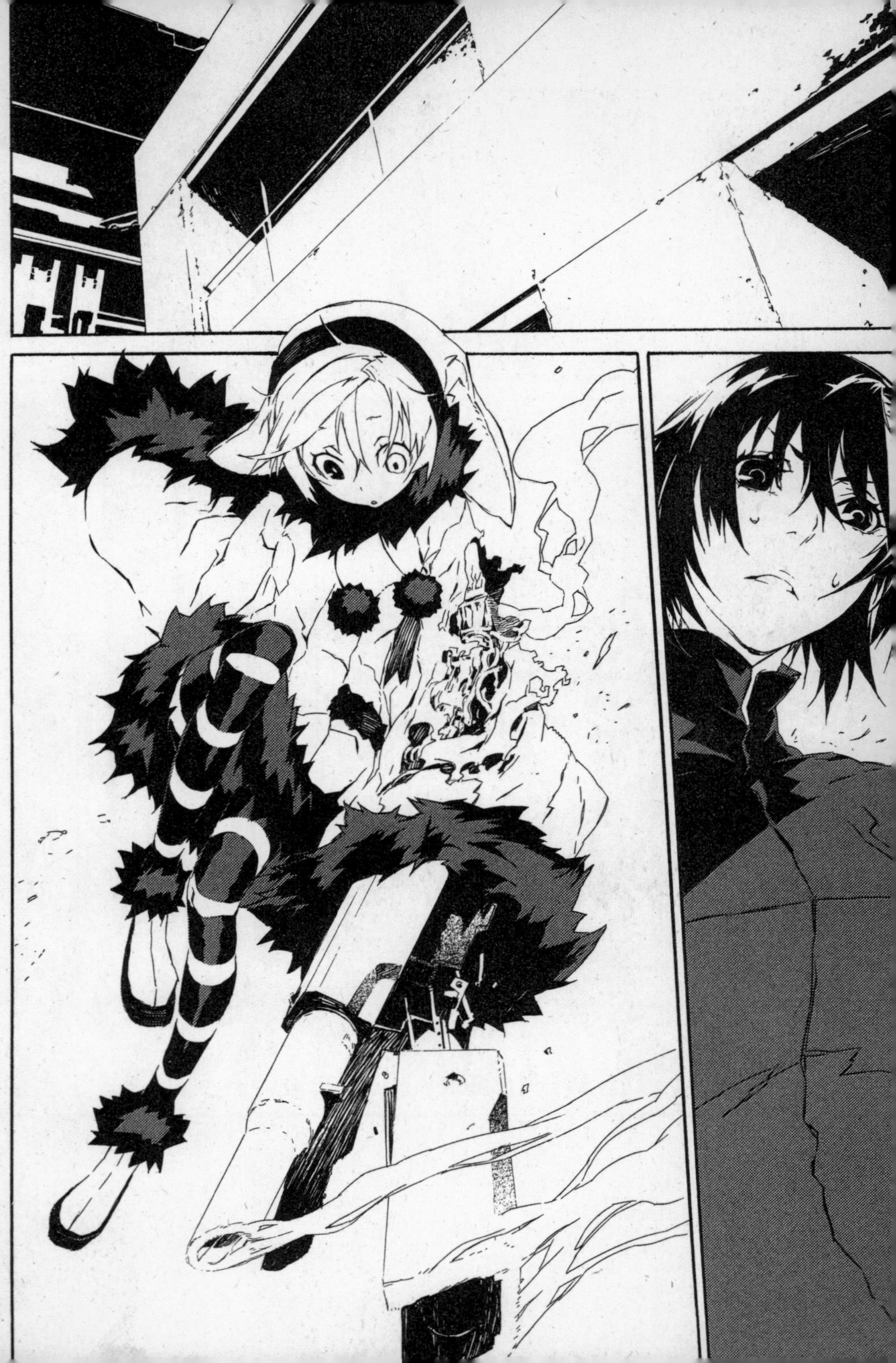

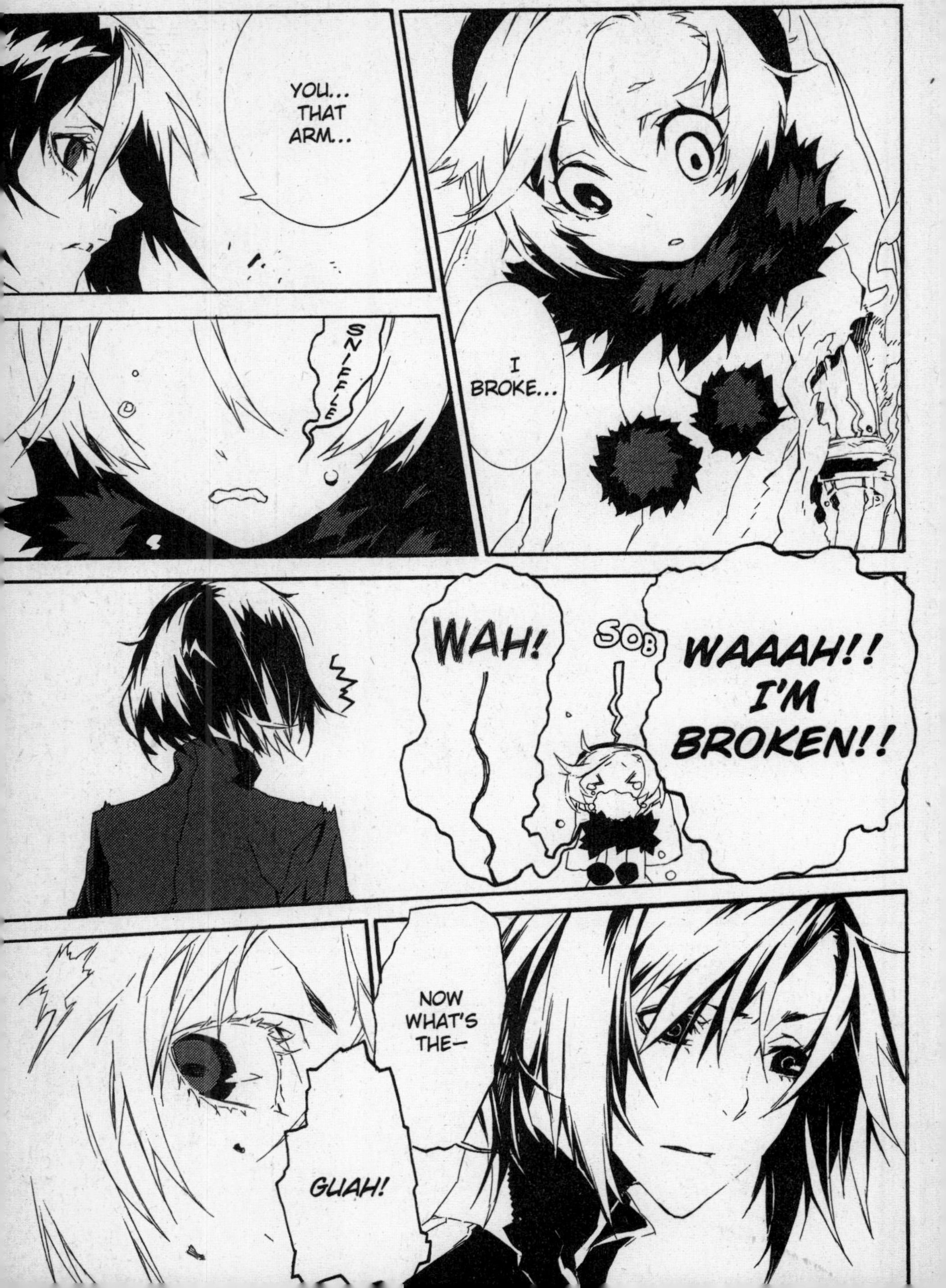
I BROKE...
YOU... THAT ARM...
SNIFFLE
WAAAH!! I'M BROKEN!!
SOB
WAH!
NOW WHAT'S THE—
GUAH!

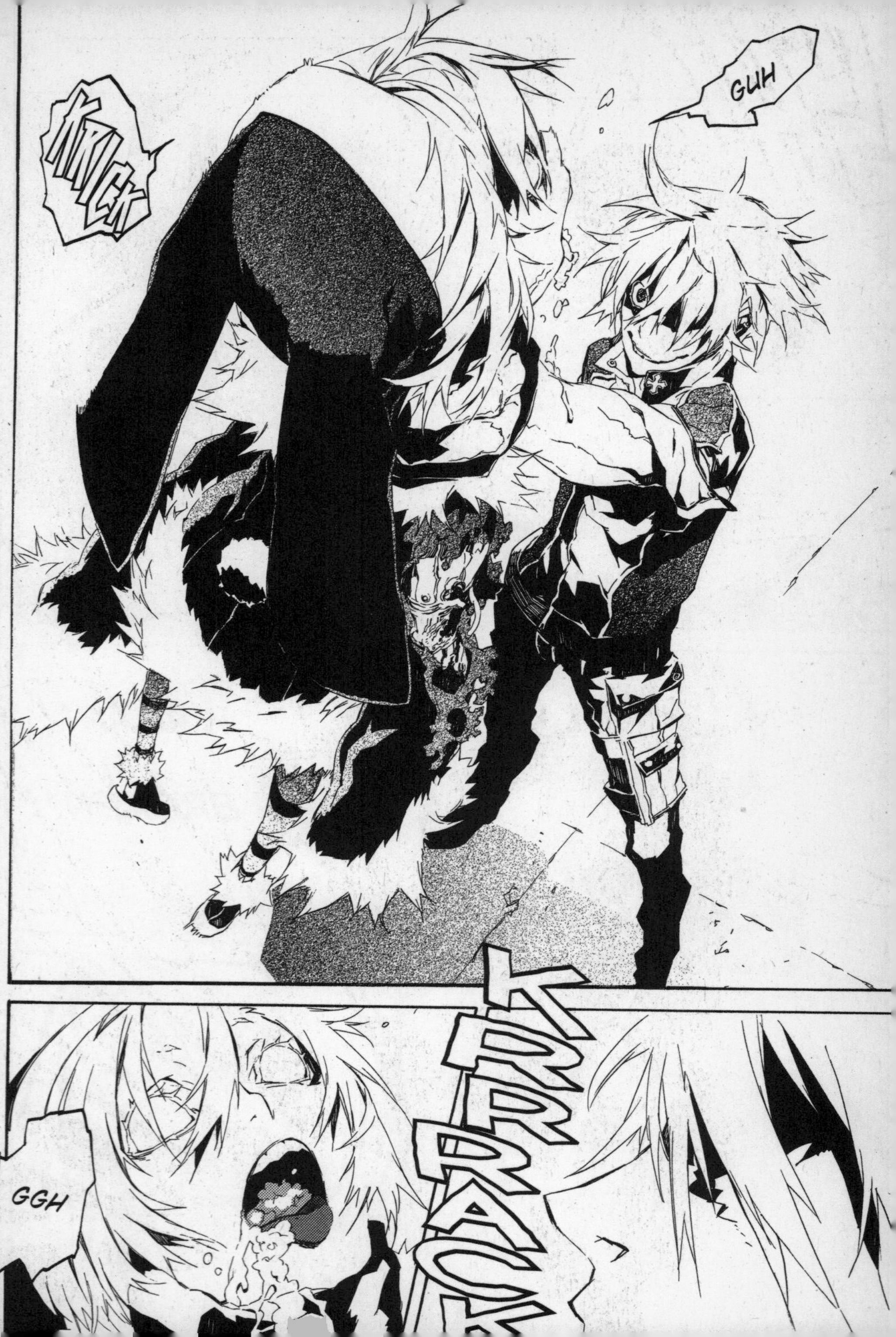
GUH
KRICK
KRRRACK
GGH

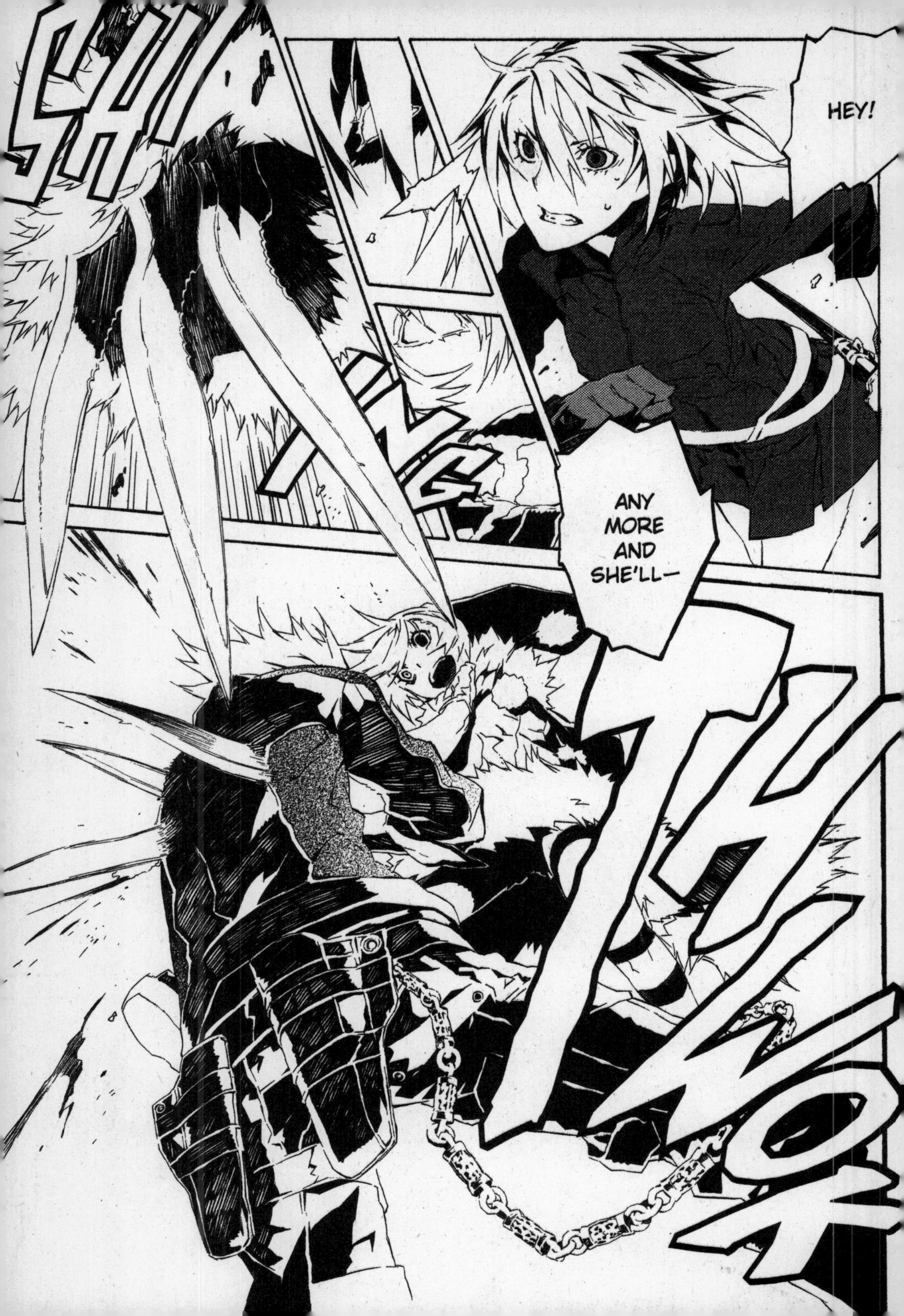
HEY!
ANY MORE AND SHE'LL—
SHA
THWOK

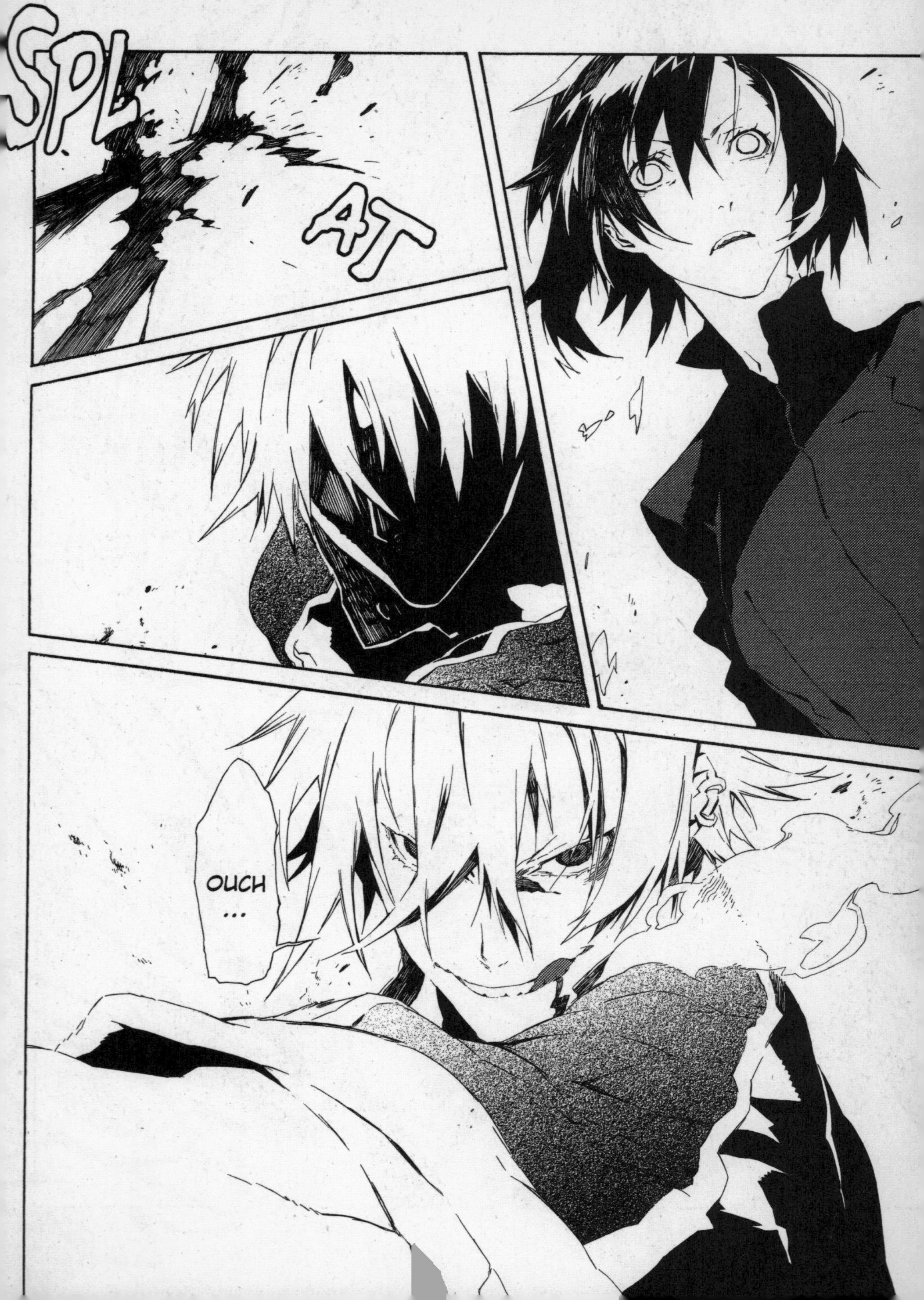
SPLAT
OUCH ...

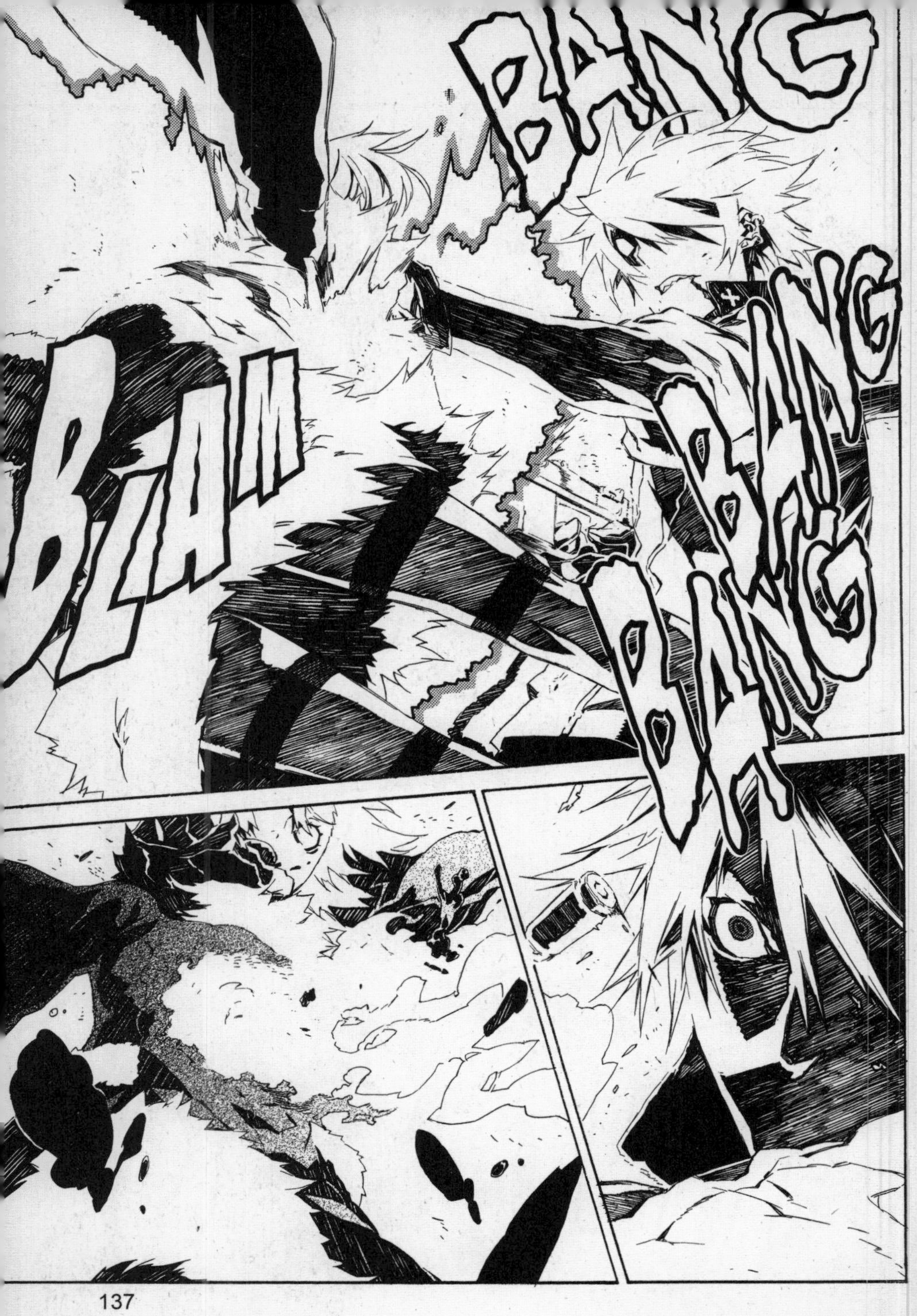
BANG
BANG
BANG
BLAM

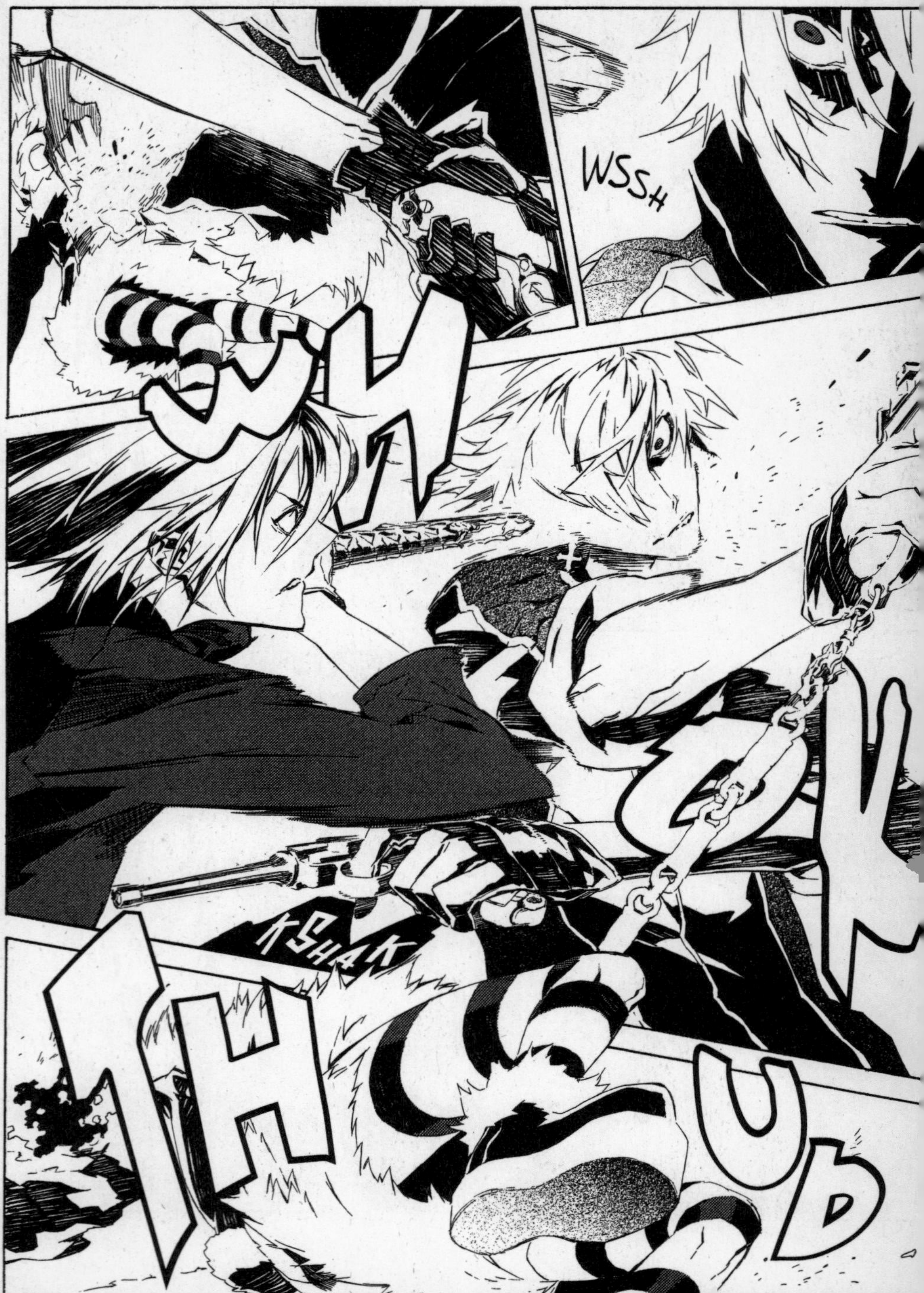
WSSH
KSHAK
THUD

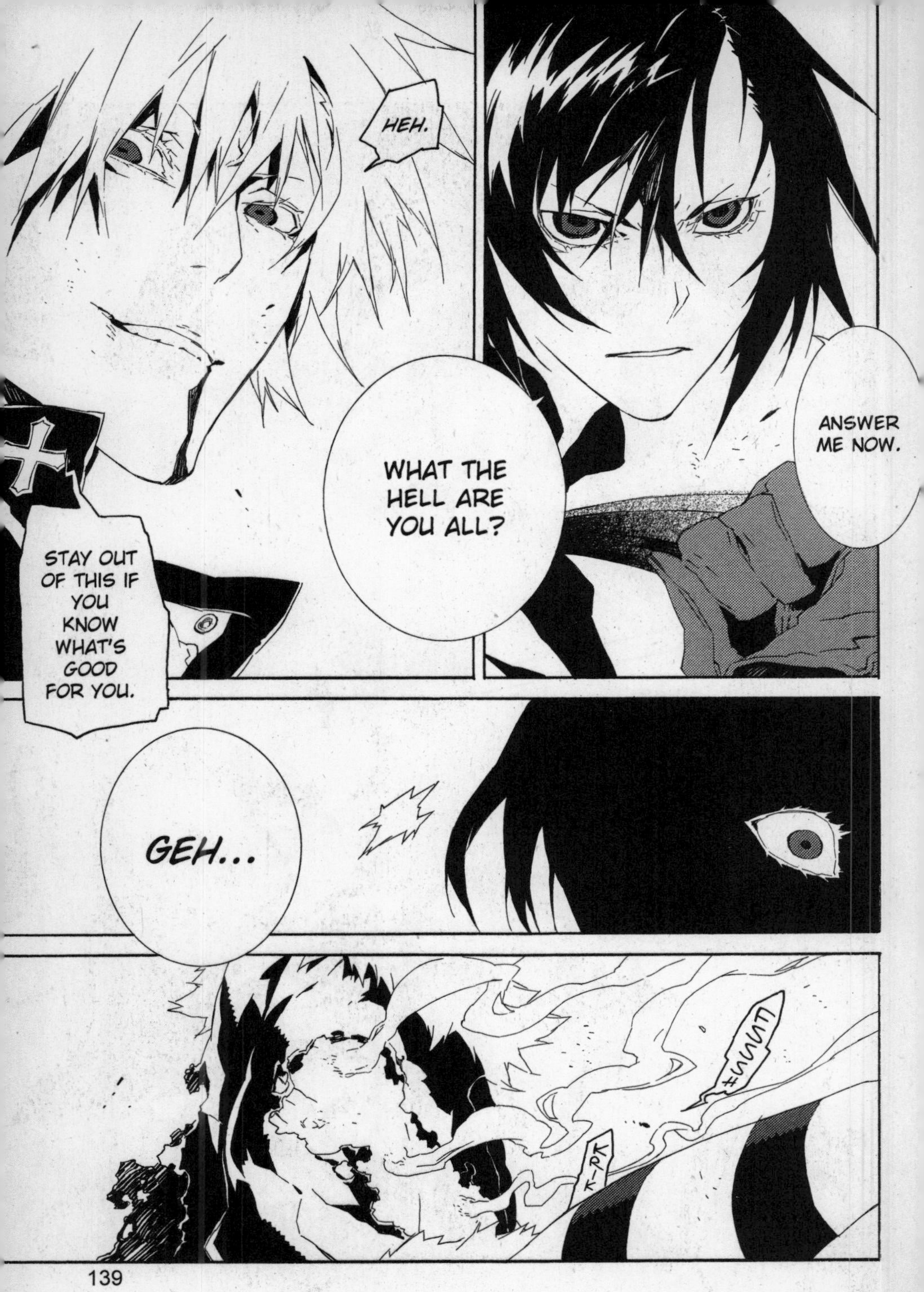
ANSWER ME NOW.
WHAT THE HELL ARE YOU ALL?
HEH.
STAY OUT OF THIS IF YOU KNOW WHAT'S GOOD FOR YOU.
GEH...
HUUUT
KRIK

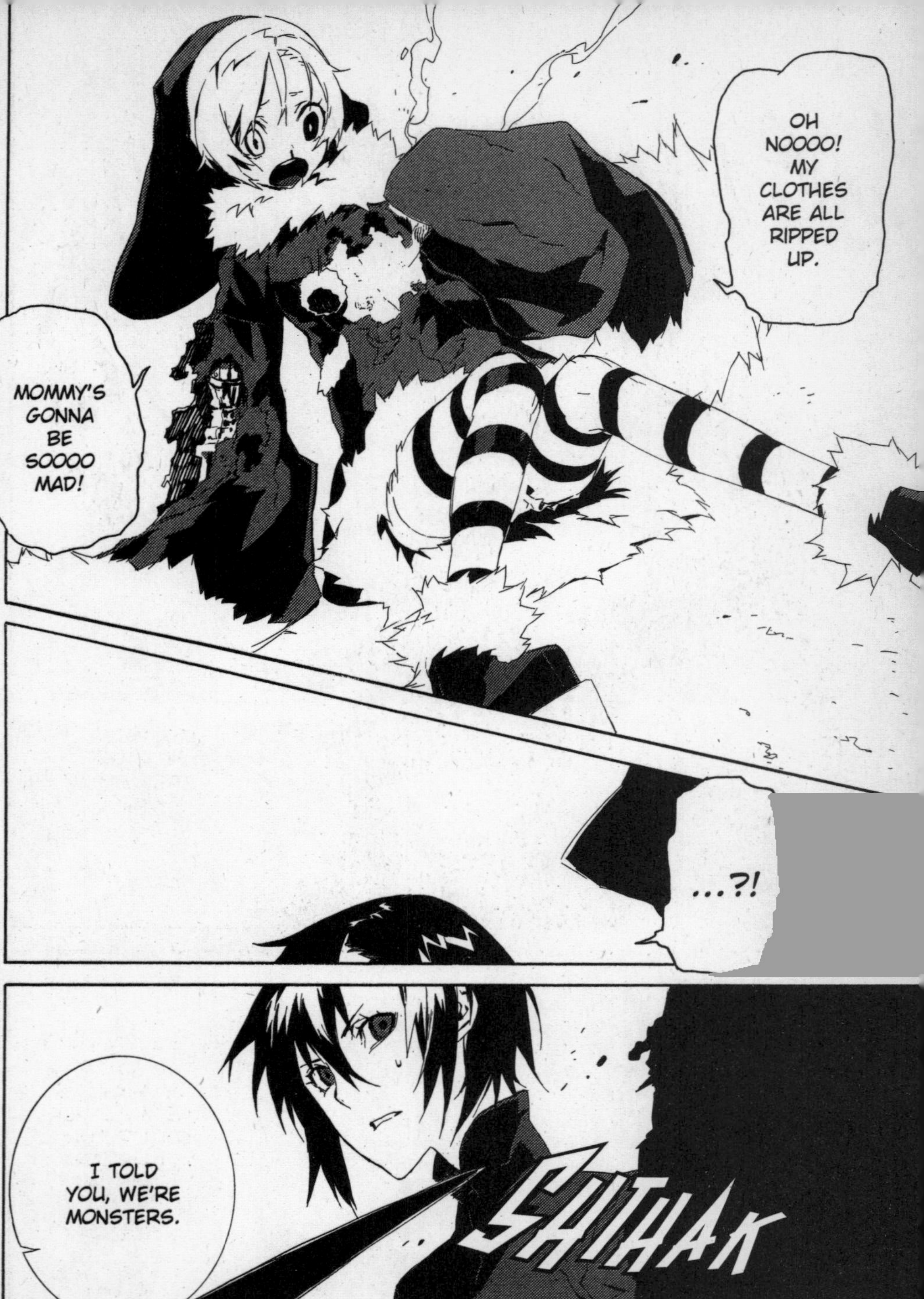
OH NOOOO! MY CLOTHES ARE ALL RIPPED UP.
MOMMY'S GONNA BE SOOOO MAD!
...?!
I TOLD YOU, WE'RE MONSTERS.

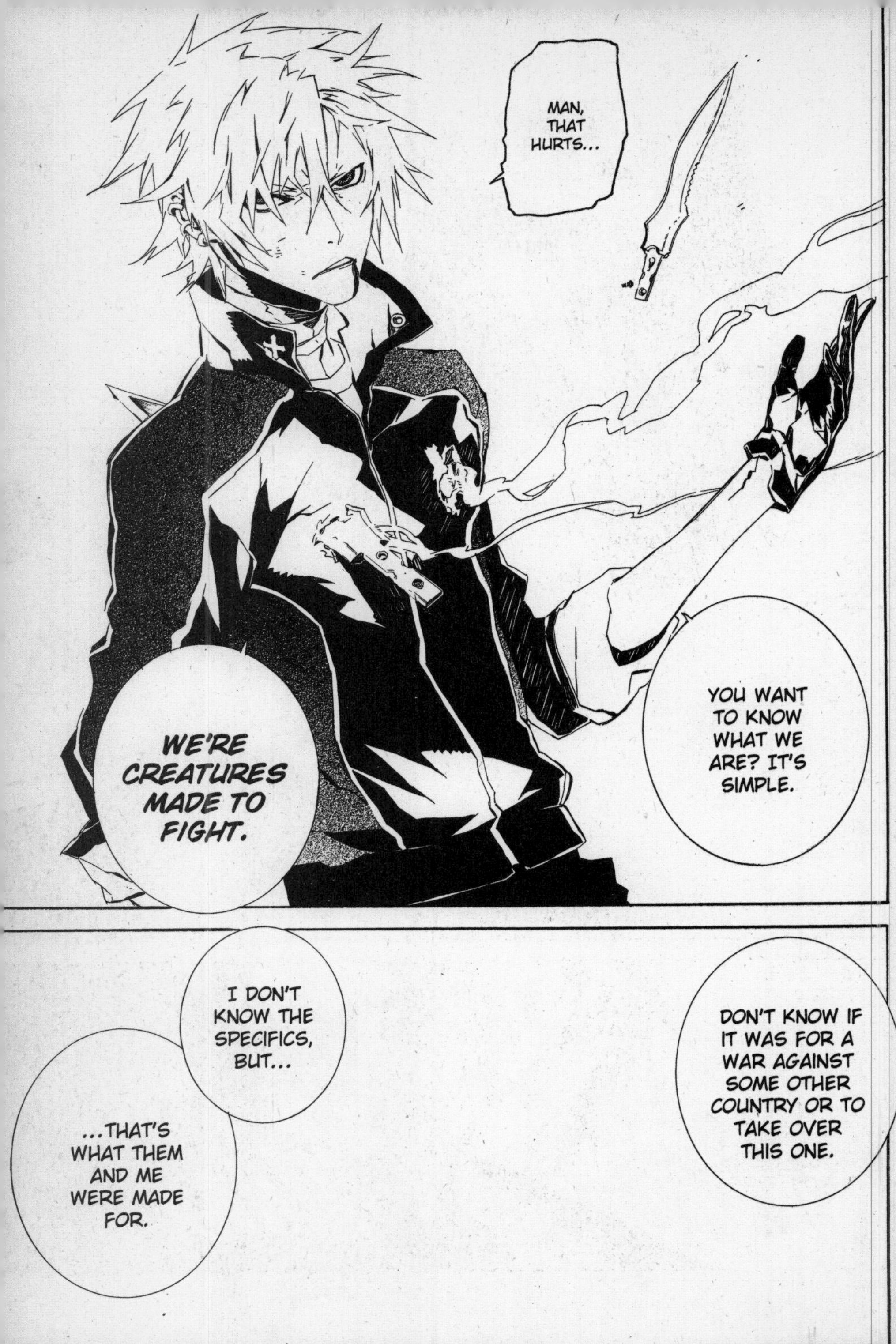
MAN, THAT HURTS...
YOU WANT TO KNOW WHAT WE ARE? IT'S SIMPLE.
WE'RE CREATURES MADE TO FIGHT.
DON'T KNOW IF IT WAS FOR A WAR AGAINST SOME OTHER COUNTRY OR TO TAKE OVER THIS ONE.
I DON'T KNOW THE SPECIFICS, BUT...
...THAT'S WHAT THEM AND ME WERE MADE FOR.

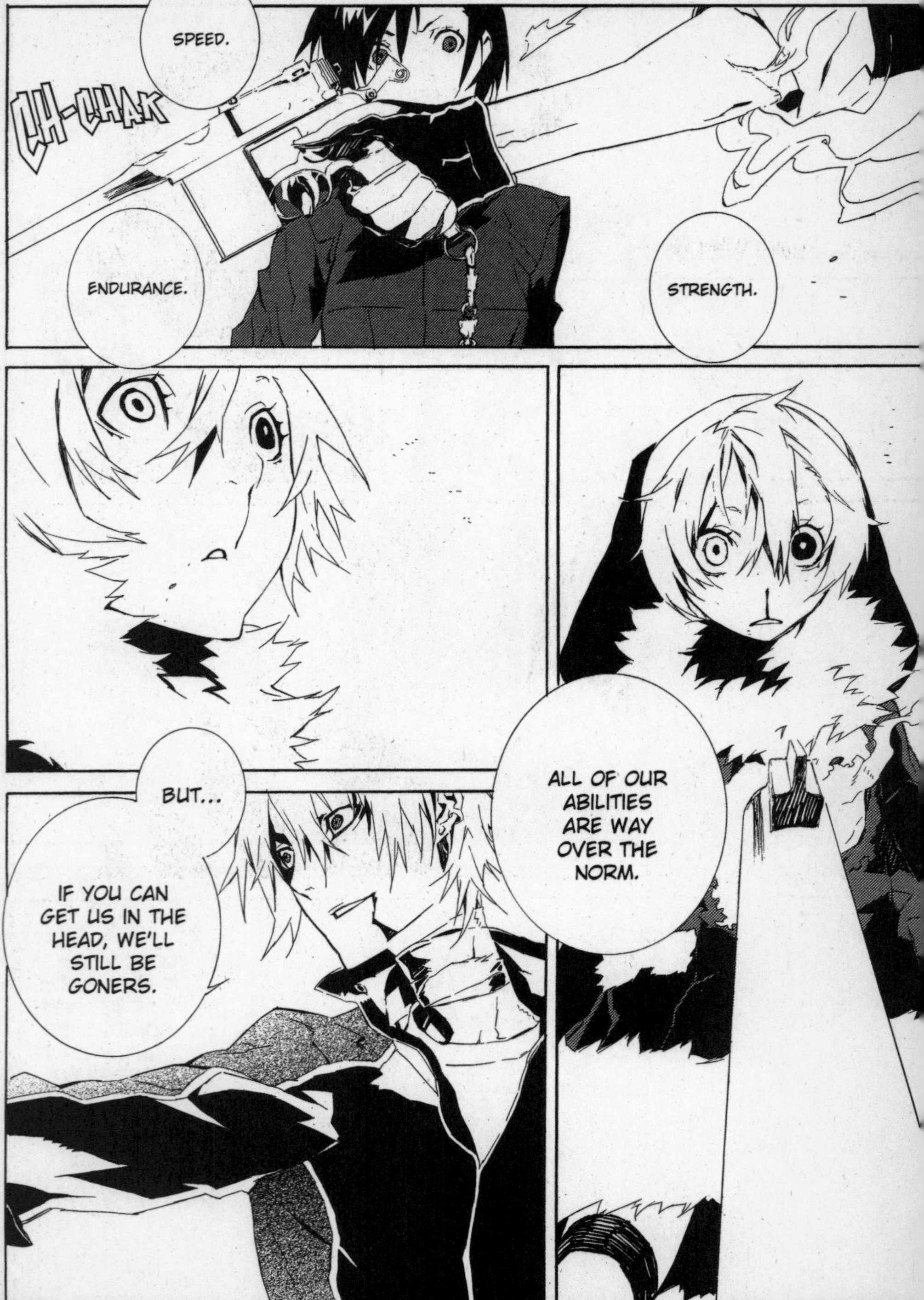
SPEED.
CH-CHAK
STRENGTH.
ENDURANCE.
ALL OF OUR ABILITIES ARE WAY OVER THE NORM.
BUT...
IF YOU CAN GET US IN THE HEAD, WE'LL STILL BE GONERS.

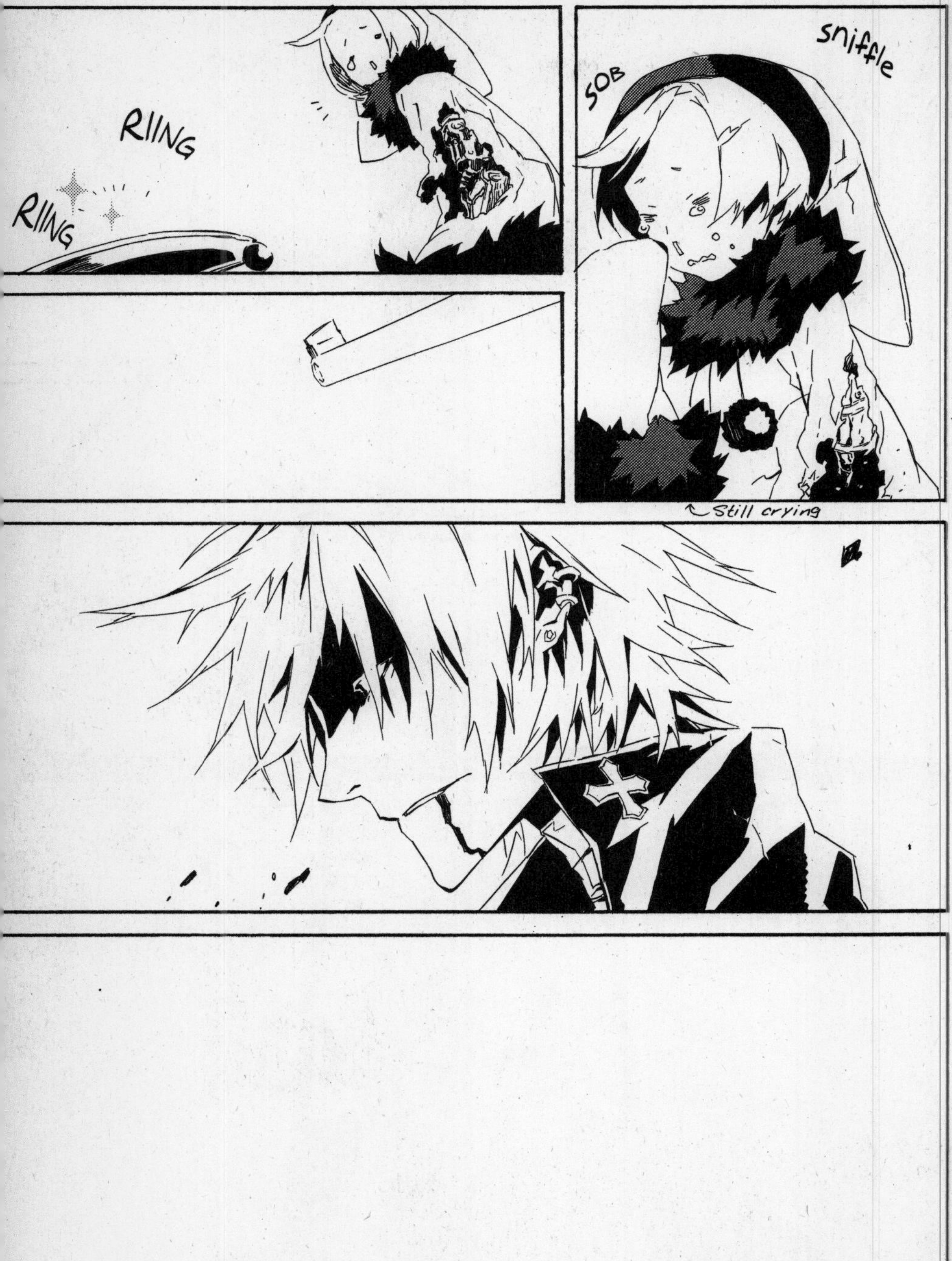
SOB
sniffle
Still crying
RIING
RIING

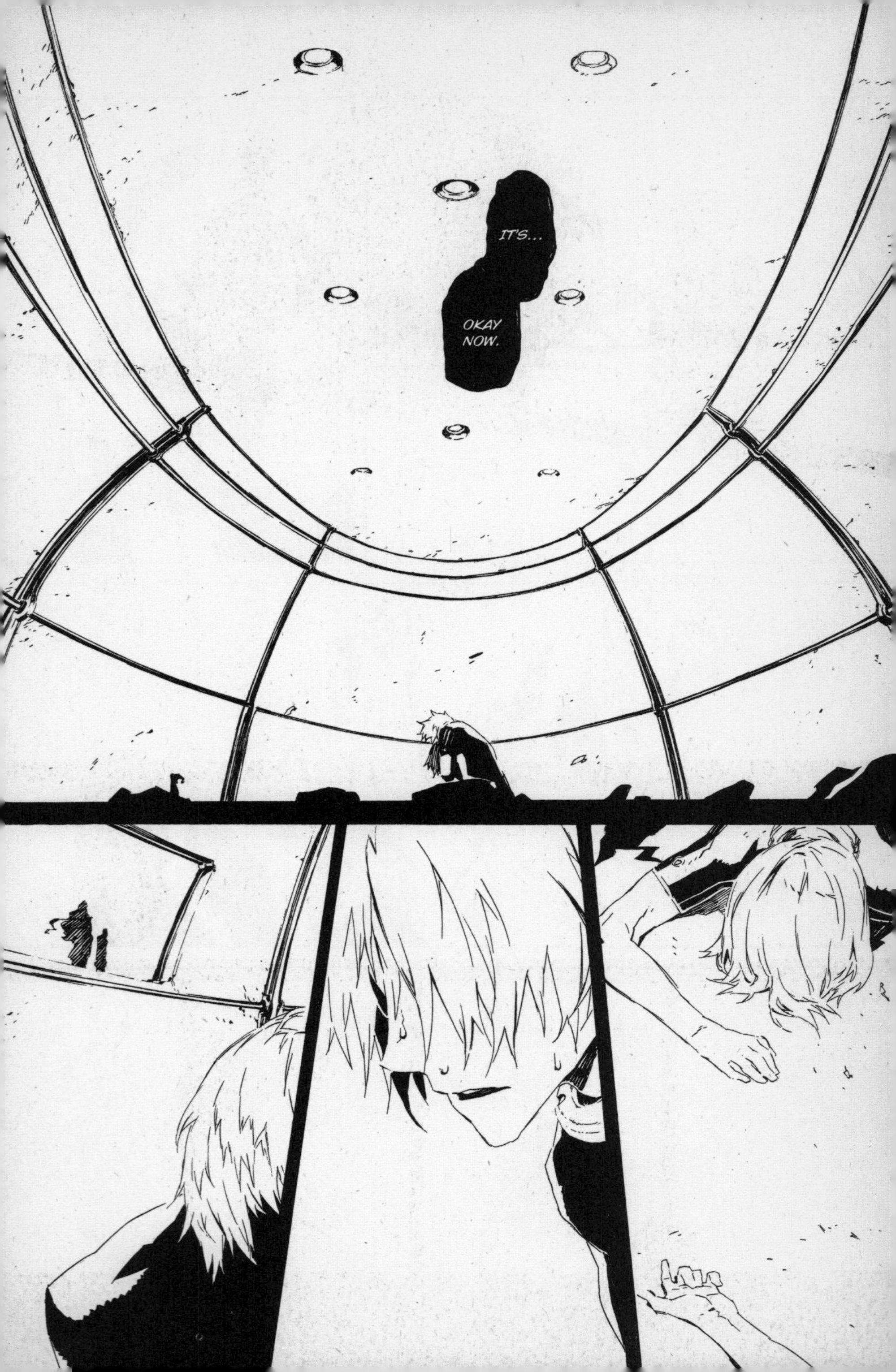
IT'S...
OKAY NOW.

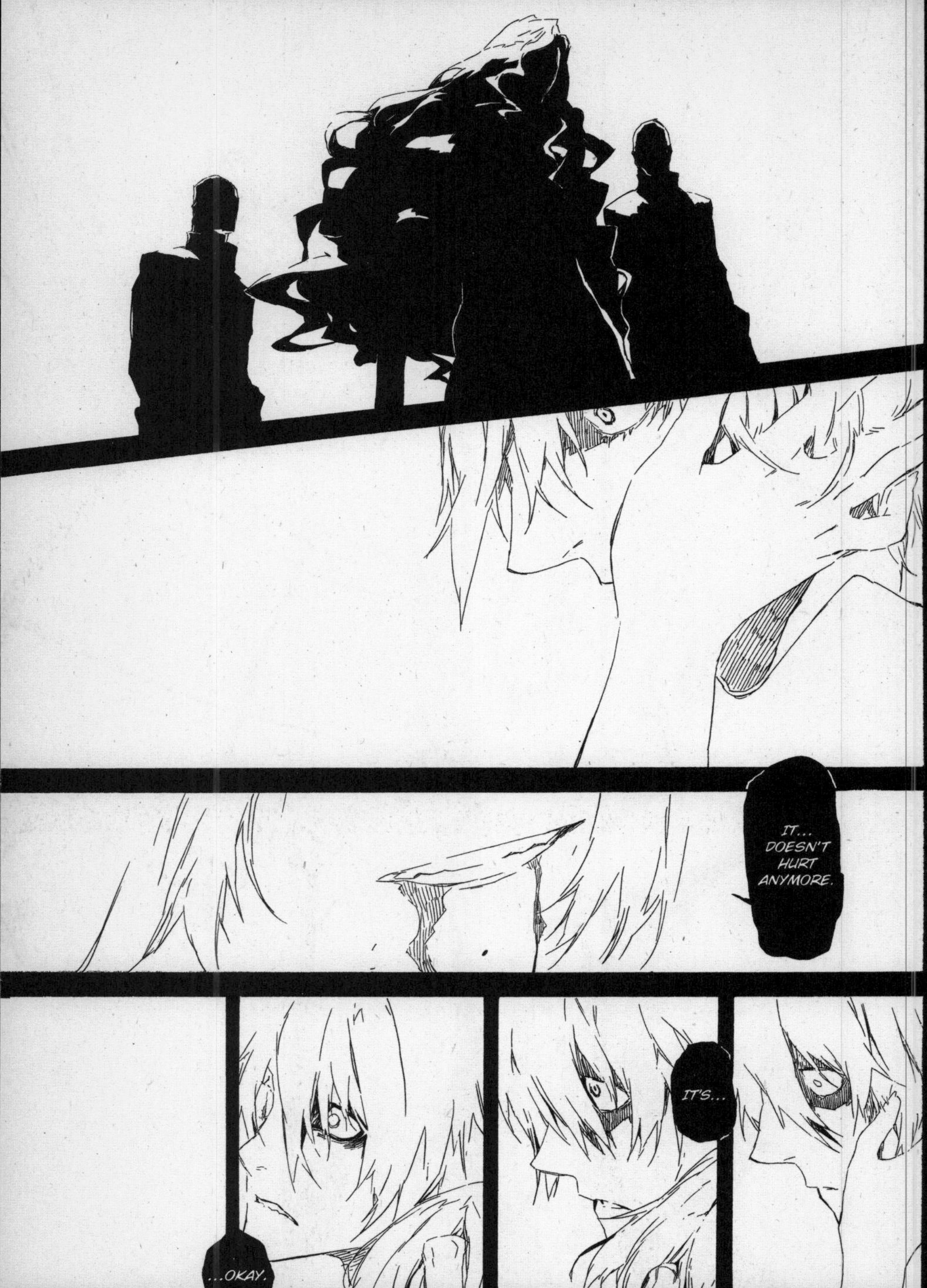
IT... DOESN'T HURT ANYMORE.
IT'S...
...OKAY.

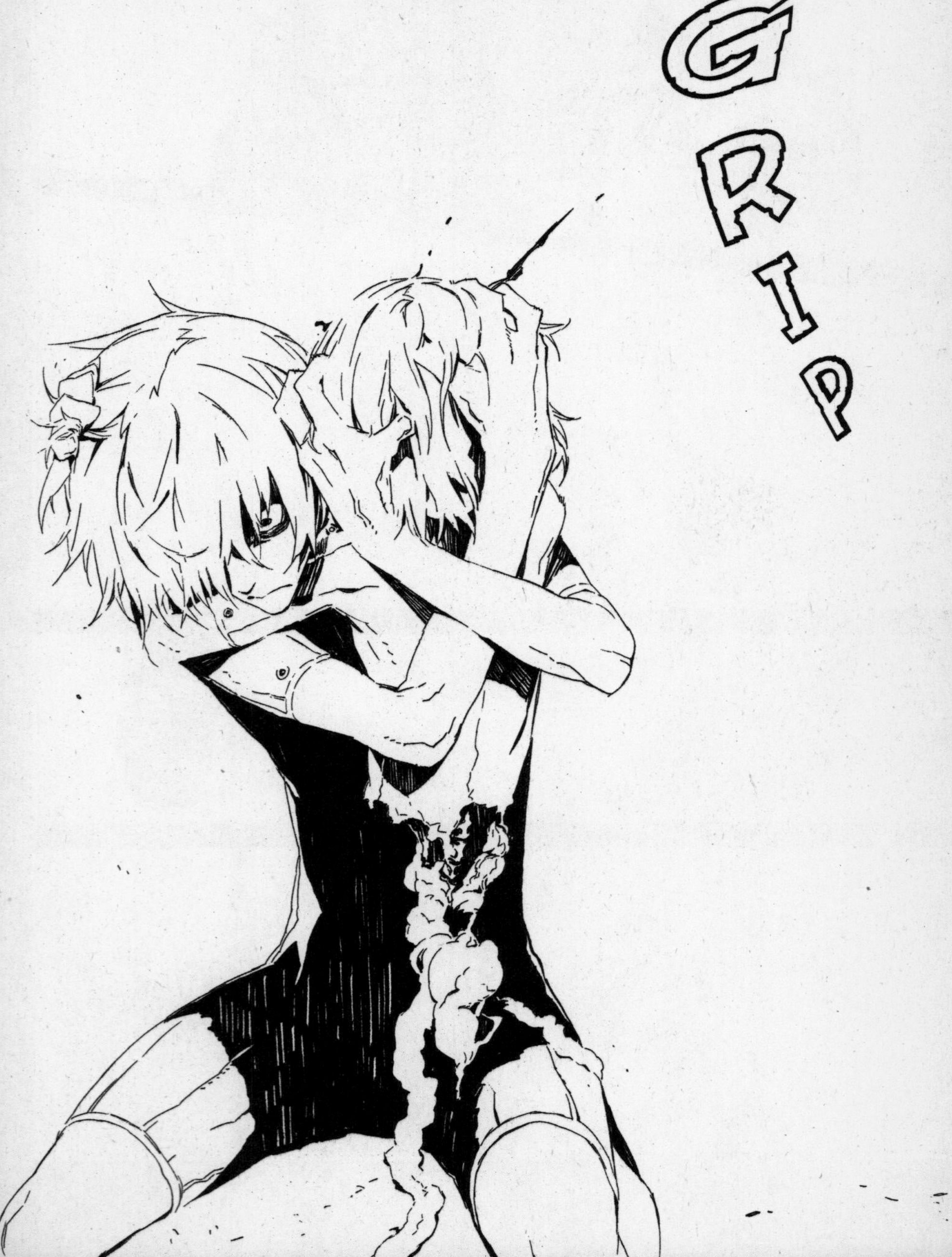
GRIP

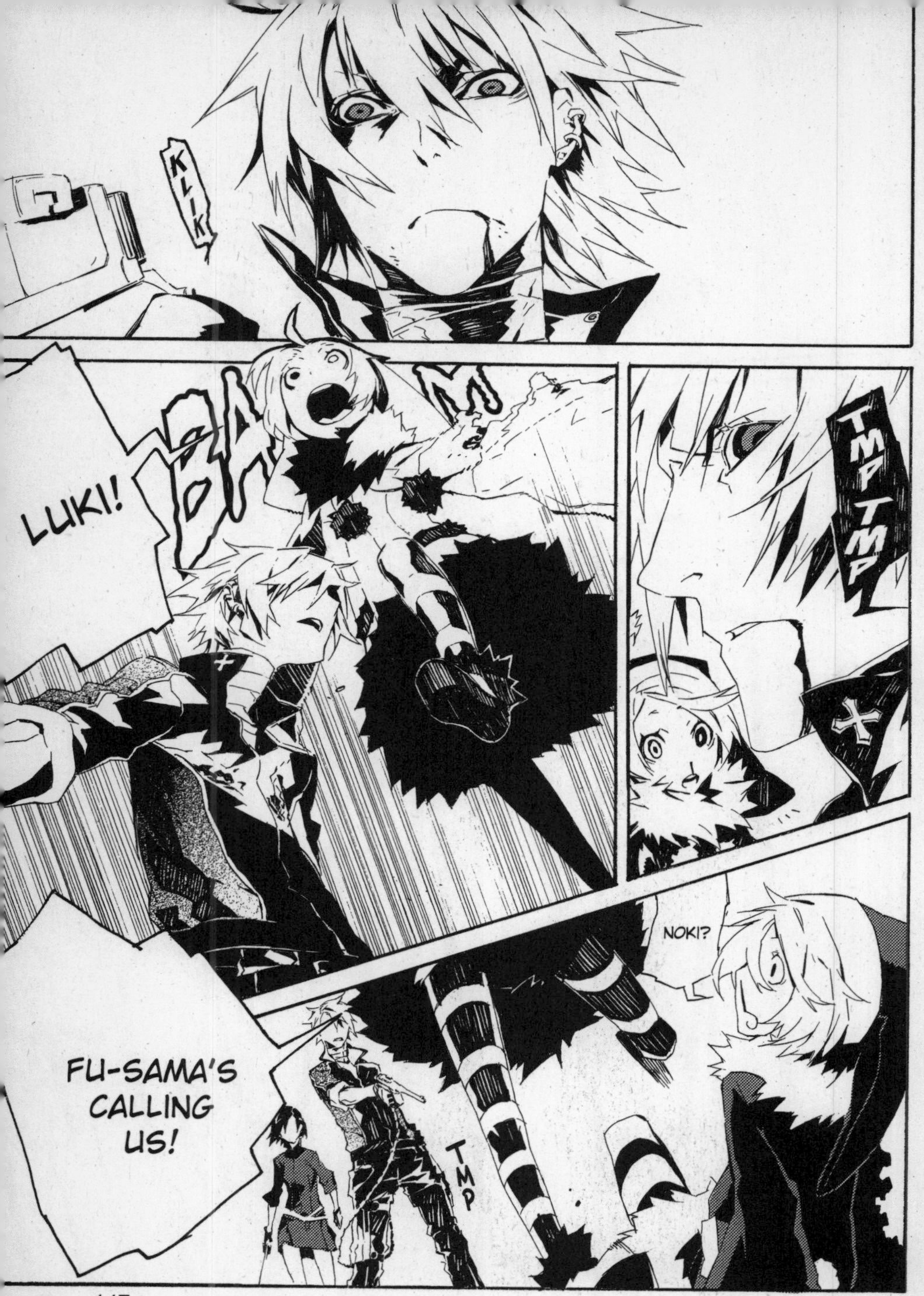
KLIK
TMP TMP TMP
LUKI!
NOKI?
FU-SAMA'S CALLING US!
TMP

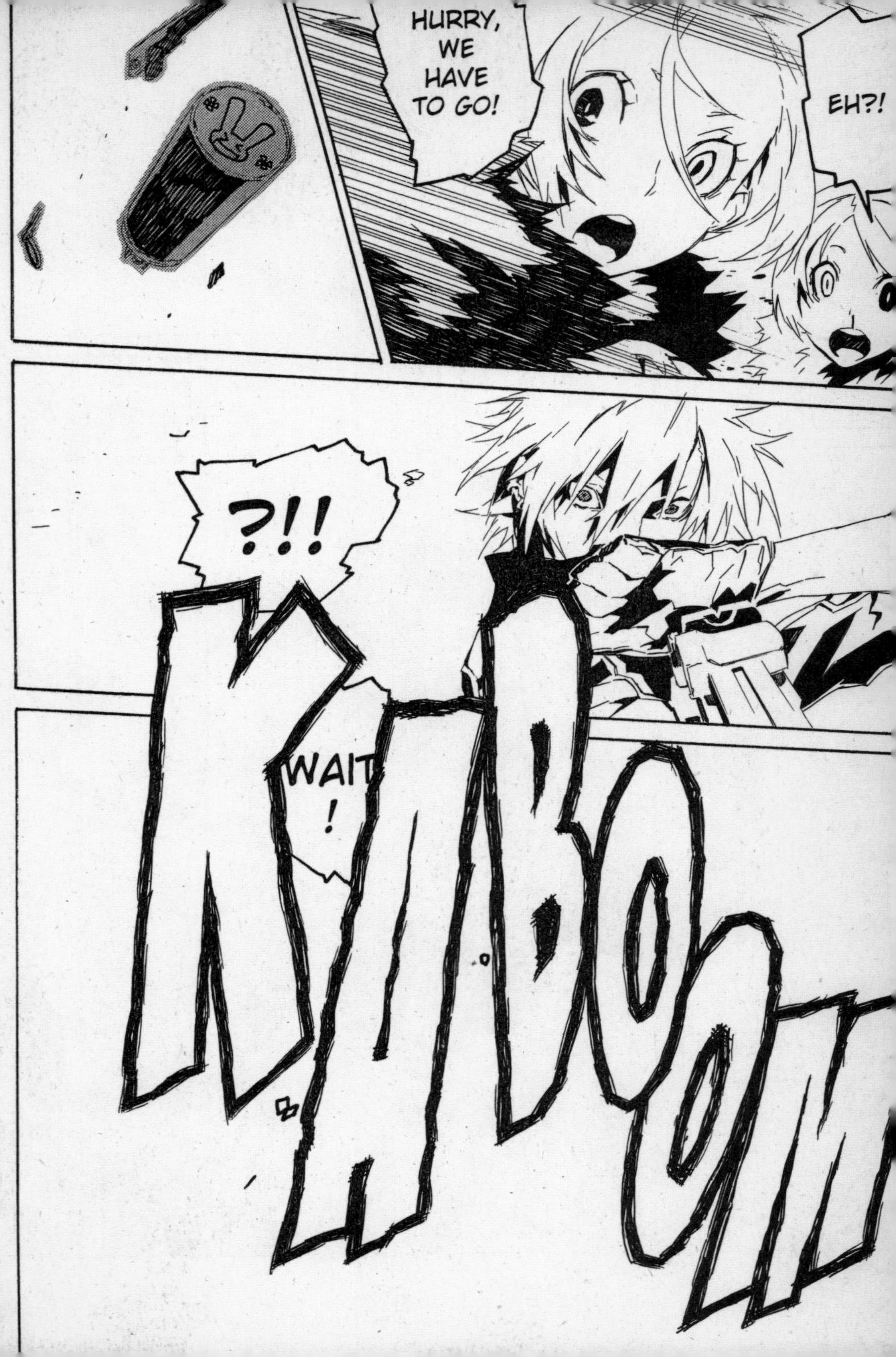
HURRY, WE HAVE TO GO!
EH?!
?!!
WAIT!
KABOOM

#20 Pink & Black VI

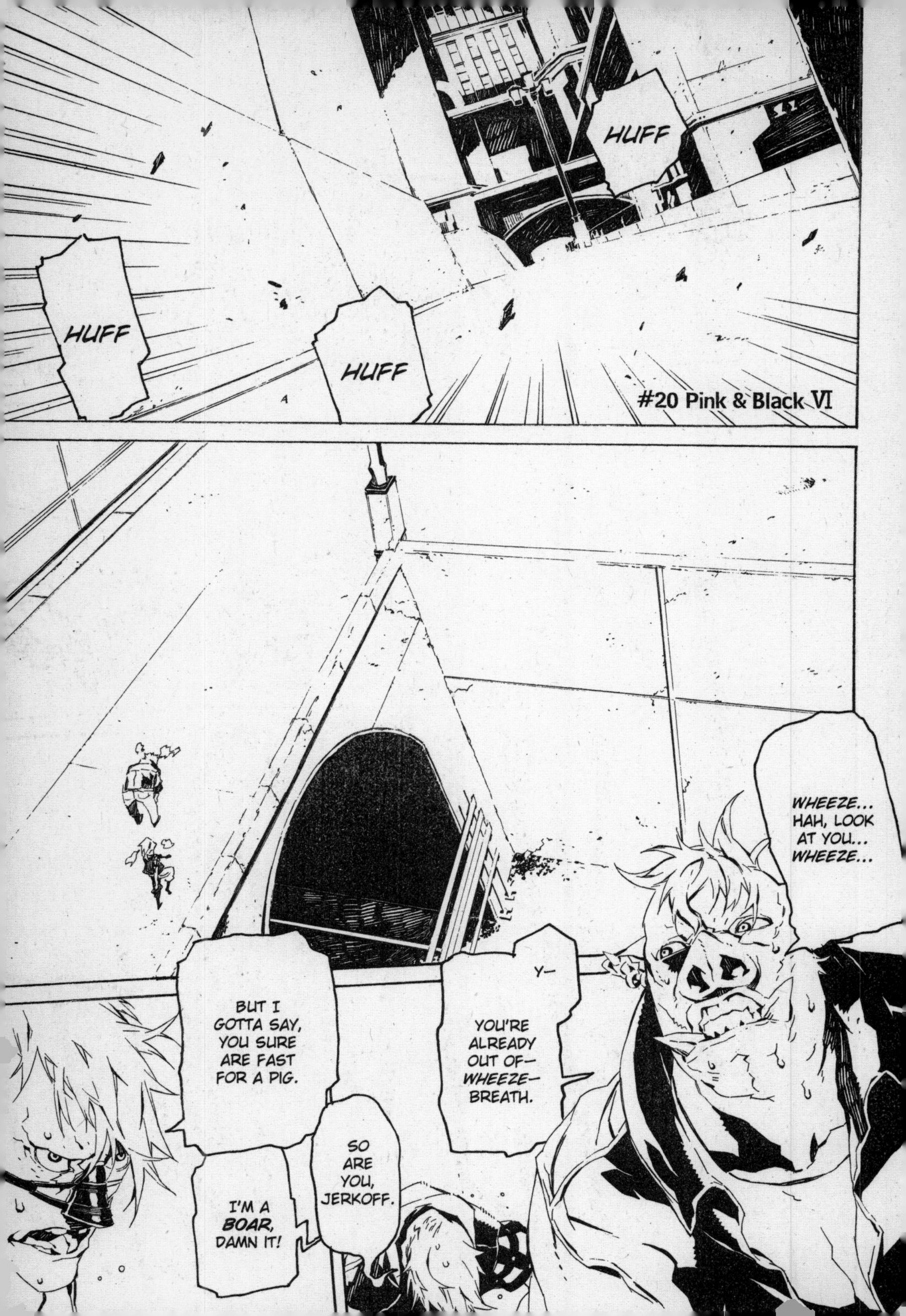
HUFF
HUFF
HUFF
WHEEZE... HAH, LOOK AT YOU... WHEEZE...
Y—
YOU'RE ALREADY OUT OF—WHEEZE—BREATH.
BUT I GOTTA SAY, YOU SURE ARE FAST FOR A PIG.
SO ARE YOU, JERKOFF.
I'M A *BOAR*, DAMN IT!

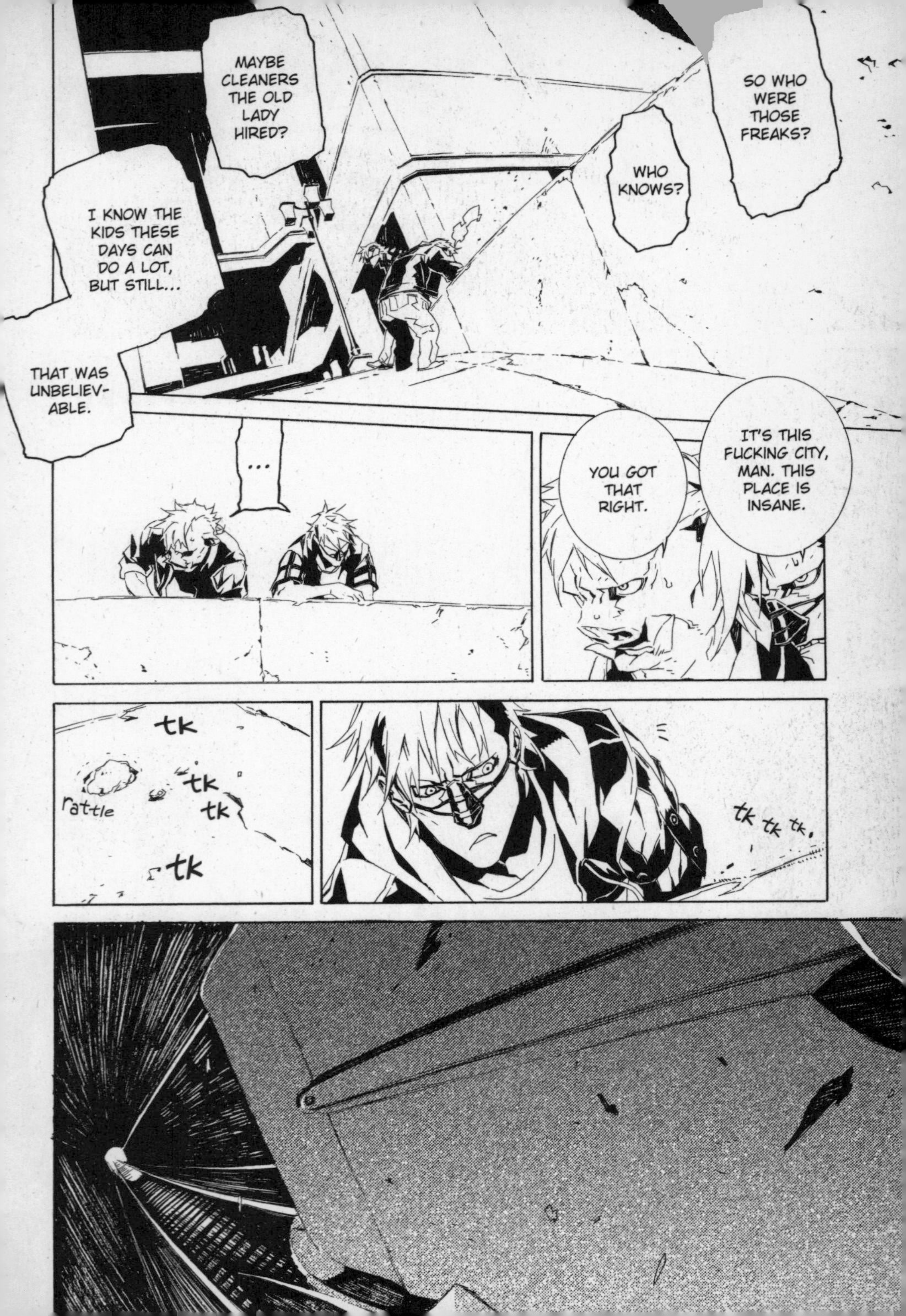
SO WHO WERE THOSE FREAKS?
WHO KNOWS?
MAYBE CLEANERS THE OLD LADY HIRED?
I KNOW THE KIDS THESE DAYS CAN DO A LOT, BUT STILL...
THAT WAS UNBELIEVABLE.
IT'S THIS FUCKING CITY, MAN. THIS PLACE IS INSANE.
YOU GOT THAT RIGHT.
...
tk tk tk.
tk
tk
tk
rattle
tk

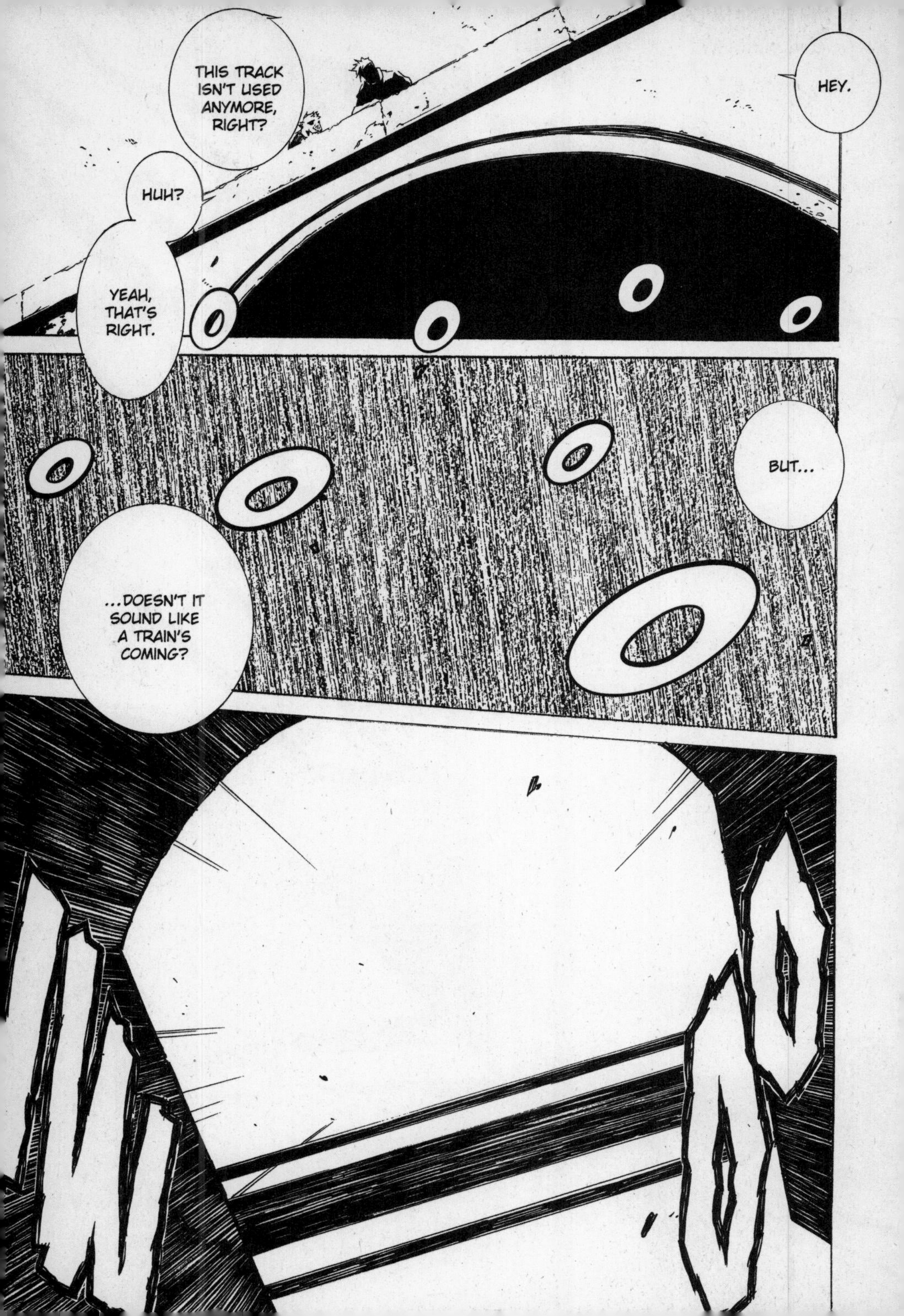
HEY.
THIS TRACK ISN'T USED ANYMORE, RIGHT?
HUH?
YEAH, THAT'S RIGHT.
BUT...
...DOESN'T IT SOUND LIKE A TRAIN'S COMING?

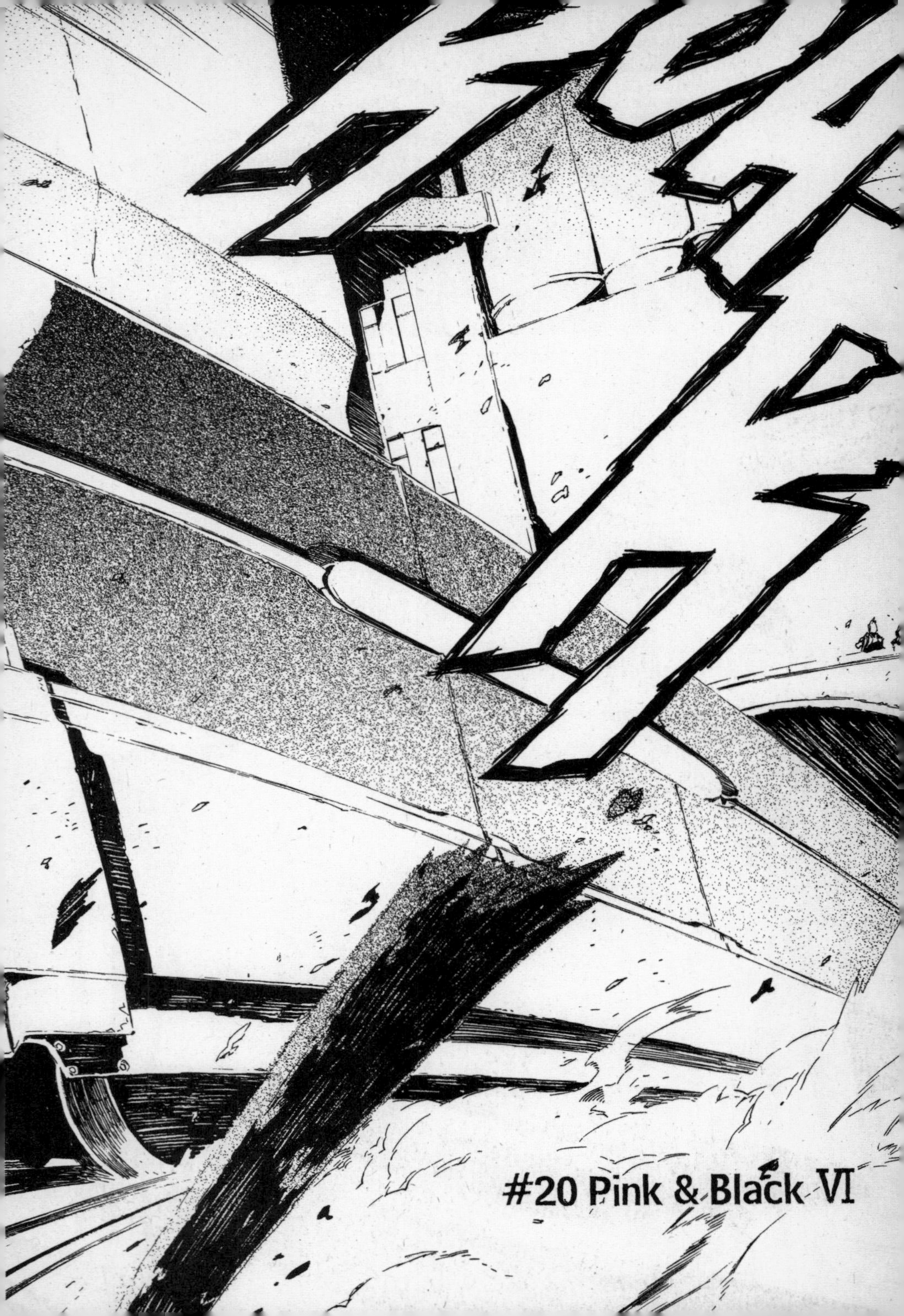

#20 Pink & Black VI

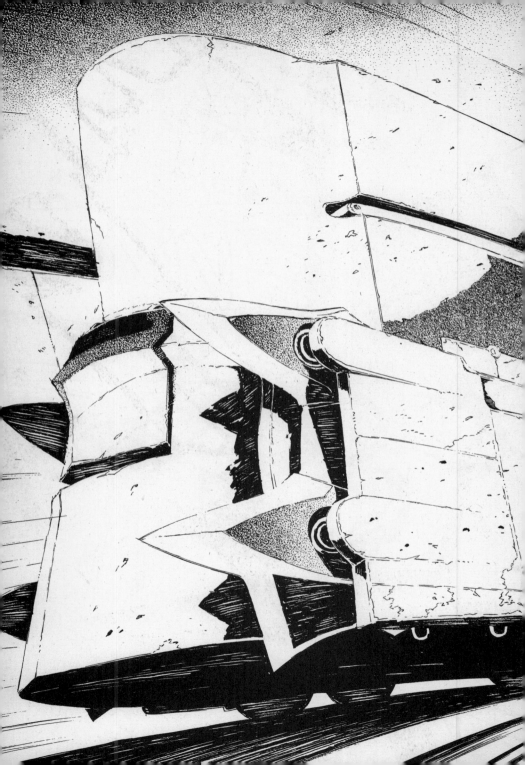

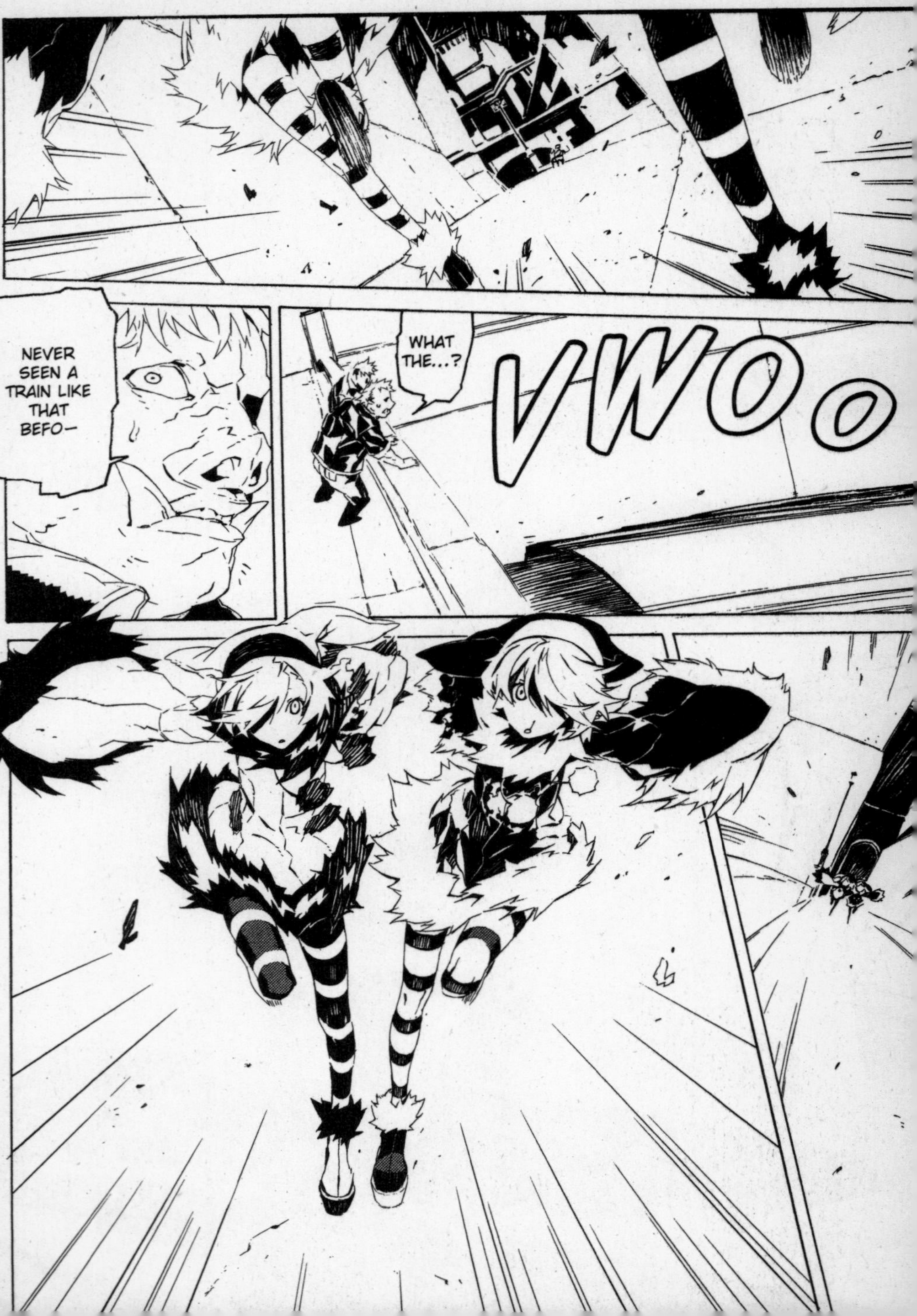
WHAT THE...?
VWOO
NEVER SEEN A TRAIN LIKE THAT BEFO–

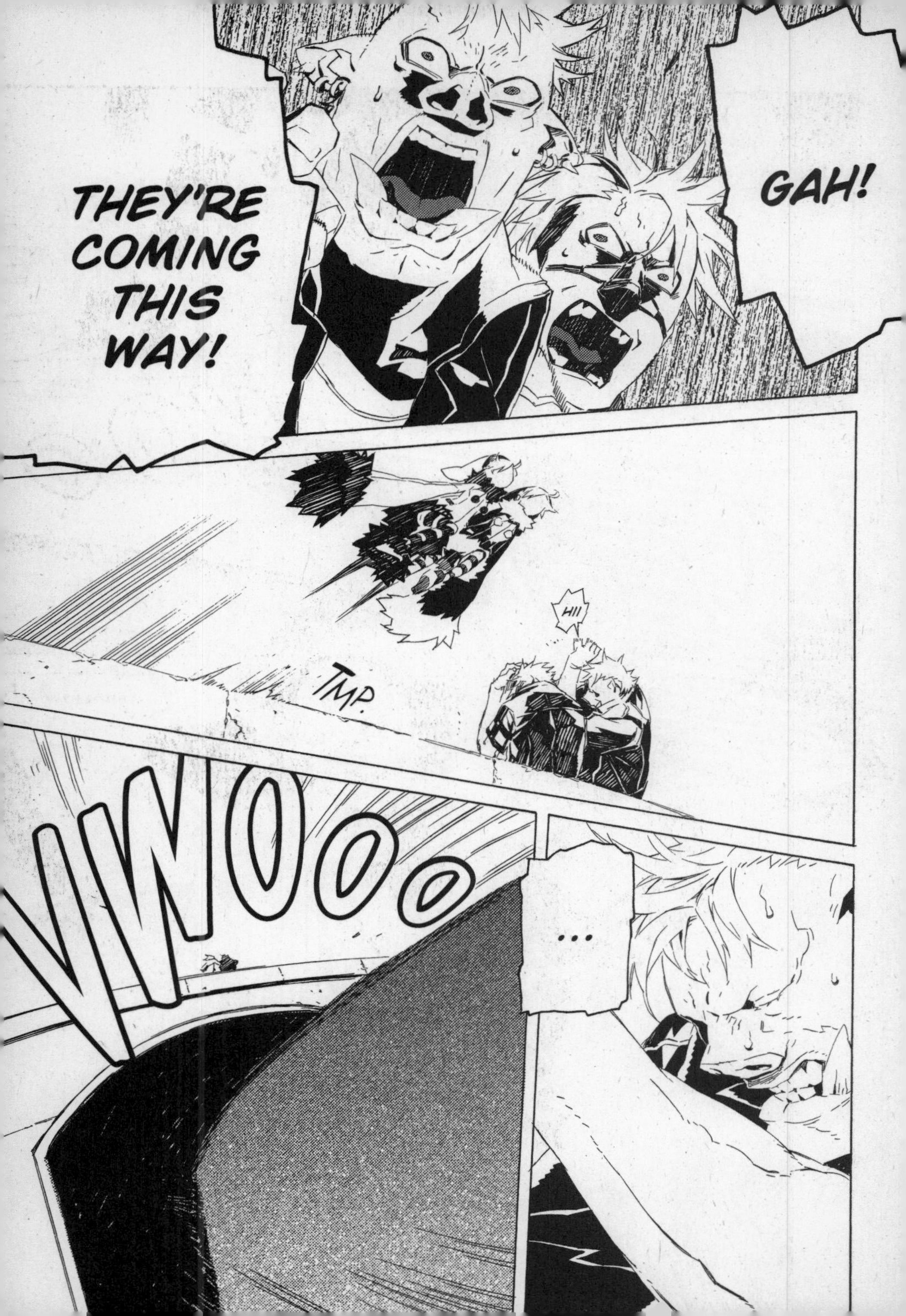
GAH!
THEY'RE COMING THIS WAY!
HII
TMP.
...
VWOOOO

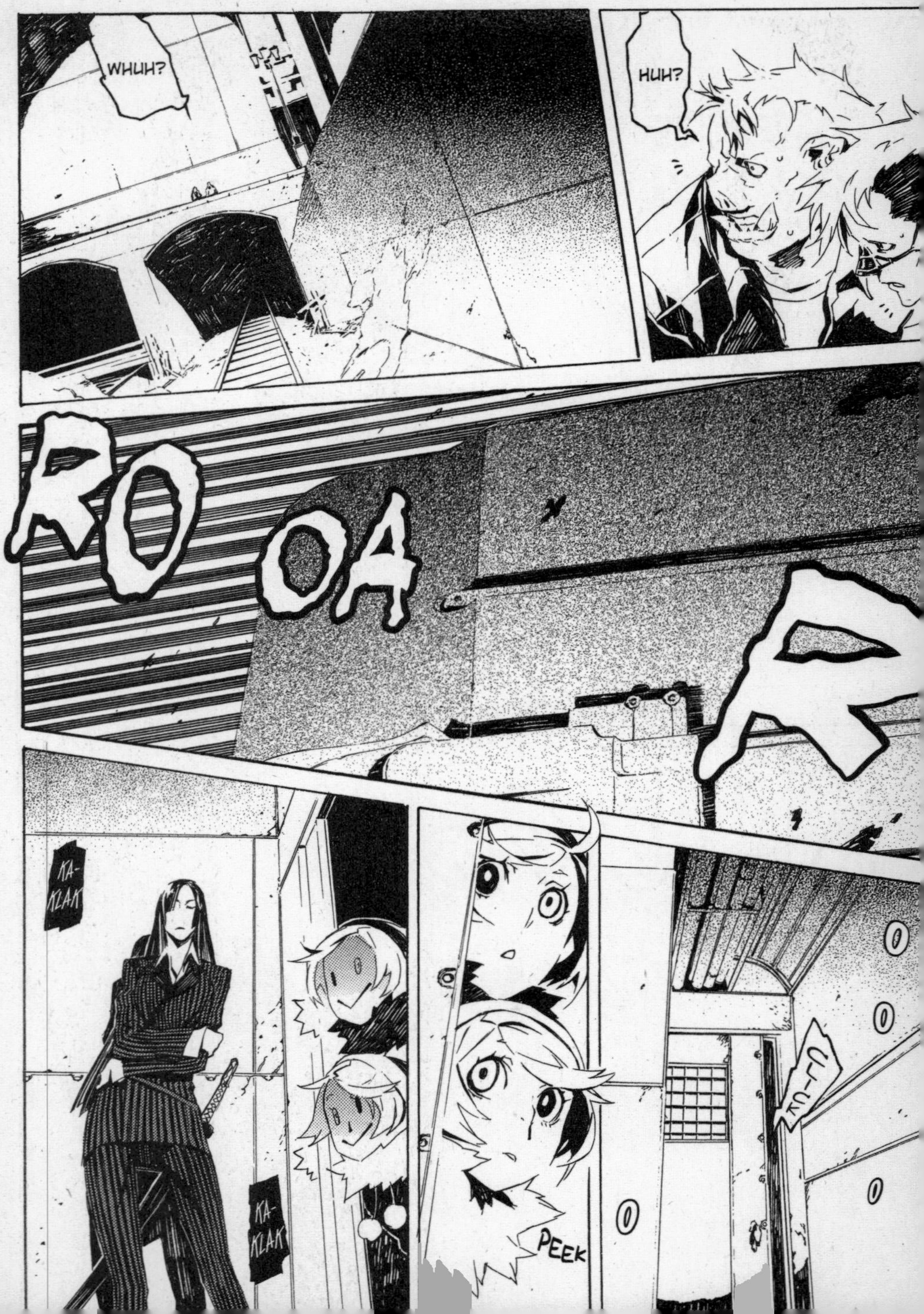
HUH?
WHUH?
ROOAR
KU-LU
PEEK
KA-KLAK
KA-KLAK

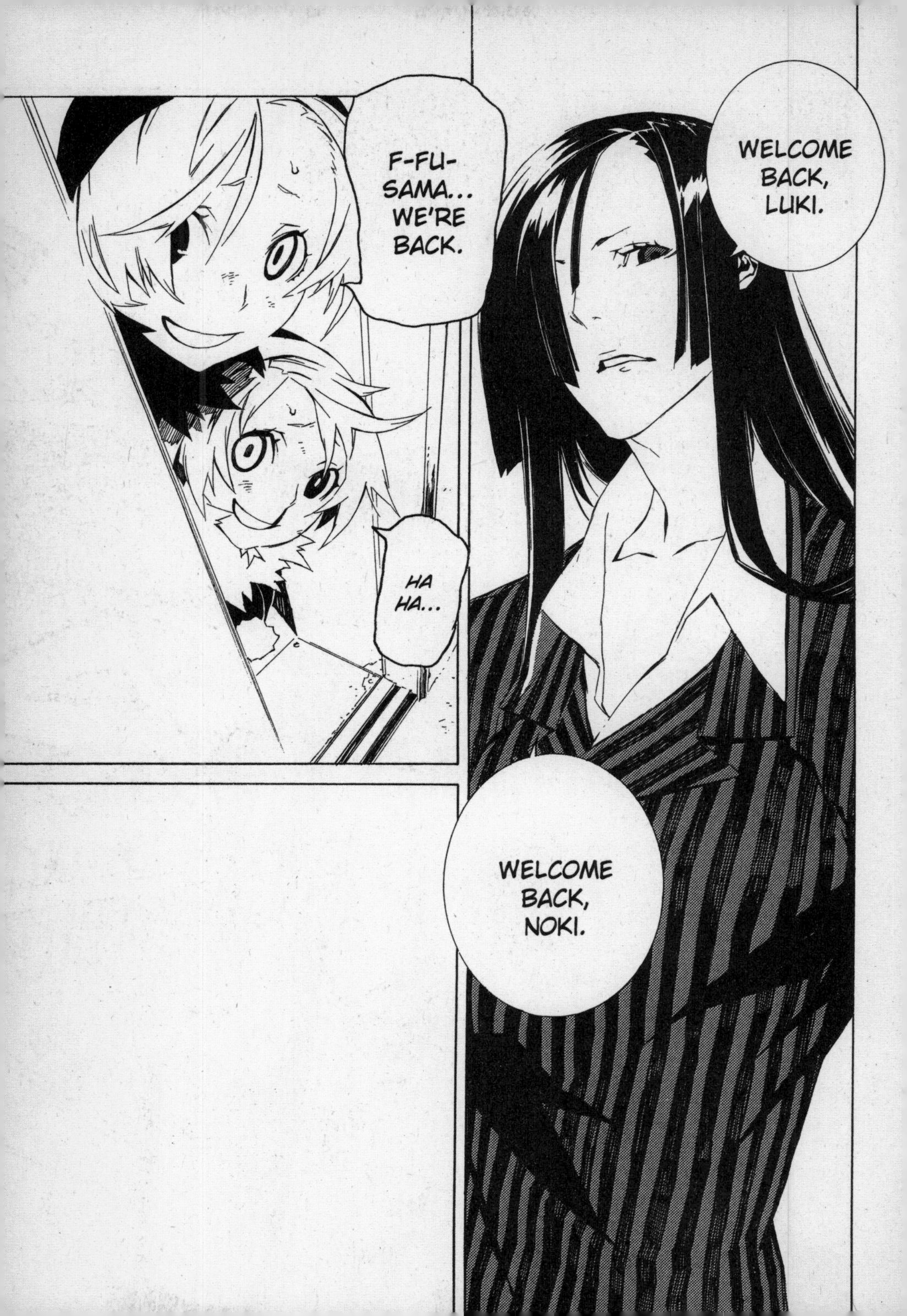
WELCOME BACK, LUKI.
WELCOME BACK, NOKI.
F-FU-SAMA... WE'RE BACK.
HA HA...

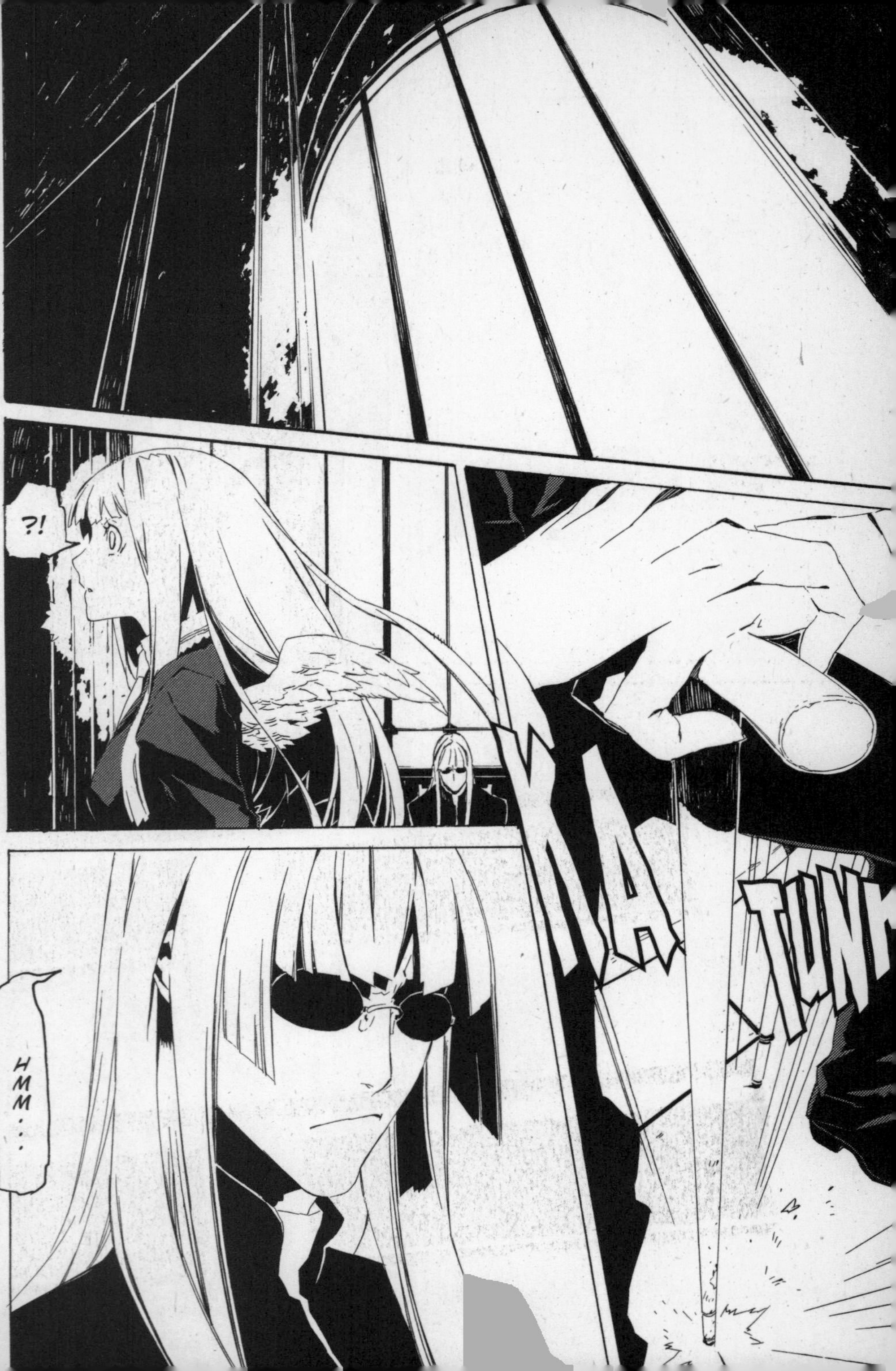
?!
TUNK
HMM...

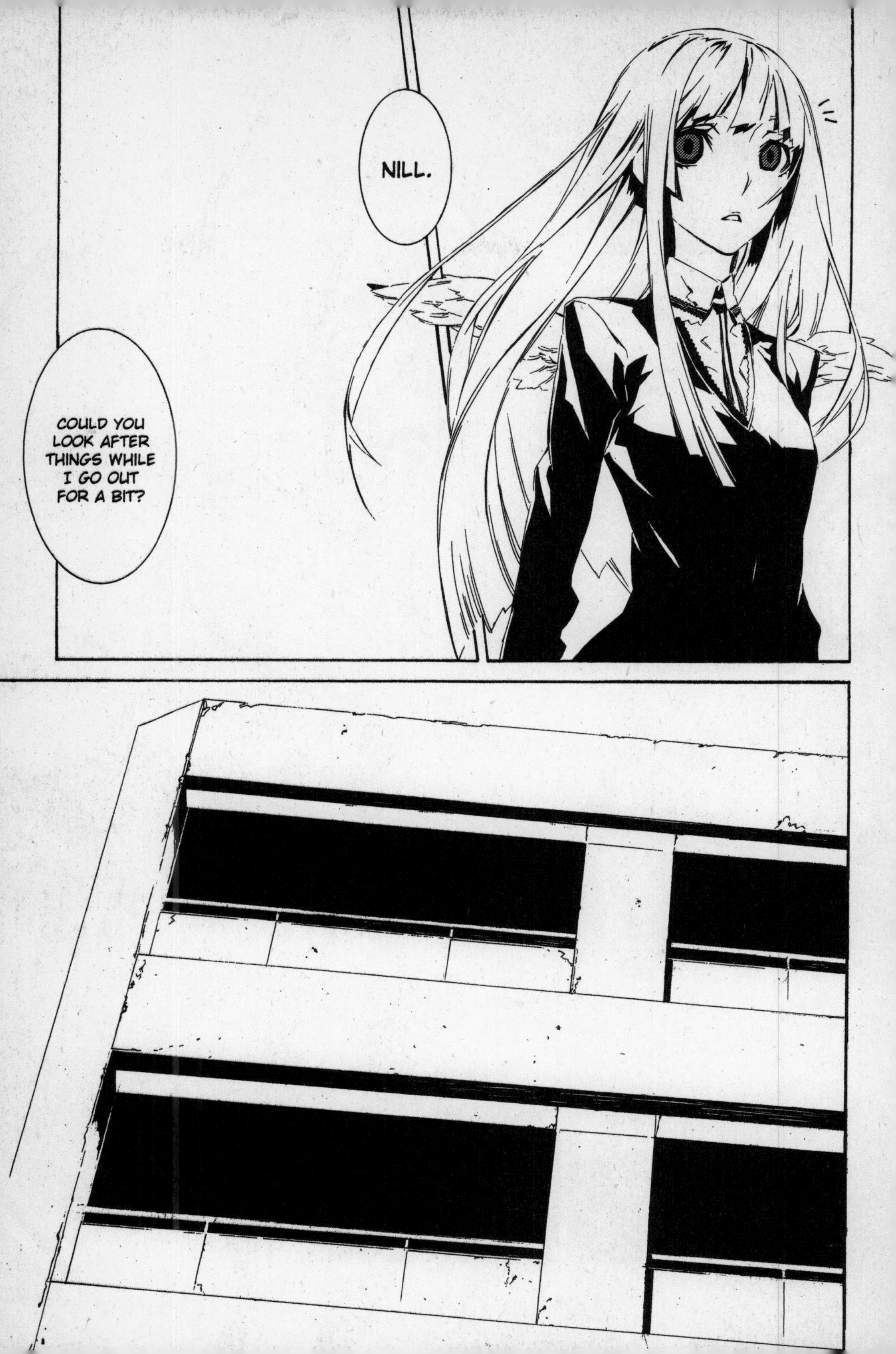
NILL.
COULD YOU LOOK AFTER THINGS WHILE I GO OUT FOR A BIT?

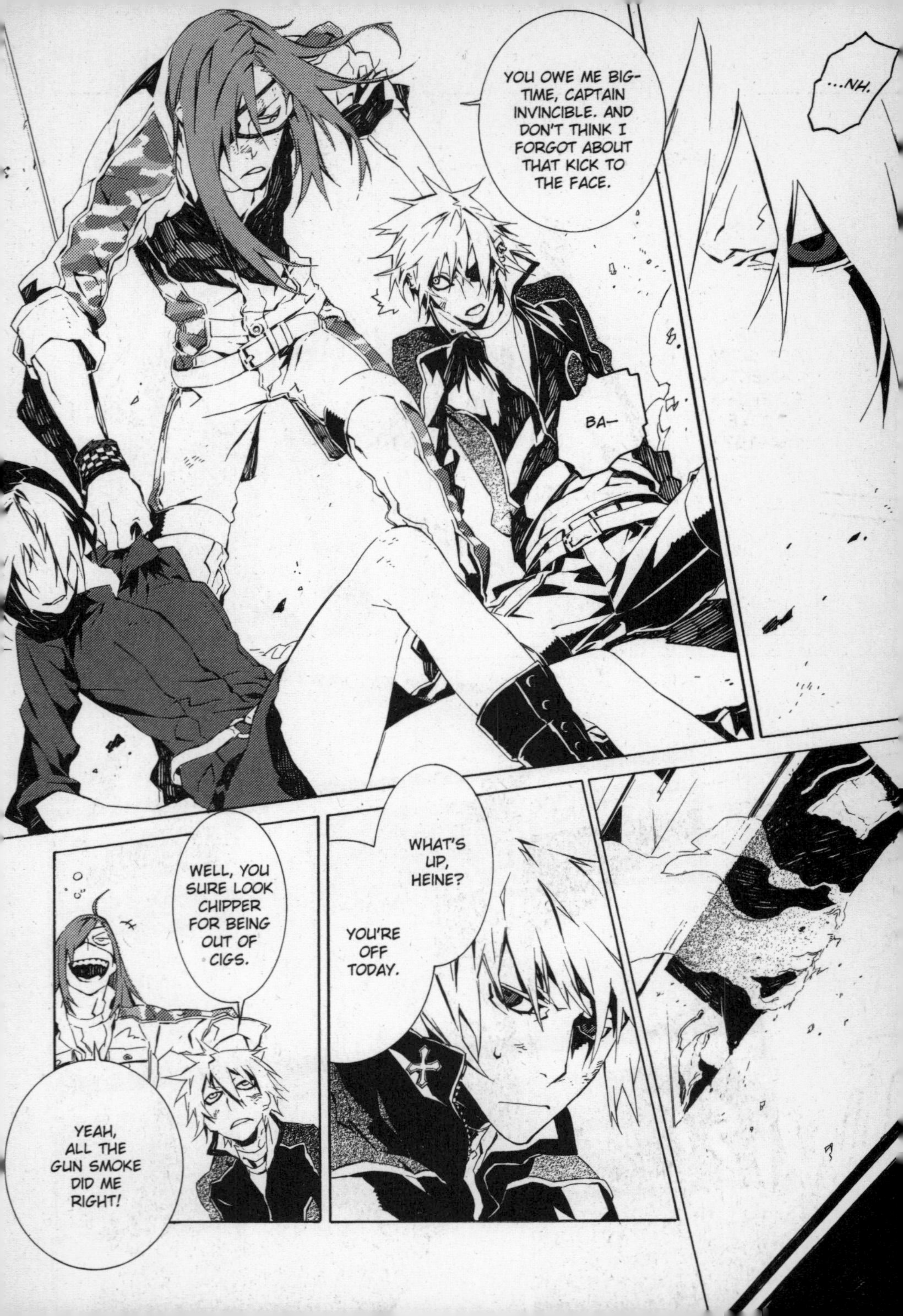
...NH.
YOU OWE ME BIG-TIME, CAPTAIN INVINCIBLE. AND DON'T THINK I FORGOT ABOUT THAT KICK TO THE FACE.
BA—
WHAT'S UP, HEINE?
YOU'RE OFF TODAY.
WELL, YOU SURE LOOK CHIPPER FOR BEING OUT OF CIGS.
YEAH, ALL THE GUN SMOKE DID ME RIGHT!

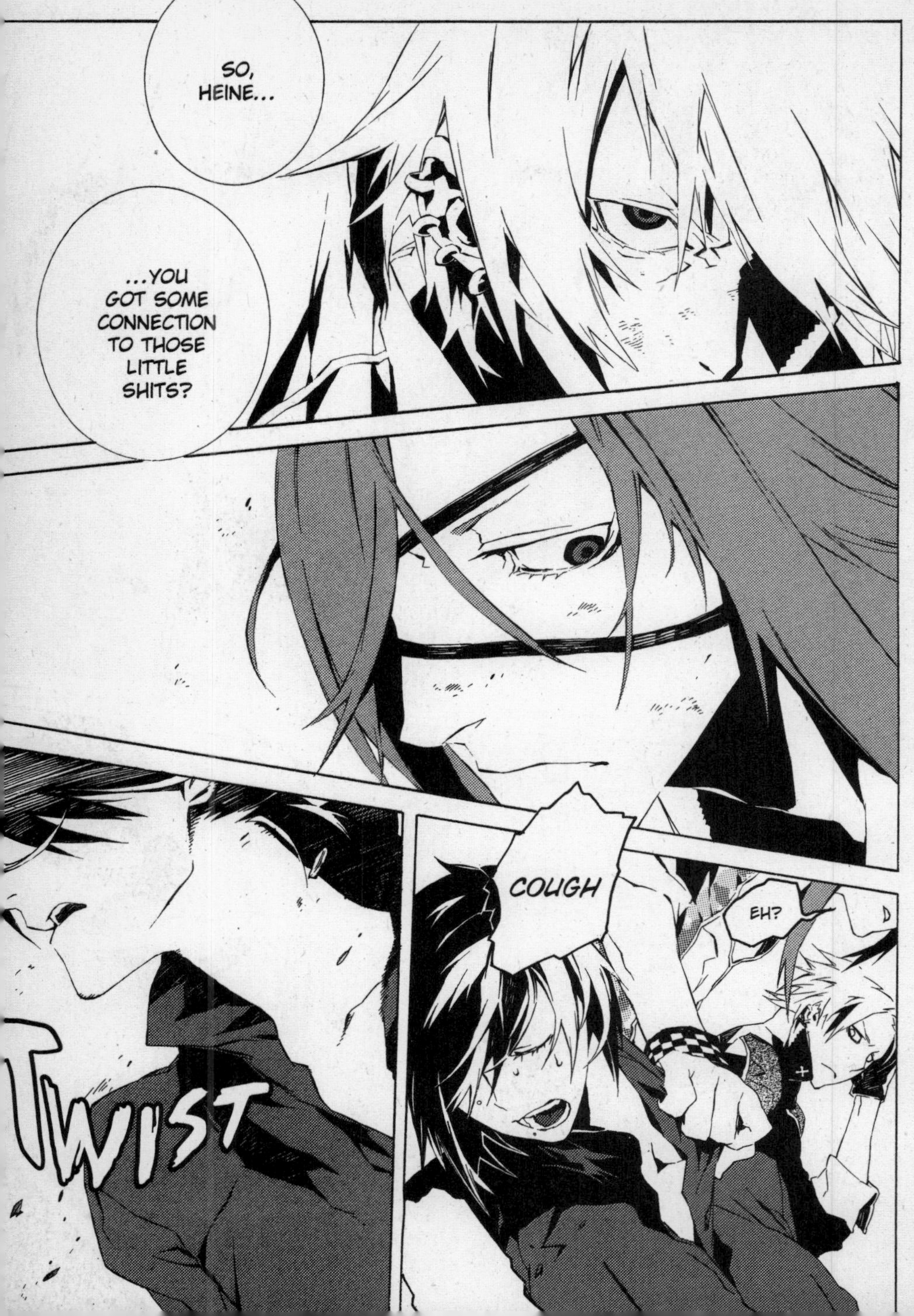
SO, HEINE...
...YOU GOT SOME CONNECTION TO THOSE LITTLE SHITS?
COUGH
EH?
TWIST

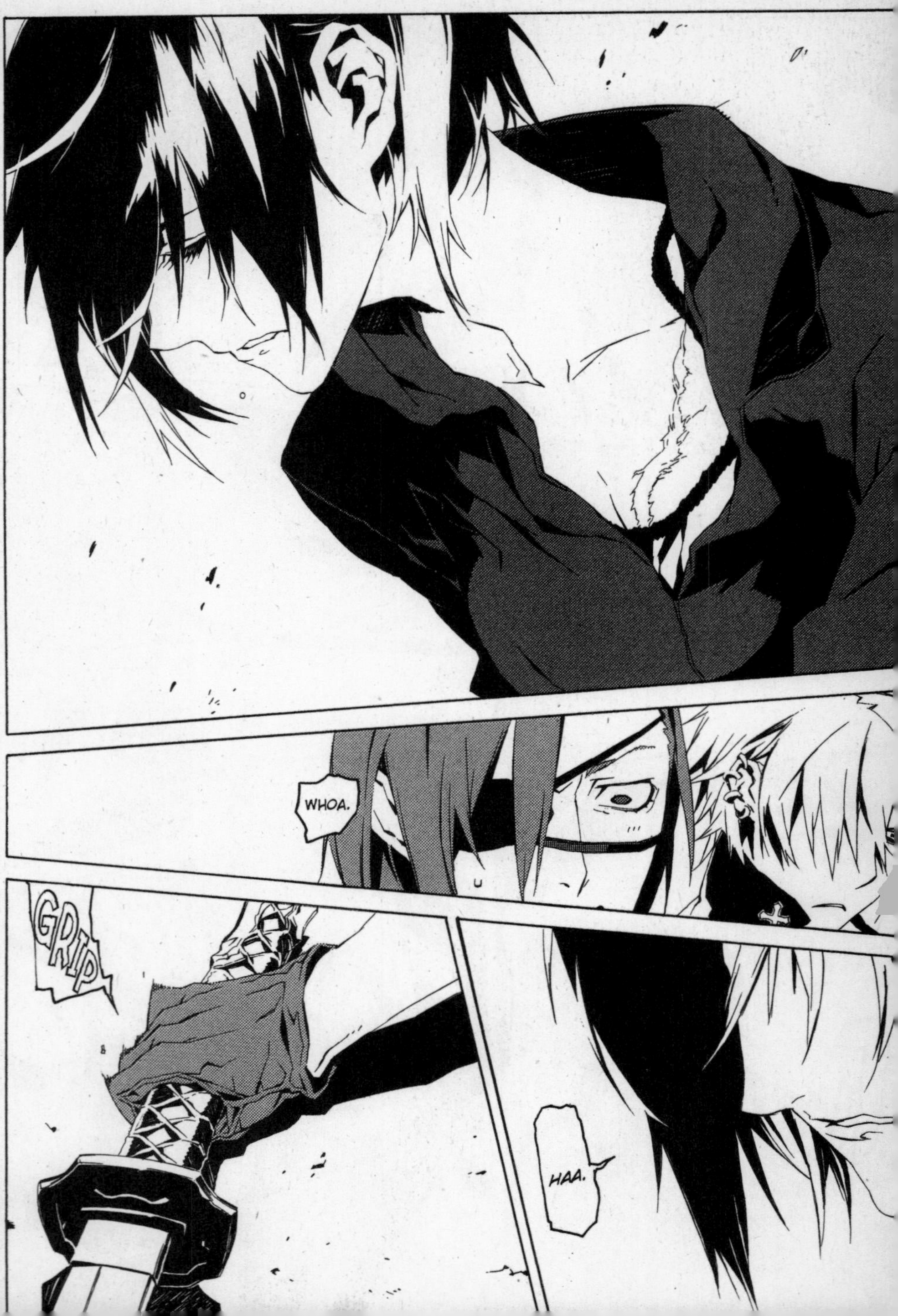
WHOA.
HAA.
GRIP

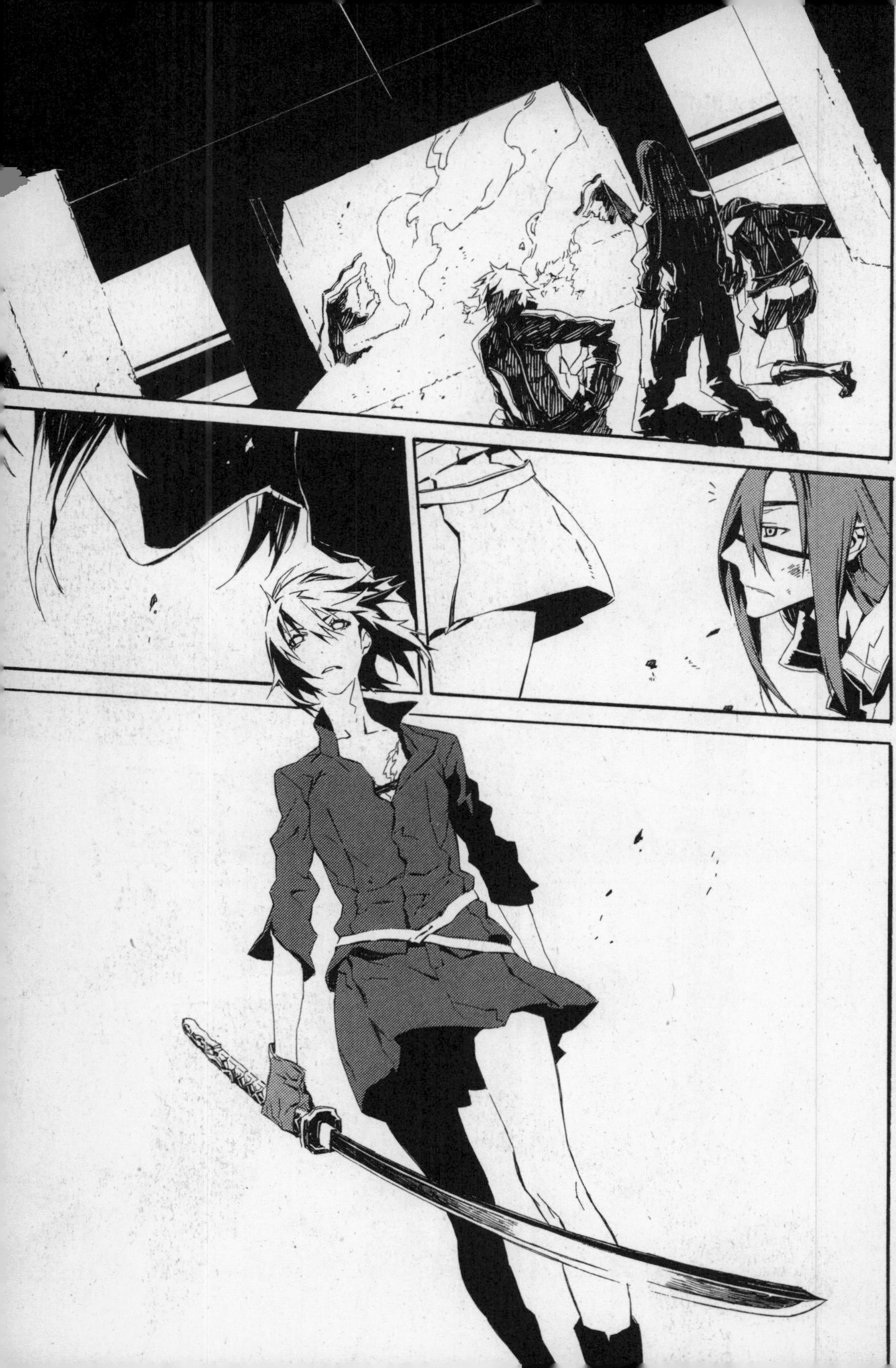

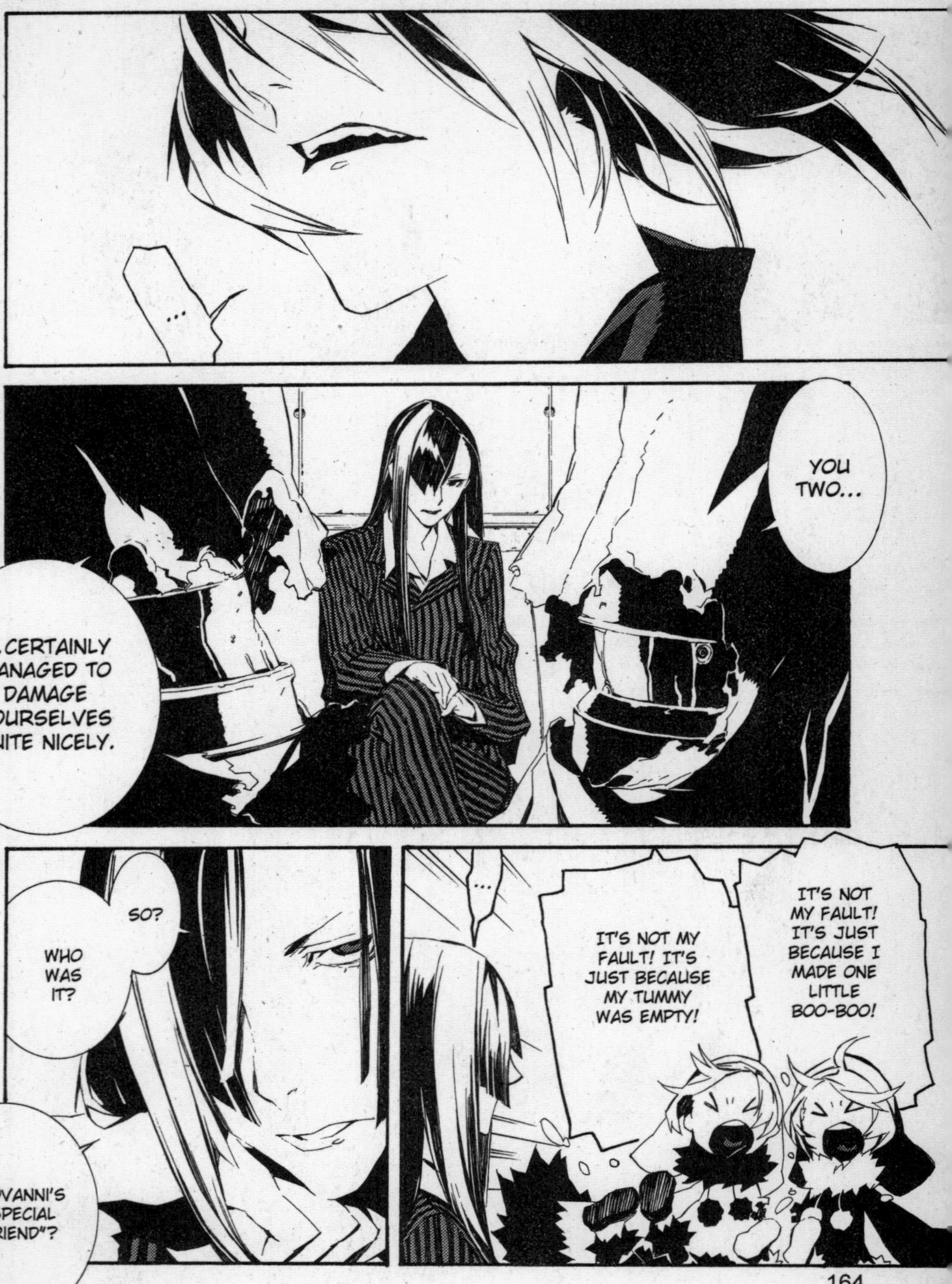
...
YOU TWO...
...CERTAINLY MANAGED TO DAMAGE YOURSELVES QUITE NICELY.
IT'S NOT MY FAULT! IT'S JUST BECAUSE I MADE ONE LITTLE BOO-BOO!
IT'S NOT MY FAULT! IT'S JUST BECAUSE MY TUMMY WAS EMPTY!
...
SO?
WHO WAS IT?
GIOVANNI'S "SPECIAL FRIEND"?

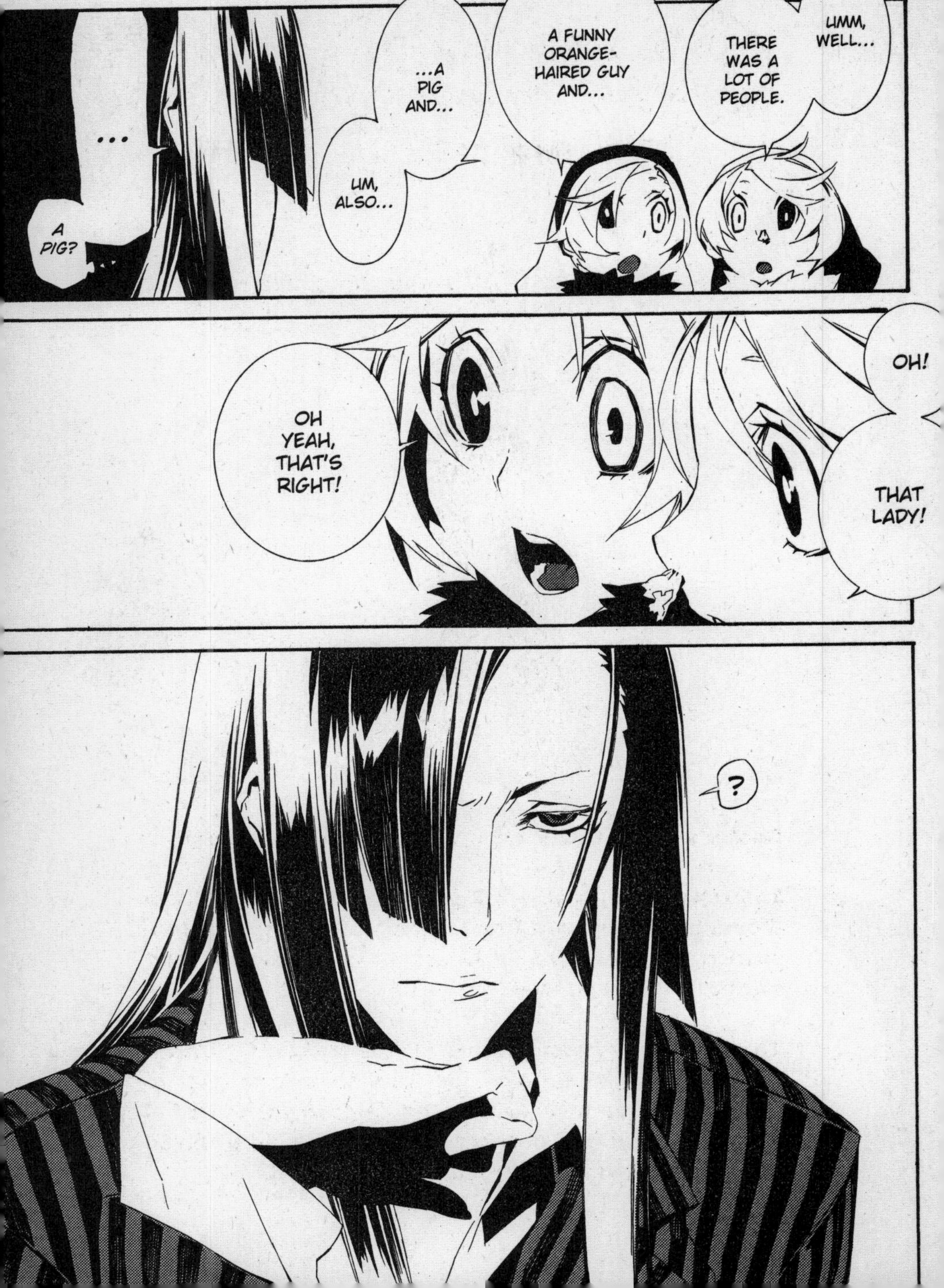
UMM, WELL...
THERE WAS A LOT OF PEOPLE.
A FUNNY ORANGE-HAIRED GUY AND...
UM, ALSO...
...A PIG AND...
...
A PIG?
OH!
THAT LADY!
OH YEAH, THAT'S RIGHT!
?

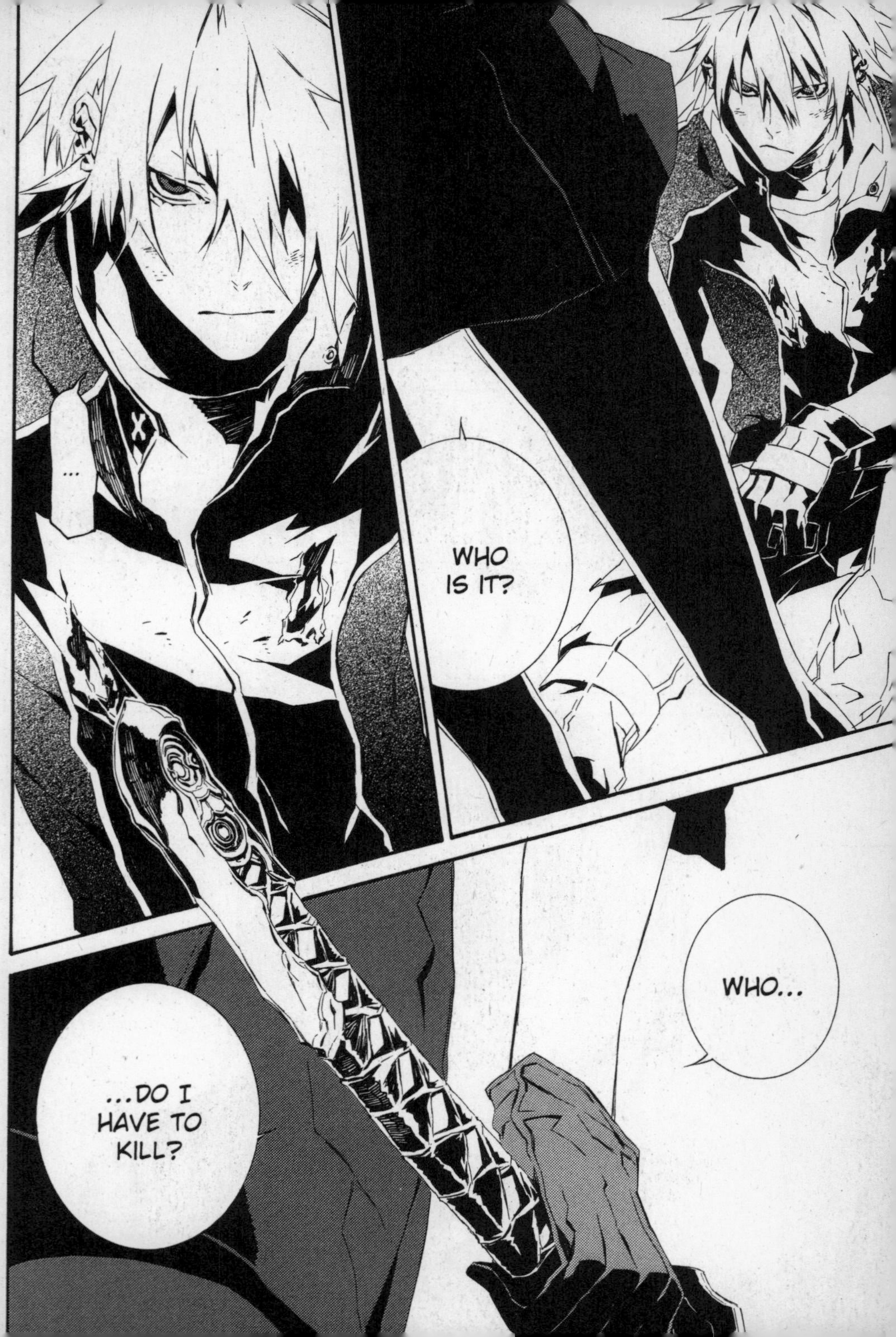
WHO IS IT?
...
WHO...
...DO I HAVE TO KILL?

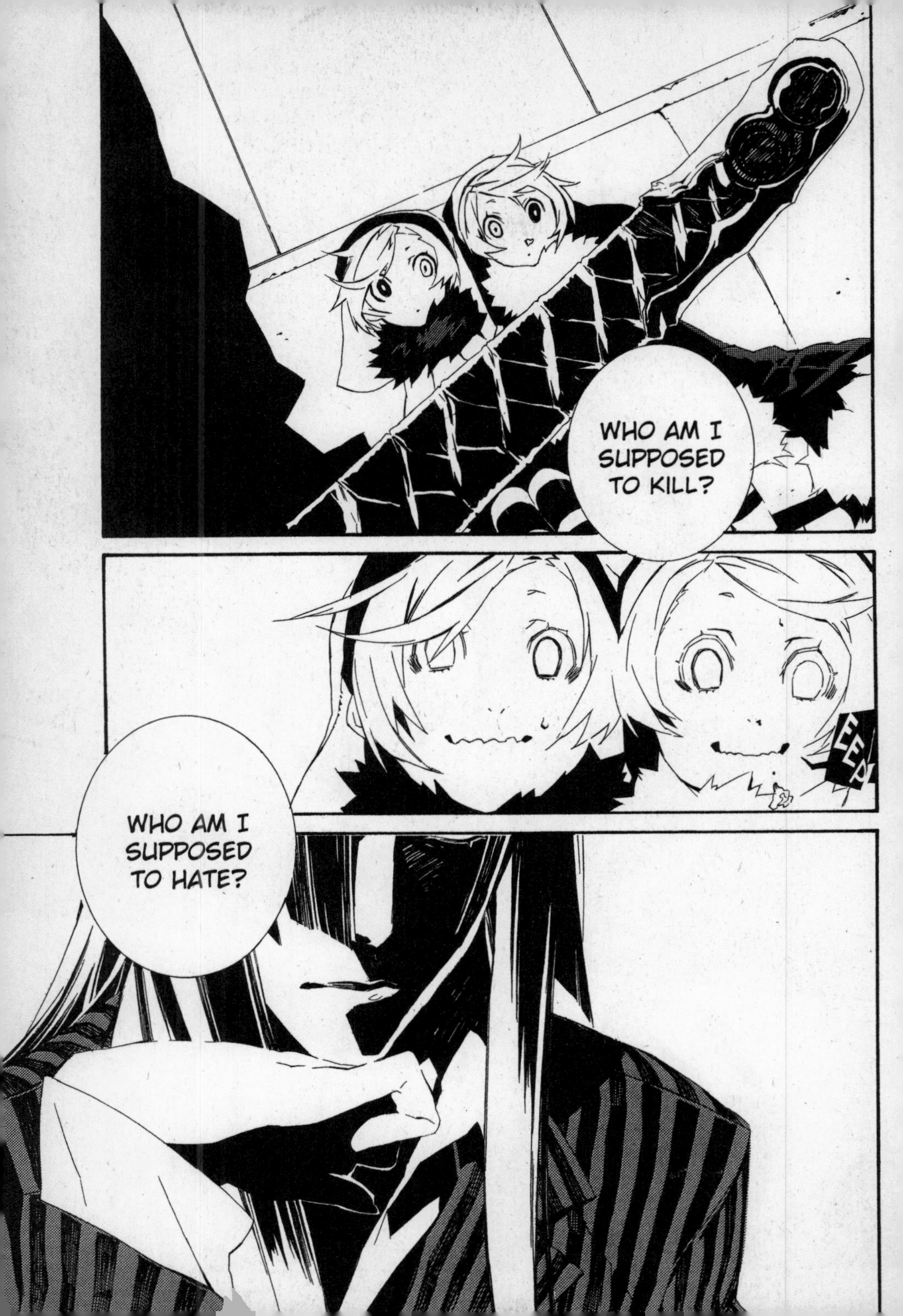
WHO AM I SUPPOSED TO KILL?
EEP
WHO AM I SUPPOSED TO HATE?

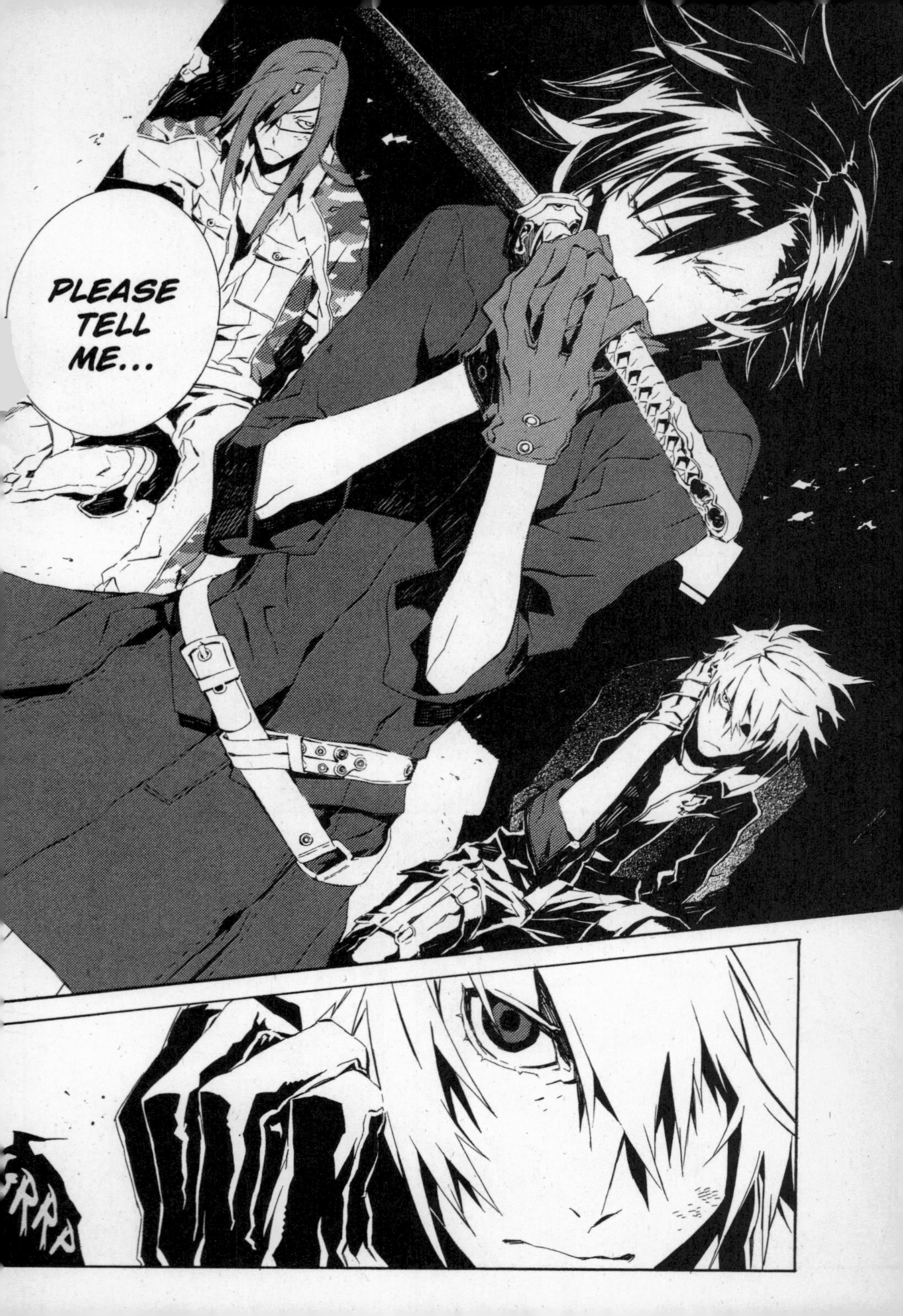
PLEASE TELL ME...
SRRR

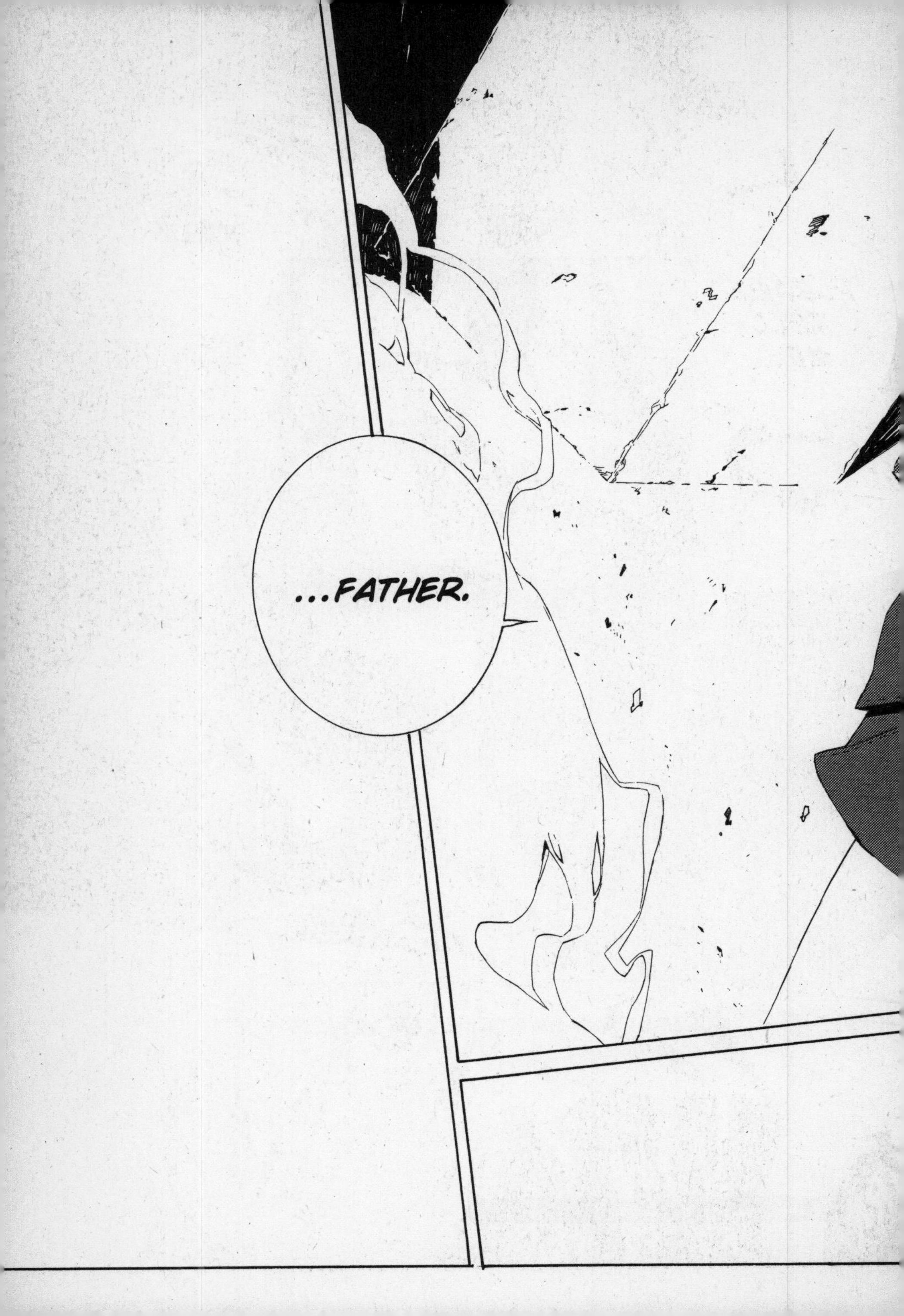
...FATHER.

HOW LONG WILL I HAVE TO LIVE...

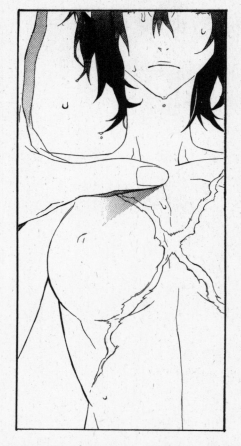

...UNDER THIS BURDEN OF VENGEANCE?

TO
BE
CONTINUED

Extra: Hardcore Twins

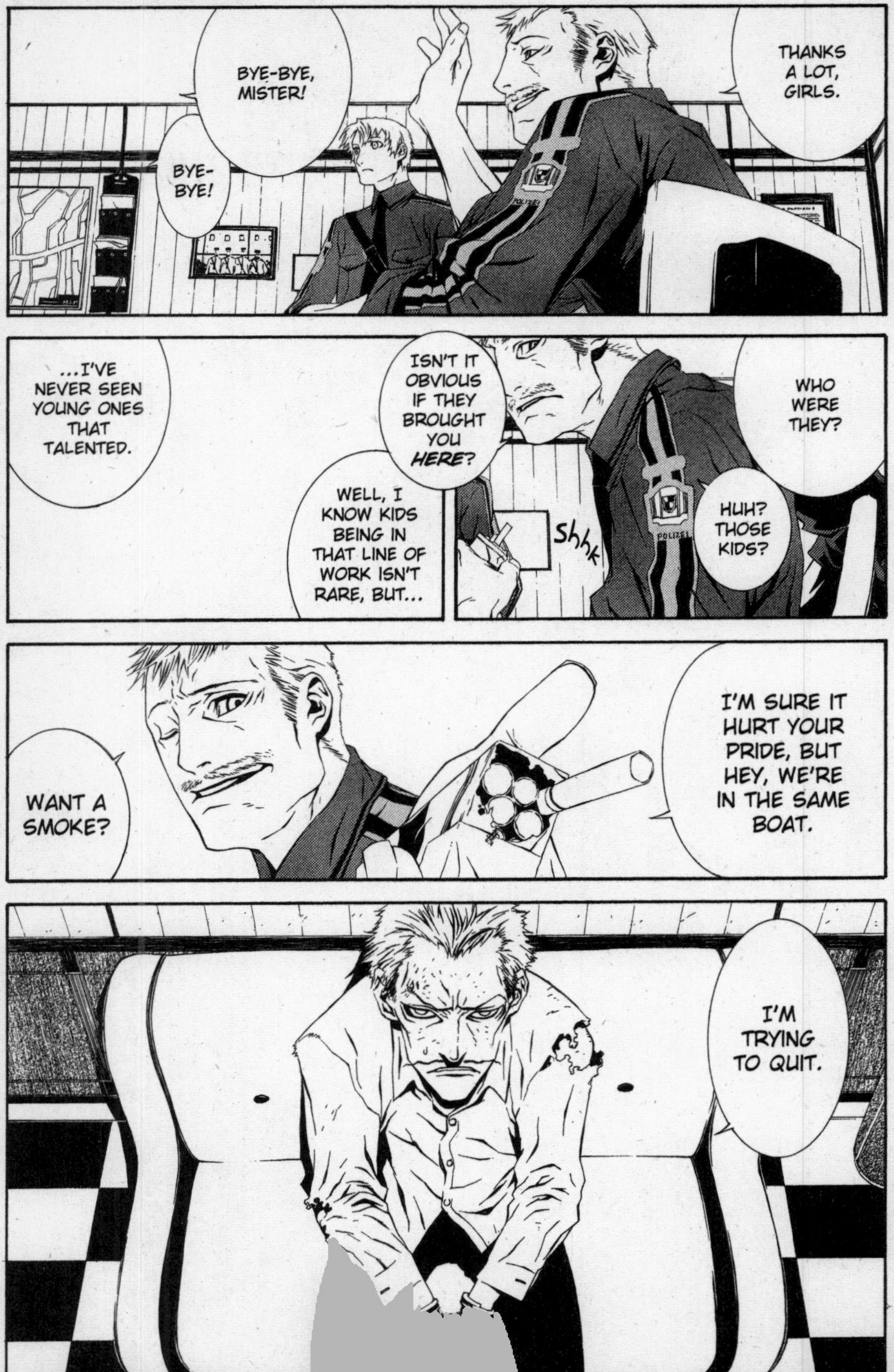
THANKS A LOT, GIRLS.
BYE-BYE, MISTER!
BYE-BYE!
WHO WERE THEY?
HUH? THOSE KIDS?
ISN'T IT OBVIOUS IF THEY BROUGHT YOU *HERE*?
Shhk
WELL, I KNOW KIDS BEING IN THAT LINE OF WORK ISN'T RARE, BUT...
...I'VE NEVER SEEN YOUNG ONES THAT TALENTED.
I'M SURE IT HURT YOUR PRIDE, BUT HEY, WE'RE IN THE SAME BOAT.
WANT A SMOKE?
I'M TRYING TO QUIT.

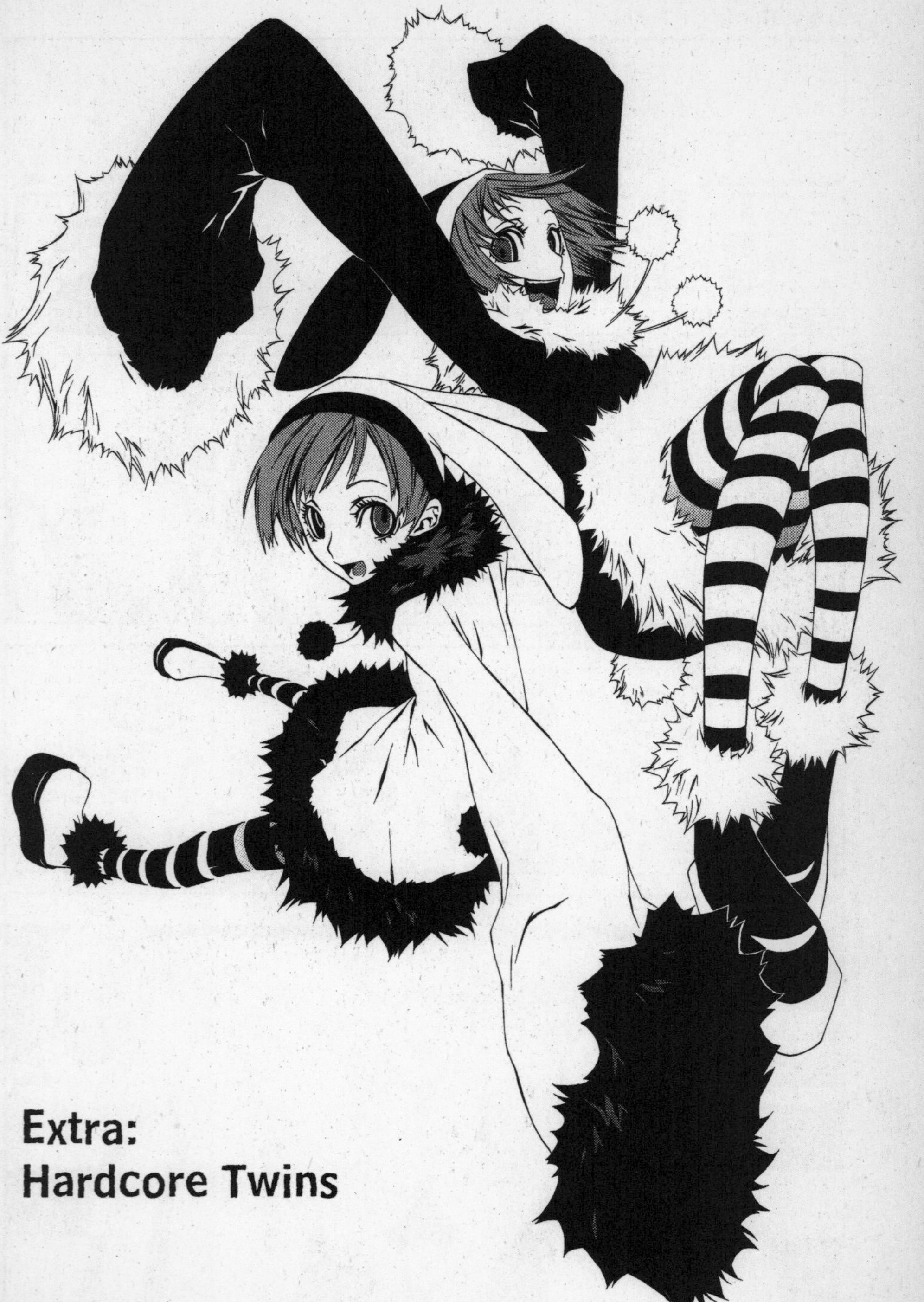

Extra:
Hardcore Twins

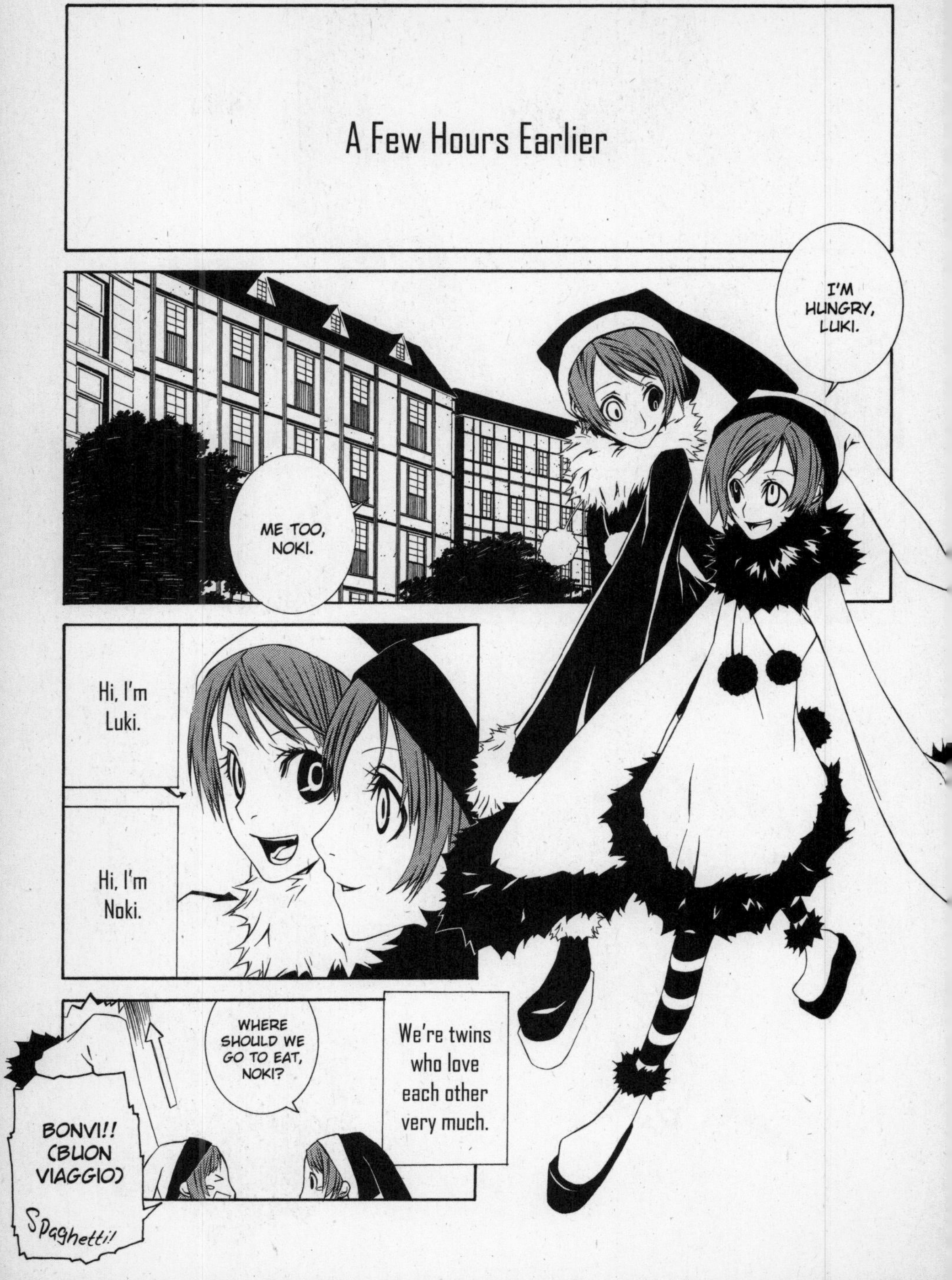
A Few Hours Earlier
I'M HUNGRY, LUKI.
ME TOO, NOKI.
Hi, I'm Luki.
Hi, I'm Noki.
We're twins who love each other very much.
WHERE SHOULD WE GO TO EAT, NOKI?
BONVI!! (BUON VIAGGIO)
Spaghetti!

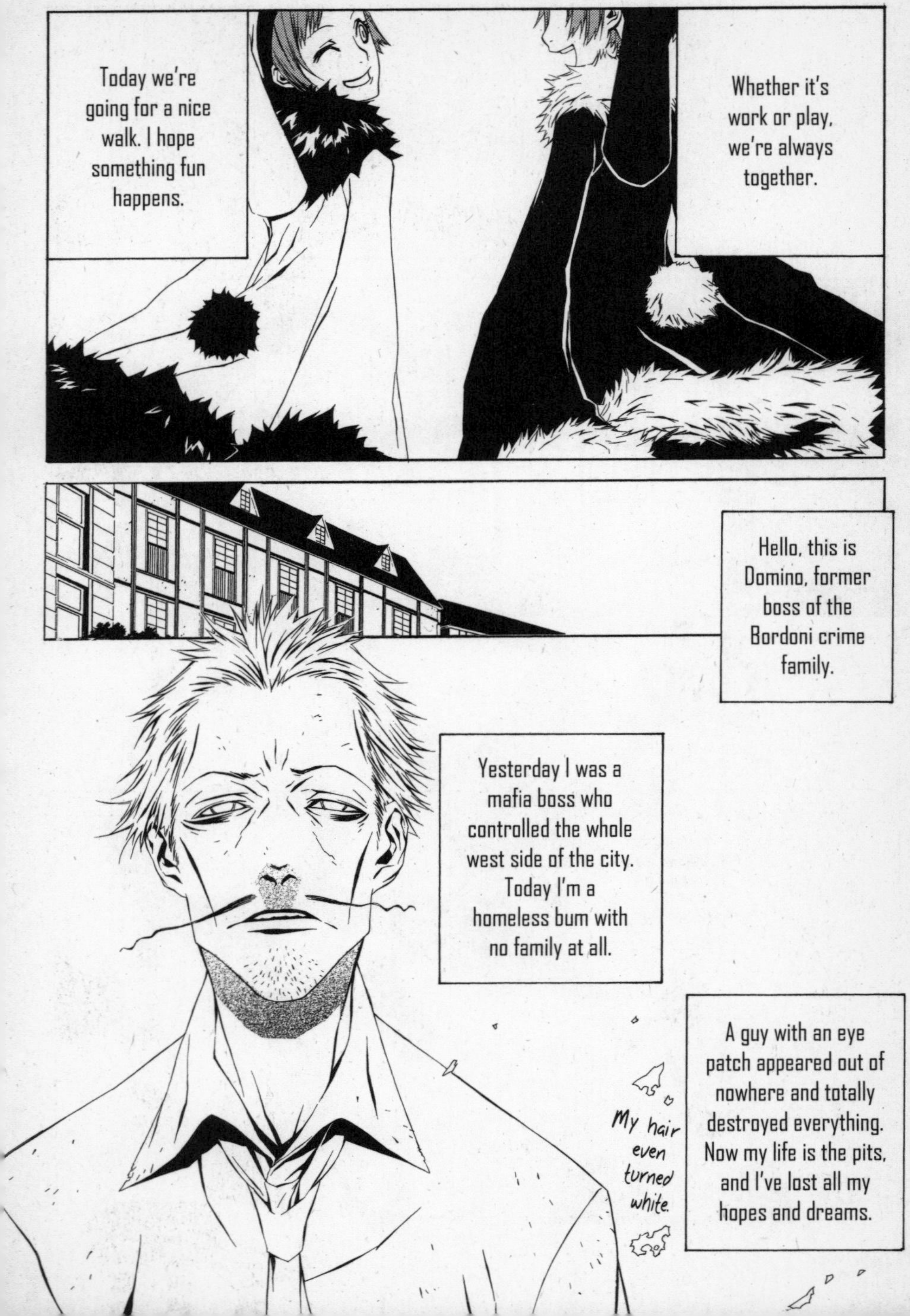

Whether it's work or play, we're always together.
Today we're going for a nice walk. I hope something fun happens.
Hello, this is Domino, former boss of the Bordoni crime family.
Yesterday I was a mafia boss who controlled the whole west side of the city. Today I'm a homeless bum with no family at all.
A guy with an eye patch appeared out of nowhere and totally destroyed everything. Now my life is the pits, and I've lost all my hopes and dreams.
My hair even turned white.

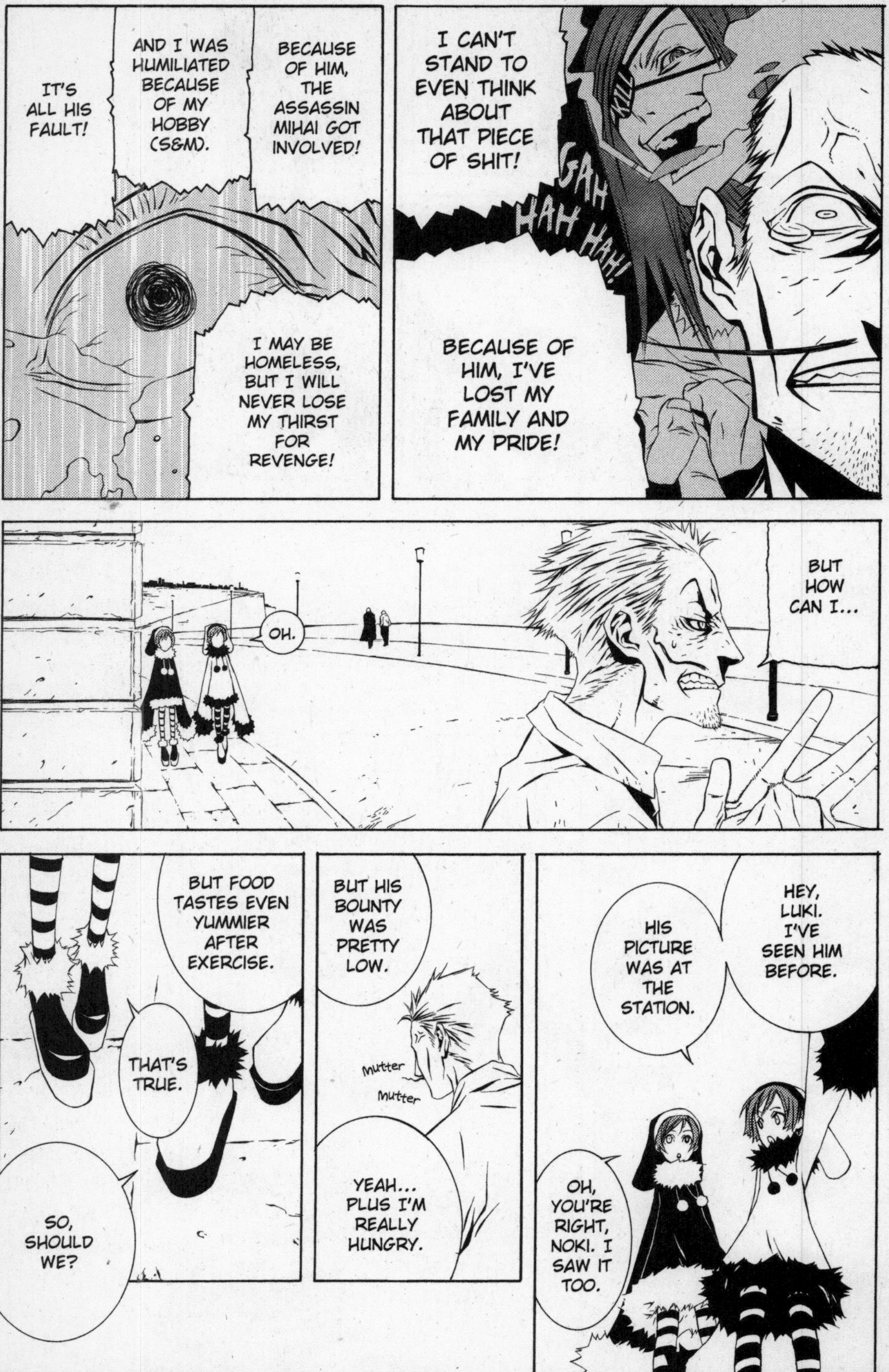
I CAN'T STAND TO EVEN THINK ABOUT THAT PIECE OF SHIT!
GAH HAH HAH HAH!
BECAUSE OF HIM, I'VE LOST MY FAMILY AND MY PRIDE!
BECAUSE OF HIM, THE ASSASSIN MIHAI GOT INVOLVED!
AND I WAS HUMILIATED BECAUSE OF MY HOBBY (S&M).
IT'S ALL HIS FAULT!
I MAY BE HOMELESS, BUT I WILL NEVER LOSE MY THIRST FOR REVENGE!
BUT HOW CAN I...
OH.
HEY, LUKI. I'VE SEEN HIM BEFORE.
HIS PICTURE WAS AT THE STATION.
OH, YOU'RE RIGHT, NOKI. I SAW IT TOO.
BUT HIS BOUNTY WAS PRETTY LOW.
Mutter
Mutter
YEAH... PLUS I'M REALLY HUNGRY.
BUT FOOD TASTES EVEN YUMMIER AFTER EXERCISE.
THAT'S TRUE.
SO, SHOULD WE?

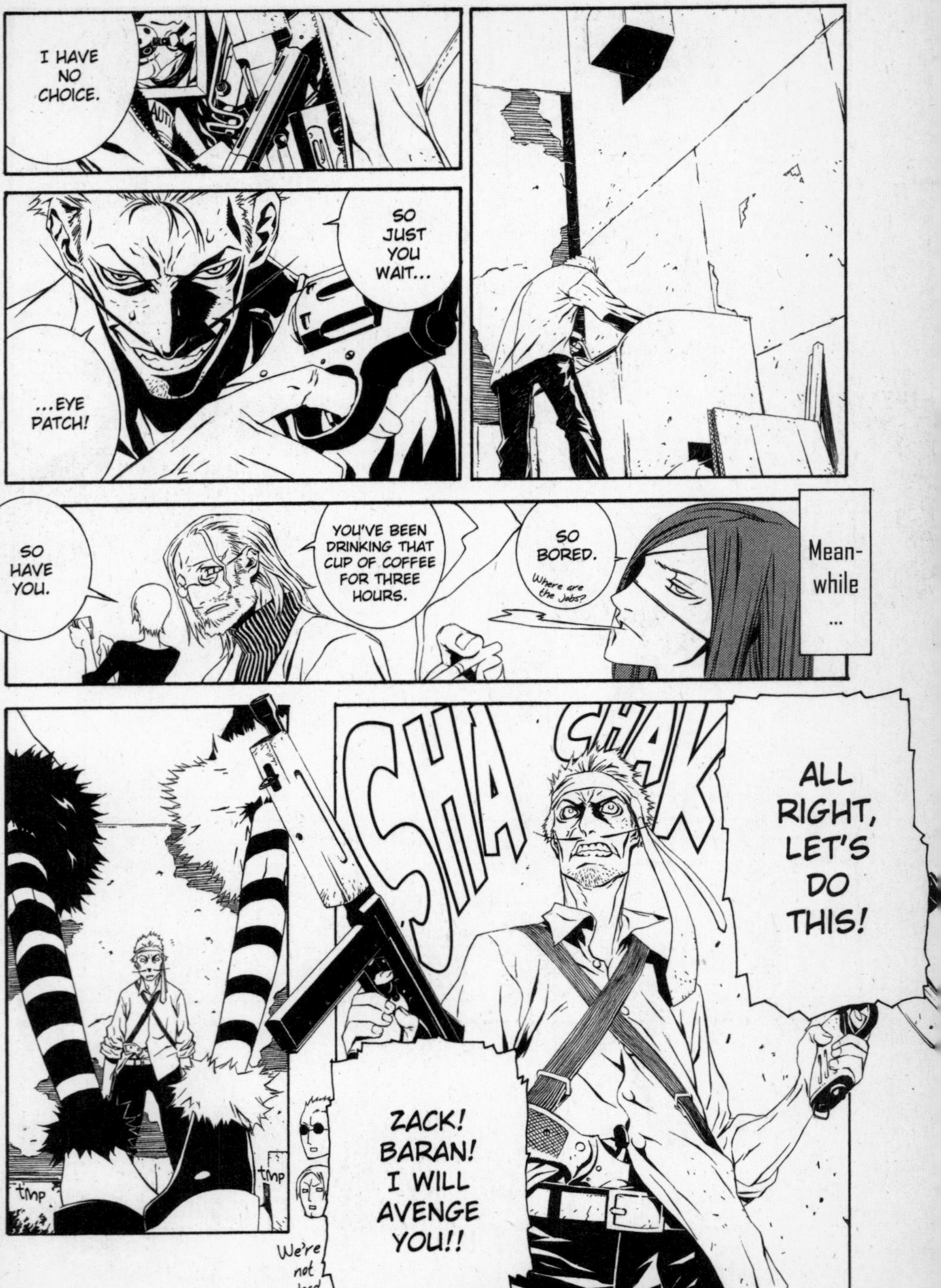
I HAVE NO CHOICE.
SO JUST YOU WAIT...
...EYE PATCH!
Mean-while...
SO BORED.
Where are the Jobs?
YOU'VE BEEN DRINKING THAT CUP OF COFFEE FOR THREE HOURS.
SO HAVE YOU.
CHA
CHAK
ALL RIGHT, LET'S DO THIS!
ZACK! BARAN! I WILL AVENGE YOU!!
We're not dead.
tmp
tmp

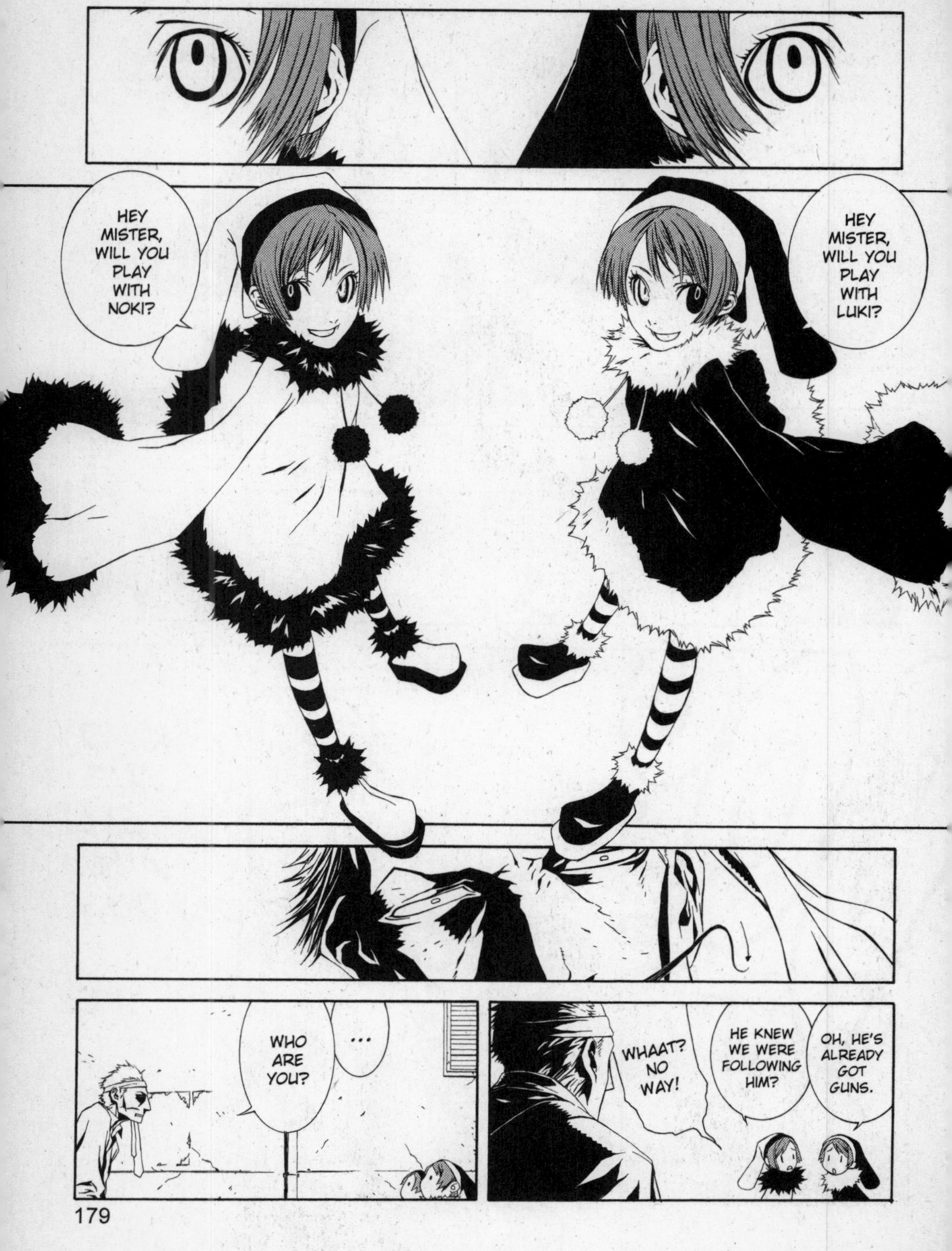
HEY MISTER, WILL YOU PLAY WITH LUKI?
HEY MISTER, WILL YOU PLAY WITH NOKI?
OH, HE'S ALREADY GOT GUNS.
HE KNEW WE WERE FOLLOWING HIM?
WHAAT? NO WAY!
...
WHO ARE YOU?

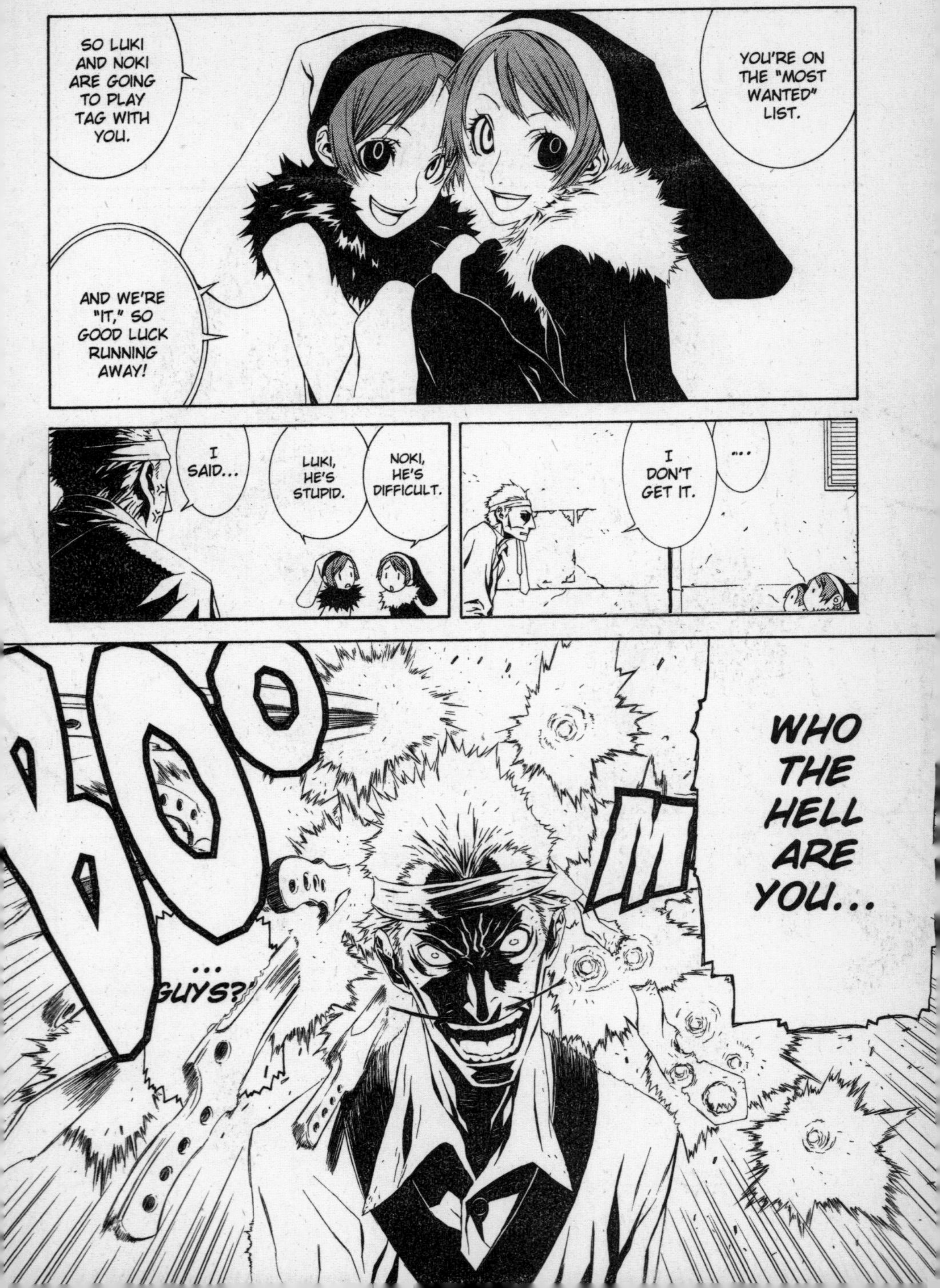
YOU'RE ON THE "MOST WANTED" LIST.
SO LUKI AND NOKI ARE GOING TO PLAY TAG WITH YOU.
AND WE'RE "IT," SO GOOD LUCK RUNNING AWAY!
...
I DON'T GET IT.
NOKI, HE'S DIFFICULT.
LUKI, HE'S STUPID.
I SAID...
WHO THE HELL ARE YOU...
BOOM
...GUYS?

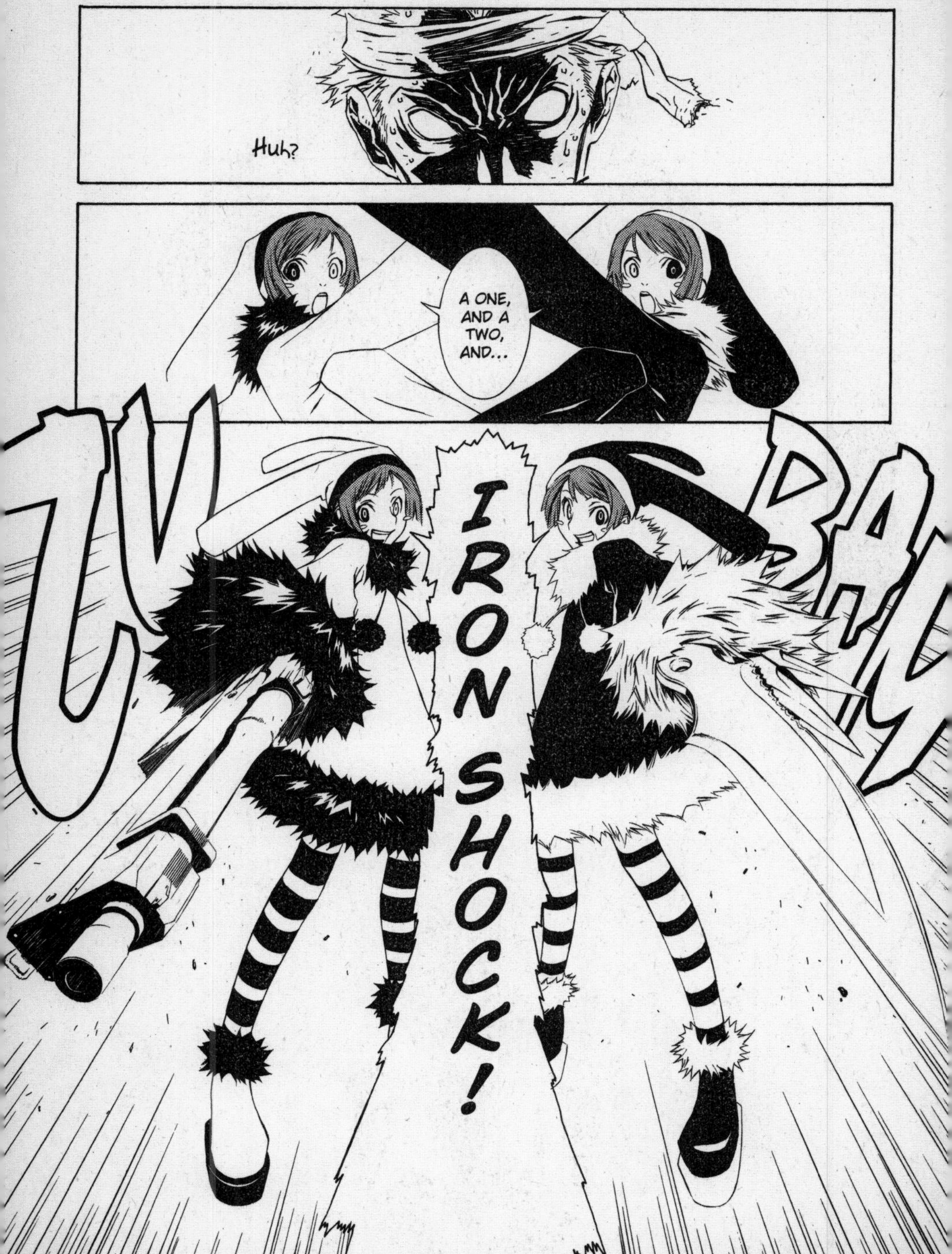
Huh?
A ONE, AND A TWO, AND...
BA
IRON SHOCK!
ZV

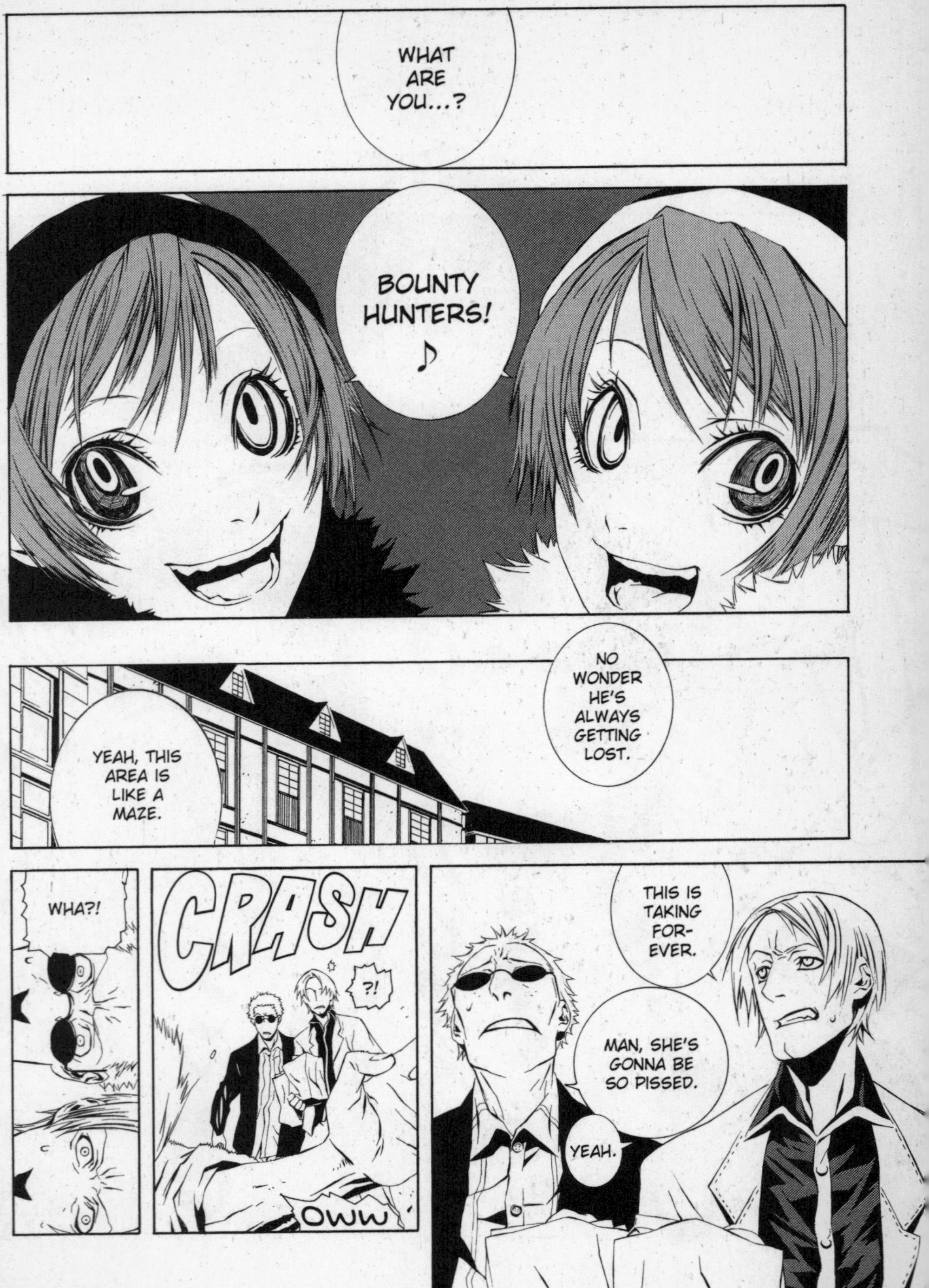
WHAT ARE YOU...?
BOUNTY HUNTERS! ♪
NO WONDER HE'S ALWAYS GETTING LOST.
YEAH, THIS AREA IS LIKE A MAZE.
THIS IS TAKING FOR-EVER.
MAN, SHE'S GONNA BE SO PISSED.
YEAH.
CRASH
?!
OWW
WHA?!

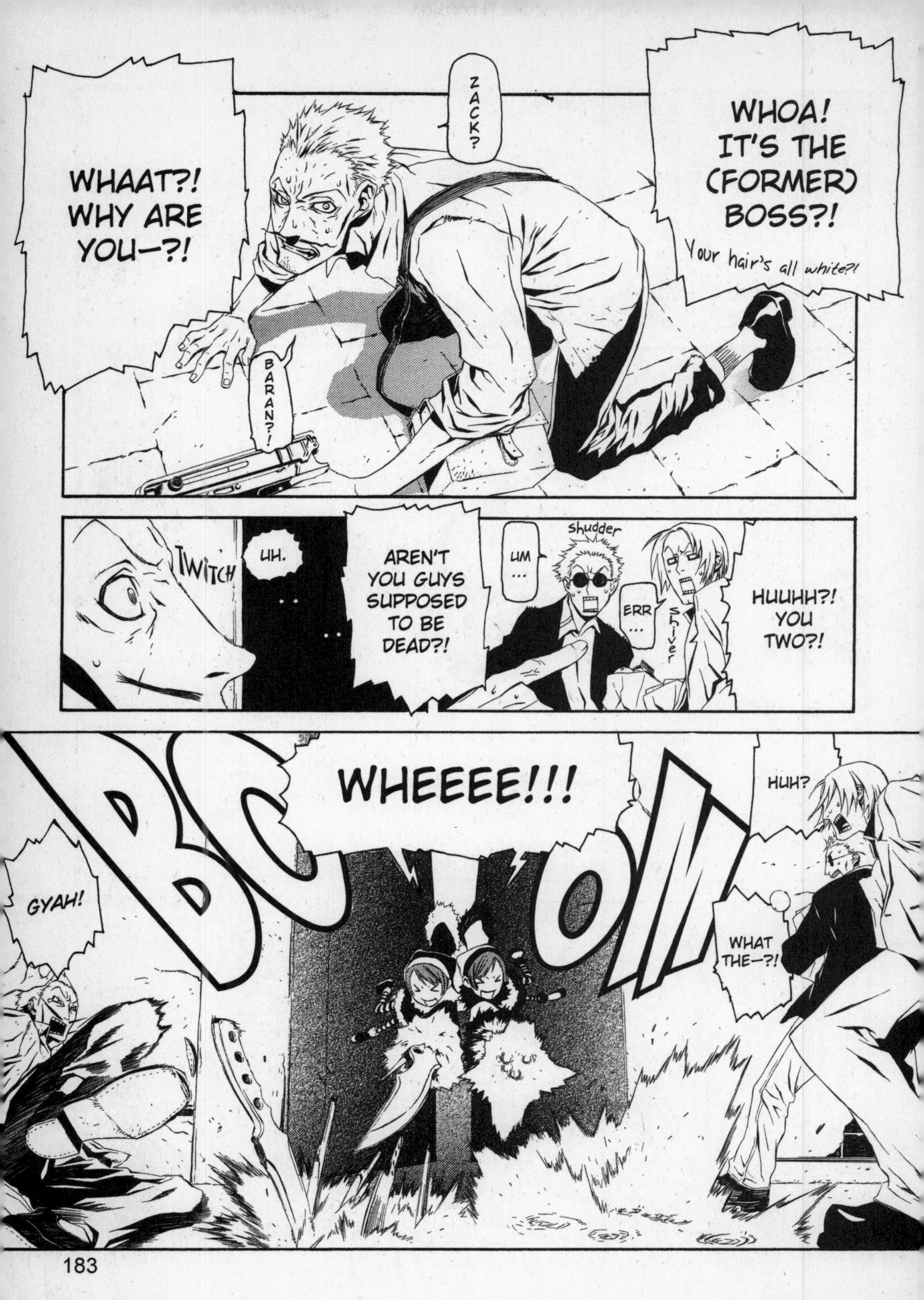
WHOA! IT'S THE (FORMER) BOSS?!
Your hair's all white?!
ZACK?
WHAAT?! WHY ARE YOU-?!
BARAN?!
HUUHH?! YOU TWO?!
shiver
ERR ...
shudder
UM ...
AREN'T YOU GUYS SUPPOSED TO BE DEAD?!
UH.
TWITCH
HUH?
WHAT THE-?!
WHEEEE!!!
BOOM
GYAH!

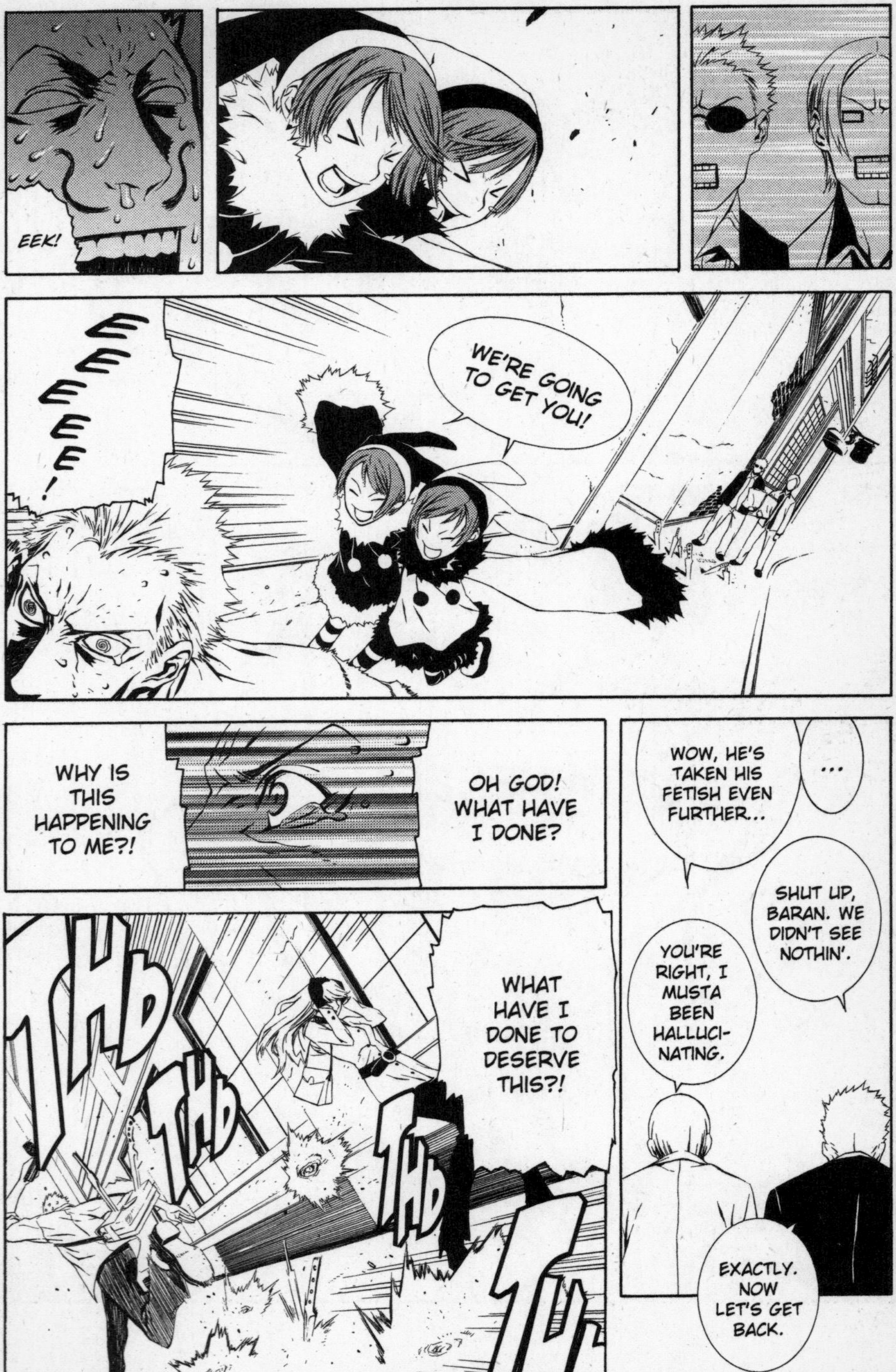
EEK!
WE'RE GOING TO GET YOU!
EEEEEEE!
...
WOW, HE'S TAKEN HIS FETISH EVEN FURTHER...
SHUT UP, BARAN. WE DIDN'T SEE NOTHIN'.
YOU'RE RIGHT, I MUSTA BEEN HALLUCI-NATING.
EXACTLY. NOW LET'S GET BACK.
OH GOD! WHAT HAVE I DONE?
WHY IS THIS HAPPENING TO ME?!
WHAT HAVE I DONE TO DESERVE THIS?!
THD
THD
THD

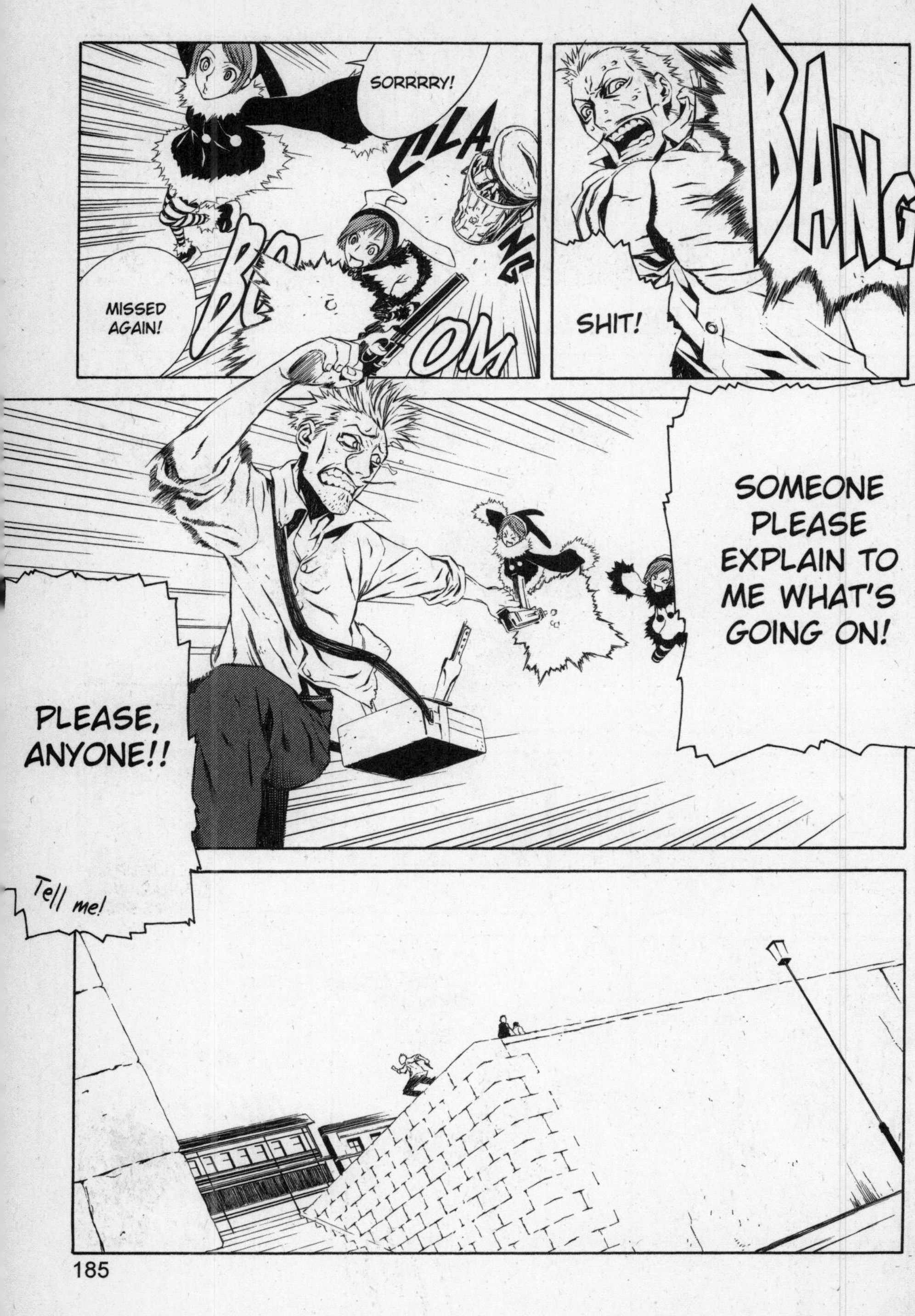
BANG
SHIT!
SORRRRY!
CLANG
BOOM
MISSED AGAIN!
SOMEONE PLEASE EXPLAIN TO ME WHAT'S GOING ON!
PLEASE, ANYONE!!
Tell me!

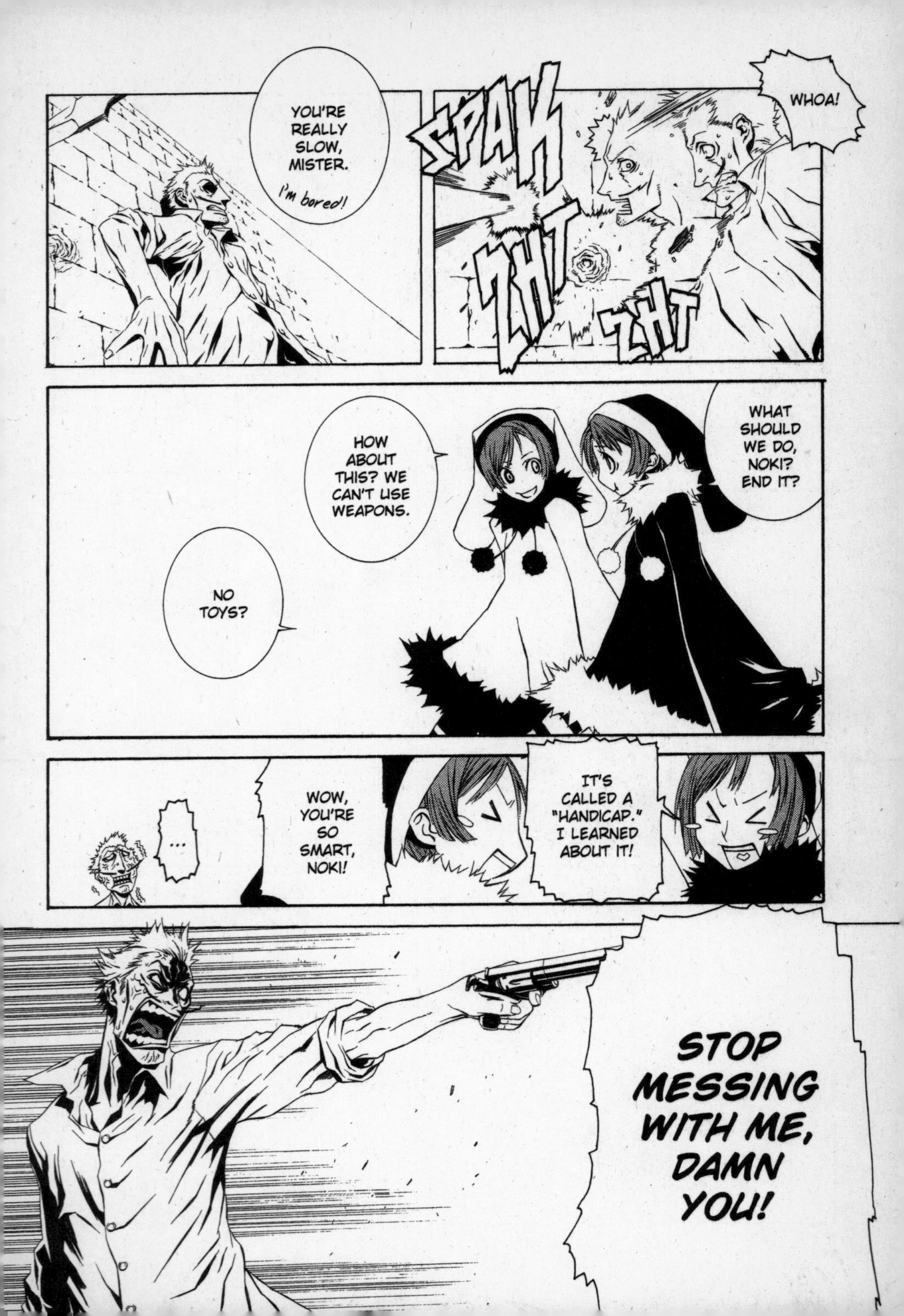
WHOA!
SPAK
ZHT
ZHT
YOU'RE REALLY SLOW, MISTER.
I'm bored!
WHAT SHOULD WE DO, NOKI? END IT?
HOW ABOUT THIS? WE CAN'T USE WEAPONS.
NO TOYS?
IT'S CALLED A "HANDICAP." I LEARNED ABOUT IT!
WOW, YOU'RE SO SMART, NOKI!
...
STOP MESSING WITH ME, DAMN YOU!

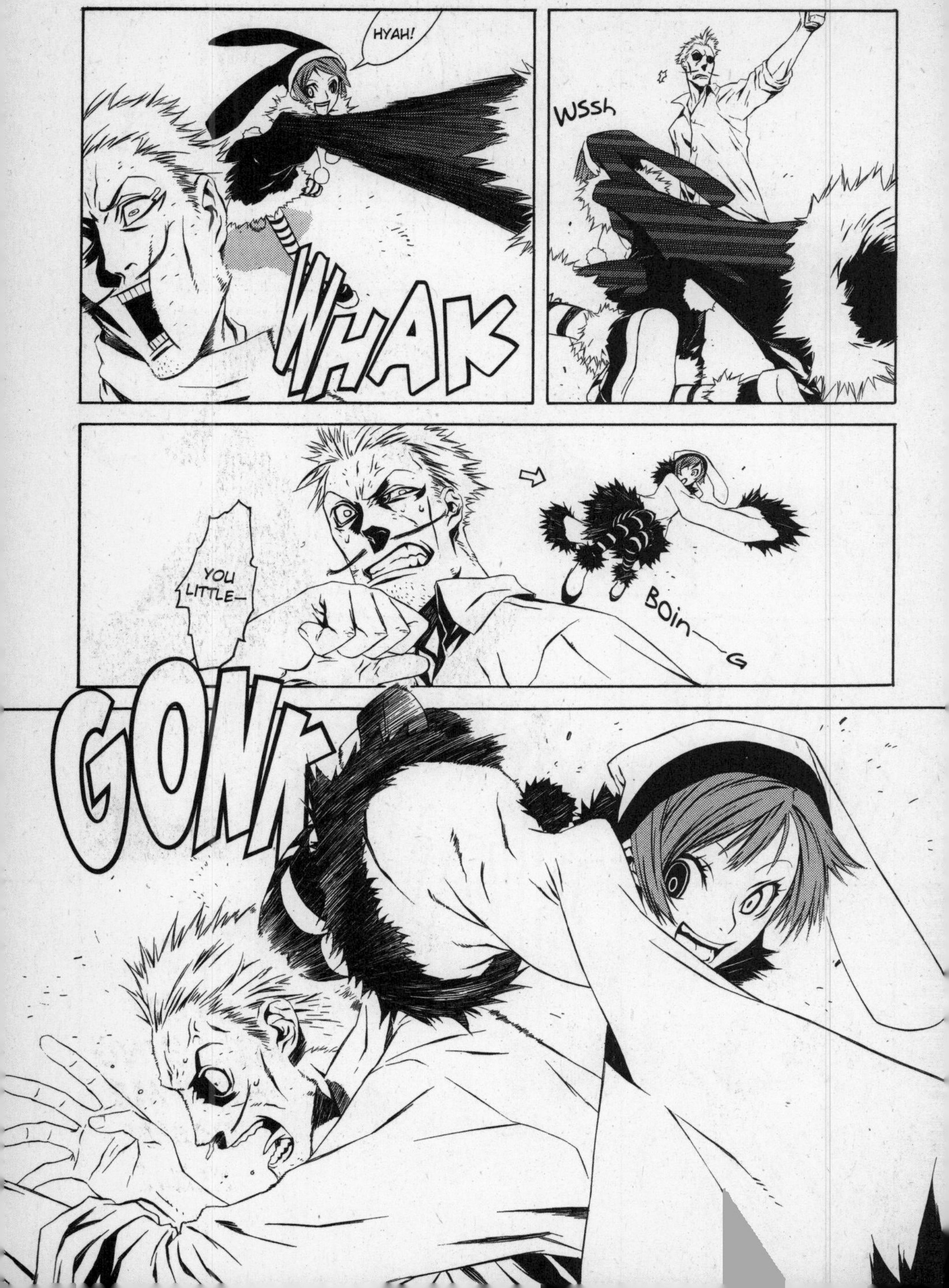
WSSh
HYAH!
WHAK
BOin—G
YOU LITTLE—
GONN

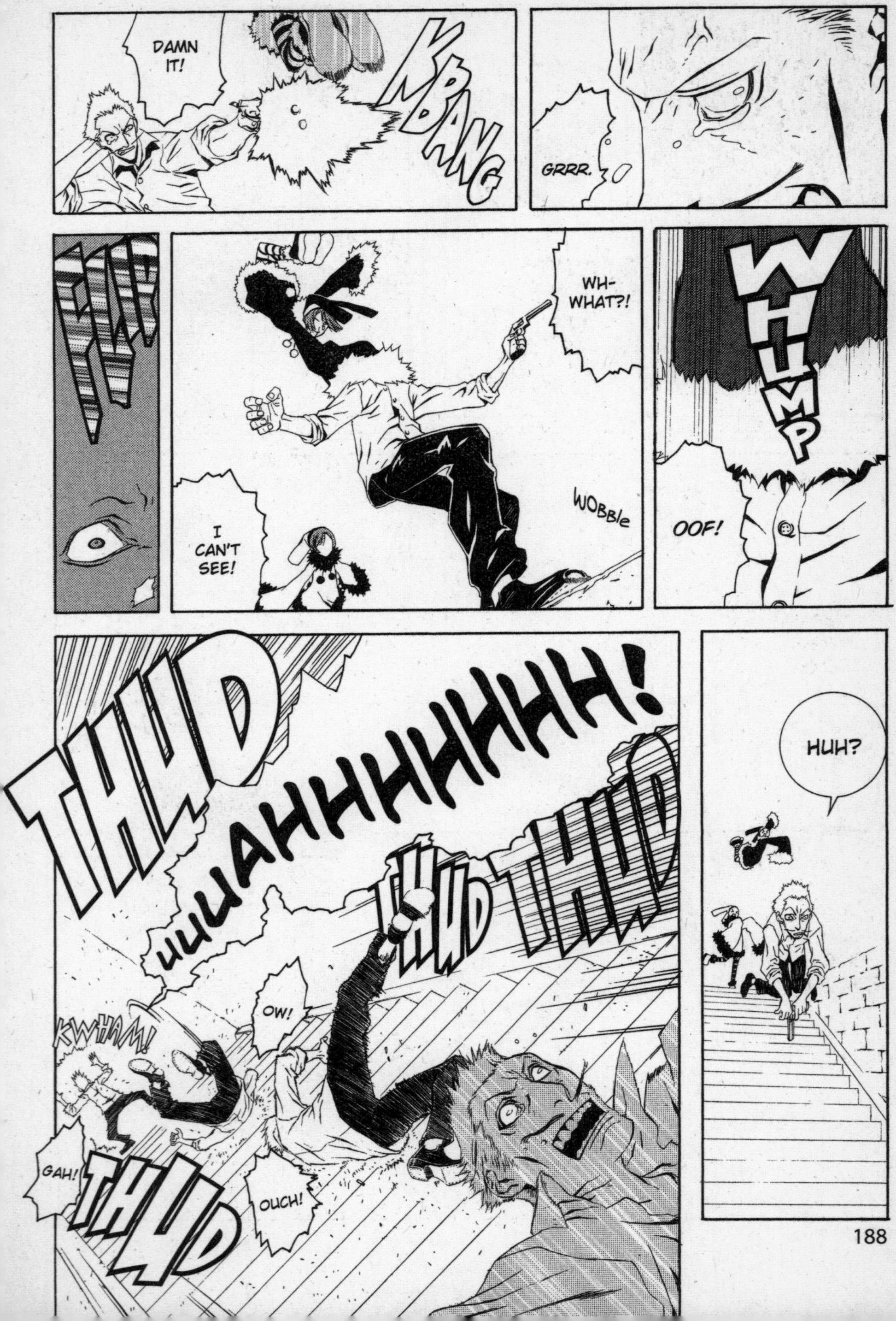
GRRR.
DAMN IT!
KBANG
WHUMP
OOF!
WH- WHAT?!
WOBBle
I CAN'T SEE!
HUH?
THUD
UUUAHHHHHHHH!
THUD
THUD
OW!
KWHAM!
GAH!
THUD
OUCH!

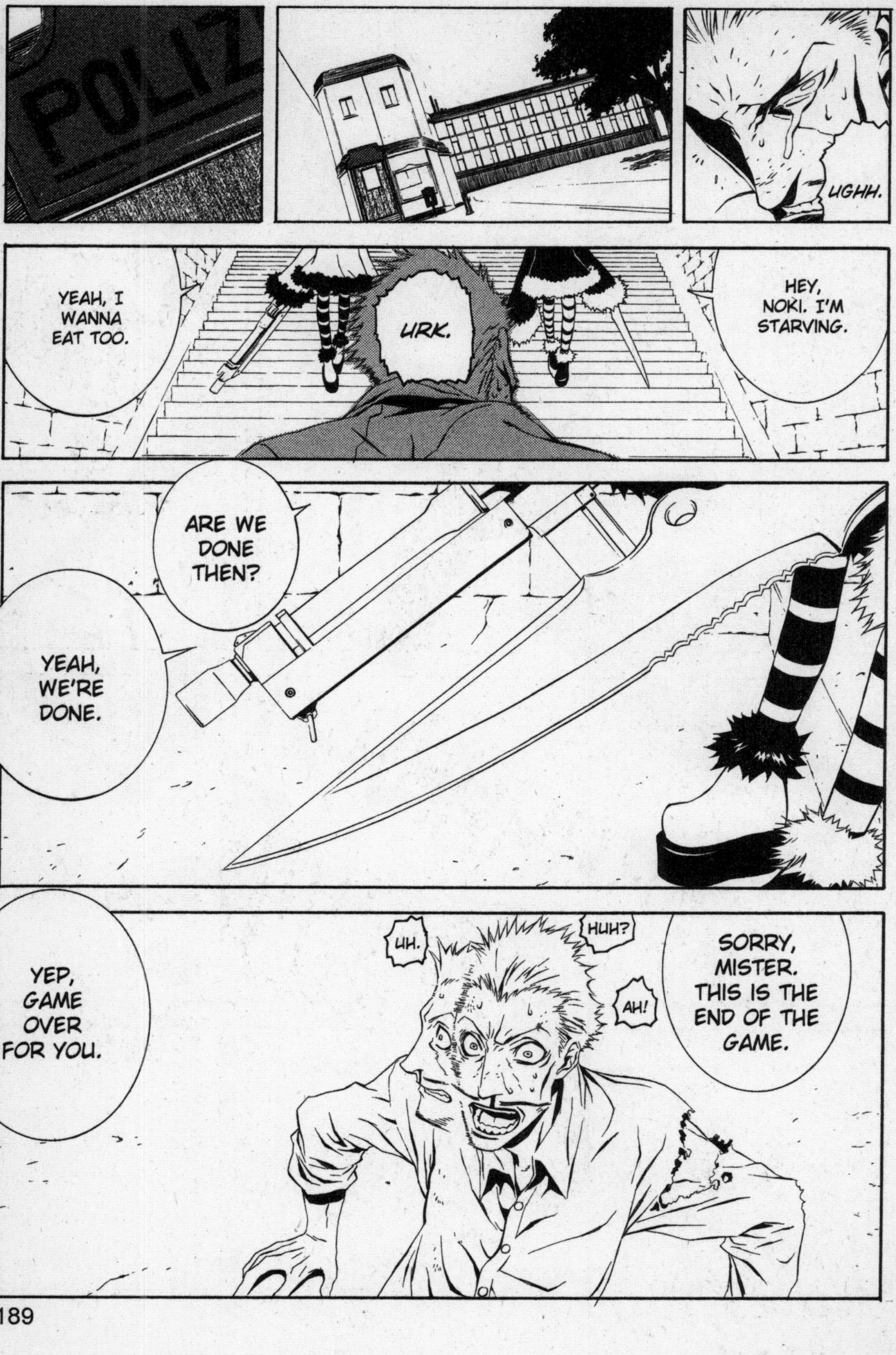
POLIZ
UGHH.
HEY, NOKI. I'M STARVING.
URK.
YEAH, I WANNA EAT TOO.
ARE WE DONE THEN?
YEAH, WE'RE DONE.
SORRY, MISTER. THIS IS THE END OF THE GAME.
HUH?
UH.
AH!
YEP, GAME OVER FOR YOU.

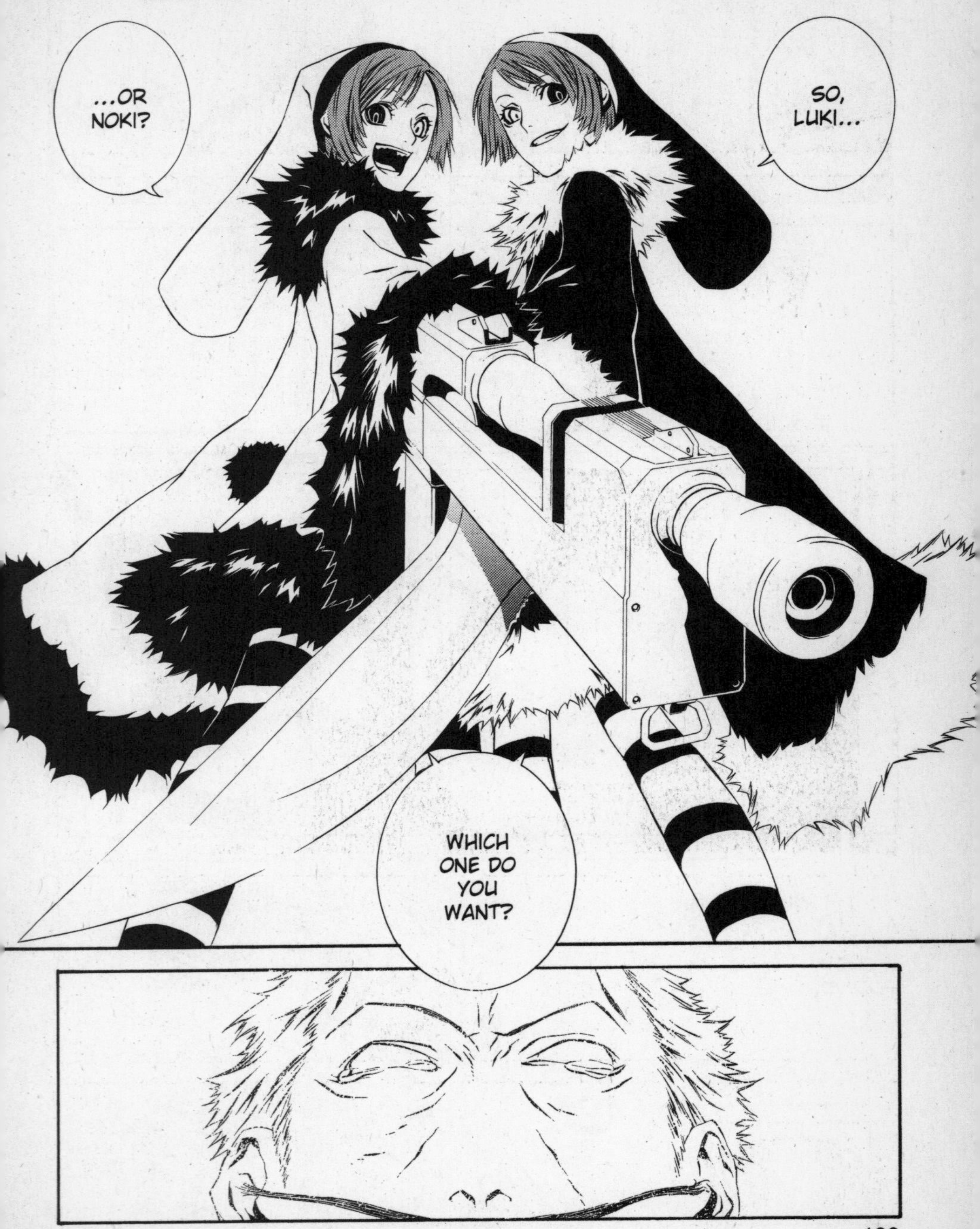
SO, LUKI...
...OR NOKI?
WHICH ONE DO YOU WANT?

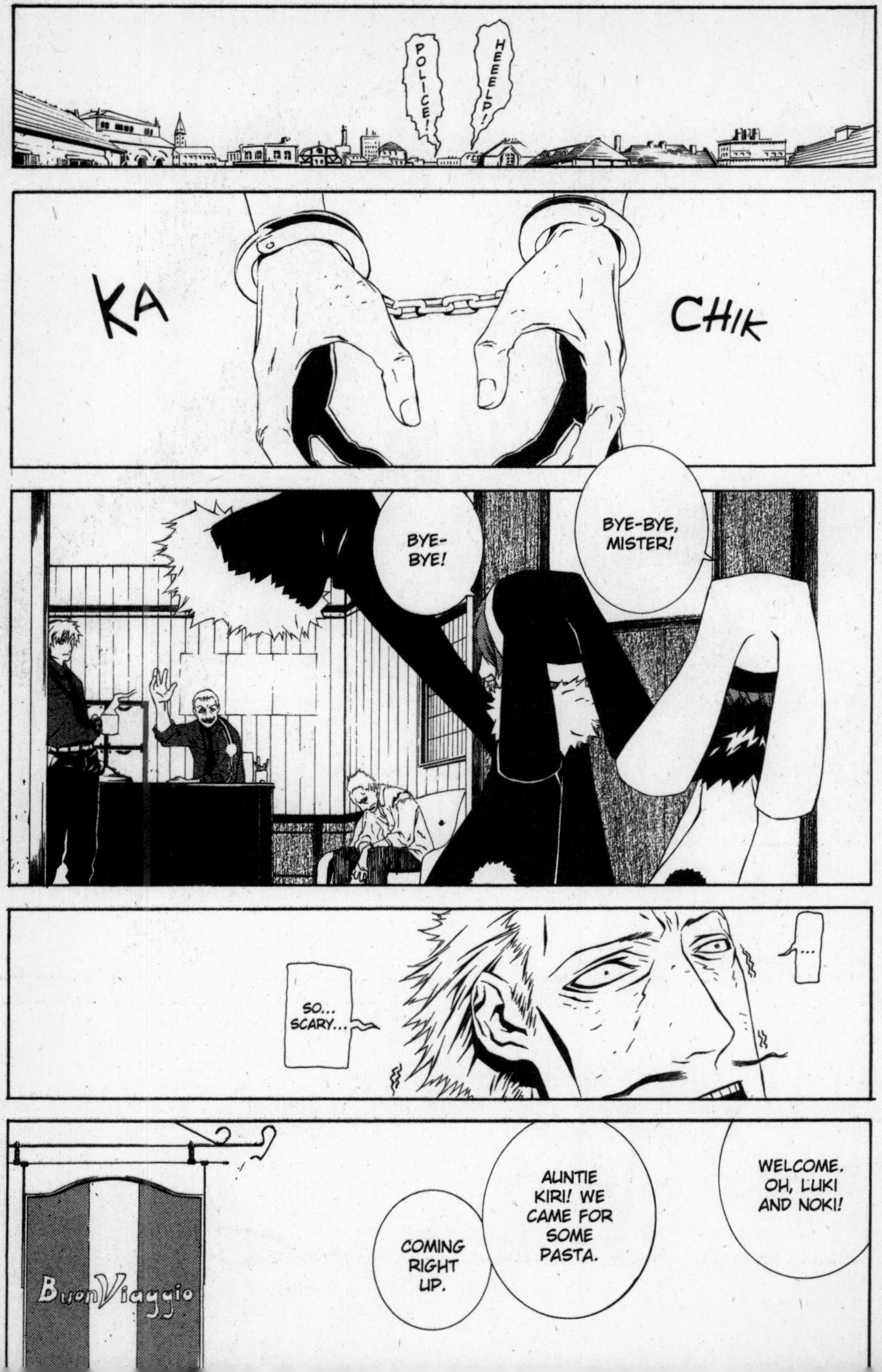
HEEELP!
POLICE!
KA
CHIK
BYE-BYE, MISTER!
BYE-BYE!
...
SO... SCARY...
WELCOME. OH, LUKI AND NOKI!
AUNTIE KIRI! WE CAME FOR SOME PASTA.
COMING RIGHT UP.
BuonViaggio

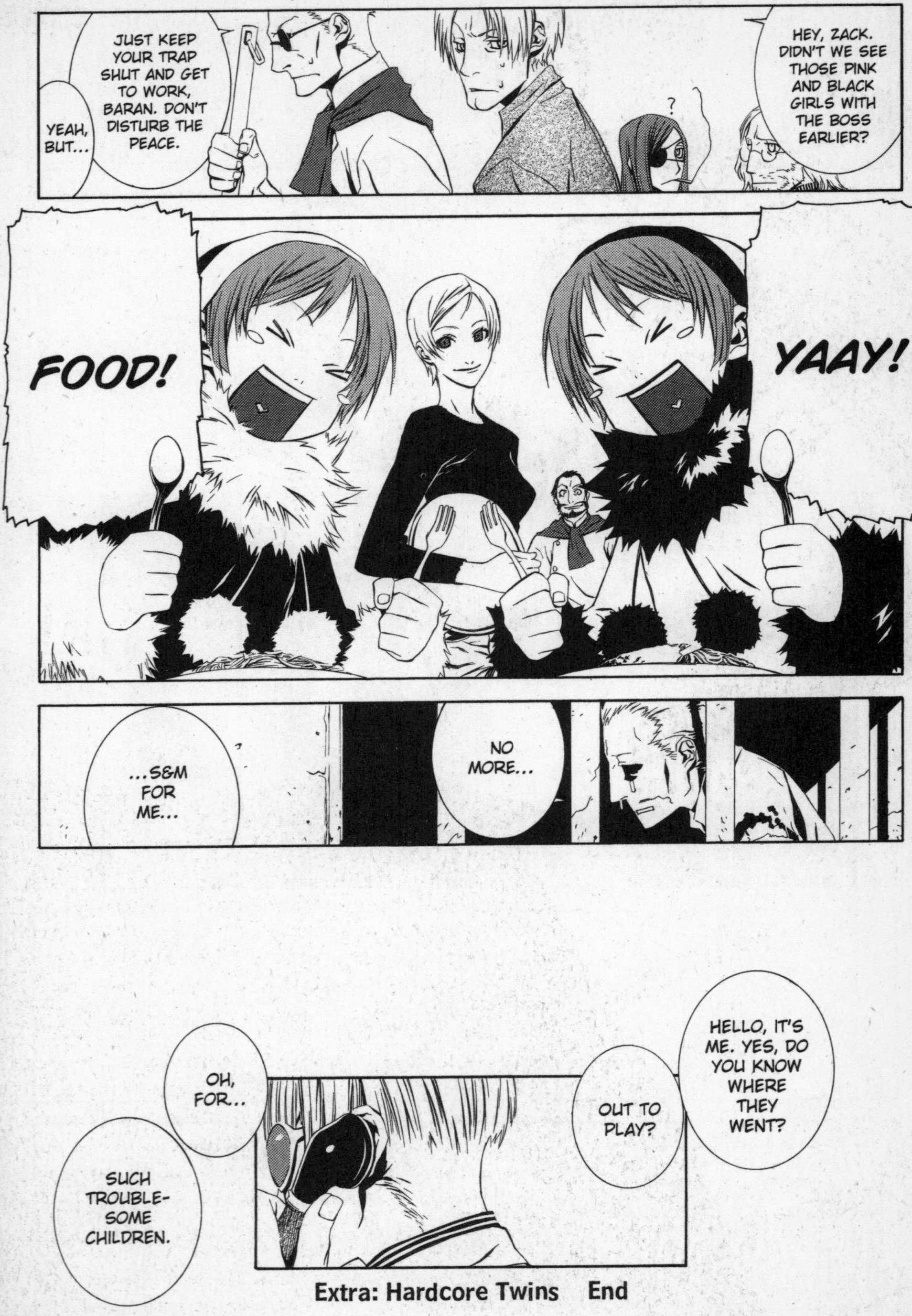
HEY, ZACK. DIDN'T WE SEE THOSE PINK AND BLACK GIRLS WITH THE BOSS EARLIER?
?
JUST KEEP YOUR TRAP SHUT AND GET TO WORK, BARAN. DON'T DISTURB THE PEACE.
YEAH, BUT...
YAAY!
FOOD!
NO MORE...
...S&M FOR ME...
HELLO, IT'S ME. YES, DO YOU KNOW WHERE THEY WENT?
OUT TO PLAY?
OH, FOR...
SUCH TROUBLE-SOME CHILDREN.

Extra: Hardcore Twins End

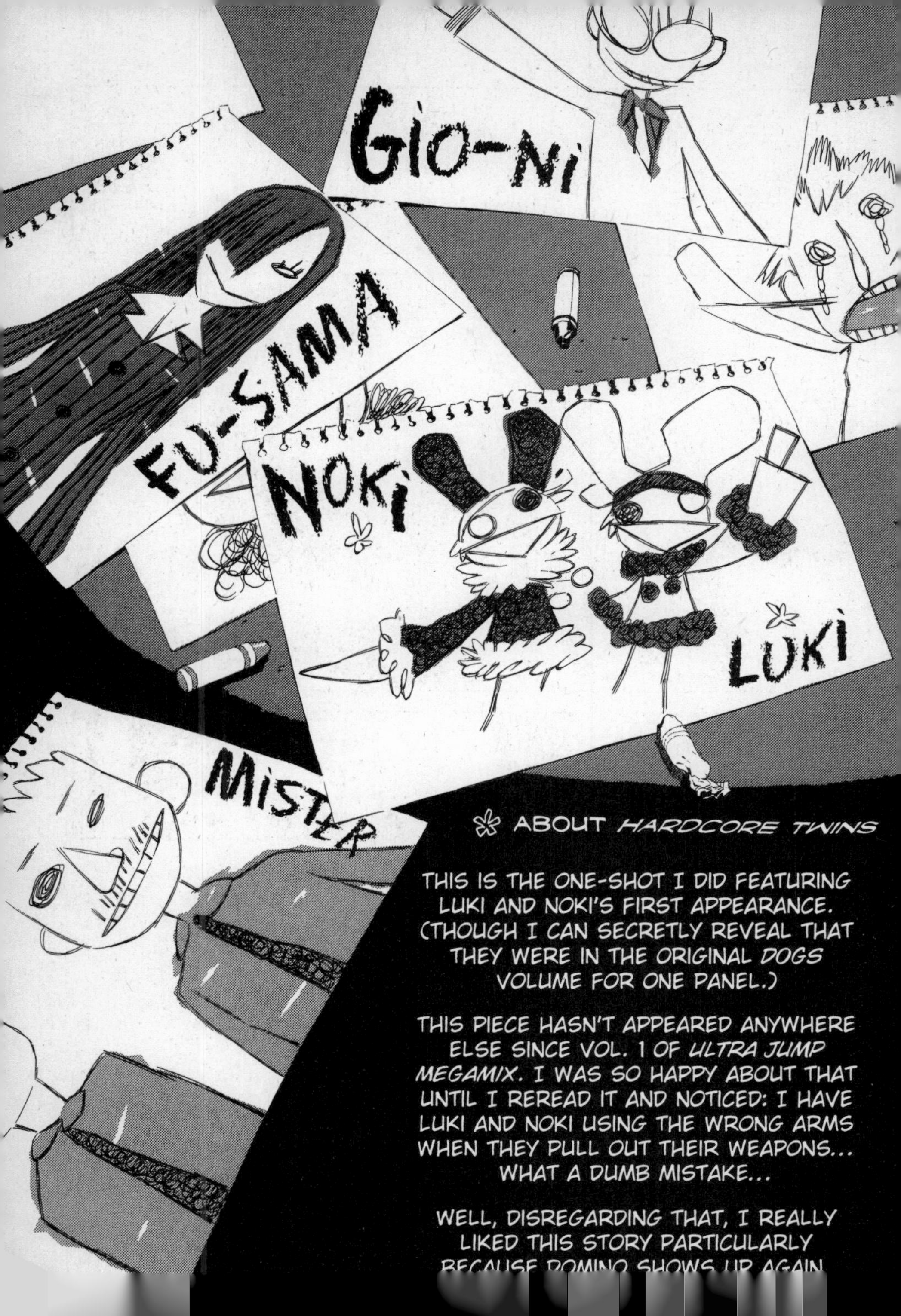
GIO-NI
FU-SAMA
NOKI
LUKI
MISTER

✿ ABOUT *HARDCORE TWINS*

THIS IS THE ONE-SHOT I DID FEATURING LUKI AND NOKI'S FIRST APPEARANCE. (THOUGH I CAN SECRETLY REVEAL THAT THEY WERE IN THE ORIGINAL *DOGS* VOLUME FOR ONE PANEL.)

THIS PIECE HASN'T APPEARED ANYWHERE ELSE SINCE VOL. 1 OF *ULTRA JUMP MEGAMIX*. I WAS SO HAPPY ABOUT THAT UNTIL I REREAD IT AND NOTICED: I HAVE LUKI AND NOKI USING THE WRONG ARMS WHEN THEY PULL OUT THEIR WEAPONS... WHAT A DUMB MISTAKE...

WELL, DISREGARDING THAT, I REALLY LIKED THIS STORY PARTICULARLY BECAUSE DOMINO SHOWS UP AGAIN.

SPECIAL THANKS
Iko Sasagawa
Kuroame
TOMO

SERIES EDITOR
Satoshi Yamauchi

BOOK EDITOR
Rie Endou

ORIGINAL DESIGN
LIGHTNING

ABOUT THE AUTHOR

Shirow Miwa debuted in *UltraJump* magazine in 1999 with the short series *Black Mind*. His next series, *Dogs*, published in the magazine from 2000 to 2001, instantly became a popular success. He returned in 2005 with *Dogs: Bullets & Carnage*, which is currently running in *UltraJump*. Miwa also creates illustrations for books, music videos and magazines, and produces doujinshi (independent comics) under the circle name m.m.m.WORKS. His website is http://mmm-gee.net.

DOGS: BULLETS & CARNAGE
Volume 2

VIZ Signature Edition

Story & Art by
SHIROW MIWA

Translation & Adaptation/Alexis Kirsch
Touch-up Art & Lettering/Eric Erbes
Cover & Graphic Design/Sam Elzway
Editor/Leyla Aker

VP, Production/Alvin Lu
VP, Publishing Licensing/Rika Inouye
VP, Sales & Product Marketing/Gonzalo Ferreyra
VP, Creative/Linda Espinosa
Publisher/Hyoe Narita

Printed in the U.S.A.

Published by VIZ Media, LLC
P.O. Box 77010
San Francisco, CA 94107

10 9 8 7 6 5 4 3 2 1
First printing, December 2009

VIZ SIGNATURE
www.vizsignature.com

www.viz.com

Hey, you're reading the wrong way.

Badou's right—this is actually the end of the book.

To properly enjoy this VIZ graphic novel, please turn it over and begin reading the pages from right to left, starting at the upper right corner of each page and ending at the lower left.

This book has been printed in the Japanese format (right to left) instead of the English format (left to right) in order to preserve the original orientation of the artwork and stay true to the artist's intent. So please flip it over—and have fun.